The Double Life of
GEORGE SAND

The Double Life of
GEORGE SAND

Woman and Writer

A CRITICAL BIOGRAPHY BY

RENEE WINEGARTEN

Basic Books, Inc., Publishers

NEW YORK

Library of Congress Cataloging in Publication Data

Winegarten, Renee.
   The double life of George Sand, woman and
writer.

   Bibliography: p. 321
   Includes index.
   1.   Sand, George, pseud. of Mme. Dudevant,
1804–1876.   2.   Novelists, French—19th century—
Biography.   I.   Title.
PQ2414.W5   843'.7   [B]   78-54501
ISBN 0–465–01683–9

For Debbe, my mother,

and Asher, my husband

Prologue

~~~~~~

THE WOMAN who is the subject of this book was born, only fifteen years after the outbreak of the French Revolution, into a world of turbulent self-inquiry. Throughout her long life, in diaries and memoirs, in letters, in novels, plays, and essays, she struggled to understand herself as a woman and as a human being. It was not easy, and she did not always succeed. But she tried, and she was perhaps the first woman to make the attempt with such enduring consistency and on such a scale. As an eminent contemporary of hers observed, in an age when the "question" or the "cause" of woman was coming to the fore, she told what none had told hitherto about woman and the inner life of her sex.

Contents

~~~~~~

Contents

PART IV
The Road to Independence

PART V
Queen and Mother

PART VI
Woman of Action

PART VII
Sphinx

[x]

In this age devoted to completing the French Revolution and to beginning the Human Revolution, equality between the sexes being part of equality between men, a great woman was needed. Woman had to prove that she could have all our manly qualities without losing her angelic ones: that she could be strong without ceasing to be gentle: George Sand is that proof. . . . she bequeathes to us the right of woman which draws its proof from woman's genius. . . . Thus the Revolution is fulfilled.

Victor Hugo
"Obsèques de George Sand"

PART I

Education of a
Writer

CHAPTER

1

The Thirteenth Poplar

 HE solitary horseman was returning home after spending the evening with his friends in the little town of La Châtre in central France. After crossing the bridge, he had to make a sharp turn at the thirteenth poplar. That rainy September night, his horse reared at a pile of stones. The rider was thrown, his neck broken. So perished at thirty years of age Maurice Dupin, grandson of Maurice de Saxe, the military hero and notorious womanizer; great-grandson of another notorious libertine, King Augustus II of Poland; and father of Aurore, who was one day to be celebrated as novelist and inspiring Muse from Boston to Saint Petersburg under the name of George Sand.

When Maurice Dupin died so tragically on September 16, 1808, Aurore was four years old. She had barely known her father. He had carried her on his shoulder in the streets of Paris and had made much of her, but most of the time he was away from home, serving in Bonaparte's army. For a short while they had been together in Madrid, where Maurice was aide-de-camp to General Murat, to whom he had presented his daughter dressed in a replica of his own hussar's uniform. It was then quite common for people who secretly wished that their small daughters were sons to dress them in masculine attire. General Murat thought the child was a boy at first, or pretended to do so.

At the moment of her father's untimely end, Aurore was too young to understand what death meant. It was only later that she came to realize fully how she had been deprived of her natural guardian and protector. A cruel destiny had taken from her the tender, all-loving creature who would have sympathized with her, understood her, pardoned, consoled, advised her, maintained her equilibrium. She would pause in later years at the thirteenth poplar, trying to commune with her father's spirit, seeking his counsel. She idealized her lost father as the incarnation of her best self.

When she eventually wrote one of her finest works, her autobiography, she astonished her readers by devoting most of the first twenty-eight chapters to a doctored account of her father's life (adding, on one occasion, to his letters an expression of his love for her that he had omitted to include, such was her deep need for fatherly affection). She stressed the physical resemblance between them—the large handsome dark eyes and dark hair—that years afterward made Maurice Dupin's comrades-in-arms recognize her at once as his daughter. And she found in his character, as she liked to interpret it—in his high courage and love of risk, his impetuous manly ardor, his frank and open manner, his delight in music and play-acting, his contempt for social convention, his devotion and tormented sacrifice for love—the precursor and model of her own nature. It was a model she imagined and shaped in her need and tireless quest for self-understanding.

Because he died at thirty, Maurice Dupin remained in the shadowy memories of his imaginative daughter as a young man. For her, the father figure would not be settled, sober, mature, but a brilliant apparition, ever young, at once ideally protective and yet strangely in need of protection. Such would be the father figures in her novels, from the long-suffering and all-watchful English hero Ralph in *Indiana*, to the guardian spirit Hebronius, otherwise eponymous hero of *Spiridion*, who always appears in the dazzling shape of a young man. So, too, she would eventually look for guardians in the most unlikely places, among men who, more often than not, were younger than herself; and, in the end, among men young enough to be her sons. Her appreciation of her relationship with father and son would become confused, so that in her maturity she could apostrophize her father as follows: "Well, my young father, my friend, my child . . ." Contributing to the enduring vision of father as son were the memories of her grandmother, with whom she spent her formative years.

For the news of Maurice's fatal accident broke the lives of two women: his wife, Sophie, and his widowed mother, Marie-Aurore de Saxe, Mme Dupin de Francueil. His mother fled out of the house, half demented, and threw herself on the body of her only son, who had been the sole object of her affections. Back at the house, his wife collapsed, indifferent to Aurore's cries and caresses.

What was Maurice Dupin really like? How far did he resemble the ideal vision that his daughter would so sedulously strive to preserve in her attempt to fill the gap left by his terrible and futile death? He was undoubtedly a charming and gifted boy, indulged by and uniquely devoted to his adoring mother until he was old enough to find feminine interests more suited to his years. Educated by a private tutor, Deschartres (who was later to be his daughter's), he was not particularly studious but had inherited his mother's passionate love of music. Much to her distress, Maurice decided to follow in the footsteps of the victor of Fontenoy, his grandfather Maurice de Saxe, bastard offspring of a royal line, in quest of fame and fortune. It was a moment when Bonaparte's armies had not yet crossed the Alps, when careers were open to talents and men of obscure birth were rising to be generals and even rulers.

Meanwhile, in 1799, when he was twenty-one, Maurice had fathered a son by one of his mother's servants, Catherine Chatiron, a carpenter's daughter. Mme Dupin had dismissed the girl with an allowance, but with considerable indulgence for the time, she paid for the boy's upbringing nearby. Maurice's unacknowledged bastard, Pierre Laverdure, otherwise known by the more poetic-sounding name of Hippolyte Chatiron, was to play quite an important role in the life of his half-sister, Aurore. There was at least one other local mistress of Maurice's, and there may have been other bastard children of his—Aurore later thought so, though she was not always correct in identifying them. Mme Dupin thoroughly disapproved of these country adventures, but Maurice, who had always been spoiled, did not like being thwarted.

In the army, Maurice was welcomed everywhere as the grandson of Maurice de Saxe, but his advancement was relatively slow. He was delighted with his uniform and its effect on the ladies, enjoying the favors of several while campaigning in the Rhineland. The cost of equipping him with horse and suitable accoutrements was not small, and he was soon burdened with debts, which his spendthrift habits (and later his taste for gambling) did nothing to lessen.

However, at the start of Bonaparte's Italian campaign, Maurice was promoted lieutenant for his gallantry on the field of Marengo in 1800. In Italy, he fell for the charms of a woman some five years his senior, whom he first knew as Mme Collin, wife of a quartermaster general. Attractive, hot-headed, she returned Maurice's passion. Only she was not Collin's wife but his mistress, and she left him—his years and assumption of marital authority counterbalancing the wealth his position had enabled him to amass—to become the lieutenant's. She even lent Maurice money she had acquired in gifts from her former protector.

The lieutenant was not eager to settle down. He had no intention of marrying "la petite Collin," as he airily alluded to her in his letters to his mother, who expressed her anxiety and displeasure. The seriousness of the liaison had become fully apparent to her when "la petite Collin" turned up in La Châtre on Maurice's heels. His perennial lack of funds prevented him from keeping his mistress, and he actually persuaded her, much against her will, to go back to Collin, who then accused Maurice of stealing gifts that he (Collin) had made to his companion. This unsavory affair was patched up with the return of a diamond to Collin. But the liaison did not end there.

Throughout the winter of 1801–1802, Maurice and his mistress were seen together in Paris, where he gambled and lost considerable sums, and he was then obliged to borrow money in order to be able to gamble—and lose—again. When he was moved to Charleville in 1802, she followed him there. He persuaded her to sell her jewels and belongings and invest the proceeds in a dress shop, so that she would be able to live by dressmaking (work that she had done before). As the sale did not provide sufficiently for the purpose, he borrowed an advance on his pay. Apparently, several children, at least one of whom was a son, were born of this irregular union. The exact number is not known; all of them died in infancy.

Then in the autumn of 1803, Maurice's companion again became pregnant. A month before the child was born, Maurice Dupin and his mistress, whose real name was Sophie-Victoire Delaborde and who was now thirty, were married at a civil ceremony in Paris. By this fortunate development, Aurore came into the world as their legitimate daughter, a fact that was to be of immense consequence to her future standing and rights and a constant source of resentment to her half-brother Hippolyte, five years her senior, offspring of an equally low-born mother, a male heir to boot, who would always have to play second fiddle.

Why Maurice decided, after four years, to make Sophie his wife—whether on a sudden generous impulse or out of a sense of obligation—it is unlikely to have been for the reason their daughter would proclaim *ad nauseam* in her works in later years: the desire to rehabilitate an unfortunate girl, degraded by society, who had sacrificed all for him and had been purified and redeemed by his love. (Only in one conservative version would she privately admit that her father had fallen into bad company and had made a garrison marriage.) In order to marry Sophie, Maurice had to practice an act of gross dissimulation upon his doting mother, to whom he had given no inkling of his intentions. At that time it was necessary to have the public consent of the parents of the parties to a marriage. Maurice contrived to elude this legality by stating that Mme Dupin's whereabouts were unknown, although he was perfectly aware that she was residing at her home in the country. Nor did he hasten to inform her afterward of the *fait accompli* or of the birth of Aurore. Mme Dupin, whose suspicions had been aroused, was left to find out for herself that her beloved only son had contracted a misalliance.

There were several reasons why Mme Dupin was dismayed by Maurice's marriage to a woman whom she considered "a camp follower," and by no means the greatest was her son's disregard for her own feelings. In those times, and for long afterward, marriage was largely a business transaction whereby the bridegroom and his family expected to better their social and financial position, and the bride of decent family hoped at least not to lessen hers. The man was supposed to put his heart where there was a sizable dowry and prospects, on pain of being regarded as an undutiful wretch and improvident fool. In the upheaval of the Revolution and the social topsy-turvydom of Bonaparte's imperial ascent, many a man contrived to place his foot on ambition's ladder through a prudent marriage.

In 1804 Mme Dupin was no longer quite so wealthy as once she had been. After a lucky escape from consummating her first marriage to a diseased debauchee by his timely demise, she had married Maurice's father, the experienced, cultivated, elderly tax collector of the Châteauroux district and hence a man of considerable means, whom she called "my papa" and who died in 1786. Their elegant style of life during the old regime, the depredations of the Revolution, and later Maurice's expenses made inroads into her fortune. In 1793 she had bought the mansion and estate of Nohant, attached to a charming little hamlet on the road from La Châtre to Châteauroux. There, Marie-Aurore lived the modest life of a country gentlewoman who liked to entertain her friends at a good table.

Like any mother of her station, Mme Dupin must have been hoping for her dashing son to marry into a family of rank and means that would be able to aid his military career and stabilize his finances. But there was a more private, deep-seated cause for her discontent at his action. As the illegitimate daughter of Maurice de Saxe by Mlle de Verrières, an accomplished *femme galante*, or courtesan, euphemistically known as an actress (whose real name was the more plebeian Marie Rinteau), Marie-Aurore felt too close to the world of equivocal amours for comfort. What was her own mother but a more elegant and more elevated version of the type of woman her son had chosen to marry? Besides, her mother's sister, another *femme galante*, had once been counted among M. Dupin's mistresses. As a girl, Marie-Aurore had struggled hard to obtain recognition of her status as Maurice de Saxe's natural daughter, and she had known humiliation. By dint of living a blameless life, considerably aided by a temperament she obviously inherited from neither parent, Marie-Aurore had managed to shake free of her mother's and her aunt's world and rise into sober matrimonial respectability. She did not particularly want to be reminded of what she had worked so strenuously to avoid.

What was she to do? Was there any possibility of having the marriage annulled? She made discreet inquiries of the mayor of the fifth arrondissement, only to be given a picture of the newly legitimized ménage that might have been painted by Greuze just before his death in 1805. Though in straightened circumstances, the couple appeared to be living in touching harmony: the household was scrupulously clean, the husband devoted, the wife occupied with the children and observed giving suck to the new infant. Mme Dupin gave up. Learning that his mother was on a visit to Paris, Maurice had the baby brought to her. For the very first time, Aurore played what was to become her favorite role. She conquered, consoled, and reconciled. A religious wedding ceremony took place, attended by Mme Dupin herself.

Those early years remained in Aurore's memory, aided by Sophie's, as a period of unalloyed happiness. She played "boy's games" with her cousin, Clotilde Maréchal, the daughter of Sophie's sister Lucie and her husband, who were living in the same building. Another playmate was Caroline Delaborde, whom Maurice treated as his own child. The daughter of Sophie by "a previous marriage," though actually by an unknown father, and five years Aurore's senior, Caroline used to tell her half-sister fairy tales. Placed for safety's sake between four straw-bottomed chairs, Aurore would compose aloud an endless series of tales about princes and princesses, an early token of her imaginative precocity. Once, though, she and Caroline were left with their aunt and uncle Maréchal for two or three months, when Sophie went to join Maurice, who was stationed at Montreuil in the spring of 1805, where the emperor's forces were massing for the invasion of England.

In 1806, a son was born who, though living in 1807, did not survive. What Aurore's attitude to this brother was, we do not know. Afterward, she had no recollection of him. Sophie was again pregnant toward the end of 1807, and these repeated pregnancies (she was now thirty-three) must have made her fear for her looks and her power to hold a husband who was not only five years younger than she but also a susceptible charmer subject to the temptations of an officer's life. She was about seven months pregnant in April 1808 when, in the grip of jealous suspicions, she impetuously set out with Aurore on the long journey to Madrid, where Maurice was serving as aide-de-camp to General Murat, commander of the French army of occupation.

The moment she chose was not a fortunate one. In March and April, Spain was seething with discontent. On the second of May, in Madrid, Spanish patriots rose in revolt against the French invaders and were executed by Murat's soldiers, in a scene of carnage lastingly imprinted on the collective memory by Goya. It was the signal for the War of Independence that gave the term guerrilla warfare to the language.

However, the pregnant Sophie was enjoying the social round with Maurice. Aurore was left in an upper room in Murat's headquarters, the Palacio de Buenavista in the Calle de Alcalá, supposedly in the company of a Spanish maid who, as soon as the parents' backs were turned, decamped. Not yet four years old, the child amused herself quite happily by trying out theatrical poses in front of the mirror, or so she recalled afterward.

On June 12, 1808, Sophie gave birth to another boy. Seeing how weak and exhausted her mother looked, Aurore was afraid for her and showed no interest in her new brother, Auguste. It was not long before the parents had cause to fear that there was something wrong with the child's eyesight. Such was the atmosphere of bitter hostility in Spain that Sophie, superstitious and distraught, convinced herself that the doctor had deliberately blinded the child out of hatred for the French. Auguste was only two weeks old when the family set out to return to France in the train of General Murat, to whom the emperor had assigned the throne of Naples. The journey was a terrible one, and

Sophie now paid a heavy price for her jealousy and rashness in following Maurice to Madrid. As the fighting spread, the coach in which Sophie and the children were traveling was requisitioned for the wounded, and they made part of the journey by open cart under the burning July sun. Food was scarce. Aurore and her brother were suffering from hunger, fever, and the itch when, after many vicissitudes, they reached Nohant at the end of July.

For the first time Aurore saw the large but simple country mansion that was to be her home. Her grandmother kissed her, dirty and scabby as she was, and soon nursed her back to health. But little could be done for the blind infant, who lingered only until September 8. The parents were sick with grief at the loss of their son. A week later, Maurice Dupin himself was dead.

By the time she was four, then, Aurore had lost two brothers. Although she was born on July 1, 1804, she long believed that her true birthday fell on July 5 (the date on which she would always celebrate it, even after she knew the true one); that she had been born abroad a year or two earlier; and that her birth certificate really belonged to another child who had died in infancy. This odd rigmarole, which she retailed in her autobiography, surely covers deep-seated fears and uncertainties about her identity that, in reality, have little to do with dates and potential rivals eliminated by fate, and much to do with the situation in which she found herself after her father's death.

What was she? What was her true nature, what her destiny? With such questions few females were supposed to be concerned. She was only brought to be preoccupied with them by her vulnerable position. Where did she really belong? Were her loyalties due to her royal ancestors and their ambitious, energetic, haughty, bastard offspring or to the members of her father's aristocratic family who had done their best to break the liaison with her mother? Or, if not to them, should her loyalties tend to her mother's side, a family of Parisian street vendors and shopkeepers, "actresses" of the most dubious sort, forced by poverty and the struggle for life to sully themselves in the eyes of high society but nonetheless proud of their plebeian resilience and, above all, tough?

Eventually, she would make a conscious choice between these opposing elements, driven to do so by circumstances and by the actions of her kinsfolk. Yet basically, her idea of her own identity was never really fixed. She would have to invent herself. Had her father lived, he might have helped her toward a balanced sense of self, by his mere presence enabling her to disentangle herself from her mother. In that case, it is perhaps unlikely that she would ever have become a writer; certainly not the kind of introspective and highly variable writer that she was in the beginning. Through her father's tragic death, Aurore was left at the age of four to the mercies of her volatile mother and her possessive grandmother, in their bitter struggle for the sole pledge he had bequeathed to them.

CHAPTER

2

~~~~~~~~~~~~~~~~~~~~~~~~~~~~~~~~~~~~~~~

The Pawn

OHANT was plunged into mourning. While the two women abandoned themselves to grief and despair, and Hippolyte could not stop crying, the four-year-old child, dressed in black, sat stunned by her mother's side. Remembering those long hours many years later, Aurore would advise a bereaved friend to exercise self-control for the sake of the children. But her mother and grandmother had lost too much by Maurice's death to consider the child. Mme Dupin was the first to realize what was happening and arranged for Aurore to have a young playmate, her maid's niece, Ursule, future faithful retainer, who was brought to the house carefully attired in black. From that time forward, Aurore felt as if there were a dark screen between the present and the early years before her father's death, a period that grew ever more to resemble an idyll of parental tenderness as distance increased.

Neither Mme Dupin nor Sophie had much cause to like each other, but in the six or seven weeks that the couple had spent at Nohant, the two women had submerged their distaste and their differences for Maurice's sake. Privately, Sophie was wounded by Mme Dupin's condescension and could avenge herself only in secret by typically Parisian mockery. Mme Dupin saw in Sophie a vain, frivolous, jealous woman, no longer young, who had taken her son away from her and ruined all her plans for him. If either could find qualities in the other, it was only occasionally.

Mme Dupin was not a passionate woman, except where her son was concerned. Sensibility and reason disputed her nature. Her manners and style were those of the eighteenth century. Dressed in a long-waisted, dark silk gown, regardless of neoclassical fashion, and never without a lace-trimmed cap upon her fair wig, she made a sober impression. The destructive wit of Voltaire, to whom she had appealed for protection in her younger days, left her largely indifferent to religion. Her sensibility was shaped by Jean-Jacques Rousseau. M. Dupin once brought home the author of *La Nouvelle Héloïse* (an occasion when all three were so moved that they burst into tears).

Extremely well read, Mme Dupin was a woman of critical spirit and independent judgment. Such gifted women, frustrated in other respects, found a unique source of power in the exercise of their maternal instincts. Little was now left to her but the chance to mold another human creature, Maurice's daughter (for, though well-disposed to Hippolyte, she did not feel so strongly about him). In Aurore, she saw another self; she saw her son as a child, the opportunity to relive her sole happiness, to avoid the same errors. What she forgot was that the relationship between mother and son is distinct from that between grandmother and granddaughter. She overlooked the abyss of years. Sometimes, struck by the physical resemblance, she would even absentmindedly call her granddaughter "Maurice" or "my son." It was a possible role for Aurore to assume, but she would not be willing to do so for her grandmother's benefit.

Sophie was governed neither by sensibility nor reason. She was not governed by anything. She was all instinct and impulse. A pale-skinned beauty with dark hair and weary eyes, she was obsessed with her looks. Moreover, she suffered from a sense of inferiority vis-à-vis women whose privileged upbringing had endowed them with social graces and savoir-vivre. Unlike her mother-in-law, who bestirred herself only with difficulty, Sophie always kept busy, washing, ironing, mending, making dresses, trimming hats, even constructing a grotto in the garden to delight Aurore and her friend Ursule. Aurore admired her mother's energy and inherited it. Where Mme Dupin was calm and deliberate, inclined to stoicism, Sophie was quick, violent, unpredictable. At one moment she could be reading one of the moralizing tales of Mme de Genlis to Aurore, who sat dreaming of a fantasy world in the shadows thrown by the fire upon a green silk screen; at another she could administer a cuff that would sharply arouse the child from her reverie.

If Mme Dupin had known adversity, especially during the Revolution, Sophie Delaborde had known the gutter. Both Sophie's parents were dead by the time she was seventeen, which was then considered the marriageable age for girls, whatever their station, and she suffered the common fate of those who were beautiful, unprotected, and poor. There were gaps in her life history before she had thrown herself into Maurice's arms in Italy, gaps that naturally she was not keen to fill. She had passed as the wife of another military man, a certain Charles-Denis Vantin, otherwise known as Saint-Charles, to whom she had borne a child; but she could not have been his wife, since he was later married during her lifetime. Nothing is recorded about the fate of their child. Later, she fell in with the man who was Caroline's father and whose name is unknown. Aurore's aristocratic relations would always draw the line at associating with Caroline Delaborde, the mystery surrounding her birth being thought particularly disreputable. Sophie was certainly in dire straits when Collin found her on the streets of Paris and took her to Italy as his wife.

Then there were so many children she had borne and lost, of whom Caroline and Aurore were apparently the sole survivors. Clearly, the sponge method of birth control, known in France by the last decade of the eighteenth century, had not reached Sophie's level, or had proved fallible. What was her conduct toward her offspring likely to be? In general the attitude to children had begun to improve by the middle of the eighteenth century, but there remains the notorious example of Rousseau, the friend of humanity who consigned all his infants to the foundling hospital. This was by no means an uncommon practice for women who had conceived legitimate, as well as illegitimate, children. Parents were then inclined to be either casual or demanding, or both at different times. The notion that a child's earliest years were crucial for his or her later development had not yet become a commonplace. (Indeed, Aurore was only beginning to glimpse it by the early eighteen forties.)

Sophie's reactions to her children were probably variable, dependent upon the conditions of the moment: She loved them tenderly or found them a nuisance. Some women did not even have her excuse of poverty or vulnerability. In respectable bourgeois circumstances, Mme Balzac put out to nurse her son Honoré (born five years before Aurore), visiting the child only rarely. At eight he was sent to a rigorous boarding school. Small wonder that he could exclaim bitterly, "I never had a mother," and that his grudge against her lasted as long as he lived. In comparison with his childhood, Aurore's, though not without pain, might even appear privileged.

After all the disasters that had overtaken Sophie in 1808, she was tired. It was winter, and the countryside was desolate. She hated Nohant, that house in the middle of nowhere, miles away from the bustle and the pleasures of Paris, from her sister and her friends. She longed to escape from her frigid, patronizing mother-in-law; from her husband's former tutor, Deschartres, who had always done his best to thwart her; from the hostile servants. Of course, she could take Aurore with her to Paris, but . . . Mme Dupin had advanced such very convincing arguments: the child's best interests and a supplementary annual allowance, provided Sophie gave up her guardianship.

The difficulty was that since Maurice's death, Aurore had developed a veritable passion for her mother, who did not like cloying dependence at all. If Mme Dupin could call her granddaughter "Maurice" or "my son," Aurore could project herself into her father's supposed role as Sophie's adoring protector. Her mother explained that she was going to Paris, that she could no longer stay away from her other daughter, Caroline (who had been placed in a modest boarding school where, indeed, for the most part she would remain). Caroline, after all, had no kind grandmother to look after her. Besides, Aurore would be following with her grandmother in a fortnight. On January 28, 1809, Sophie signed the document that gave Mme Dupin complete authority as Aurore's legal guardian, and shortly afterward set off for Paris and a new life. Her inner struggle had lasted some four months.

It was Mme Dupin's custom to spend the winter season in Paris. At that time, the journey by her private berlin took three or four days, with overnight stops along roads infested with highwaymen. In Paris she could visit or receive her friends and attend the concerts and theaters she loved. Her pied-à-terre, with its furniture dating from the reign of Louis XVI, appeared far more luxurious than her country mansion. Even more splendid was the home of Mme Dupin's bastard half-brother, urbane abbé de Beaumont, with its magnificent Louis XIV drawing room, which Aurore was allowed to see by candlelight while her elders were playing cards after dinner.

Aurore did not forget those splendid human relics of the old regime when she came to write, but as a child she far preferred her mother's modest rooms, which she considered to be her true home. There, everything seemed more natural, more warm, more active, more fun. She could play with her half-sister Caroline (on Sunday leave from boarding school) and her cousin Clotilde Maréchal. A devoted friend of her parents, Louis-Mammès Pierret, was always at hand. Anything her mother said, did, or admired appeared enchanting. Aurore's passion for her mother fed on this contrast between the elderly who, though kindly, seemed so slow, mannered, or remote, and the quick verve of those who made up her mother's milieu.

This was the very ambience from which her grandmother longed to wean her. But, of course, such an end could not be achieved all at once. Who was this fellow Pierret, and what precisely was his relationship with Sophie? In any case, this dubious atmosphere was not for her granddaughter. Mme Dupin wanted to be able to form Aurore's taste and critical judgment. This aim could scarcely be achieved if the child were permitted to consort with mediocrities. Her dream was to produce a refined young girl, endowed with all those accomplishments deemed essential for acceptance in polite society, a girl who would ultimately be fitted to enter into the solid kind of marriage Maurice had failed to make. Perhaps—supreme ambition—she might marry into the aristocratic side of the family, finding a partner among the offspring of her cousins, René or Auguste Vallet de Villeneuve, grandsons of M. Dupin by his first marriage. Such considerations of matrimony, entertained while the object of them was still a small child, then formed a large part of the interests of a lady of Mme Dupin's station. All too soon, Aurore learned about her grandmother's plans through the servants and was much troubled by them throughout her childhood.

In the early years after Sophie yielded her rights over Aurore to her mother-in-law, mother and child would see each other during Mme Dupin's annual winter visits to the capital, at first daily, then afterward only on Sundays. Later during the year, Sophie might pay a visit to Nohant, sometimes remaining there as little as a month. The long separations were painful to the child and only increased her idealization and adoration of her mother and her mother's style of life. She had plenty of time to dream. Moreover, Mme Dupin was not always wise in the way she carried out her resolve. On one occasion during this early period, Caroline appeared at Mme Dupin's Parisian pied-à-terre asking to see Aurore and was refused admittance. Aurore could hear Caroline's sobs, and she was deeply upset by this unexplained prohibition. Mme

Dupin was moved to grant that Aurore might see Caroline at her mother's, but would not allow the unfortunate pariah to darken her own doors.

Such disturbing incidents contributed to the heightened emotional sensibility of the imaginative child. As Sophie came to rely more and more upon the pretext of Caroline's need for her in order to explain her long absences, it was inevitable that Aurore should feel jealous toward her half-sister. Caroline in her turn would know jealousy of Aurore. Each imagined that the other had a greater share of their mother's love. Their relationship would eventually become cool and guarded. More than twenty years later, Aurore would hotly deny any jealousy of Caroline, when accused of it by her mother.

On several occasions Aurore was to write that children hear everything. The girl overheard her grandmother as she sat discussing Sophie with royalist friends; she overheard servants, unsparing of a woman of their own class who had married above her station. At Nohant, the servants were divided into two parties: those who took her mother's part and those who did not. In so far as she understood their words, Aurore assumed that disapproval rested upon her mother's social position, upon erroneous interpretations of her character, not upon her reputation. Her own passion for the underdog and for justice was aroused. She defended her mother in the only court that mattered, in her innermost heart.

Aurore's early awareness of differing viewpoints made her an observant child. Moreover, she could read at four, and she was about five when she learned to write. The fairy stories of Perrault and Mme d'Aulnoy delighted her. Her grandmother, who had met Gluck and was familiar with the work of the leading eighteenth-century composers, gave her lessons in music from an early age. The child would sit entranced beneath the old harpsichord with a favorite dog, as her grandmother ran her stiff fingers over the keyboard. Music formed one of the principal accomplishments of a lady, whose chief aim was to please, as did dancing, sketching, the ability to turn a phrase, to converse with charm and wit, to compose an interesting letter. As well as a feeling for music, Mme Dupin succeeded in inculcating some of these, notably penmanship (for her granddaughter would be one of the world's most singular, brilliant, and prolific letter writers); but throughout her life Aurore cared little for dancing and was famous for her lack of conversation.

On the whole, Mme Dupin was not much satisfied with the result of her efforts to impress upon Aurore the virtues of *tenue,* or good manners, ladylike bearing, and a proper sense of decorum. Her grandmother believed that there was a correct style for performing each action, however trivial, a form of social elegance that must be acquired early. Mme Dupin spoke gently, but she addressed the child with the formal "vous" and objected to any familiarity of speech whether with the servants or herself.

When Aurore was seven, Mme Dupin entrusted the more formal part of the child's education to the remarkable pedagogue who had been her son's tutor and who was already in charge of that of Aurore's half-brother, Hippolyte. Variously mayor of Nohant, farm manager, and general adviser to Mme Dupin, in demand for his medical skills, Deschartres at fifty was still a handsome figure, rather vain as well as pedantic. Many years later, Aurore would tell Flaubert that her tutor grotesquely combined genuine learning with a total lack of common sense. The children called him "the Great Man." Indulgent with her, he was more severe with the lazy and fractious Hippolyte. Aurore's feelings toward Deschartres were ambivalent. She never forgot that he disliked and opposed her mother (who returned his animosity in kind); nor did she forget that, despite his faults, she owed him a great deal.

As for Hippolyte, he made his half-sister's life a misery in the manner of small boys. When she was little, he teased her, stole her dolls, knocked them about, and made her cry. She admits that at times she hated him, but she went on playing with him because, naturally, she adored him as well. Their sibling rivalry, now subdued, now rekindled, would endure. It would be sublimated in the ideal relationship between the eponymous hero of her novel *Jacques* and Sylvia, who may well be his half-sister. Hippolyte, destructive, fond of rather brutal practical jokes involving animals, was the torment of his tutor's life. For a few months in 1811–1812, the boy was dispatched to a boarding school in Paris, but he made such a nuisance of himself there that he was restored to the supervision of Deschartres.

The lessons the children received consisted of the same subjects, grammar, French versification, arithmetic, to which would be added Latin and botany (though Deschartres skipped "the mystery of generation and function of the sexes" essential for understanding it, in Aurore's later view). The only difference between Aurore's lessons and Hippolyte's was that hers tended to be shorter. It was then quite customary in enlightened households (as it had been for generations) for girls to participate in a fairly desultory way in their brothers' lessons, despite the widespread prejudice perpetuated by Rousseau that girls, whose main purpose was to please, did not need the same academic instruction as boys.

Certainly, compared with the extraordinary education that Germaine Necker, afterward Mme de Staël, received some forty years before as the daughter of an eminent banker and political figure, an education that made her into a bizarre child prodigy who could hold her own among the luminaries of her neurotic mother's salon, Aurore's schooling appears unsystematic and more ordinary. Compared with the education she would have received had her mother taken her to Paris, it looks striking and even impressive for the time, complemented as it was by her grandmother's lessons, not only in music but in geography, history (which Aurore loved in its romantic and literary aspect), and above all, literature. Her grandmother encouraged her to express her personal appreciation of what she read and allowed her, in her compositions, to "decorate" somewhat the dry evidence of her sources by developing a character here or elaborating a description there. These signs of facility of expression and of an imaginative gift delighted Mme Dupin. The inclination to embroider was never to fail Aurore, and this is one reason to be wary of those marvelously fluid dialogues, suggestive of virtually superhuman recall, which she would include in her account of her early years.

Aurore alternated between assiduity and indifference in her lessons, or so she said afterward. The enduring prejudice against pedantic females (which she shared) may have led her to underplay some aspects of her desire for instruction. She made light of her Latin, for instance; but according to one of her grandmother's letters, Aurore felt the need to learn and would even insist on being taught Latin. Her grandmother had managed to instill in her the habit of work (which is so essential a part of a writer's armory), and for this Aurore would later be devoutly grateful.

Meanwhile, in the winter of 1811–1812, lessons in the social graces continued in Paris, where Aurore shared with an aristocratic little friend, Pauline de Pontcarré, the services of a dancing master (one of the dancers of the Opéra), a writing teacher, and a music mistress. A drawing teacher, said to be the daughter of Greuze, was engaged for Aurore alone. During that winter, Aurore felt she was seeing rather less of her mother than on previous visits to Paris.

However, Sophie came to Nohant later in the year. Aurore left her mother a note in childish hand—the first letter to come down to us—before her idol's departure: "How sorry I am not to be able to say goodbye. You see how[. . .] upset to leave you. Goodbye, think of me and be sure I won't forget you." And as a postscript: "Put your answer behind grandpa Dupin's portrait." Genuine distress, the need to assert and prove her attachment, the appeal for affection, with an added touch of conspiratorial romance, already formed part of her feeling about separation from her mother.

About this time, when she was seven or eight, Aurore was given passages from the dramas of Corneille and Racine to learn by heart. It is Corneille who seems to have left the deeper imprint, with his scenes of courageous self-conquest and self-abnegation, of high-souled heroic generosity. As the news of Napoleon's army, lost in the snows of Russia, filtered to Nohant, the imaginative girl began to have dreams of ambition and elevation. She fancied that she grew wings, flew over the Russian steppe, and guided Napoleon's legions safely home; or else she swooped down upon the enemy forces with a flaming sword, like some theatrical divinity, and put them to rout. Once, by touching the emperor with her sword, she made him invulnerable. Such were the waking dreams that came to her while she was trying to learn the verses of Corneille or Racine. Her mother would have to love and pay attention to a little girl who could save the army and protect the greatest military genius.

There was no means of putting this love to the test, for Mme Dupin did not visit Paris in the winter of 1812–1813, nor did Sophie go to Nohant during 1813. Not until December of that year, when Aurore accompanied her grandmother to the capital, did she see her mother for a brief period. Toward the end of January 1814, Aurore and her grandmother were back in Nohant.

Not long after their return, Mme Dupin suddenly fell seriously ill. Recovery was slow. Intense pain made her irritable and difficult. She began to rely more heavily upon her servants, especially her maid, Julie, head of the party opposed to Sophie, who arrived at Nohant in April 1814 for a month's visit. Aurore now realized that, as a result of her grandmother's illness, she was going to see even less of her mother, who made no secret of her continuing dislike of Nohant, particularly under Julie's ascendency, whether her daughter were confined there or not.

As the hour for her mother's departure drew near, Aurore begged to be taken with her. If considerations of a good education, a fine marriage, and wealth were to be weighed against poverty with her mother (who would lose her supplementary allowance if she broke the contract with Mme Dupin), then without hesitation Aurore chose poverty. For a moment, the headstrong Sophie yielded or appeared to yield to her daughter's pleas. After all, Sophie mused, she could again open a dress shop in the provinces, where she and her two daughters could earn their living by honest toil. She would make inquiries and would come for Aurore when all was ready. This "secret plan" filled the nine-year-old with joy. However, the idea that the battered Sophie, who knew what real poverty meant, could seriously consider returning to a life of precarious toil, aided by a small child and another not much older, seems unlikely in the extreme.

Aurore waited desperately for a further sign from Sophie, but there came none. Just as the child had done two years earlier, she wrote a letter begging her mother to leave word, before going away to Paris, behind her grandfather's portrait. But already Sophie had had second thoughts. When her mother was gone, Aurore ran to the portrait and found nothing. The "secret plan"—or the emotional tie it stood for—continued to fill the child's dreams for several years to come, even though her mother's letters became less frequent, even though the suspicion had entered Aurore's mind—surely never to be eradicated—that she loved more deeply than she was loved.

The element of trust, essential for solid, lasting human relationships, was being undermined by the situation in which Aurore found herself, by the erratic nature of Sophie's affection and conduct. The pattern was already beginning to take shape, the pattern of intense, wild exaltation and idealization in the early stages of a relationship, eventually followed by doubt, by a sense of betrayal, and all too often by disgust for those whom she had previously thought sublime and devoted. And she would later endow some of her novelistic characters with this awareness of a lack of proper balance and true judgment.

Aurore soon had cause to feel guilty at her disloyalty toward her grandmother. One day, during dinner, Mme Dupin fell into a sort of catalepsy. Aurore's fondness for her grandmother—as for so many others—was strengthened by the sight of her infirmity. These distressing attacks would recur at intervals. Mme Dupin could still give Aurore brief lessons, but she tired easily; her judgment of people was affected by her dependence on her servants; she was no longer the matriarch in total command. For long periods, Aurore was left to her own devices.

It was during her grandmother's decline that Rose, a maid who was otherwise very attached to Aurore, began to exceed her office. Without always realizing what she was doing, Rose would administer, in private, sharp corrective slaps. Hippolyte knew about these, but he said nothing "as he never liked making enemies." Here, Corneille came to the girl's aid. She met this trial with stoic fortitude and in silence. She told no one, and she forgave the injury. As she would later express it, ". . . I found my vengeance in my heroism and in the forgiveness I bestowed on my maid."

On the domestic scale, it is a repetition of the sublime moment in Corneille's play *Cinna*, where the Emperor Augustus conquers himself and pardons the conspirators. Instead of exacting vengeance in the accepted sense, by having them put to death, he avenges himself nobly through his clemency, by proving his moral superiority to those who have wronged him, to the world at large, and above all, to himself. By some powerful instinct of pride, which those who believe in heredity might attribute to her royal and aristocratic ancestry, the child glimpsed a greater inner satisfaction in vengeance through pardon. Magnanimous self-sacrifice allowed her to feel superior, and that was what she needed more than anything to counter the sneers she overheard about her adored mother; the uncertainty of her own position, entirely dependent upon her grandmother's patronage; the fact that she did not know where she really belonged.

Not only public political upheavals—Napoleon's abdication, his return from Elba, his defeat at Waterloo, the presence of the Allies in Paris—but, on the private plane, her grandmother's continuing ill health meant that Aurore remained at Nohant between January 1814 and November 1817. It may seem surprising that, given the state of Mme Dupin's health, Sophie did not evince more active concern for her daughter's welfare.

After Hippolyte enlisted in the Third Hussars and went off to join his regiment in March 1816, Aurore spent a good deal of her time by herself, absorbed in her own private world. She read poetry, Homer's *Iliad* and Tasso's *Jerusalem Delivered* in translation. She loved Tasso's epic, with its balance of fragile and energetic ladies, and adopted his characters, placing them in adventures of her own devising.

At about twelve, too, she began to write. These early efforts took the form of descriptions of a moonlit summer night or of the countryside where she loved to walk, descriptions of nature that were later to be her forte. She was dissatisfied with her written sketches, because they never seemed to equal the spontaneity of her first impressions or the charm such scenes possessed in her imagination. Her grandmother praised these descriptions to all and sundry. One, sent to her mother, aroused Sophie's mirth. There was not likely to be much encouragement from that quarter. If Aurore gave up writing for a while, she never stopped collecting material and making up stories in her head.

In her fantasy world, there arose a strange figure whom she named Corambé, part novelistic character, part spiritual ideal. Corambé appeared in her imagination as a beautiful, eloquent, talented creature, to be loved as a (male) friend or as a sister, and to be revered as a spiritual being—now masculine, now feminine, now completely sexless. An endless narrative was woven about this unearthly marvel of kindness and goodness who, while suffering innumerable trials and tribulations, consoled Aurore in hers. In a secret corner of the wood in the garden, she set up an altar to this celestial being, to whom she devoted a veritable cult. In Corambé's ability to charm by word and song there remains a strong suggestion of precocious literary ambition, while through the cult there pierces a hint of self-worship, since Corambé is (like Aurore) both martyr and angel of consolation. When the altar was discovered by one of her peasant companions, she destroyed it. But if the cult itself ceased, the inner weaving of a poetic narrative about an ideal being, source and object of tender affection, witness of her profound need for sympathy and her urge to self-expression, continued until she published her novel *Indiana* some sixteen years later.

Life for Aurore was not all secret fantasy, though. She also roamed and romped with the peasant children, swineherds, shepherds, the sons and daughters of farmers and farm workers, playmates through whom—as well as from her own observation—she doubtless learned far more about the earthy aspects of country existence and about the natural cycle than she was later prepared to admit. This was an unusual phase of her upbringing, for there was no suggestion on her grandmother's part that these peasant children might not be fit companions for a potential lady. In the open air, she grew remarkably vigorous and was thought strong for her age and sex. Energetic activity became essential to her, the reverse of her grandmother's lassitude and inaction, which offered a warning example to the girl as she adjusted her pace to Mme Dupin's fragile steps.

Although Mme Dupin was not a believer, it struck her that Aurore's conventional accomplishments would be incomplete if she were not to prepare for First Communion. Purely in this spirit, the unregenerate Voltairean deist arranged for Aurore to take instruction from the curé of La Châtre; purely in this spirit, Aurore followed her grandmother's wishes. However, the girl acquired then her distaste for confession, which she seems to have associated with injudicious probings into questions of chastity and which in any event she considered humiliating. The old lady attended the rite, which took place in La Châtre in March 1817. Her circle of friends, the worldly churchmen, the "old countesses" ridiculed by Sophie (who doubtless conveyed her own mockery of them to her daughter), had come into their own with the downfall of the Corsican upstart and the restoration of Louis XVIII, and they reinforced Mme Dupin's fundamentally royalist sentiments as well as her increasing conformity. Religion *à la mode* appeared as an instrument of stability (or of reaction, depending on the point of view). At the least, it had again become part of social decorum.

In the summer of 1817, two events occurred that, in very different ways, were to have lasting effects upon Aurore's development. The first was the visit to La Châtre of a company of strolling players and musicians. At the impressionable age of thirteen, Aurore was enchanted with the dramas and operas presented by the strolling players. The theater would remain one of her favorite diversions. Indeed, hers was an age enraptured by the theater. Throughout her life, much of it later devoted to writing for the boards, her heart would beat faster as the curtain was about to rise. Not only the actors themselves but true devotees among the spectators are people fascinated by questions of identity and self-definition, by the search for a role, by the varied, magical opportunities the stage provides for assuming different ones and becoming lost in them.

Between altar and greasepaint, dreams and tomboy escapades, staying up late to read and write in her room or neglecting her lessons, Aurore was becoming difficult for a much weakened old lady to control. Whenever the girl was dreaming about joining her mother, she stopped being interested in her books, which at other times she would devour as if insatiable in her will to learn. After all, her studies would be of no use in the humble kind of life she would lead with her mother. Mme Dupin loved her granddaughter, but she was also very conscious that she was conferring a favor by giving Sophie's child an education and prospects, a favor of which the recipient seemed totally unaware. She expected obedience and gratitude; she expected love in return. She was disappointed.

The second, shattering event—even more subtly destructive, perhaps, than Sophie's abrupt departure at the beginning of 1809, or her disinclination to come to Aurore's rescue—occurred when, provoked by Mme Dupin's maid, Julie, the girl let slip that she was longing to be with her mother. This indiscretion, duly reported to Mme Dupin, deeply wounded the sick old lady. At first, she refused to see Aurore. Then, when the girl was brought to her bedside, she told her, in a voice quivering with bitterness, all that she knew about Sophie's past (probably less than the whole truth, many of whose details remain in shadow). In her loneliness of spirit Mme Dupin spared nothing, made no allowances for dire poverty or adverse fate, and roundly qualified her daughter-in-law as "a fallen woman." Worse still, she hinted that even Sophie's present mode of life was not above suspicion and that it would be dangerous for Aurore to live with her mother. Only by this drastic method, she reasoned, could she hope to save Aurore from the consequences of her ignorance and folly.

Stunned by these shameful revelations, Aurore returned to her room and wept without relief. Even in middle age, when writing her autobiography, she heavily scratched out a number of lines at this point in her life story. The girl who had soared in dreams above the Russian steppe to save Napoleon and his legions was in despair, humiliated by the humiliation of the object of her deepest affections. It was one thing for her mother to be despised for her lack of birth or breeding, but quite another for her to be deemed worthy of contempt, debased and shamed before her adoring daughter. If her mother betrayed her in one way, her grandmother did so in another. From despair and wounded pride, Aurore moved to profound scorn for the rest of humanity. Scorn was the only way she could preserve her own self-esteem and superiority.

Months passed. Sullen, defiant, Aurore complained of being bored at Nohant, of being left to herself without a companion of her own age and tastes, without a proper master. Mme Dupin then made a decision that contradicted her Voltairean principles, one that she herself would come to rue. It was the traditional means for dealing with recalcitrant girls: the convent.

CHAPTER

3

Still Waters

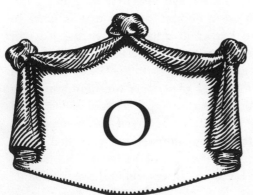

O N January 12, 1818, Aurore passed through the portal of the Convent of the English Augustinian Sisters in the rue des Fossés-Saint-Victor in Paris. The two years and three months that she was to spend in purple uniform, cloistered behind its high walls, would leave a permanent mark on her imagination. Mme Dupin was herself well acquainted with the rambling old edifice, since she had taken up voluntary residence there during the interval between the death of her first husband and marriage to her second, this being common practice for respectable, unprotected ladies who wished to preserve their reputation. During the Terror, part of the convent functioned as a prison, and Mme Dupin had been incarcerated there for withholding valuables from the revolutionary government. (By a strange chance, at roughly the same period, though doubtless in a less aristocratic quarter of the building, Sophie, then a small-part actress, was held—her crime being the performance of a counterrevolutionary song.)

By the time Mme Dupin brought Aurore to the English convent, it had long reverted in entirety to its proper use, and under the Empire and the Restoration it had become one of the most fashionable religious houses in Paris, with strong aristocratic connections. The nuns came of good British recusant family, as did the majority of the pupils, the remainder being French girls of the nobility or the higher bourgeoisie. If Mme Dupin wished to bind her granddaughter to her own caste, she could not have made a wiser choice.

Aurore's first impression as she entered the cloister was of extreme cold. Here, there could be no late rising and keeping of late hours, as at Nohant. The girls, who shared an unheated dormitory, rose at six and washed in icy water. While it was still dark, they attended mass, breakfasted on bread and tea at seven, and began lessons just as it was growing light. But, whatever the physical discomforts, for the first time Aurore was thrown into the close company of girls of her own age and interests who, apart from the fact that they appeared to come from more settled families than hers, were roughly in the same situation. She was only thirteen, after all, and relieved to find in the new life and new companions of the convent an escape from the emotional tensions and upheavals caused by the rivalry between her mother (who mocked the whole undertaking) and her grandmother.

Mme Dupin seemed rather unreasonably aggrieved that Aurore was accepting the new experience so philosophically. She had decided that Aurore should take no holidays, in order that her granddaughter might gain the utmost benefit from her studies. Meanwhile, she remained in Paris until the spring, anxious to be at hand. Twice a month during this period, Aurore left the convent for her grandmother's pied-à-terre, the home of abbé de Beaumont or of the Villeneuves, but she had come to prefer the society of her new friends and to dislike the sharp contrast these outings provided. Just before leaving for Nohant, on May 11, Mme Dupin wrote to Aurore: "It is five o'clock in the morning. . . . I am thinking of you, my dear child, and want to say goodbye again before I go. . . . To prove to me that you are touched by my care and affection for you, work hard . . . profit from the large sums I am spending on you, that is the only means of not making me regret them. . . ."

What the Convent of the English Augustinian Sisters provided was a kind of superior "finishing school." Although her grandmother thought her well educated for her age, at first Aurore was placed in the "little class," consisting of about thirty girls aged from six to thirteen or fourteen. Any special lessons took place in one of several convent parlors, with the pupil on one side of the grille and the teacher on the other. For dancing lessons, given by a spry eighty-year-old master who had served under Marie-Antoinette, the girls were free to ignore the grille. There were also lessons in music, drawing, the social graces. In addition, Aurore studied Italian and made rapid progress in English, a necessity since the nuns spoke little else. She would remain grateful for her ability to read Shakespeare and Byron in the original, but nonetheless afterward she professed to hold a very poor opinion of the convent's educational standards. Yet this establishment was probably among the best available to girls at that period.

Aurore lost no time in joining the "devils," as the wilder girls were called. Led by an Irish girl, the band of "devils" of the "little class" found plenty of opportunity for practical jokes and were endlessly in fits of giggles. During general silence, in the overheated emotional atmosphere of an enclosed community, they scribbled notes to each other, questioning and affirming their love.

One of the traditions of the "devils" was a marvelous game called "rescuing the victim." Like Aurore, who had read at Nohant a story that, if not by the egregious Mrs. Radcliffe herself, was of a similar character and written by one of her numerous imitators, the girls were captivated by the Gothic mode, with its imprisoned heroines, mysterious apparitions amid gloomy romantic ruins, and villainous persecutors of injured innocence. The convent in its prison or punishment aspect lent itself to such dread imaginings, mirror of a possible female fate. Though the house had been founded in the French provinces in the Middle Ages, it was established in Paris in the seventeenth century on an ancient site. Its cellars may even have merged into the old city's network of underground passages.

The game of "rescuing the victim" consisted of an adventurous exploration of the crumbling convent cellars in quest of the incarcerated heroine whose voice (so the more suggestive maintained) could sometimes be heard pleading plaintively behind the walls as she rattled her chains. Years later, when she described the convent cellars in her autobiography, Aurore imparted to them the weird air of one of Piranesi's etchings of imaginary prisons, with their frightening staircases that lead nowhere. But the game itself she saw as a collective novel in action, and when she came to write of convents or monasteries in her own books, like *Lélia* or *Spiridion*, the mysterious, seemingly haunted crypts and underground galleries of the English convent would reappear, not just as romantic paraphernalia in the manner of Ann Radcliffe or "Monk" Lewis, but as a remembered part of a daring, pleasurably fearful, and real experience of her girlhood.

The poetry of the cloister and of the religious life also appealed to her. She was drawn by one side of her nature—the contemplative, solitary, dreamy side—to the chapel, paved with the memorial stones of the exiled British recusant dead. In its candlelit penumbra a veiled nun might be glimpsed kneeling in prayer. She loved the convent garden with its great horse-chestnut trees, and the quiet of the cemetery. As the months passed, she grew better aware of the convent hierarchy: its well-born mother superior and nuns and its proletariat in the shape of the humble lay sisters who performed all the unpleasant menial tasks. With her keen and already experienced gift of observation, she noted one of the nuns who was interested in astronomy and who was thought to be a freethinker, and another who bitterly regretted having taken vows. (These would later appear as monks in *Spiridion*.) Sometimes, she could hear the blasphemous oaths of the market people in the street outside. Nothing was simple.

As "Madcap," one of the leading lights of the mischievous "devils," which she would remain for about a year or eighteen months, and as self-styled "generalissimo" of the band, Aurore fell afoul of the disciplinarian Mlle D., a teacher whom she chose not to name in full. Promoted to the "big class," Aurore went back to her old classroom to collect her books. Mlle D., smarting under some real or imagined insult, promptly locked her in the book cupboard. (This incident, too, would reappear in *Spiridion*, in the episode where Alexis is left locked in the monastery library.) As for Mlle D., she was granted Aurore's pardon, the special Cornelian magnanimous forgiveness that allowed the detested creature to feel the full force of her victim's "superiority."

"Devil" or not, however, Aurore managed to obtain the protection of one of the most respected and admired members of the community, Mother Alicia Spiring. It was long customary in religious houses for nuns to adopt a few of their pupils as "daughters." Aurore explained to Mother Alicia how she already had two mothers in Sophie and her grandmother; how the three of them contrived to make each other suffer; how she needed a wise and good mother whose affection would be stable and undemanding, and would give her some idea of her true identity. "I don't know yet what I am or what I can be," she confessed to Mother Alicia. It was really what she saw as either inadequate or excessive demands by her mother and grandmother that made her seek out Mother Alicia. What she needed was an ideal mother, of the kind she had read about in books, to replace her own unreliable and disappointing parent. She needed a dream object of perfection, quietude, and justice, to venerate "above myself," a living Corambé, as it were. Mother Alicia became, from the summer of 1818, "my ideal, my sacred love, the mother of my choice."

From Nohant came her grandmother's letter, expressing satisfaction that good Mother Alicia was taking Aurore under her wing and containing the usual admonitions concerning drawing and dancing, admonitions that may well have fed Aurore's sense of her own value and importance. Already, among the staff at Nohant, she was known as "our young lady." "Beware, my dear, of weakening the talent given you by nature," wrote Mme Dupin. "Begin with the most difficult; what is easy comes all by itself. . . . I am so desirous of seeing you perfect in mind and body, and you have so many gifts if you want to use them. . . ." For Aurore's fourteenth birthday, Mme Dupin managed to arrange for some flowers and presents to be sent to her granddaughter:

If only I could send you as a bouquet a magnificent cherry tree by the corner of the château, it is so laden with fruit, its branches are bending over. . . . As long as I live I want to celebrate your birthday, provided you will console me for the loss of him who gave you life; and I hope for that consolation from your efforts to improve yourself, from your good behavior and your gratitude to your grandma who loves you dearly.

Mme Dupin never forgot that once, when she was weeping by her son's grave in the grounds at Nohant, Aurore had whispered, "Dear grandmamma, I shall console you."

During those months when her daughter was in the English convent in Paris, what had become of Sophie, whose home was in the city? She had been asked by Mme Dupin not to take Aurore out, but she came once a month to visit her daughter, and they spoke through the grille in the convent parlor in the presence of one of the sisters—or so Aurore remembered some years later. The girl felt that her mother had no sympathy for her moments of exaltation, indeed, that Sophie tried to repress them. It seemed to her that her mother no longer cared about her. Whether this impression was partly the result of Mme Dupin's successful maneuver in placing the girl out of her mother's reach in the convent or the result of Aurore's new interests and new well-born friends, little is heard of Sophie during her daughter's convent years. It may well be that, rather than Sophie's moving away from her daughter at this time, as the latter suggests, it was Aurore who was growing away from her mother.

Among Aurore's convent friends were some whose families were household names and with whom she was to correspond for many years, right up to the creation of a new life and personality. Louise de La Rochejaquelein, for instance, was the daughter of a famous heroine of the revolt of the Chouans against the revolutionary government, whose memoirs Aurore had read at Nohant and would later use. Another close friend was Emilie, daughter of Baron de Wismes. These girls, with Aimée and Jane Bazouin (illegitimate daughters of a wealthy land-owner) would all marry into the nobility.

Aurore's deepest attachment was to Fannelly de Brisac, whose Gascon accent delighted her. Fannelly, who made the first move in initiating the friendship, was (Aurore would remark) the "sole being" in life in whom she felt she could place perfect trust and whose affection she knew would never falter, whether they were together or not. Convent schools often tend to foster such warm and elevated associations. For Aurore, the unquestioning Fannelly remained the model friend whose equal would be hard to find.

Nonetheless, the convent frowned on excessively close friendships between the girls, who were forbidden to kiss, to write letters to each other, and to walk in twos. The pupils attributed these rules to piety and had little difficulty in getting round them. Being confined behind convent walls, their dream was of freedom—the freedom to return to their families, the freedom some thought they might enjoy in marriage, for which they were being groomed so carefully. Affecting to be bored, they dreamed about pleasures, balls, travel, clothes, life in society. Yet sometimes, in dread of marriage and the world, they contemplated a life of solitude and renunciation, preferably in the Swiss Alps.

There was fear of the future, of the unknown, but the marvelous thing about the convent from Aurore's point of view was that nobody knew much about the past of her companions or about their family life. Each girl was free to confide or conceal what she thought fit, and it seems unlikely that Aurore would have told anyone about her mother's history or about the pain its revelation had caused her. Writing to Emilie de Wismes some years after leaving the convent, Aurore could inform her friend that, up to and including her convent years, she had never experienced any sorrow. On the other hand, she had talked "in secret" to a chosen few about her father's love child, who was suddenly promoted to Hippolyte *de* Chatiron. Nothing seems more revealing of her social inclinations toward the nobility than the intrusive "de" with which she ennobled her part-peasant illegitimate half-brother.

In December 1818, Mme Dupin came to Paris on her annual visit. Worried by declining health, she was more anxious than ever about what might become of her granddaughter if she herself were unable to pro-tect her. In addition to the usual visits to abbé de Beaumont and to the

Villeneuves, she took Aurore to see her friends, the "old countesses," in an attempt to forge closer links between her granddaughter and the nobility. A number of potential suitors were introduced. Aurore, not yet fifteen, did not take much notice of them. Mme Dupin returned to Nohant in April 1819, disappointed.

It was toward the spring of 1819 that Aurore began to settle down. She made good progress in Italian and English, if not in social graces, and to her great delight she had been allowed to move from the dormitory to a cell of her own, where she could dream of Nohant or play her grandmother's harp. About this time, she felt the urge to write. Already in the previous year she had written a satirical account of events in the convent in letters to her grandmother, who enjoyed it, but it had led to trouble, because the mother superior had opened the letters, much to Aurore's indignation.

Now, she took to composing poetry, a few lines of which have survived. She also produced a pious tale (now lost) in which the hero, named FitzGerald, and heroine became respectively priest and nun. Significantly, her friends preferred in the tale her portrayal of a mother to her dull hero and heroine who were apparently not in love with each other. The character of the mother presumably had some basis in life. Afterward, she tried a pastoral novel that fared no better and that she destroyed. Then, as once before with her attempts at description, she gave up writing, as she found more pleasure in her imaginings than in the end product. The self-indulgent dream of Corambé was not interrupted. However, she had acquired the useful literary habit of noting down her impressions, as a result of which her companions gave her the nickname "Calepin," or "Notebook."

She was soon to gain another, more in keeping with her surroundings. That winter, she had been struck by a painting that hung in an ill-lit corner of the chapel, "The Agony in the Garden," at the moment when it was illuminated by a ray of sunshine. This fleeting moment of poetry moved her as she looked up from reading the *Lives of the Saints* during the afternoon period of prayer and meditation. Another painting whose subject was Saint Augustine as he heard the words *"Tolle, lege"* encouraged her to look again at the Scriptures, but to little effect. The fact was that, by the summer of 1819, when she turned fifteen, she had grown tried of being a "devil" and needed some more powerful and worthwhile aim for her directionless emotions. Mme Canning, the mother superior, had perspicaciously qualified Aurore as "still waters." The waters were beginning to be ruffled.

As night was falling, Aurore made her way into the simple, white-washed chapel. It was dimly lit by the silver lamp above the sanctuary. A breath of honeysuckle wafted through the open doorway. Through the chapel window, Aurore observed a star high in the heavens that seemed to be intently gazing down at her. Lost in reverie, she thought she heard a voice whispering, *"Tolle, lege."* Deeply shaken, she wept and believed. She had unexpectedly found faith at last. Once her heart was won, all doubts and reasonings were abandoned. Ignoring her grandmother's cool advice to beware of "superstition," she threw herself wholeheartedly into a life of piety.

In Jesus she perceived an unshakable friend, an ideal brother, a perfect father to replace the one she had barely known. Her idea of the Savior merged with dim memories of her father; sometimes she almost saw her father in the very guise of Jesus. Then she had to take care not to address Jesus as "my father" in her prayers.

To her spiritual director, the gentle Jesuit abbé de Prémord, Aurore related the change in her feelings, and in a three-hour session she told him the story of her life. It was the first of many varied accounts that she was to give to friends and later to the public in the years to come. Abbé de Prémord and Mother Alicia were naturally pleased with her "conversion." As a token of her commitment, she made her communion for the first time since she had done so in La Châtre. They were less impressed, though, when she announced her intention of becoming a nun, or even a lay sister. Had she forgotten, Mother Alicia inquired, her grandmother's wish that she should marry? But Aurore's imagination had been captured by the self-abnegation of Sister Helen, one of the humbler members of the community, a simple if fanatical lay sister upon whom she now sought to model herself.

Aurore, or "Saint Aurore" as she became known to her fellow pupils, was not, even at fifteen, a girl to do things by halves. She had found an exalted, virtuous, heroic role after her own heart. The habit of self-scrutiny was not enough. Soon she was tormented by scruples and occupied with austerities that made her ill. Her mother and grandmother came to learn of her spiritual excesses, and they grew alarmed. Abbé de Prémord quietly advised her to quit this dangerous exaggeration. He pointed out to her that in her excessive scruples a good deal of pride commingled, unbeknown to her, under the guise of humility. As a penance, she must return to the pursuits suited to her years.

This was not too difficult for a fifteen-year-old. Afterward, she realized that the wisdom of abbé de Prémord had saved her from losing her wits or taking the veil. All the same, the idea that she might become a religious would not be quickly abandoned, even though an incident in the convent gave her pause. On one occasion, overhearing Sister Helen's sobs, she became convinced that the poor woman was being "victimized" by her superiors. The persecuted religious joined the images and episodes of convent life that were to pass into Aurore's books: the painting illuminated by the sun's declining rays, the mysterious voice heard in the chapel, the single star glimpsed as a symbol of spiritual solicitude, the music and the poetry of the religious life. What abbé de Prémord had succeeded in inculcating was "the life of the soul," as Aurore would later call it, the essence of spiritual awareness and spiritual disquiet that in modern times would characterize the pupils of certain religious schools, whether these pupils had faith or not.

Once Aurore had recovered from religious mania, she entered upon a period of great contentment. The would-be nun merged into the would-be actress and playwright. To remind her of her delight in the strolling players who had visited La Châtre a few years before, there were amateur theatricals, for which Aurore wrote charades and playlets, choosing the performers and the costumes. On the mother superior's saint's day, the pupils had been accustomed to perform some tearful moralizing drama by Mme de Genlis. Now Aurore constructed a comedy, which she adapted from Molière and which gave much innocent pleasure. She was allowed a great deal of freedom. Indeed, just as she had formerly been the idol of the "devils," so it seemed she was now the darling of the virtuous. At the peak of this achievement and popularity, Mme Dupin, seriously perturbed lest Aurore might really be developing too passionate an attachment to the community, removed her from the convent on April 12, 1820. They lingered for a few days in Paris, visiting the opera, before returning to Nohant together. Aurore was heartbroken.

Yet the spiritual gains of convent school life were never to be forgotten. Aurore had met there a girl who gave her an idea of true, trusting friendship: Fannelly de Brisac. She had found, too, in Mother Alicia the embodiment of disinterested motherly solicitude, the first of her ideal substitute mother figures. And above all, in Jesus she had discovered, if only for a brief while, the ideal father, the undeviating guide and companion. What earthly affection would ever be able to match that glimpse of perfect love?

CHAPTER
4

A Taste of Freedom

HAT spring of 1820, Nohant was at its loveliest to greet the returning heiress. She awoke at nine, ran to the window, and looked out on the flowering trees. From the distance came the haunting chant of the Berry plowmen that she had not heard for more than two years. No more uniform, no more trivial regulations about how to dress one's hair, no more discipline—she was free! Her grandmother had ordered Aurore's favorite delicacies. The staff as well as Deschartres treated her with the deference due to the young lady of the house.

One matter was privately bothering Aurore. The prospect of an arranged marriage ran counter to her secret dream of possibly one day taking the veil. It seems hardly surprising that the question of marriage would loom so large in her fiction when the matter darkened her adolescence, not to say her childhood. Mme Dupin, now over seventy, might appear more pressing in her dread of leaving her granddaughter without a protector, but Aurore herself was full of the convent's exalted notions of heroic duty and service. Marriage for the fresh, high-minded girl of fifteen signified the unknown, the relinquishment of her own will in submission to an unpredictable master, as well as a source of troubled curiosity, of attraction and repulsion. It was the common fate, but did she want it now, or could she contrive to postpone it? On the one hand, what core of integrity might be lost? On the other, what experience might have to be forgone? Her maid Rose, who had formerly treated her so roughly, newly married and blatant in sensuality, now made Aurore tremble in a different way.

By the matrimonial standards of the gentry of the day, convent-educated Aurore represented quite a good match for, say, a childless, middle-aged widower of position. Provided with a sizable dowry, she would eventually bring to her husband the property of Nohant as well as the income from the Hôtel de Narbonne, a large mansion in Paris. On her father's side, there was little to query about her family tree, for the blood royal of her bastard ancestors counted for more than the rank to which any of her likely suitors might aspire. But the major drawback for anyone attracted by the dowry of the sole heiress of Nohant was her dubious and unpredictable mother. At the height of the Restoration, with its vain attempt to turn back the clock, the prospect of having to endure Sophie in the drawing room quite erased the entrancing effect that might be caused by discreetly alluding to one's future wife as a descendant of the Polish royal house. In all likelihood, the first condition made by any suitor who valued his rank (and who did not?) would be the banishment of mother-in-law.

This was a proviso Aurore felt she should not allow. Her mother failed to be touched by such filial delicacy and unworldly renunciation. Sophie had no head for such niceties of sentiment. Aurore could not marry without her mother's consent, Sophie had informed her as they said goodbye in Paris, consent that she, Sophie, was not likely to give to any arrogant fellow who would show her the door. Earlier, Sophie had urged Aurore to follow the worldly course, but now she seemed resentful because it had produced a girl educated in the very style that made her feel inferior. On no account would she set foot in Nohant until her mother-in-law was dead, cried Sophie, adding that their reunion might well be taking place sooner than Aurore thought. The girl was deeply shocked by this cruel response. For the first time she glimpsed something odd in her mother's embittered gaze, some element of irrationality that made her shudder.

In addition to her yearnings for conventual calm or for some heroic role, her doubts about marriage and her filial scruples about an arranged "brilliant" match, perhaps there was also, as Aurore would later suggest, the secret dream of finding a twin soul, of being free to choose. Her reading of poetry and fiction would tend to keep before her what she would afterward call "idle dreams of happiness." Such dreams were thought to be suitable for her years, but were unlikely often to be realized in the marriage market of her era. All these conflicting hopes and half-conscious desires were enough to induce a strain of adolescent melancholy that mingled with her joy at reunion with childhood friends, with her pleasure in the Berry landscape she loved, with her growing understanding of her grandmother's true stature.

Then, in the autumn, Hippolyte came home on leave for three months. At first, the dashing sergeant of hussars, who looked so much like his father, and the imaginative, observant girl eyed each other cautiously. But soon their old intimacy returned. It was largely through Hippolyte that Aurore's tastes began to change direction. It was he who introduced her to riding. Placing his half-sister on a handsome filly, Colette, he told her to hang on. Girl and beast took to each other at once. If Aurore showed any hesitation, Hippolyte tapped Colette with his whip, and they were off. In no time at all, they were jumping hedges and ditches. Never before had Aurore possessed a creature to dominate and control, one who responded to the merest touch. Never before had she known such grace, such sensual excitement, such an impression of risk and danger overcome, such a vivid awareness of life itself, such freedom.

In a brief while, the one-time scrupulous moralizer of the convent had acquired the daring of a hussar. With her dark abundant hair pushed under a man's cap, she could at last see herself in the role of one of Tasso's disguised warrior heroines, or as some "femme forte" of the Fronde—Mme de Chevreuse, Mme de Longueville—who occasionally donned masculine garb and who plotted recklessly for high stakes.

Certainly, Aurore already had something of the courage and ambition of the seventeenth-century "femme forte," as yet incapable of outlet. Sometime after her sixteenth birthday, she had composed a portrait of the noble and just human being, applicable to members of either sex, but in particular a substitute for the model of the "femme forte," rooted in the seventeenth-century heroic code, a model she found unsuitable for modern civilization. No manuscript survives of this plan, published many years later after being retouched. The portrait bears the stamp of an imperious will, a demanding and ambitious nature, such as Aurore already was in embryo, in her hunger for the highest fame that belongs to those endowed with greatness of soul.

She recognizes no distinction of sex in the claim to the heroic role. The code remains the same for the commander of men or the mother. It was not that she wanted to be a man. With one part of her being what she desired, in conjunction with woman's compassion, was man's heroic virtues. She wished to have the qualities of her father at Marengo, in an age when women were supposed to be timid and submissive. The rather self-righteous portrait suggests a readiness to embrace hard toil and struggle to achieve one's end: an ideal of magnanimity to be understood and acknowledged at least by a small elite of kindred spirits.

There now entered the stage a potential member of this elite, a striking and enigmatic young student, introduced by Deschartres (who knew his father). Stéphane Ajasson de Grandsagne, two years older than Aurore, was a hard-working classical scholar, destined to devote himself to medicine and scientific learning under Baron Georges Cuvier, the founder of comparative anatomy. Since her return to Nohant, Aurore had been helping Deschartres in his medical rounds, and the unworldly pedagogue thought it would be a good idea if Stéphane were to give her lessons in physics and anatomy to add to her study of osteology. Stéphane brought limbs for her to draw, and she borrowed the skeleton of a little girl from a local doctor. All this was by no means quite as extraordinary as might at first appear. The studies of the young Mme de Genlis included osteology, for instance, some knowledge of bone structure being helpful for women engaged in nursing, one of the few serious activities considered proper to the sex. (The nurse or angel of mercy was a power-based role to which Aurore constantly gravitated, unlike her later admirer, Elizabeth Barrett Browning, who would scorn the fact that "Every man is on his kness before ladies carrying lint.")

Stéphane, or Stény, as he was known to his friends, thus made his first appearance in the prestigious role of teacher, as the guide who could enable his pupil to better herself through study, a role of immense importance at a time when female education was so sketchy. He was, indeed, the first of several to play this important part for Aurore. Everything about him was likely to arouse compassionate interest. His family was noble, but ruined. The youngest of ten children (some of whom blotted their escutcheon by their disorderly style of life), Stéphane was thought to be suffering not only from excessive Faustian study but from consumption. His dark, cadaverous good looks, sardonic expression, and doomed Byronic air, known from the later lithograph by Achille Devéria, must have been fascinating when he was eighteen.

One of those young men of whom great things are expected and who appealingly fail to live up to expectations, Stéphane would prove nonetheless quite a remarkable figure of the improvident eternal student, educationist, and scientific popularizer. He made no secret of his advanced views and his atheism—indeed, in virtually glorifying the atheism and materialism of the poet Lucretius, he would later be sufficiently well-known to be mentioned as an authority by the critic Sainte-Beuve. Between Aurore, ingenuously ambitious for instruction, and the studious, inquiring though erratic and unprincipled Stéphane, there must have been stimulating discussions, even if they could not agree on fundamentals. Their conversation was not entirely confined to erudite matters, though, for he taught her to shoot. When he left to pursue his studies in Paris, they wrote to each other, with or without Mme Dupin's knowledge (letters that have since been either concealed, lost, or destroyed). Despite his noble birth, his poverty and uncertain position presumably ruled him out as a formal suitor. In any case, similarity of age or interests was not then the first criterion for matrimony.

Toward the end of 1820, Aurore could write to one of the girls she had known in the convent how much she felt she had changed in a few months. The love of risk and danger in galloping through the countryside, the long, serious talks with Stéphane (whom she did not mention) offered a glimpse of a different life. "As I sit by the fire . . . poking the coals," she wrote, and it is already a novelist's observation, "I keep turning over in my mind the past, the present, the future. I am astonished how circumstances, character, viewpoint keep changing all the time." After Hippolyte had returned to his regiment, she remained alone at Nohant with her grandmother and Deschartres. Despite occasional dark presentiments of the future, she spent agreeable hours with her harp, her guitar, her sketching, and, above all, her books. She hoped that in the spring she would be going to Paris with her grandmother and would be able to see Mother Alicia.

While Mme Dupin and Deschartres played the ritual game of cards after dinner, Aurore would go up to her room and scribble her reflections and memories in a green notebook. ". . . You cannot imagine what pleasure I find in rereading my recollections several months later," she wrote to Emilie de Wismes in January 1821. She liked to read and write from ten o'clock at night until two or three in the morning. After four or five hours sleep, she went out riding. Then she would join Mme Dupin at breakfast, and make music or read to her. Aurore told Emilie that she would not change her own simple mode of life for her friend's round of social pleasures under the protection of an adored father.

A new suitor had made himself known among the various names proposed by relatives, friends, neighbors. This was one of Bonaparte's generals, fifty years old, disfigured by a saber cut but "vastly rich."

His cause was being urged by Aurore's middle-aged cousin, René Vallet de Villeneuve, who pointed out the advantages of an older man of established position but youthful spirit as compared with some untried youth whose character might well prove unreliable. Mme Dupin, despite her own more or less agreeable style of life with her elderly second husband, despite the fact that such arrangements between spring and autumn were common enough, did not favor the match. She thought the general too old for her sixteen-year-old granddaughter and would not consent to any ban on Sophie.

There was to be no visit to Paris and Mother Alicia after all. One winter morning, Mme Dupin was found lying unconscious on the floor of her room. With the help of her maid Julie and of Deschartres she came round, but she was paralyzed in one side, temporarily blind, and her mind began to wander. Aurore was horrified to witness the final decay of that fine intelligence, just when they were growing closer. Her own high spirits as a young child had been subdued so that she might keep pace with her grandmother's slow tread. Now, in the energy of her youth, she was confronted with the tragic experience of senility. The contrast made a powerful impression upon her, young as she was, an impression that was never to be forgotten. The insistent call of life and living before it was too late would form the ground bass of her conduct in later years.

After the stroke, Mme Dupin knew lucid intervals when her condition noticeably improved; but it was during the nine months of her grandmother's final collapse that Aurore's character was firmly molded. During those months, she tasted a form of freedom that could have been experienced by very few girls of her generation. When not yet seventeen she was placed in virtual control of the household and domain of Nohant. There was no sign of Sophie, who "could not" or "ought not" to leave Caroline (now twenty-one and on the verge of matrimony). Aurore could do more or less as she pleased. She acquired a taste for being in charge of others and, especially, of herself.

True, much time was spent helping Julie and the maids look after her grandmother, who often did not know the difference between night and day. To humor Mme Dupin, Aurore might sit with her throughout the night, reading to her and trying to keep awake by means of black coffee or her grandmother's snuff. But early every morning, she would ride for several hours, accompanied only by her groom, André, and she could let her thoughts wander as she galloped through the burgeoning countryside. Deschartres took her with him when he went luring quail, encouraging her to wear the local masculine smock and gaiters for crouching in the damp cornfields.

A "true peasant," she walked in clogs and rode in all weather, she told one friend of convent days. To Emilie de Wismes, she confided that sun and wind had turned her complexion the color of snuff. In a man's cap and ankle-length double-breasted overcoat, a gun on her shoulder, she trudged the plowed fields in search of small game. Emilie failed to be suitably shocked by these revelations. Notwithstanding her social round, or because of it, she felt rather envious of Aurore's riding, hunting, and shooting exploits, and longed to emulate them. That there was a strong element of play-acting and showing off in these exploits seems undeniable. Dressed in a long overcoat, Aurore could, in some distant village, be taken for a government surveyor, or so she said in order to enliven her letters to Emilie, letters that already reveal a gift for spirited dialogue as well as a brisk sense of humor.

Hours not spent in healthful and energetic pursuits in the fresh air were devoted to reading. Chateaubriand's *Le Génie du Christianisme*, inadvisedly lent to her by her confessor in La Châtre—a work whose seductive prose she had been reading to her grandmother shortly before the dreadful stroke—clashed in her mind with *The Imitation of Christ*, which Mother Alicia had given her, and doubtless also with her discussions with the unbeliever Stéphane. Thirsting for knowledge, Aurore could not but reject the sacrifice of intellectual inquiry required by the author of *The Imitation of Christ*.

With the (surprising) permission of her spiritual director, abbé de Prémord, she devoured the works in her grandmother's library, to which she had been given the keys. After the moralizing novels of Mme de Genlis she consumed books of philosophy and poetry in no particular order: seventeenth-century *moralistes*, eighteenth-century *philosophes*, together with Dante and Shakespeare. In reading without guidance or discipline, she nonetheless came to think for herself. For instance, she sympathized with the liberation of Greece, in whose cause Byron would later perish, although throne and altar and Deschartres were against it. It was in this way that she helped to educate herself, supplementing the training in languages, sketching, music, and manners usually deemed sufficient for females. She would always retain a hint of the private insecurity and the public opinionated air of the self-educated.

Two great writers of different periods, both inordinately concerned with themselves, aroused her lasting interest. The first of these egoists,

Montaigne, with his fine, amused introspection, penetrating good sense, and outspoken candor, led Aurore further along the way she was already going in her fondness for puzzling over her own nature and its vagaries, for recording her reactions in private notebooks. The second, a greater thinker though a less attractive personality, author of fiction, confessions, works on politics and society, became her guiding spirit. Rousseau it was who would wean her from religious orthodoxy to the religion of the Inner Light of his Savoyard Vicar, thus encouraging her growing inclination to rely upon her own responses rather than upon authority in any form.

Books meant more to her than ever. Accompanied by one of her dogs, she loved to go to some quiet retreat in the grounds where she would lose all sense of time as she read Chateaubriand's *René* or the poems of Byron, acquiring from them as from Shakespearean characters like Hamlet and the melancholy Jacques a pleasurably misanthropic view of life. All the world seemed a stage, the men and women merely players. She read, too, Mme de Staël's bizarre novel *Corinne*, that paean to Italy, to spontaneity, and to the exceptional superior woman. Corinne personified the inspired woman artist, doomed by her very genius to be misunderstood by the mediocre, to be unhappy in love, and to find no equal. Through her books, Aurore knew some contentment, in spite of the human tragedy she was witnessing daily, in spite of Byronic despair and the momentary attraction of suicide by drowning. (She later evoked this period of intense reading in pages of great charm, to be echoed with delight by a grateful Matthew Arnold.)

Possibly the high-spirited girl drew from those ill-assorted acquaintances, Byron and Mme de Staël, encouragement of the urge to shock. One day in May 1821, her conservative cousin René Vallet de Villeneuve arrived at Nohant to learn how she liked to stand at the window wearing Deschartres's dressing-gown and tall antique headgear in order to astonish the passersby (who must have been few in that hamlet). He had come at Mme Dupin's request. The old lady, in one of her brighter moments, was drawing up her will, and she wished him, after her death, to replace her as Aurore's guardian. To this he freely consented. One year older than the unfortunate Maurice (and the son of M. Dupin's daughter by his first marriage), René owned one of the most beautiful Renaissance homes in the country, the château of Chenonceaux. An urbane nobleman of exquisite manners and keen wit, he lectured Aurore on decorum, discussed Ossian with her, enlarged her outlook, encouraged her to write (another abortive attempt at a novel being the result), rode with her, and joined her in target shooting at the door of the winepress. She looked up to René as a father. He promised to return in the autumn with his son, Septime, an officer of hussars.

Meanwhile, Aurore had been troubled about the salvation of her Voltairean grandmother's soul, but she did not want to upset the old lady by mentioning the subject to her. Instead, she wrote to abbé de Prémord for advice. He thought that Aurore was right in following her humane instincts. Not all the members of the clergy whom she encountered were to prove so delicate, either in this matter or where her own personal life was concerned. While the indulgent abbé de Prémord refrained from inquiring about her private feelings, her confessor, the curé of La Châtre, who had heard rumors about her association with Stéphane, tried to probe her. She proudly cut him short, and never returned.

Indeed, friendship with Stéphane, with his reputation as a freethinker, was not likely to raise Aurore's standing in a small provincial town like La Châtre. Gossips thought there must be something sinister in her piety if she could be seen with Stéphane. Besides, no well-bred girl rode about the countryside like a man; or shook hands, English style, with local youths (Gustave Papet, Alphonse Fleury, Charles Duvernet, whom she had known since they were little). Something of this gossip had been conveyed to Sophie, who corresponded with Dr. Decerfz, Mme Dupin's trusted physician in La Châtre.

Moreover, Stéphane, studying medicine in Paris, had called on Sophie and had tactlessly let fall that her daughter was of "martial character" and that he had been giving Aurore lessons in her room at Nohant. Would he have been so indiscreet if he had anything to hide? Notwithstanding her dubious past, Sophie did not see any incongruity in writing to her daughter in a high moral tone. She accused the girl of neglecting her grandmother, implying that with such unladylike behavior—resembling that of a hussar or dragoon—Aurore would never find a decent husband. Sophie demanded to know what use all her daughter's erudition would serve if and when she were married.

Aurore's pride was outraged, and from her reply to her mother on November 18, 1821, some idea of her expectations and hopes from matrimony may be gleaned. In a tone of profound, exaggerated respect, which did nothing to mask her own sense of superiority and her angry contempt for her mother, she wrote, with a few passing digs at Sophie's neglect: ". . . to judge me in this way, you would have to know me. . . . Why should a woman be ignorant? Can't she be educated without being a blue-stocking?" After all, an educated mother would be able to give lessons to her sons (no mention of daughters). "I shall not be looking for a man capable of becoming his wife's slave, for he would be a fool, but I don't think an intelligent man would approve if his wife were to pretend to be timid and shrinking when she was not."

Was Aurore truthful in declaring to her mother that she was not on sufficiently intimate terms with Stéphane either for him to have a correct estimate of her character or when protesting the propriety of their conduct during the lessons in her room? Perhaps at the age of seventeen, under her beloved grandmother's roof and with her own lofty ideals and intellectual ambitions, she might be allowed the benefit of the doubt, doubt that would not necessarily preclude on the young people's part both mutual attraction and interest in each other. Surprisingly, Sophie professed to be satisfied by Aurore's asseverations, although she had not missed any of the harsh digs aimed at her unmotherly conduct. But if there were any hint of danger, Sophie expected to be told of it by Dr. Decerfz, in which case nothing would prevent her from "rushing" to her daughter's side. A dispassionate observer might consider that Sophie already had cause enough to "rush" to Nohant. But Caroline's wedding was approaching in the second week of December.

In the closing months of the year, Mme Dupin was failing fast. She consented to receive the last rites, principally in order to please Aurore, who did not forget how she interrupted the priest to say, "I believe in that" or "That does not matter much," thus preserving her independent spirit to the last. On December 22, she said to Aurore, "You are losing your best friend." Those were her last words before she died on December 26. Her granddaughter took a sorrowful private farewell before facing the world of the indifferent.

Aurore's months of freedom were at an end, but they had sufficed to transform her into a girl of proud, independent mind, careless of the opinion of those she scorned.

In the first days of January 1822, true to her grim prophecy, Sophie arrived at Nohant accompanied by her sister and brother-in-law, Lucie and Armand Maréchal, Aurore's godparents. They had come for the reading of the will, which named René Vallet de Villeneuve as her guardian. Aurore had gladly consented to his guardianship, and she anticipated a pleasant life of elegant cultivation at Chenonceaux, under René's protection. He had observed that her tie with her mother was weakening of itself and had simply advised her to do nothing to strengthen it. Now, her mother, free to express all her accumulated bitterness against her dead mother-in-law, refused to be considered "unworthy" to act as her daughter's guardian and would not yield her parental rights to René. After being named deputy guardian by the local magistrate, René left Nohant in the third week of January.

Aurore had high hopes for René and poured out her gratitude to him, her resentment and scorn at the behavior of her mother and godparents, to whom she alluded in a contemptuous pun as "les maréchaux," or "the marshals." Sophie had no intention of remaining with Aurore at Nohant and "consented" to take her to live in Paris, in Mme Dupin's pied-à-terre in the fashionable rue Neuve-des-Mathurins (the street where Mme de Staël had died nearly five years before). She was enjoying the exercise of parental authority of which she had been deprived for so long, and a quarrel, the first of many, ensued. In the account Aurore gave to René, Sophie remained speechless and turned pale with fury, while "as for me, cool contempt came to my aid. . . . She spared me her revolting kisses, but hurled taunts as sour as acid, or rather, as herself, during dinner."

Once in Paris, Sophie contrived to make her daughter's life a misery. She was passing through the menopause, with all that crisis may mean in terms of pain or fear to a once beautiful woman. Her seventeen-year-old convent-educated daughter, well provided for, independent in spirit, could only invite comparison with herself at the same age, when she had suffered extreme poverty and subjection. Aurore in the freshness of youth served as an object of love and loathing, a constant reminder to Sophie that her own day was over. Only in the exercise of her will and authority could Sophie at last obtain some slight revenge for the way fate had treated her. She made a mockery of Aurore's passion for books, which she saw as another sign of "eccentricity," and had no understanding of her daughter's lofty dreams and ideals. Aurore's only weapon was her sense of superiority, expressed either in outward submission or in silence, which only enraged Sophie the more.

A trivial incident was to have major consequences, as one of the strongest formative influences of Aurore's youth. René de Villeneuve called to take Aurore to dine at his home in Paris. Sophie, standing on her dignity, sharply observed that his wife might have come herself. René was annoyed. His wife would never set foot under Sophie's roof, he retorted. He left without a word to Aurore, and he did not come back. The effect upon the girl was shattering. Her father's nephew, her grandmother's favorite, her guardian and protector had abandoned her to her fate. Could he not have written to her to say that, in spite of everything, he would always be ready to help her in time of need? Surely, his wife could have made a show of politeness to Sophie, which her mother would probably have accepted as true coinage. René had seized on the first pretext to rid himself of a burdensome duty. Where, if not among her father's family, would she find protection? Was she fated to know nothing but betrayal?

She might have reflected that the charming René had not returned with his son, Septime (her grandmother's hope as a husband for Aurore), in the previous autumn; that it was René who had thought a rich fifty-year-old general offered a suitable match for her. His brother Auguste, with whom she did not feel so close (or, in another version, René's snobbish wife) had told her plainly that if she persisted in staying with her mother instead of retiring to a convent until she came of age, she might be acting in accordance with religion and duty, but she would never make a "good" or socially acceptable marriage. So she might just as well find herself what husband she could. Why not settle for some honorable commoner? One can guess what impression this suggestion must have made on the proud great-granddaughter of Maurice de Saxe, a girl whose imagination had fed on high deeds and who had willingly opted for her father's family.

Aurore wept at their abandonment of her, and she brooded on it. To accept their code she would have had to recognize her own "inferiority." That was impossible, as well as untrue. She forgave René in her heart, as she had once forgiven her maid Rose, or Mlle D. in the convent, which meant that she consoled herself with her private superiority. The opportunity for vengeance would come years later through literature, when she could add to one of her father's letters, which she published in her autobiography, an aspersion on the virtue of René's mother omitted by Maurice; or when she could point out that the Villeneuves were not themselves of old stock but had risen in class through their wives. Vengeance would be hers in her public (though sometimes ambivalent) rejection of their class and their prejudices in her novels; in her contempt for the cant of high society; and later, in her increasing devotion to "The People" from whom she had sprung. As regards her mother, Aurore's revenge would be rather more subtle.

The way in which all her grandmother's careful plans for her protection had been swept away in a moment gave Aurore a healthy disrespect for the prudence that might so easily be mocked by a turn of fate. Now she was at the mercy of her mother's changeable moods, foul temper, and imperious whims. Details of the tyrannical persecution she suffered at the hands of her mother and her aunt and uncle, later elaborated in her journal in the form of letters, recall at times the cruelties inflicted on Richardson's Clarissa. She did not give these details in her autobiography because (as she rightly observed) they would seem "improbable."

Why Aurore did not seek respectable temporary refuge in a convent, as her grandmother had formerly done, remains obscure. Perhaps the taste of freedom she had so recently enjoyed made her dread what she had once desired. Sophie, after allowing one brief visit to the English convent, forbade her to return there. To abbé de Beaumont, Sophie complained that Aurore was using the convent as a pretext: that she was really meeting a young man with whom she was having an affair. The English convent was not far from the lecture rooms where Stéphane might be found. Stéphane, after all, would be one of the rare friends in Paris to whom she might unburden herself. Abbé de Beaumont was persuaded to question Aurore. Her response was outraged silence and the rupture of relations: the movement of wounded pride with which she tended to meet imputations against her virtue. Those who loved her should understand and sympathize with her; by the mere query they revealed their distrust. That betrayal was a far more serious crime than any she might or might not have committed.

The break with her father's family was thus complete. Sophie had had her way. But, now that Aurore was living with her, Sophie did not know what to do with her superior daughter. The obvious course was to marry her off as quickly as possible, and then Sophie could return to her old life with Pierret in attendance. At the same time, Aurore herself, who could not envisage living under this strain until her majority at twenty-one, began to see in marriage an escape from her mother's capricious tyranny.

At the home of a friend of abbé de Beaumont's, Sophie had met a well-to-do couple who kept open house at Le Plessis-Picard, their fine mansion in extensive grounds near Melun, not far from Paris. A retired army captain in his early forties, Jacques Roëttiers du Plessis vaguely remembered meeting Maurice Dupin during Bonaparte's Italian campaign. He had led a wild life in his youth as an officer but had settled down since his marriage to a wealthy young girl, Ange, though he remained fond of the bottle. Of their five daughters, four were dressed as little boys, because Jacques wanted a son. Bluff Jacques assured Sophie that nothing was easier than to marry off a girl with a dowry, and so, on March 21, 1822, Sophie took Aurore to stay with her new-found friends for a fortnight. Sophie then returned to Paris, leaving her daughter, whom she described to all and sundry as giddy, odd, and a blue-stocking, to fend for herself among people unknown to her.

In both Jacques and his wife, however, Aurore found nothing but kindness. She came to regard Jacques, whom she called "mon père James," as a substitute father, and Ange, whom she liked to name Angèle and who replaced her shabby and unsuitable wardrobe, as a true mother. At Le Plessis-Picard, there was little opportunity for literary pursuits. Still in some ways a child, Aurore threw herself into leading the children's games. The house was much frequented by the military stationed at nearby Melun and Fontainebleau.

What exactly was this milieu in which Sophie had unceremoniously dumped her daughter? Afterward, Aurore would describe it in one version as loud and frivolous, with a hint of impropriety. It was, she declared, far too free and easy for a young person left without any guide. Angèle, though kindly and generous, was not sufficiently serious-minded to protect her from the dangers of such a milieu. Some idea of the atmosphere and talk of the household may be deduced from the excremental jokes favored by Jacques's sister, as well as from the social gatherings at the home of Colonel Borel and his wife, a couple whose raffish style shocked all the prudes in the district in the novel *Jacques*, in which Aurore drew on some of her recollections of life with the Roëttiers du Plessis family.

Aurore had not been in the house more than a few days when she met a thirty-year-old sublieutenant in the regiment formerly known as the Legion of Lot-et-Garonne. Prosper Tessier would not be her only admirer at Le Plessis-Picard, but he paid assiduous court to her as they rode together through the leafy grounds. She became infatuated with him. One day, in May, he coolly invited her to become his mistress. If she refused, he would leave forever, since he no longer felt master of himself. A week later, he was gone, leaving Aurore deeply wounded. Here was a man who said he loved her, but he could leave and forget her. True, a less honorable man would have seduced her instead of making his departure, she reflected later.

It was nonetheless painful to her pride to be the one who was abandoned, especially after her mother's abandonment of her as a child, especially after her recent desertion by the Villeneuves. "You have understood how cruel it is for a woman's self-esteem to find herself abandoned . . ." says the eponymous heroine of one of Aurore's fresh, early short stories, *Lavinia*, a dark Portuguese Jewess recalling to her British former lover how he had compromised her and left her at eighteen. Aurore may well have concluded that, if there were any abandoning to be done in future, she would not be the victim.

The encounter with the elusive sublieutenant spanned two visits that Aurore made to the house near Melun, in the spring and early summer of 1822. When she had returned to Paris on April 3, after her first fortnight at Le Plessis-Picard, James and Angèle came to the capital for a short stay and chaperoned Aurore at the restaurant or the theater. One April evening, they were sitting eating ices at Tortoni's, on the corner of the rue Taitbout, when a tall, slim young man of military bearing, evidently well-known to her gregarious friends, joined them either by chance or design. The newcomer evinced great interest in Aurore and whispered to Angèle that he had found the girl who would be his wife. Casimir Dudevant thus entered Aurore's life in the midst of the Tessier episode. He was, indeed, a sublieutenant in the same regiment as Tessier's.

On April 24, Aurore returned for a second stay at Le Plessis-Picard that lasted, with one brief interruption, until June 18. Casimir Dudevant joined Aurore in the children's games, and she enjoyed his company. They became friends. By chance or design, Casimir's approach was skillful, given the circumstances. When he asked for her hand, he said that he desired her own unhurried consent before her mother's formal approval. This was refreshing in view of all the numerous applications that had been made by those who had heard of the dowry but had never actually set eyes on the heiress. It gave her the feeling that he was disinterested and that she was still free to choose. Nor did he speak of love at first sight and pretend to any great passion. He candidly envisaged their marriage in terms of steady companionship and quiet domesticity.

She was struck by his frankness and his kindly manner, and touched by the delicate little attentions he paid to her alone. Nothing could be more attractive to Aurore at that particular moment. She had just been disillusioned in her infatuation for Tessier. Perhaps Casimir's Gascon accent reminded her of Fannelly de Brisac, her ideal friend of convent days, who came from Nérac, the very region where Guillery, the Dudevant estate, was situated. In Casimir she saw the good-hearted guide and protector she had always felt she so desperately needed.

Casimir Dudevant, who thus caught the seventeen-year-old Aurore on the rebound, was the illegitimate but acknowledged son of the recently ennobled Colonel Dudevant (raised to a barony under Napoleon in 1811). His mother, of whom little is heard, had been one of Colonel Dudevant's servants. Two years after Casimir's birth, his father had married a lady. The marriage being childless, the natural son would be entitled to half his father's estate under the Napoleonic Code. Still, Casimir's immediate prospects were not particularly bright. The marriage would thus be an improvement of his position, but, though respectable, it could hardly be regarded as brilliant from Aurore's standpoint.

When Casimir met Aurore he was nearly twenty-seven. He had studied at the military academy of Saint-Cyr, and in addition he had obtained a diploma in law in 1821. Army life as he had known it since 1815, when the days of Napoleonic glory were over, consisted largely of the boredom of garrisons and what that entailed, including a taste for heavy drinking. Sophie, at first inclined to smile upon Casimir's suit, suddenly bethought herself of her own experience of regimental existence, suggesting that he had led "a disorderly life." Whether that was so or not, suffice it to say that here was the classic situation of Aurore's fiction: the union of a convent-educated young girl with a man considerably her senior in years and experience. Aurore, though, was doubtless not quite as innocent and ignorant as her heroines, or as she later liked to make out, having heard and observed much despite her youth.

On the day Casimir was accepted, Aurore wrote in her diary: "June 2nd. Trinity Sunday. 7 or 8 P.M.—unimaginable happiness . . . several happy days." Thanks to Sophie, however, the engagement hung in the balance for several months. It was even broken off at one stage. There were lengthy negotiations with Baron Dudevant about the settlement. Sophie insisted upon the *régime dotal*, or dowry system, which the baron, aided by Aurore, opposed because this arrangement reflected upon the husband's honesty as well as the wife's discretion. This system, traditional in southern areas of France, allowed the husband the use of his wife's income from the dowry but did not allow him to touch the capital. Should there be any profits from the husband's transactions with her money, the wife could not share in them. The system tended to lead to frequent loans and law costs. In taking her stand upon the dowry system, Sophie performed her last (though eventually beneficial) act of parental authority.

The wedding took place on September 17, two months after Aurore's eighteenth birthday. At the wedding feast, she looked radiant. She had triumphed. She had escaped at last from her mother's "hateful and unbearable yoke."

What other course had been open to her? Marriage had been in prospect since childhood. She might have waited longer, reflected more deeply, but her mother scarcely gave her the opportunity. Submission to Sophie until of age or retreat to the convent would have been difficult for Aurore to accept after her months of freedom immediately before the death of her grandmother. Now, as she thought, a new kind of freedom, in the company of a good-hearted husband, a solicitous companion, who would henceforward be able to protect her against upheavals of the sort she had hitherto known, was awaiting her at Nohant. The exalted dreamer, the avid reader, the persistent scribbler, the devoted assistant nurse, the would-be "femme forte," the seeker for truth and for some noble role was, after Millamant, about to dwindle into a wife.

PART II

The Domestic Scene

The Little Woman

Believe me, the worst fate is that of a woman who is not totally occupied by an interest in clothes, the tittle-tattle of her set, or lofty self-satisfied virtue. . . . women who need affection harbor for too long the illusions of youth and are continually exposed to painful disappointments.
Mme Jules Gaulthier, letter to Stendhal, June 5, 1834

The slave is never more worthy of contempt than in blind submission which convinces the oppressor that his victim is born for slavery.
Charles Fourier
Théorie des quatre mouvements

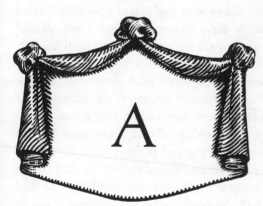

A NEW character takes the stage, a girl seemingly as different from the inquiring and independent spirit or the willful defier of social conformity as could be imagined. The young wife of sublieutenant Dudevant (who resigned his commission a month after their wedding, to devote himself to his new estate) had found a ready-made role that she was determined to play to the best of her considerable ability.

After a brief stay with their friends the matchmakers at Le Plessis-Picard, the young couple traveled with Hippolyte to Nohant, where they arrived at the end of October 1822. Aurore seemed to be happy. Years afterward (in a study of the early stages of a marriage in her novel *Jacques*, pages that would arouse the astonished admiration of the future George Eliot), Aurore would describe the pleasurable awakening of her newly married heroine, Fernande. After a long and tiring journey, Fernande awoke to find herself at the country estate of her husband, the wealthy Captain Jacques. Perfectly ordinary things were a source of deep pleasure to her. Fernande's gaze wandered from the silver-fringed silk curtains of the bed to the serene expression of her husband, and from the Japanese porcelain coffee cup he was holding to the silhouette of the maid. "The rose-tinted light of the lamp, the bluster of the wind outside, the pleasant warmth of the room, the softness of my bed, everything was like a fairy tale, a child's dream. I would doze off and wake up every now and then to feel cradled by happiness. . . ." Fernande was experiencing a return to the womb, a cherishing she had not known at the hands of her thoroughly odious and vulgar mother, one of the numerous "bad mothers" who people Aurore's fiction.

As the newcomer, however, the fictional heroine was more tactful than Casimir would prove to be in making alterations to the estate, in the course of which he was to kill off Aurore's old pet dogs, sell those of the horses as were no longer useful, and clear away some of her sacred childhood haunts in the little wood. Her protagonist, Captain Jacques, generously offered to change the view from the house, if his wife disliked it. "Let us make no changes in the places you love," cried Fernande. "How could I possibly have tastes different from yours? Do you think I have eyes of my own?" Jacques was grateful to her, since his home held very dear family memories. For someone so deeply affected by the sensations of everyday existence as Aurore and, because of her widely divergent royal and plebeian ancestry, so uncertain of her proper place in life, the memories of her father and grandmother associated with Nohant and of her own childhood there gave her an almost pre-Proustian sense of her own being and reality.

There were the graves of her father and grandmother to visit in the grounds. In the library were ranged the books her grandmother had loved, books with which she had dreamed away the summer days in the little wood that bordered the road to La Châtre. In the simple dining room facing the cool stone-paved entry, her grandmother had entertained old friends, survivors of the prerevolutionary era. Here, in the soil of Nohant were such roots in reality as she, the inveterate dreamer, possessed. Here, she would lovingly share her small treasury with Casimir.

The elderly bachelor jack-of-all-trades, Deschartres, who had remained in charge of the estate since Aurore's enforced departure with her mother some ten months before, noted toward the end of November 1822 that Casimir was of a very gentle disposition: ". . . he has something of the Gascon's impetuosity without his bragging, he loves his pretty wife as much as she loves him— . . ." And Deschartres told his correspondent that, "between ourselves," Casimir could flatter himself in having found "a very agreeable mistress of the house," who was likely to become more so with experience. However, the sight of the ostentatious happiness of the newlyweds increased his own melancholy. He was determined to retire (and would do so in the following year). Despite his slightly patronizing attitude to the new master, natural in an old retainer, Deschartres bears witness to the evident connubial bliss of the young pair and confirms Aurore's later contention that the finest moment in marriage is the first.

Just as she had thrown herself into being a "devil" or a "saint" in the convent, or a "hussar" under Hippolyte's guidance, so Aurore now determined to play to the full the role of the little wife. She would prove to everybody that she could be what a proper wife was generally expected to be, pliant, good at household management, concerned solely with her idolized husband's well-being, to which, of course, she should subordinate her own. Instinctively, it would seem, she yearned to be mastered. She resolved to act the "slave" to his "master" in the way that subordinates have traditionally absorbed the values of their lords and reflect the unprepossessing image the latter have of them. Moreover, the full weight of social pressure, custom, and convention was bearing down upon her, and she doubtless submitted the more readily to them now because she found that she was pregnant.

In the early stages of pregnancy, she felt quite ill from loss of blood, dizziness, and vomiting. Dr. Decerfz (the family physician who had earlier conveyed tittle-tattle to Sophie) saw to it that she spent most of the month of December in bed. Whatever her fears and joys, it was natural that she stressed the latter when writing to her old friend, Emilie de Wismes, at the end of January 1823. Emilie had conveyed her own doubt and alarm about matrimony and child-bearing, understandable enough in an age of high mortality among both mothers and infants. Aurore sought to allay these apprehensions (in herself as much as in her friend). Yet the mother-to-be appeared to recall with nostalgia the single state. "I shall not write you a sermon to give you a taste for marriage," Aurore assured Emilie, "because that will come to you just as well as to any other girl, and besides, your present state is so pleasant and so happy that I do not see why you should be in a hurry to change it." The recollection of her own vulnerability and motive for haste lies behind that poignant phrase. Aurore discounted the physical ills of pregnancy, which she felt would be outweighed by its ultimate rewards. "Meanwhile, you cannot imagine what contentment you experience on feeling the baby stir in your womb. And what delightful plans you make for him."

There followed one of the most revealing passages ever to be written by that (at times) most candid of letter writers. The young bride of a mere four and a half months had already analyzed her position. She confided in her friend:

> I agree that the vexations arising from the difference of tastes, of characters, are only too real, in most married households. A girl needs must also be thoroughly convinced that it is *absolutely impossible* to find a person whose temper and tastes resemble her own in every respect since . . . whether Nature has worked well or ill, she has certainly never used the identical mold for two people.

What, then, was to be done?

The solution was difficult, grand, and likely to appeal to her equally idealistic convent-bred correspondent.

> One of the two partners must, I believe, renounce himself completely on marriage, and should sacrifice not only his will, but his opinions, should decide to see through the eyes of the other, love what he loves, etc. What torture, what a life of bitterness, when you are united to someone you loathe! What miserable uncertainty, what a charmless future, when you marry someone you do not know! But also what an inexhaustible fount of happiness, when you obey in this manner the person you love! . . . No need to inquire whether it is the man or the woman who has to *remake* the self in this way on the model of the other, and since *omnipotence is on the side of the beard,* and since, besides, men are incapable of such devotion, it is necessarily ourselves who have to yield to obedience. . . . One must love, and love one's husband a great deal to reach that point and to know how to make *the honeymoon* last. Like you, I had a poor opinion of marriage until I became devoted to Casimir and if I have changed, it is only as regards myself and I should not venture further to pronounce upon the happiness others may find therein.

It had not taken Aurore long to perceive the reality of the situation— but the torture, the bitterness, the charmless future, already glimpsed with such perspicacity, were dismissed as too intolerable to contemplate. She was bearing Casimir's child; there must be a noble way out, through a love so great that it would require the total denial of the self. For, of course, she must love the father of her unborn child, deemed in her passion for generalization to be, like all men, incapable of such sacrifice. Despite her imperious will and the force of her urge to dominate, Aurore was prepared to sacrifice her will and her opinions, "to see through the eyes of the other, love what he loves . . ." to *remake* herself, in short, upon the model in Casimir's mind's eye, and to become a little woman.

For whom was this extravagant sacrifice of her own nature and her own instincts and interests to be made? The worthy Casimir was, as the poet Heine would remark years later, a thoroughly ordinary fellow. He possessed no great talents, no remarkable qualities of mind, no high ideals; he had not been encouraged to think for himself, nor was he particularly interested in analyzing his own feelings and drawing conclusions from them, like his young wife. His character and actions were not all that interesting to himself. For music and books, without which Aurore could scarcely breathe, he cared not a jot.

He had not married out of any grand passion. What he wanted was a quiet life with a perfectly ordinary girl who would make a pleasant home, serve as pliable bedfellow, bear his children, defer to his greater age, experience, and masculine wisdom. He thought he had married a normal country gentlewoman who shared his interest in country pursuits, in looking after the estate, in hunting and hunting parties of the sort favored by his father at Guillery. (And, of course, he had married such a person, who happened also to be rather more complex.) He did not expect to find himself the object of a great love and the cause of so total a sacrifice (if indeed he was aware of it). Small wonder that he began to think his young wife rather silly and full of romantic, bookish notions.

All the same, despite his conventional expectations and attitudes, Casimir was soft-hearted, good-natured, kindly enough in intention. He gave up hard drinking when he married and set out to be an indulgent husband ready to gratify his young wife's whims where he felt he reasonably could. If only Casimir, with his mediocre outlook, had not married the girl whom Henry James would one day call a sister to Goethe, he might well have led the untroubled life he sought. One may suspect that his childhood and upbringing as the servant's bastard had not been entirely happy and that he had been made to know his inferior place. Indeed, he had much in common with Hippolyte, who became his bosom friend. It was delicacy and sensibility that Casimir lacked above all, qualities he was not likely to have acquired in the casual amours of the garrison or the local Gascon village. From the veiled hints in Aurore's fiction, it may be deduced that he did not succeed in matching the ecstatic expectations she had acquired from her reading or her masturbatory imaginings. But sexual dissatisfaction would not be expressed until much later.

In some ways the hard winter of 1822–1823 seemed long to the pregnant Aurore, especially as she had abandoned her books and all concern with the things of the mind in her determination to be the sweet little thing she thought Casimir wanted. In the lengthy hours when he was out hunting, which he pursued with an ardor he seldom revealed for anything else, she took up sewing for the first time and found, as she prepared the layette, that she quite enjoyed its creative and recreational aspects. At the end of May, she was thought fit enough to make the long journey to Le Plessis-Picard and thence to Paris with Casimir. In Paris, they went frequently to the theater. It was there one evening, during the intermission, that she felt the first pains. At six o'clock in the morning, on June 30, 1823, in a furnished apartment in the Hôtel de Florence, rue Neuve-des-Mathurins, their son was born. Aurore's first glimpse of the new creature was, she would say later, the loveliest moment of her life. Her Parisian doctor kept her in bed longer than she afterward thought was absolutely necessary. In accordance with Rousseau's advice, she herself breast-fed the infant, which she believed greatly tired her. Tired or not, she was proud and happy to show off the new baby to her friend, Jane Bazouin, who came to see her at the Hôtel de Florence.

With the birth of her son (named Maurice after her father), Aurore had indeed found the great love of her life, to compensate in so far as possible for the shortcomings of the imperceptive Casimir. The maternal passion and extreme possessiveness that she would reveal for Maurice, her acute nervousness about his well-being, may often appear excessive. Her exaggerated determination to be seen as the good, caring mother would be one form of reproach for her own mother's neglect and ill-treatment. It would also provide an outlet for domination supposedly denied by the conventional role of submissive female domesticity she had assigned to herself.

This intense concentration upon Maurice was surely encouraged by Casimir's decision to return to Nohant a few days after his son was baptised on July 24, with Sophie and Baron Dudevant (represented by a proxy) as godparents. What pressing business urged Casimir to leave his wife and infant son in Paris for some ten days at this crucial moment, less than a month after the birth, when Aurore was in a state of mingled exaltation and exhaustion? Deschartres had not yet retired. Husband and wife took a fond, tearful farewell. To Aurore, left alone with her baby and the disputatious maids, the brief separation seemed endless:

> Tuesday night.   How sad it is, my good little angel, my dear love, to be writing instead of talking to you, to know you are no longer here beside me, and to think that today is only the first day. How long it seems and how lonely I feel! I hope you will not be leaving me often, because it hurts me a lot and I shall never get used to it. . . . I shall never be able to get used to living without you; I am dying of boredom; . . . If you were like me, dear love, if you were bored, if you hadn't a moment's pleasure in my absence, you would soon be back. . . . If I had had to be separated from you altogether before our marriage, I should have gone mad, and now I should die.
>
> Good-night, my love, my dear little puss, I am going to bed to cry all alone into my pillow. . . . Write to me soon . . . above all, write to me about yourself, tell me you love me, that you will always love me the same. As for me . . . I shall only repeat that I adore you, that I love you as much as one can love on earth . . .
>
> Wednesday morning.   . . . You had a bad [night] too, poor little diddums, shaken up in the coach. At least you thought of your dear little wife, didn't you? . . . Maurice slept well last night, took the breast well this morning, and has done his wee-wee and business, etc., well.

And so it went on, at insufferable length, this demand for the affection of which she had always, rightly or wrongly, felt deprived (both by her mother's indifference and her grandmother's well-meant nagging); this attempt to prove an affection she perhaps already feared she might not feel; this sense of hurt, as yet unexplored, at Casimir's departure. (A few days later came the more characteristic reproach: If you had listened to me, you would not have gone to Nohant and we could have left together a fortnight later.)

Fortunately, Jacques and Ange Roëttiers du Plessis came to Paris and relieved Aurore's boredom somewhat by taking her to the theater. Sometime in August or September, when staying with her friends at Le Plessis-Picard, Aurore repeated the theatrical success she had known in the convent. Together with a retired actor from the Théâtre Français, the young mother appeared in a farce before the colonel and officers of hussars garrisoned at Melun, the numerous guests staying at the mansion, and the assembled society of Melun itself. In the role of old Mother Ragot, where Aurore's youthful looks were at variance with the words she spoke, she had the audience in fits of laughter. The gay, resourceful amateur actress could not seem further from the bored and mawkish little woman of a few weeks before, terrified of loneliness. After the play, there was a fine ball and supper. And then the colonel in his turn invited everyone to a ball, where Aurore, who did not care for formal dancing and who always lacked small talk, reverted to her silent self. Her social timidity provided yet another contrast with the potential artist absorbed in the creation and exuberant projection of a role.

On her return to Nohant that autumn, Aurore wrote to her friend, Emilie (who had waived her doubts about matrimony and had married the Vicomte de Cornulier in June), about her happiness in four-month-old Maurice as he kicked about naked on the carpet, where his doting father romped joyfully with him. She painted a charming domestic picture for her friend. Nonetheless, Aurore ventured to admit that she wished she had two or three friends who could come and join her in sketching or singing.

> My dear Casimir is the most active of men, coming in, going out. . . . I can hardly manage two or three hours reading in the evening. But I have read somewhere that for perfect love it is essential to have similar principles and souls, with contrary tastes and habits. I am tempted to believe it, and besides I don't know whether I could love my husband more if he were a poet or a musician. I don't think I possibly could. And you? You are no doubt truly happy, and have no regrets about being married.

she wrote revealingly to Emilie.

Already, by October 1823, after just over a year of marriage, after having originally aimed at the total dramatic sacrifice of her intellectual tastes for love of Casimir, Aurore was feeling nostalgia for friends who shared her fondness for drawing and music and was finding time for a few brief snatches of evening reading. The dangerous (and suggestively prophetic) dream of union with someone who shared her tastes, with a poet or musician, had entered her head. However, she was still anxious to convince herself as much as Emilie that she adored her husband, that they were indeed kindred souls, even if they so manifestly differed in other outward respects.

A month later, she was again confiding to Emilie: "I am still living in solitude, if you can consider yourself to be alone when you are together with a husband you adore. While he is out hunting, I work, play with little Maurice or read. I am now reading the *Essays* of Montaigne, my favorite author." It was the quaint, ingenuous-seeming style of Shakespeare's contemporary and source that she lauded to Emilie, yet what she must gradually have found as she reread that tolerant and questing spirit was the invitation to acknowledge and follow the inclinations of one's own nature: the very opposite of what she was trying to do in her marriage.

But what exactly was one's own nature? Montaigne himself had revealed in his own incomparable manner how changeable, contradictory, odd, and inexplicable his own character was, and he had actually reveled in the discovery. He had made a virtue out of what would commonly have been regarded as a want of rigid consistency. At nineteen, following Montaigne's example, as she examined her own variable conduct in the past and the present, Aurore could not but be struck by the contradictions apparent in herself, by her own bizarre amalgam. Why not, after Montaigne, continue to probe into so fascinating a subject as the self, while making, as he did, a virtue of one's own rich oddities and contradictions?

The active Casimir, meanwhile, was following the established pursuits of the country gentry. Deschartres had retired in August, leaving Casimir in full control, with which Aurore did not seek to interfere. The new master would soon be taking an interest in local politics, but now he was devoting the time not spent in hunting to the amelioration of the house and estate. Aurore had to admit that he had made considerable improvements, but nothing seemed quite the same. It was almost as if the past were erased, while a dull, monotonous present projected itself into an uncertain future. Was this all there was to life, or all there was to be in her life? By the spring of 1824, Maurice was weaned. The young mother fell into an apparently causeless melancholy. Suddenly, at breakfast, tears would well into her eyes for no obvious reason, but in reality they were from depths of chagrin and frustration. Nothing could cheer her, not even the piano Casimir had sent for, despite the fact that funds were low after his program of improvements.

The decision was taken that they would move away from Nohant, where neither was at ease, and try to look for a home in the neighborhood of Paris. Given the state of their finances and other purely common-sense considerations, it seems an extravagant and foolish move. In May 1824, they were staying as paying guests with their friends at Le Plessis-

Picard, where they knew they would always find plenty of company and social activity. In the latter part of June, Casimir returned alone for a short visit to Nohant. Aurore was upset when she did not hear from him.

The fact was that Casimir had aroused his wife's jealousy by flirting with a certain Mme Lambert, while Aurore had countered with a mild flirtation of her own. Aurore complained to him about Angèle's "tyranny" in persuading her to go to balls and parties. "She made out that I didn't dare show myself to the hussars in your absence because I was so beautiful that I should certainly be carried off, and other jokes of a similar nature"—a phrase that reveals both the tone of the household and Aurore's rather pathetic attempt to play the teasing little doll. The repetitious protestations of undying love to the beloved angel continued, together with the new injunction, underlined, to *"sleep alone."* The foundations were being laid for her later skilled depiction of the torments of jealousy.

On Casimir's return to Le Plessis-Picard in July, there occurred a trivial incident that, because it wounded her inordinate pride, lingered long in Aurore's memory. As the little child-wife, Aurore was larking about with the younger girls, throwing sand at each other, while the rest of the company was taking coffee in the drawing room that looked out on the terrace. Though reprimanded when some sand accidentally went into the coffee cups, Aurore continued the childish game. The exasperated Casimir delivered a resounding slap, in public (worse, then, than the private buffets of the maid Rose). This public humiliation bit deep and must have marked a serious deterioration in the relationship, though little was to be observed outwardly.

Casimir went off to look for a place to live before returning to Nohant at the end of August. Aurore's letters show her thoroughly subdued, at the very lowest point in her role of submissive wife. "I am very glad that you have nearly fixed on our home. I don't doubt we shall be all right there, and since you have thought it suitable and comfortable, you need not bother about my consent before settling. I am sure I shall like it there. . . ." She did not feel like making a journey of inspection all by herself. Now that her guardian angel was no longer at hand to watch over his little family, she wrote to Casimir, the slightest thing made her nervous.

The furnished house Casimir had rented at Ormesson, near Enghien, in the environs of Paris, stood in an English garden decorated with a fountain and fake tombs. But this doll's house was fairly isolated, and the roads were bad. No sooner was the "little family" installed there, in September 1824, than Casimir found an excuse to be off to Paris "on business." Sometimes he stayed away at night, leaving Aurore alone with Maurice and a maid, the manservant sleeping in an outhouse. Aurore could see that these absences were no compliment to herself.

It was during the autumn of 1824, at Ormesson, when she was feeling at a very low ebb indeed, that Aurore again took up Montaigne's *Essays*. She had good reason to feel humiliated as a woman (a humiliation to which her own excessive self-abasement and self-denial had contributed not a little). In Montaigne she could find no comfort on that score. In the main, her favorite author did not have a very high opinion of women; his own marriage had been a mere matter of utility, and for him hetero-sexual love stood much lower than his rare friendship with the poet and magistrate Etienne de La Boétie. Was it true that women were inferior beings, incapable of such disinterested, noble friendship as theirs? After the example of Montaigne and La Boétie, a meeting of minds, was it not possible that other kindred souls did exist? Perhaps she had been mistaken in trying to convince herself that Casimir was her soulmate. Perhaps, somewhere, there dwelt her own equivalent of Montaigne's companion. The dream of perfect friendship seemed all the more alluring in the comparative isolation at Ormesson.

The Ormesson experiment did not last long. By the second week of December, Aurore was staying with her aunt and uncle Maréchal, miser-ably trudging the muddy streets of Paris looking for a modestly priced flat. This time, she herself was in charge of the search. At last she found a furnished apartment in the rue du Faubourg-St-Honoré. That winter of 1824–1825, she saw some of her old friends of convent days. What she could not recover was the faith she had known in the cloister. Aurore told her troubles to abbé de Prémord, who advised a retreat. But on withdrawing to the English convent, she found that there was to be no going back. Through some facets of marital experience, especially the bond of motherhood, she had moved too far from that kind of austere unworldliness.

Aurore did what many frustrated women do when they are unhappy. She bargained with her dressmaker, lost money at cards, and she had bought a very handsome black velour hat that, she assured Casimir, was a great bargain at forty francs instead of forty-eight, besides being everlasting. That black velour hat is a perfect symbol of her relation-ship with her husband in those early years. When eventually Aurore came to write with subtlety of the gradual decline of a marriage, in words that found an echo throughout Europe and beyond, she was writing out of her own experience. When she created women who were lonely, a prey to nerves, hysteria, and mysterious illnesses; who saw themselves as their husbands saw them (that is, as irresponsible children or virtual idiots) and were crushed by the sight; who deferred to their spouses in uncomprehending frustration—she had not far to look. She had only to examine her own heart, for she herself was one of them.

CHAPTER
6

Mirror-Image

. . . true Love is not in the sexual instinct at all . . .
Charles-Augustin Sainte-Beuve
Volupté

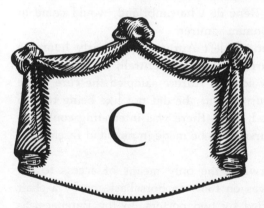

HANCE brought about one of the most important and influential episodes of Aurore's early married life, singular in its nature, unique in her annals, lasting in its direct and indirect effects upon her imagination, her personality, and her conduct. The chance event was the visit of her convent companions, the sisters Jane and Aimée Bazouin, in June 1825, to Nohant, whither Aurore had repaired after the failure of her attempt to settle in Ormesson or Paris. Prey to numerous physical ills, ranging from rheumatism to (as she thought) consumption, about which little was then known, Aurore was in a sorry nervous state. Her solicitous friends hit on the idea of inviting her to come to Cauterets, the newly fashionable spa in the Hautes Pyrénées, where they were going to spend the summer.

Just turned twenty-one in July 1825, Aurore set out by carriage with Casimir, two-year-old Maurice, and two servants for Cauterets. During the journey, Casimir betrayed his boredom at this new move by his bad temper, while Aurore tried to hide her tears. At the ascent to Cauterets itself, however, astonishment at the unexpected grandeur and

[67]

beauty of the scene took possession of Aurore, hitherto familiar only with the gently rolling contours of Berry or Brie. Nestling in the fold of mountains draped as if in a soft green baize, their peaks snow-tipped even in high summer, the growing village of Cauterets offered simple accommodation and a cure for all ills. Day and night could be heard the thunderous descent of the pure mountain torrent that traverses the center of the village. At once, the impressionable Aurore was captivated by the sheer loftiness of the setting in which she found herself.

The fashion for taking the waters had grown during the early years of the century, and some spas had served as a backcloth for celebrated (and not so celebrated) love affairs. In October 1816, at Aix-les-Bains in Savoy, the susceptible poet Alphonse de Lamartine had encountered Mme Julie Charles, the doomed Elvire of "Le Lac," after spending his youth in "dissipation" and gambling. Only a few months before Aurore arrived in Cauterets, the poet Alfred de Vigny had married Miss Lydia Bunbury, whom he had met at Pau in the Pyrenees. To Cauterets itself that aging Don Juan, François-René de Chateaubriand, would come in quest of his "Sylph," a young woman admirer.

The fact that Casimir sometimes left Aurore in the early hours to hunt eagles and chamois, returning only at nightfall, encouraged the neglected wife to seek out new society. Aurore sampled the cure, since that was the purpose of the journey, but she did not like being told to spend the rest of the day in bed, when there was interesting conversation to be had and exciting excursions to be made in new and fascinating company.

In 1825, and for long afterward, the only means of access to the mountains beyond Cauterets was on foot, on horseback, or by a chair with shafts attached to it carried by two porters. In the Pyrenees, as Aurore negotiated the narrow ledges and rocky inclines, some of the courage that she seemed to have lost during the early years of her marriage returned. While her friends, Jane and Aimée, languished among the other ladies in semi-invalidism, Aurore, her various ills momentarily forgotten, could be found climbing boldly after Casimir, who turned to remark that she was making a spectacle of herself.

Another young woman proved equally intrepid. This was Zoé Leroy, the unmarried daughter of a Bordeaux wine merchant. Vivacious, intelligent, Zoé was a few years older than Aurore. The two young women took to each other at once. Soon, the new companions were deep in discussion on religion, love, friendship, marriage. Very conscious of her superior intelligence (as of Aurore's), though also aware of the lack of any practical outlet for it, Zoé helped to revive Aurore's confidence in her own worth and abilities, which had been suppressed through her submission to Casimir's masculine view of female incompetence. Later, Zoé would, by her example, encourage Aurore to resume reading the historical works that (so the young wife averred) she had abandoned out of conventional notions of futile and distasteful female pedantry. "I still have some years left to me," she would tell Zoé, and, health permitting, "I shall put them to good use."

Zoé formed part of a lively circle of friends who had come to Cauterets from Bordeaux. The most striking figure in the Bordeaux group to attract Aurore's attention was a swarthy young man of distinguished appearance, features of classical Greek regularity, sensuous mouth, flashing dark eyes, and irresistible dark curls. Endowed with a ready wit and a plausible manner, Aurélien de Sèze officiated, at twenty-five, as deputy public prosecutor in his native city. He came of a noted royalist family, his uncle having been the lawyer who unsuccessfully defended Louis XVI when the king was on trial for his life. As for himself, he would remain loyal to the senior branch of the Bourbon house (as distinct from the junior Orléans branch). At Cauterets, Aurélien de Sèze was officially in attendance upon a young lady of means, Mlle Le Hoult, to whom he was expecting to become engaged.

He was diverted from this intention by the diminutive Aurore's fathomless dark eyes and her air of mysterious melancholy beneath an outward gaiety of manner. It was not long before he was pointing out the scenic beauties to her and telling her, in tones of deepest respect, about his mother and his sister, Indiana (whose name Aurore would borrow for the heroine of her popular novel). Aurore was touched by this note of filial and brotherly esteem, a note that would always awaken contrasting bitter recollections of her own family experience.

Once, though, Aurélien failed to take the right tack when he cynically inquired, "What is virtue, in the meaning you give it? A convention, a preconceived idea?" Perceiving the error of this approach, he assured her that he was being ironic. More to their mutual satisfaction, they discussed whether dull or passionate souls enjoy greater happiness in this life, characteristically opting for agony rather than atrophy. These discussions about motives and manners were balm to Aurore's deprived soul. She delighted in Aurélien's forensic gift of expression, his air of impassioned interest in her observations. How easily they understood each other at a word, a glance! Was it conceivable that she had met, in Aurélien, her friend, her La Boétie, her kindred soul?

One day, when Casimir was away hunting, they rode out to Saint-Savin, the once-important medieval village that, from its fortified romanesque church, dominates the Argelès valley. There, Aurélien confessed that he felt nothing for the frigid and mediocre Mlle Le Hoult. It was Aurore he loved, adding that she was in love with him also. Her feeble efforts to discourage him merely increased his ardor. The following day, they made a more strenuous excursion into the mountains, to the Lac de Gaube. In a small boat on the still mountain lake, whose clear blue waters are dominated by the majestic snowcapped peak of Vignemale, Aurélien traced the first shared letters of "their" name, AUR, in mystic bond. Afterward, as Aurore waited alone with him for her porters, under an overhanging rock, he pursued his advantage. Aurélien was hoping for an avowal from her that, despite her feeling for him, she declined to make. Offended by her doubts about his sincerity, he neither spoke to her nor looked at her for three entire days.

Up to this point, Aurélien had behaved like the typical experienced Don Juan of the watering places, and nothing more readily confirms that impression than the ritual three-day silence. His early manhood, like that of his half-brother, Amédée de Raymond, had been far from saintly. When Aurélien was about twenty, his mother could be found inquiring about his mistresses and about a child, nearly two years old, whom she had not seen. Later, he would confess to Aurore that he had known only casual amours. Doubtless Aurore secretly suspected at first, against the current of her feelings, that he might be a mere womanizer.

The three-day coldness was too much for her resolution. Learning that Aurélien was making the long excursion to Gavarnie with Mlle Le Hoult and her family, Aurore lost her head. Despite Casimir's objections, she insisted that they join the party. Impulse and obstinancy were combined. It was the first occasion when Aurore's private feelings tempted her to commit an act of public folly. It would not be the last.

On the long ride back from the stupendous spectacle at the Cirque de Gavarnie through the wild, rocky gorge at Gèdre, the party stopped in the evening at the enchanting mountain village of Saint-Sauveur. A dance was in progress and, in the garden, with lights and music in the background, Aurélien succeeded in convincing Aurore that he loved her deeply enough to renounce her. Unable totally to master his ardor, however, he took her in his arms and kissed her on the cheek. On another occasion, he even urged her to resist him. The grandiose setting against which they both made their lofty Cornelian efforts to sublimate their passion, the great snowy heights, the pure raging cataracts, clearly influenced their responses. Purity was in the air they breathed.

It was also a notable feature of the literature of the age. Lamartine, who never tired of the virginal purity of women in his poetry, fathered several illegitimate children. Vigny, while dreaming of pure spirit, would note some years later in his secret diary, in Greek letters, that he had spent the night with two sisters from Charleston. The critic Sainte-Beuve would console himself with prostitutes while vowing a pure and undying love for Victor Hugo's wife. These examples could be multiplied. There was often, among the masculine writers of the period, a complete divorce between the ideal pure love, the theme not only of literature but of actuality, and the need for physical release with some less elevated woman who might well be treated with brutality. If Aurore decided not to yield, Aurélien could always find consolation elsewhere. She would have to console herself with virtue.

Aurélien took to calling Aurore his "darling sister," owned to her that hitherto he had wasted his life in casual affairs, that he had experienced nothing more than sexual pleasure, that he had never met any woman like her before. When he found a moment for a private farewell in the grotto at Lourdes (where they had gone with Casimir), he vowed "in the presence of majestic Nature" to love her always as his sister and his mother, and to respect her as he did them. In so doing, he doubtless impressed upon Aurore the interesting notion that it was not the mistress but the mother who deserved esteem and respect. This was another reason for trying to maneuver oneself into the role of the good mother.

From the Pyrenees, Aurore and Casimir traveled northward early in September, with Maurice and their small retinue, to Guillery, her father-in-law's home not far from Nérac, on the very edge of the desolate Landes forest that extends to Bordeaux. It was the first time that Aurore had seen her husband's birthplace, a mansion of modest proportions, without any of the charm of Nohant. The hills around Guillery, thickly wooded with cork oak and pine, were infested with foxes and wolves. Life for the gentry there seemed to consist of endless hunting parties in which Aurore joined fervently, while dreaming of Aurélien de Sèze.

A month later, Aurore and Casimir paid a visit to the dignified city of Bordeaux. Zoé did all she could to facilitate Aurore's meetings and communications with Aurélien. Casimir came upon the pair at a compromising moment when Aurore was leaning in tears upon Aurélien's breast. She threw herself at Casimir's feet. A stormy explanation followed between husband and wife. Casimir, though hurt and angry, forgave her, meekly going so far as to allow his wife her freedom but putting her on her honor. All three now rose to the sublime heights upon which Rousseau had lingered so lovingly in *La Nouvelle Héloïse* when conveying through letters the emotions of Julie, her lover Saint-Preux, and her husband Wolmar—with the admiring Zoé in the role of Claire.

By the sheer force of her imagination, her will, and her personality, Aurore had contrived to elevate to the dramatically noble and heroic level at which she dreamed of living, first the smooth womanizer Aurélien and then the prosaic, nearly indifferent Casimir. Zoé, too, began speaking of the formation of an idyllic little group—that recurrent romantic utopia—whose members would all delight in their own virtue. It was no mean feat on Aurore's part to have accomplished, all unknowingly, this form of purification and elevation while dealing with the brute reality of human passions and human clay. The day following the grand scene in Bordeaux, when Aurore found herself with Casimir and Aurélien in a carriage on the way to La Brède (the country home of Zoé's parents), she was able to revel in "the joy of being cared for and consoled by two beings so dear to me." She was already capable of "loving," albeit in different ways, two men at once.

On her return with Casimir from Bordeaux to Guillery, Aurore, in a state of exaltation, began one of her most significant early literary undertakings: a journal in the form of letters addressed to Aurélien de Sèze, and to be shown to him at some later stage. At last she had found a sympathetic audience, a soulmate whom she felt was interested in her slightest move, her every thought. This was what she had been thirsting for—the discovery of another self into whose attentive ear she could pour the details of her everyday life, her responses to them, her dreams and aspirations. The letter journal to Aurélien allowed her to linger complacently on every dramatic minute of their adventure in the Pyrenees. It also provided her with an opportunity to compose the story of her life, a theme that had lain under the surface like a hidden spring, seeking an outlet for expression. This theme burst forth in the letter journal to Aurélien, assuming the form of a sketch for an autobiographical novel adapted to the taste of this particular well-bred royalist reader.

For Aurélien's benefit, Aurore shaped her life as the noble young innocent, abandoned or persecuted by her family, the theme being that of nobility of soul and virtue misunderstood. In this touching "aristocratic" account of the early years leading up to her marriage (where her grandmother undergoes a fictitious deathbed conversion and, for the first time, assumes the important place she would keep thereafter), Aurore intersperses vivid speeches and dialogues that can scarcely be strictly accurate but that already reveal the considerable dramatic gifts of the budding novelist.

What Aurore was trying to formulate here, for her own benefit as much as for Aurélien's, was an understandable version of all that had so far happened to her. She was longing to probe the mystery of her life as a girl and a young married woman, to attain to the secret truth of character and motive, but as yet she could only write her story in terms of the books she had read. So she makes much play with her early infatuation for the unsatisfactory sublieutenant Prosper Tessier, while naturally omitting to mention the undying love she had so often professed for puss and diddums, her husband.

In her urge toward self-understanding as a woman, Aurore probably invented the observer who puzzled over her nature as she did herself: " 'Put my mind at rest,' he said to me. 'Tell me what you are. I cannot understand you. Are you a coquette, are you frivolous, sensitive, well-read, are you an ordinary or a superior woman? . . .' 'I am everything you may care to imagine,' I replied, and fled." Aurore would have liked to find the clue to the mystery of her personality. To Jane Bazouin, wounded by her friend's sudden neglect at Cauterets, Aurore offered excuses drawn from Montaigne: ". . . I am eccentric, inconsistent, capricious." The aggrieved Jane was not impressed by Aurore's casuistry about her contradictory character. "You vainly blame all your faults on your character, your eccentricity and caprice. I accuse your heart alone. You know it has always been fickle, faithless," Jane retorted unambiguously.

In contrast, as it seemed to Aurore, Aurélien had guessed her inner sufferings, and through him she knew the joy of being appreciated at her true worth. He helped to restore her faith in her own potential as a superior being through his respect for her wit and intelligence. He restored, too, her self-confidence as a woman, by choosing her in place of the handsome Mlle Le Hoult, by affirming Aurore's superiority to all the other women he had known, since with her alone he was experiencing the deep spiritual union of two hearts and minds. A woman would indeed have to be lacking in vanity if she were not gratified by this achievement.

At this period, though, Aurore's view of herself was thoroughly confused. While yearning to be recognized as a superior being, an exceptional woman whose dreams still gave her wings to soar above the earth, she continued to play the part of the poor little creature she had enacted for Casimir. Assuring Aurélien that she was feeble and ignorant, she hastened to place herself under his protection, for he was learned, experienced, infallible: ". . . in your company I am no longer anything but what you would have me be. I no longer care for my opinions, tastes, habits, if you want me to change them; stay forever *my guardian angel.*" As previously for Casimir, she was busy "remaking" herself for Aurélien. Another role she allotted to Aurélien was that formerly performed by Stéphane Ajasson de Grandsagne: the important part of mentor. She tried to find merits in Lewis's lurid though influential novel *The Monk*, which Aurélien had recommended. She dreamed that Aurélien stood behind her as she wrote and corrected her mistakes. There was no means of reconciling her two opposing images of herself—as the weak, humble, docile pupil on the one hand and, on the other, as the elite soul, contemptuous of the mediocre society at Cauterets or Guillery. These contradictory images would long continue to provoke an inner struggle.

For Aurore, the charm of the love affair with Aurélien was the fact that it was firmly rooted in self-sacrifice and virtue. The lovers had, and would always have (she thought), the immense satisfaction of knowing that they were pure. They were living a novel, a dream of the sort that, according to vulgar souls, could not be realized on earth. And because their exceptional love was a commerce of souls rather than of senses, it must endure. This did not prevent Aurore from questioning Aurélien about his love life. Nor did it prevent her from teasing her guardian angel as well as herself with visions of his spirit seated beside her bed, and with invitations to come to her in her sleep. Sexual curiosity and sensuality would keep breaking in, and indeed, at several moments in the Pyrenees or Bordeaux, one cannot help wondering whether Aurore might not have been on the brink of yielding to Aurélien's pressing suit.

There was a rude descent from the heights, however, and harsh words were spoken, when Casimir discovered Aurore's revealing journal on the eve of his departure for Nohant early in November. (The discovery of incriminating papers in Aurore's fiction, a device that may now seem so far-fetched, was a serious hazard in an age when people often had to rely on communication by the written word and perhaps had learned to say more in writing than in speech.) Still, here was another opportunity for Aurore to go over the favored ground—her early life and recent events—in a long letter aimed at placating her husband, while at once demonstrating her lover's good faith and justifying herself. This letter of confession, handed to him on his return to Guillery, gives a subtly different interpretation from the letter journal to Aurélien.

The thrust to the ideal, so essential a part of her character, is emphasized in her words to Casimir: "If you strip our conduct of the lovely colors in which it appeared clothed to us, if you lower us to the level of vulgar souls, if in a word you ever succeed in convincing me that he is despicable and I feeble and faithless, I shall never get over it." Aurore was well aware of the harsher realities or cruder aspects of existence. When a mere girl, she had witnessed sickness, senility, and death. She had caught a glimpse of her mother's sordid early life; had read her father's letters and knew about his mistresses; and (in a fit of pious prudery) had recently destroyed her grandmother's collection of obscene eighteenth-century lampoons. Moreover, she knew something of what she called "sublieutenant's" coarse manners and speech from the military company at Le Plessis-Picard, from Casimir and Hippolyte. Perhaps it was partly this very knowledge that fueled the drive to the ideal, without which neither she nor many of her immediate literary contemporaries, whatever their sexual proclivities, could live. They may have been inwardly divided and frequently hypocritical, but without the ideal neither they nor their age can be understood. Here, Aurore is already, at twenty-one, an exemplary figure.

A more commonplace view of the triangle was expressed by her half-brother, Hippolyte, to whom Casmir had unburdened his sorrows at Nohant. Rising to the defense of his sex and also plainly revealing his suppressed hostility toward Aurore, Hippolyte found Casimir far too indulgent. In his opinion, what Aurore needed was a good thrashing. She was infuriated not only by Hippolyte's failure to stand by her but by his masculine clichés, especially as this high line was being taken by one who, in all likelihood, had eloped with Emilie Devilleneuve, the heiress whom he had married after getting her pregnant.

All the same, Casimir's indulgence quickly led Aurore to seize the advantage. After inviting Casimir to forget the mistaken code of honor, to stop being her husband, lord, and master, and, significantly, to become her father instead, Aurore went on to patronize him: "Your mind has never been cultivated, but your soul has remained as God created it, worthy of mine in every way." She had misjudged him. How unhappy she had felt when obliged to confine herself to trivial ideas and occupations! How pleasurable it would have been to write down an account of her day and read it to him, so that he could share in her feelings!

Now that he "understood" her, she had a plan for his cultural improvement. They would learn languages together. He would read to her while she sat sketching. They would profit by the interesting books in the library at Nohant, and discuss what they had read. (She would not, however, "insist" that he enjoy music—she would play only when he was out.) This project for improving Casimir's mind was, surely, a grave miscalculation, since it placed him in the subordinate position; and it shows, too, how tenuous was her grasp of his character and capabilities as well as of reality. She was carried away by her role and by rosy visions of mutual trust and understanding. What she was envisaging was a complete reversal of roles current in the nineteenth century (and beyond), where the intellect was the masculine prerogative and where the man was supposed to educate the woman to his own level. Casimir made a genuine effort to comply: He even offered to give up hunting. But the seeds were being sown for his eventual hatred of her intellectual superiority.

The stay in the Pyrenees, then, was to have wide-reaching consequences for Aurore. She had lived, in those few short weeks, a high-toned adventure in which she had contrived to conduct herself like the virtuous wife in a drama or novel, somehow managing to persuade Aurélien and Casimir to play the parts of noble lover and equally noble husband. She had found the opportunity to compose at least two versions of her early life and recent love affair, with elaborate justifications of her conduct, attuned to different readers. In addition, she had discovered, as she thought, in Aurélien the mirror-image of herself. Her meetings with Zoé and Aurélien had reminded her of her courage, her ambition, her superior soul, and suggested to her that she had been neglecting her talents. By the end of the year, she had recovered enough independence of mind to differ from Aurélien about a lady who had converted to the Protestant faith. And it is interesting that she took her stand on a woman's ability to think deeply about religious matters and her right to act upon her conclusions.

Certainly, Aurore had been unfaithful to Casimir, in imagination if not in deed. She had analyzed her feelings for Aurélien and Casimir and decided that she loved one "more" and the other "better": a nice distinction. There had been moments when she had felt embarrassed and guilty about deceiving Casimir, when she had been obliged to endure his embraces while dreaming of another. And then she had been forced to find explanations for her conduct that might placate Casimir, something hateful to her self-esteem. She could not bear to be in the wrong. If only one understood her properly, she never was actually in the wrong.

Aurore had no desire to be involved in a banal sexual adventure. Like most of her generation, of both sexes, she yearned for an ideal love between soulmates. It was only in the following months and years that she was able to reflect upon the merits and the demerits of trying to live a novel *à la* Rousseau. There was more than one sense in which Aurore would never forget the Pyrenees.

CHAPTER
7

The Lost Years

Man has a given sum-total of energy. . . . Almost all men exhaust in unavoidable labors or in the pangs of disastrous passions this splendid sum-total of energy and willpower with which nature has endowed them; but our decent women fall victim to whims and to struggles with this power which cannot find a place to catch hold.

Honoré de Balzac
Physiologie du mariage

OTHING could be quite the same after the sublimation of her feeling for Aurélien de Sèze and the creation of the noble trio. Aurore would go on corresponding with Aurélien (though most of her letters have failed to come to light); there would be visits to Bordeaux; but meanwhile, everyday life on a lower plane would go on, with all its trivialities and sorrows, pleasures and disappointments. One gain: Nothing more was heard of the clinging, poor little wife. Aurore, granted a glimpse of her worth through the admiring reflection of Aurélien, was not at all sure precisely what her potentialities were. She did not know what she wanted. The immediate consequence of the lofty scenes with Aurélien was a long period of unrest, self-doubt, and self-searching. Private dissatisfaction was revealed in constant ill-health, although she later affirmed that her chronic sore throat, bouts of quinsy or tonsillitis, migraine, various rheumatic aches and chest pains were not psychological in origin.

In the spring of 1826, Aurore returned to Nohant, having abandoned her restless search for a home in or near Paris. Once more she took up the pursuits and duties of a country gentlewoman. She concerned herself with the house. She surrounded herself with children. She served as apothecary for the local doctor (Charles Delavau), helping him in minor and often unpleasant duties on his rounds, as formerly she had helped Deschartres. In the following year she would engage with Casimir in political entertaining during the elections in La Châtre—her first contact with practical politics.

In early summer, she was habitually overcome by a strange combination of indolence and animality: "I become a bird or dog, or hare, I don't know, but I think still less than they." At such moments she rejoiced to be free of the human condition. This observation of hers suggests the active personality's gift for drawing refreshment from nature and the life force as well as the poet's imaginative ability to become the bird that hops along the gravel (the quality defined a few years earlier by Keats as "negative capability"). Of the meaning of these active and poetic energies, however, Aurore was as yet quite unaware. She only knew that she felt these incomprehensible urges, and was both disturbed and restored by them, but she could not know what inner resources for action or creativity they might portend.

A mere six months after the great plan for Casimir's cultural improvement, Aurore recognized that nothing would come of it. It was impossible to change the tastes of the sexes, she wrote to Zoé. From this remark of hers, it may be inferred that both Aurore and Casimir had given up the attempt. Their marriage bent under a strain greater than it could bear. The couple were drifting further apart, toward virtual separation. Aurore felt resentful that Casimir could travel to Bordeaux or Paris whenever he liked, but she was only too pleased to restore the control of the estate to him on his return. Her ambitions did not run in that direction as yet.

Meanwhile, her old schoolfriends wrote, praising her letters. Jane Bazouin, now reconciled, observed: "You depict all your ideas so well that you really made me toss on that stormy sea . . ." As for Louise de La Rochejaquelein, she urged: "Send me often an account *of your life* as in your last letter. I have read nothing more delightful . . ." The autobiographical theme went on exerting pressure. Still, it was one thing to be praised as an amateur for one's literary gift, as many girls doubtless were, and quite another to think of braving the entrenched prejudice against female "pedantry" and of using that gift seriously.

Her enormous energies were thus contained, or expended on domestic or local nursing tasks. It was only many years afterward that she realized how this containment had made her ill, and the theme of ignored or frustrated creativity was to recur in her work. As yet unaware of what was happening within, she could find no support in Casimir. Aurélien was far off in Bordeaux. Lacking confidence, she felt she needed a mentor, but now the noble friends were apart, they did not always see eye to eye. Astonished by her contradictory demands, Aurélien wrote on August 4, 1826: "You insult me, you accuse me of intolerance, you call me a *Jesuit* and you want a sermon on politics! . . . You call me a *hypocrite* and you urge me to convince you!" While clinging to her own views with Bonapartist tenacity, she was longing for intellectual exchange, a longing that came out as a desire to be instructed by her royalist friend, who was not attracted by political curiosity in a woman.

Nearer to hand was the dangerously intriguing young mentor of her girlhood, the materialist Stéphane Ajasson de Grandsagne, who had once written her what might be interpreted as a "declaration." During the next few years, Stéphane was to share the stage with Aurélien. That autumn, the eternal student was convalescing at his home after a serious illness. His hollow cheeks and wild eyes inspired Aurore with the compassionate if suspect and power-hungry concern that masculine weakness and sickness would always arouse in her. Accustomed to analyze her feelings, Aurore distinguished carefully between those inspired by her "father" James Roëttiers du Plessis and his wife (who were spending the winter at Nohant) and those she felt for Aurélien and Stéphane. She would call James and Angèle "my comrades if I were a man." Aurélien was a rare soulmate, whereas Stéphane, or Stény, was "everything a friend can be without inspiring love."

When Stéphane returned to Paris after engaging in the annual Shrovetide masquerade, news reached Aurore that he was still suffering from fever. What is more, he frequented bad company, money ran through his fingers, and he tried the patience of his friends. She knew his faults well enough. All the same, "*Sten.* will always be dear to me, however unfortunate he may be." Indeed, her interest in him was partly dependent upon his misfortunes. The streak of recklessness in his nature half appealed to her; it corresponded with something in her own she was struggling to subdue.

With my wish to be useful to him, if I were a man I would stand guarantor for him. But as a woman and given our respective positions, all I could secure for him is virtually nullified through the difference in sex, status, and many other things . . . which run counter to my good intentions. Cruel fetters that my friendship abhors yet accepts, for love alone, weak and inferior as it is compared with the former feeling, can break them.

Twice within a short time she had used the expression "if I were a man." She was coming to realize more intensely the disability of being a woman—a wife of a certain standing and a mother in provincial France in 1827—when her freedom to act was being curtailed. Here is the first striking expression of a growing awareness of the "fetters" of law and custom that, in April 1827, she was not prepared to break. At the time, she felt that love alone could entitle her to sever these bonds, while accepting, then as always, Montaigne's view that friendship was higher than passionate love. All the same, the idea of a break—for Stéphane? for Aurélien?—though dismissed, had crossed her mind.

It was not to Paris or Bordeaux but to Mont-Dore in Auvergne to take the cure that Aurore, constantly complaining of aches and pains, traveled with Casimir and Maurice in August 1827. The couple slept in separate rooms, Maurice sharing his mother's. The diary kept during this excursion—a mixture of intraspection, lyricism, and lively dialogue together with a plan for her autobiography—was retouched at various times over the next two years, and gives some general idea of her state of mind at moments during this period. A strong note of self-pity pervades part of the journal. She is good; why does not her mother love her? Instead, her mother has betrayed her, lied to her, abandoned her. "You have inflicted a wound that will bleed all my life. You have soured my temper and warped my judgment." In the street, the sight of any little girl being cherished by a mother aroused Aurore's bitter envy. At twenty-three, she still felt she had been deprived of maternal love as a child. Hence her insatiable need for the devotion of others, which rarely succeeded in filling the gap left by her mother's indifference.

To whom can she turn? To Zoé, to Aurélien? Stéphane is a pedant, a madman. At Nohant, she is "playing the part" of the lady of the manor. Time is passing—soon she will be old, with nothing useful achieved. Despite her private sense of advancing years and declining beauty, she is being courted nonetheless. One admirer at Mont-Dore even employs the strategy of a few days' absence, thus inspiring an unexpectedly cynical remark on love affairs at watering places. Particularly noteworthy in these mixed introspective jottings, however, is the way self-pity and self-mockery eventually yield to a kind of Stoic courage and determination: "Tireless traveler, I shall arrive!"

After their return to Nohant, relations between Aurore and Casimir deteriorated further. On an excursion with friends near the ruined castle of Châteaubrun, Casimir lost his temper with her in the presence of witnesses, who long remembered the scene. Aurore certainly did not forget the moment when Casimir struck his horse, which reared and almost crushed her. She roundly criticized his management of the beast—a form of public humiliation in a field where he felt an expert. He responded by calling her foul names. Perhaps this incident was the breaking point. Certainly when Casimir went to Paris to enjoy himself, Aurore felt completely at a loss.

During Casimir's absence in Paris, she reported to her husband that she was seeing Stéphane and his brother Jules, among others. Possibly it was from Stéphane, in his role of student of medicine, that she conceived the idea of going to Paris to consult doctors about her recurrent coughing, headaches, and bouts of tonsillitis. Stéphane with his contacts would make the appointments for her.

She traveled to Paris early in December 1827, escorted by a servant and by Jules de Grandsagne, who lodged in the room above hers in the Hôtel de Florence, where Maurice had been born four years earlier. Stéphane visited her there, engaging with Hippolyte in puerile horseplay. After some delay, Aurore was examined by leading doctors (including the eminent Broussais, whose universal panacea was bloodletting). They had no solution to her problems, though mention was made of a suggestion she had heard earlier in the provinces: an operation on her tonsils. However, Aurore, homesick for Maurice, returned to Nohant for Christmas.

In agony of spirit, she found she was pregnant. To Zoé she eventually wrote that she no longer deserved anyone's friendship, and compared herself to a wounded animal. Who was the father? Much suggests that it was Stéphane, but the matter can scarcely be proved, since their entire correspondence—with the exception of a single brief note from Aurore—has failed to come to light. Whether she went to bed with Stéphane from passion or compassion, by intention or by accident (the "surprise of the senses" to which she would allude in later writings), there is no doubt that she felt guilty and thoroughly miserable to be pregnant.

This time, she experienced none of the joyous anticipation she had known when carrying Maurice. For some while, she was confined to her room or her bed. Casimir stayed out of doors, she wrote, or if indoors, he was eating or snoring. No help came from her mother: only the usual complaints and untimely bad news of the death of her cousin Clotilde's child. Aurore gave out that her baby was due in October. By the beginning of August, she was very big. People remarked that she must be mistaken in her calculations.

During sleepless nights, Aurore could not stop analyzing her feelings. Aurélien advised her of the dangerous and destructive aspect of such relentless self-scrutiny. Let philosophers attempt to study man's enigmatic nature—ours not to reason why. He owned to her disarmingly that he was not a meditative person, that most of his life had been passed in thinking of nothing. The disparity in their temperaments was becoming apparent. He lacked her impulse to probe, her restless spirit of inquiry.

Aurore had not given Aurélien any details of her trip to Paris the previous December; she had simply spoken about an operation on her tonsils, which, he remarked in passing, he did not know were inflamed. Soon enough, however, he knew, or pretended to know, that Aurore was pregnant. Not the least surprising element in this period of her life is the arrival of Aurélien de Sèze at Nohant early in September 1828. As far as is known, he had never visited Nohant before.

This was only one of the bizarre circumstances surrounding the birth of Aurore's second child, Solange. When Aurore's pains suddenly seized her, Hippolyte ran for the doctor, who did not arrive in time. Casimir served (literally or figuratively) as the only midwife, no mention being made of any skilled maids. Aurélien (in his "sublieutenant" aspect) could be found, somewhat the worse for drink, celebrating the new arrival with the equally sozzled Hippolyte.

Two days later, Aurore was up and about, in marked contrast to the lengthy ceremonial attendant upon Maurice's birth in Paris. No wonder Aurore did not find much pleasure in Solange's "premature" advent on September 13, 1828. It was not only because she was a girl that Solange remained second best. Aurore would make it quite clear to Caron, the family's man of business, that she had no wish to experience another pregnancy. She also informed him with ostentatious emphasis that she and Casimir were sleeping apart.

The birth of "my daughter," Solange, marks a new era in Aurore's domestic life. From that moment, she began more seriously to look around for a way out of her impasse. She saw Stéphane from time to time, but little help was likely from that irresponsible quarter. Aurélien, after witnessing the birth with Hippolyte and Casimir, had returned to his legal work in Bordeaux and to the female consolations of which he had made no secret. Aurore occupied herself with the ladylike production of watercolors. She ordered pieces of music by Boïeldieu and Rossini. She sent for books, including the poems of Victor Hugo, political works by such thinkers of different liberal tendency as Benjamin Constant and Royer-Collard, as well as the memoirs of the martyred Girondin heroine, Mme Roland, one of the most influential women during the French Revolution. Plainly, Aurore was not only trying to keep abreast of literary, musical, cultural, and political developments but also inquiring into a possible female role.

There was a notable change of tone, too. She now took to favoring puns, rustic jokes, parodies of what was thought to be broad Rabelaisian humor or quaint old style, and a facetious manner. Facetiousness was often to be a sign that Aurore had made up her mind to put sorrow and humiliation behind her, to show determination and courage of the sort adumbrated in her Mont-Dore journal.

During the annual Shrovetide celebrations of 1829 in La Châtre, she could particularly enjoy dressing up as a peasant youth. "No, it is not I but somebody else," she wrote, delighting as ever in a new disguise, a new identity. In an account of the masquerade, she attributed her own sentiments to Duteil, the family lawyer, who opined that it is our fault if we fail to live: ". . . let us live in order to live. . . ." As time passed, the urge to live, whatever the consequences—that urge which, in the Pyrenees, she and Aurélien, in proper romantic fashion, had preferred to a mere dull everyday round—came to predominate.

Was Aurélien to be the answer? In May, June, and July 1829, Aurore with her husband and children spent a long stay in Bordeaux, interrupted only by a brief visit to Guillery. They saw plays, toured churches, made excursions. If Casimir's later memory is to be trusted, Aurore could often be found at the home of Aurélien who, as a rising young lawyer, was obliged to request their departure to avoid scandal.

More extraordinary was the expedition Aurore made from Nohant entirely on her own to visit her father's mistress, Félicité Molliet, in Périgueux, in November and December 1829. She later remarked of this adventure that she had been "completely free." It was the first time since her youth that she had known such freedom.

From Périgueux, she secretly traveled alone to Bordeaux. Perhaps, on this occasion, she may have become Aurélien's mistress. Still, whether she was his mistress then or not, by a trick she had contrived to do exactly what she liked. With considerable satisfaction, the great-granddaughter of Maurice de Saxe would be able to compare her Bordeaux episode with Napoleon's crossing of the Beresina when, by a simple ruse, the Corsican military genius succeeded in saving the remnant of his army in the retreat from Moscow. In just such a way had she demonstrated her will to be free.

Throughout 1829, the year that had culminated in this triumph of feminine daring, she had answered her friends' requests with examples of her writings: lively accounts of her travels and of local manners, or autobiographical fragments. There was also work on a prentice novel called *La Marraine*, which she wrote at the corner cupboard-cum-desk in her downstairs room at Nohant, and in whose pages Jane Bazouin (now married) perceived excessive scorn for humankind. Why, wondered Aurore at twenty-five, had she accomplished nothing? Her imagination galloped ahead of her, lacking direction and discipline.

Despite her literary gift (so evident to her friends) and her interest in the novel, Aurore had not yet decided to follow the path of literature, which had brought fame to a considerable number of women novelists in France from the seventeenth century onward. She did not want to risk all on a single throw, and so she also occupied herself with decorating snuff boxes, fans, little cases for visiting cards, and similar trifles, in the hope that these might eventually provide a livelihood.

What probably encouraged her to look for some work that might offer the means to a new independent life was the fact that Casimir was sleeping with Pepita, the Spanish maid, whom he shared with Hippolyte. Later, the boon companions would share the favors of another maid, Claire, along with Jules de Grandsagne and others, including possibly young Jules Boucoiran, Maurice's tutor. Aurore could adopt a Rabelaisian gusto in speaking of such affairs as Claire's pregnancy, an earthy note that contrasted singularly with her lofty aspirations elsewhere. She was not exempt from the contradiction of her day between the noble ideal of purity and the brute reality of contemporary manners where, as Stendhal put it, a pretty chambermaid was fair game.

If Casimir's extramarital affairs revealed no refined taste, his business dealings betrayed an incompetence that aroused Aurore's contempt, and she made no effort to disguise it. In 1827, he had bought land for which he could not pay. His debts led to quarrels. When, as so often, he was duped over speculation in a (probably nonexistent) brig, she charged him with engaging in business deals when the worse for drink and ridiculed his "sublieutenant's camaraderie" and masculine showing-off. He criticized her friends and she saw no reason why she should not criticize his: "The right to tell the truth is mutual. . . ."

Aurore dreamed of independence, and she began to bother about her provincial mode of dress, a sure sign that she was thinking of Paris. The place for making up her cultural backlog was obviously Paris, then the artistic and intellectual capital of the civilized world. Goethe could extol the modern metropolis: "Paris, where the highest talents of a great kingdom are all assembled in one spot, and by daily intercourse, strife, and emulation, mutually instruct and advance each other; where the best works, of both nature and art, from all the kingdoms of the earth, are open to daily inspection . . ." In April 1830, some two months after the riotous first night of Victor Hugo's much parodied poetic drama *Hernani*, which heralded the triumph of the new literature, Aurore left for Paris, accompanied by Maurice. She was going to stay with Mme Gondouin Saint-Agnan, the sister of her "father" James, a lady with whom she was accustomed to exchange Rabelaisian banter.

In the city, delightful were it not for the stink (thought Aurore), she saw Stéphane, who acted as her guide on several occasions. She ate ices under the newly refurbished colonnade of the Palais-Royal, the nightly haunt of prostitutes and gamblers. Above all, she visited museums and art galleries; heard *Fra Diavolo* by Auber and Rossini's *Comte Ory*; and saw as many plays as she could, including the latest historical melodrama by Alexandre Dumas in the new, violently frenetic taste, which appealed to her as little as it did to the aging Goethe.

In May 1830, she had her portrait and that of Maurice painted in watercolors by Candide Blaize, while calculating how much the painter earned a day and reflecting that (with a few lessons) she could do as well as he. Blaize's portrait is an image of great charm that helps to explain the effect she had on her numerous provincial adorers. Somewhat overdressed in the provincial manner, in a rose silk gown with a white ruffle, rose-striped streamers, and huge puffed sleeves, her hair piled in elaborate curls, Aurore gazes directly at the painter. Her brow is high, her large dark eyes tinged with melancholy, her small mouth set in proud and willful determination. Certainly, it is an image of extreme femininity—that of a young woman not averse to reminding her husband about her periods, in a delicate way, when it suited her to do so.

A fracas with her mother over a visit to the theater—Sophie accused her daughter of coming to Paris simply in order to "carry on"—may have led Aurore to undertake on an impulse a journey to Bordeaux. This time, she informed Casimir of her intention. Parking Maurice with Mme Gondouin Saint-Agnan, who was by no means pleased, Aurore hastened to see Aurélien. She found him grief-stricken, for he had just lost his father. This bold expedition was evidently much less satisfactory to Aurore than the one accomplished five months earlier, and it denotes the end of her wild attempt to reactivate the association with Aurélien. Another companion, more responsive to her present needs and aspirations than either Aurélien or Stéphane, was about to enter the scene.

Aurore returned to Nohant in mid-June 1830, her head full of all the artistic and political manifestations she had seen and heard in Paris. It was a moment when, provoked by Charles X's attempt to restore absolutism, the conflicting classes in French society were about to engage in violent confrontation. A few weeks before Aurore's departure for home, Achille de Salvandy had exclaimed, "We are dancing on a volcano." During the Three Glorious Days (July 27 to July 29), the Parisian populace took to the barricades, the Hôtel de Ville was captured, and a provisional government formed. General astonishment at this revelation of what the common people could accomplish rapidly gave way to greater sympathy for the disinherited, a new feeling of vigor, a sense that others, too, could seize their opportunities, if only they dared.

Though worried about the fate of her relatives in Paris, Aurore accepted an invitation to dine with her childhood friend, Charles Duvernet, at his mansion nearby, on July 30. Also present were two other young men she had known as children, Alphonse Fleury and Gustave Papet. Walking with them in the garden, she came face to face with a newcomer as he sat reading under an old pear tree. His awkward shyness aroused her interest. After dinner, as the company rode toward La Châtre, she impulsively invited the entire party to dinner at Nohant the following day and galloped off.

That very day, July 31, which saw the rise of the house of Orléans, Aurore wrote that she felt she possessed energies she did not even know she had. "One's spirit expands with the momentous happenings," she declared. The reason for this enlargement of energy was not only the upheaval of the July Revolution but the shy young man she had just encountered. At nineteen, Jules Sandeau was a delicate, dreamy fellow, with fair, curly hair, winning ways, and a student's taste for puns. Of modest origin, he was ostensibly studying law in Paris but his true ambitions were literary.

They used to meet at a bench in the wood at Nohant. She would find his hat and cane there while he pretended to hide. The little pavilion in the grounds by the road often served as the scene of their passionate encounters. To Sandeau, Aurore's manners presented a peculiar mixture of virginal timidity and boldness: Her airs seemed those of a duchess and contrasted oddly with her contempt for social conventions and her unworldliness. To the twenty-six-year-old Aurore, ever fearful of stagnation after the example of her grandmother, young Jules offered an opportunity to live, at a moment when she was wondering if she ever could. He restored her to life and hope. That was why she adored him.

In a fictional account of an escapade to join Sandeau by the banks of the river Indre, on the outskirts of La Châtre, Aurore invented a meeting in the future with a withered old woman, an imaginary self. "Why should I have any regrets?" inquires the crone, remembering the events of 1830. "I have had my full share of life's banquet." That was what Aurore longed to be able to say when her turn came. From the crone's diary, which is really Aurore's, can be gathered some idea of the outlook of the lovers and their young liberal-minded friends in the autumn of 1830. "We wanted danger, extravagance, freedom, action. . . . One fancied being a bandit, another a gypsy, a third an actor. Each one of us assumed a role." With Sandeau, the dreams of happiness, life, and liberty that Aurore had long been cherishing began to take shape in actuality.

The July Revolution was Aurore's supreme moment. It marked her views and her conduct. While some women of her acquaintance, like Mme Gondouin Saint-Agnan, took lovers but kept up a veneer of respectability, Aurore flaunted her feeling for Sandeau. This was a way of thumbing her nose at conventional, hypocritical society, of proving (to herself at least) that she was free. She joked about her local reputation as a female Don Juan, supposedly with no less than four lovers. It was in the autumn of 1830 that she read, in translation, E. T. A. Hoffmann's influential tale, *Don Juan*, which portrayed the Spanish libertine as a soul endlessly thirsting to possess everything in life, and endlessly disillusioned. (Along with many of her contemporaries in France, including Balzac, Gautier, Mérimée, and Dumas, she came under the spell of Hoffmann's brilliant fantasy and was long to reflect this particular poetic taste.)

If the common people could take to the streets and momentarily triumph in the Glorious Days, perhaps even a woman, subject to oppressive laws and customs, might seek redress through the general reversal. She proudly proclaimed herself a republican, opposed to the death penalty and keen to ameliorate the condition of the underdog. As she wrote, only half humorously, to a bachelor friend: ". . . why won't you allow that a woman may believe men can become better and happier by changing the state of a rotten society . . . ? Are our faded and worn old institutions suited to a rising young and magnanimous generation?" But in going so far as to dream of a better society achieved through masculine agency, she still expressed herself with typically feminine self-deprecation. As she was well known to be "feeble-minded and a little mad," her views were of no great consequence. "A woman is always a woman and don't think I am complaining. On the contrary, it is so pleasant to make life into a novel. . . ." Whatever her hopes, she was still very unsure of her ground, still to be seen as Blaize had painted her: femininity incarnate. Soon enough, along with the rest of her generation throughout Europe, she found her hopes for social and legal reform dashed.

Meanwhile, Jules Sandeau had been obliged to return to Paris, where he was supposed to be studying law, leaving Aurore to languish in Nohant. One day, looking through her husband's desk, Aurore discovered a package addressed to her, labeled "Do not open until after my death." It contained Casimir's will, which made quite plain his hostility to his wife, his contempt for her character. The discovery of his scorn was too much for her pride. She wanted to be a "free companion," not a burden. For eight long years she had suffered humiliation. She had wasted her precious time and affection on cold, false natures (so much, too, for Stéphane and Aurélien!). She had been dreaming of a lofty spiritual relationship with Aurélien when she could have been loving and living. Now she had the pretext that would enable her, with a clear conscience, to join Sandeau in Paris.

But what of the children? Fortunately, Jules Boucoiran was prepared to remain as Maurice's tutor. For little Solange, just two, there was no shortage of maids. Aurore informed her husband that she would divide the year between three-month periods in Paris and Nohant. All she demanded of Casimir was the personal allowance of three thousand francs allotted to her under the marriage settlement. Armed with an unfinished novel called *Aimée,* she was going to seek her fortune in the capital.

Why had it taken her so long—five years—to reach this decision?

The brief answer is because she was a woman, uncertain of herself, her gifts, and how to use them—long torn between her conventional image of herself as the weak, silly female whose views did not count and the strong-minded superior being, fully capable of thinking for herself. While she was dreaming and consuming her energies in jam-making, her masculine contemporaries of comparable energy were establishing their reputations. By the time Balzac was twenty-six he had published numerous potboilers and had completed his literary apprenticeship. Victor Hugo, two years older than Aurore, was already well known as poet, novelist, and dramatist at twenty-six. The equally precocious Charles-Augustin Sainte-Beuve (born, like Aurore, in 1804) had produced many articles, his survey of sixteenth-century French poetry, and poems of his own by 1830. She lacked their obsessive single-mindedness. Unlike Victor Hugo, she had not said to herself, "I want to be Chateaubriand or nothing." Ultimately, a price would have to be paid for her timidity (which was only partly her own responsibility, given the social pressures of the day) as well as for her courage.

Nowadays, it is difficult to appreciate the degree of willpower and courage required to take such a fateful step at that moment in history. If she failed—as Casimir clearly expected her to do—she would have to return, chastened and subdued, to mockery at home, or risk a miserable fate in the Parisian whirlpool. Aurore made no secret of going to Paris to join her lover in order to satisfy artistic urges, the desire for self-fulfillment and happiness, for freedom and life. True, she did not entirely burn her boats. She had left her children behind. But when Aurore's action became known a year or two later, the sound of the slamming of the front door at Nohant would reverberate through the civilized world even more loudly than the theatrical exit of Ibsen's Nora, which obliquely derives from it, fifty years after.

PART III

The Stormy Sea of
Literature

The Advent of George Sand

I am embarking on the stormy sea of literature.
Aurore Dudevant, letter to Jules Boucoiran, January 12, 1831

A woman under fifty who gets into print risks her happiness in the most appalling lottery. I see only one exception: a woman who writes books to maintain or educate her family. Then she should always confine herself to financial considerations when speaking of her works.
Stendhal
De l'Amour

HEN Aurore arrived in the cold and muddy metropolis early in January 1831, she plunged into the world of student Bohemia. At twenty-seven, she consorted with the friends of Jules Sandeau, medical students like Emile Regnault and Gustave Papet, law students like Alphonse Fleury and Gabriel Planet. Just as she had been the center of an intelligent provincial circle at Nohant, now in Paris, by virtue of her age and drive, she was, belatedly, the head and sole woman member of a young student group. This alone was extraordinary.

One of her circle who was later to achieve celebrity as a writer and leftist political figure, Félix Pyat, has left a description of the Renaissance-bearded radical students of his day: their long hair, bohemian existence, and private lingo, where "bourgeois" and "proper" figured as terms of insult. It was to the world of the ambitious young, soon to be immortalized by Balzac, that Aurore was introduced by Sandeau or Regnault.

It was the world, too, of those outrageous flouters of convention, the writers known as "les Jeune-France," and remembered years afterward by Théophile Gautier as a lost paradise of youth: "To be young, intelligent, fond of one another, to comprehend and partake of the sacrament of art—a finer style of life cannot be imagined, and all those who experienced it have retained an indelible impression of brilliance. . . . " Aurore, in the early months with Sandeau in Paris, knew a similar lift of the heart.

At that time, a woman of repute rarely went out alone at night. Certainly, at the theater, a respectable female would hesitate to be seen in the pit. Her place was in a box, where the seats were naturally more costly. Aurore's funds and wardrobe were limited. Her thirst to be rid of her provincial air was unslaked. In her insatiable curiosity, she wanted to do, see, and hear everything—to look at the Napoleonic battle pictures of Gros and Gérard in the Luxembourg, to read in the (unheated) Bibliothèque Mazarine, to visit the theaters she loved and see the flamboyant Frédérick Lemaître as Dumas's Napoleon or the touching mime Deburau at Les Funambules, to listen entranced to La Malibran or Paganini, to attend the Chambre des Députés, hear the Saint-Simonians who were preaching every Sunday in the rue Taitbout, witness such violent events as the sacking of the Archbishopric. On some occasions, she donned the student's dress of grey trousers, long grey frock coat, and the grey hat that replaced the leather cap, or *bousingot* (a term that at first denoted any youthful extremist or republican and was only later extended to embrace an entire literary group). This inconspicuous attire proved much more practical than voluminous fragile skirts and petticoats, and enabled her to gain access to places denied her as a woman.

In such garb she must have heard, in street, theater gallery, or cheap restaurant, a good deal more than reached the ears of most women of her class and generation, who in any case, however close they may have been to their brothers, were unlikely to be living freely among students of law and medicine on terms of complete equality. Besides, there was the pleasure of daring to elude the role assigned her as a woman, of being able to thumb her nose at all those "bourgeois" or "proper" people whom she and her student friends despised. Most of all, though, she could delight, as always, in playing a part, assuming another identity, and savoring the misapprehensions of those who were unaware of the joke.

"I am free at last," she declared, while regretting her separation from Maurice and Solange. "I want to live a little for myself. It's time." But what was she to live *on*? Her annual allowance of three thousand francs from Casimir would not take her far, nor would it give her the independence of which she dreamed. Had she really the talent that might enable her to acquire financial independence? This was just what she did not know. The very idea of complete financial independence for a married woman was unexplored territory.

Aurore had been encouraged by the local liberal politician, François Duris-Dufresne (whose election to the Chambre des Députés she and Casimir had supported) but, like other women writers of her era in a similar quandary, she suspected condescension and gallantry on his part. Nevertheless, she was armed by him with an introduction to one of his Breton colleagues, the elderly moderate liberal monarchist Comte Auguste-Hilarion de Kératry, a contemporary of Chateaubriand and (then) well-known author of a novel of the romantic agony where a priest violates a supposedly dead woman. Such satanic-sadistic episodes were all the rage among men whose imaginations had fed upon the grisly scenes of the Terror and the Napoleonic battlefields, and who seemed to require ever stronger stimulus.

At least two distinct versions exist of Aurore's meetings with Kératry. The later version, given in her autobiography, offers a highly entertaining account, with vivid dialogue, of how that quick-talking, foxy-looking gentleman received her, early one morning, in his bedroom, his young second wife still under the covers. He plainly informed Aurore that a woman should not write, that even the most intelligent female was incapable of producing a good piece of work, and that she should stick to childbearing. In the letters Aurore wrote at the time, however, she referred to Kératry in terms of respect, describing him as both gentlemanly and kindly. It may be supposed that he was indulgent in his criticism of her novel *Aimée* and that it was only gradually she perceived the underlying prejudice against women writers in his attitude.

Kératry was not the only writer she consulted. Through the mother of her friend Charles Duvernet, she had obtained a note of introduction to a more curious figure, their relative Hyacinthe de Latouche. Born in La Châtre in 1785, Latouche was the town's leading literary light. Author of *Fragoletta*, a modish and influential novel about a hermaphrodite, first editor of the poems of André Chénier, counselor of the young Balzac, Latouche had recently bought a minor paper, *Le Figaro*, which he ran as a satirical journal of opposition. He was in need of helpers. It was the moment, after the Revolution of 1830, when, owing to new techniques, literary and political journalism was on the rise.

Though noted for his sharp tongue and his extreme touchiness, Latouche received Aurore in a friendly manner. He had already acted as adviser to the poet Marceline Desbordes-Valmore, his one-time mistress. As for the aspiring author, hoping not to look overawed, she took snuff in his presence and tried not to drop any grains on his carpet with its white ground. Latouche perceived that his compatriot did not lack ability, and told her so, although he reproved her for treating art as a mere means of livelihood. At first, Aurore did not fully appreciate the immense value of his promise to be a severe critic, a promise that he kept.

So Aurore, like Félix Pyat, joined Latouche's team on *Le Figaro*, to be followed by Sandeau. She became an apprentice and dog's-body, working from nine to five at seven francs a column. Latouche ran the office from his third-floor apartment on the quai Malaquais, standing over his assistants, criticizing, slashing. In this way, Aurore's first piece or riddle, "Molinara," written at his table and under his direction, appeared unsigned in *Le Figaro* on March 3, 1831. She began to speak of being overwhelmed with work. If she had known the difficulties involved, the perseverance required, she would never have chosen this path. Yet she was acquiring the taste for literary labor; indeed, it was already growing into a passion. "Oh yes, long live the artist's life!" she cried. "Our slogan is *liberty*."

Aurore's second piece, also unsigned, a joke about the National Guard, almost brought down the law upon its obscure author's head. But, in a short while, she had become enough of a professional to appreciate how a fine or a prison sentence would have made her name. Meanwhile, in Nohant, disapproval was being expressed about her working as a journalist on *Le Figaro*. ". . . I am pretty proud of earning my living by myself," she retorted. "*Le Figaro* is a means to success like any other."

At every opportunity, Aurore liked to insist that she was writing for money. In this, she may look very much a contemporary of Guizot, who advised his compatriots to "get rich." Yet her aim was not, like theirs, money for its own or for power's sake. She was simply following Stendhal's tongue-in-cheek advice to women writers: to claim the need to earn a living if they wished to avoid the stigma and ridicule of being thought blue-stockings, part of the growing league of scribbling females. In her perpetual emphasis on writing for money alone, the lady may seem to be protesting too much.

Certainly, the hostility toward feminine intellectual effort or, as it was usually called, "female pedantry," had been bitterly resented by Mme de Staël. Her contemporary, Jane Austen, went to extreme lengths to convince everyone that she was "the most unlearned and uninformed female who ever dared to be an authoress." Less than twenty years after Jane Austen made her wry claim, the prejudice against literary women was still widely current throughout Europe, following the example of Napoleon, who remarked that women should stick to knitting. Not all the editors Aurore encountered were as well disposed to women aspirants as Latouche. Since intellectual ability was considered a masculine attribute, any woman with serious pretensions to thought appeared unfeminine, even a little weird. It is partly for this reason that Mme de Staël (whose ideas proved so influential) as well as her successors of merit were unthinkingly labeled "masculine" spirits or talents.

In the charming self-portrait she sketched in the spring of 1831, Aurore saw herself as intensely feminine. By serving as a woman journalist in a man's world, however, she ran the risk of being taken for a masculine talent, a so-called mannish woman. That was a fate—the fate of Mme de Staël—she wished to avoid. Even her mentor, the understanding author of *Fragoletta*, was inclined to see her as some sort of hermaphrodite. By declaring to all and sundry that she wrote to earn a living, to help Jules Sandeau establish himself, to educate her children, Aurore hoped to indicate that she was a womanly woman. The side effect of this attitude of hers proved important. In stressing that, for her, writing was simply a job, she loudly announced that she was not a dilettante, like so many upper-class woman novelists of the Napoleonic Empire and Bourbon Restoration. And while her most eminent predecessor, Mme de Staël, was no dilettante either, as the sole heiress of the banker Necker she certainly did not need financial reward. So Aurore was probably the first woman to demand publicly as a right a place as a purely professional writer.

Despite such difficulties as she encountered, the moment when Aurore entered the Parisian journalistic scene happened to be a propitious one for women in some respects, and not only on account of the notable growth of popular journalism. From the early eighteenth century onward, greater leisure had encouraged an increase in the number of women readers as well as in the number of authors who catered to them.

These writers included a considerable bevy of females. The vicissitudes of the Revolution, the emigration of many aristocratic families, the eventual return of the survivors, gave some women a far wider experience of the world than their forebears had known. In the field of journalism, one of Aurore's predecessors, Pauline de Meulan (the first Mme Guizot), was obliged to take up the pen when her family was ruined during the Revolution. Blamed for engaging in journalism, Mlle de Meulan wrote a spirited defense. As for the liberal-minded Duchesse de Duras, Chateaubriand's friend, who had spent some time in exile in Philadelphia, Martinique, and England, she wrote novels on the theme of social or racial inequality, largely out of a private sense of alienation.

Apart from women of rank or position, however, the nineteenth century witnessed the rise of a body of middle-class women writers. Among these were several poetesses of repute: Mme Mélanie Waldor, an officer's wife, one of Alexandre Dumas's mistresses; Mme Amable Tastu, wife of a printer and scholar; Mme Adèle Janvier, a lawyer's wife; as well as a more important figure, Mme Marceline Desbordes-Valmore, wife of an actor. When widowed, Hortense Allart's mother took to writing to support her family. Hortense Allart, one of Chateaubriand's mistresses, and her cousin, Delphine Gay, "the Tenth Muse," who married the libertine founder of the popular press, Emile de Girardin, were Aurore's contemporaries. Most of these ladies were in print before 1831.

By 1831, there was widespread interest in the subject of woman. During the eighteenth century, some leading writers from Rousseau onward had concerned themselves with the question of female education, which was much debated. Many—including a number of women—recognized that there was something very wrong with the education of girls, since it produced ignorant, servile, deceitful creatures, the phenomenon of chaste girls who turned into adulterous women. This theme—and the consequent disaster for marital, family, and social relations—was treated by the eccentric bachelor Charles Fourier in his *Théorie des quatre mouvements* (1808) and later writings. Fourier believed that fidelity in love is against nature and that sexual repression is bad. (Indeed, in his utopian Harmony, all tastes, including that of sadists, would be catered to.) Some of his notions were elaborated with wit and irony by his debtors, Stendhal in *De l'Amour* (1822) and Balzac in *Physiologie du mariage* (1829). Aurore was certainly familiar with Balzac's book. The misguided treatment of one half of the human race was, as Fourier expressed it, an obstacle to any general happiness or social progress.

Fourier, with his demand for the emancipation of women and their admission to all careers, serves as a link between the eighteenth-century apostle of perfectibility, Condorcet, and the followers of Saint-Simon. As early as 1782, Condorcet had advocated equal education and civil status for women. In 1790, during the French Revolution, he proclaimed the important truth that either no member of the human race has real rights, or else all have the same. It was during the Revolution that an almost illiterate woman, Olympe de Gouges, published her *Declaration of the Rights of Woman and the Citizeness*; that a former courtesan, Théroigne de Méricourt, chilled the blood with her revolutionary rhetoric; that members of the advanced women's clubs engaged in feminist discussions and paraded in striped pantaloons. With the fall of the Girondins, however, the revolutionary feminist movement came to a sudden end on the guillotine. How much Aurore knew about these revolutionary developments of forty years before, from her grandmother or from her own reading, it is difficult to say, for she does not allude to them.

The whole question of the role of woman was revived, along with that of the poor, the disinherited, the exploited, the outcast, by the followers of Saint-Simon's New Christianity, whose preaching Aurore heard shortly after her arrival in Paris. The founder of the new religion, Comte Henri de Saint-Simon, who died in 1825, had urged equality between the sexes. In his "Last Words" to his disciples, he declared that "my whole life can be summarized in a single thought: to secure for all men the most free development of their faculties." (This would be the basic quest of intelligent women, whether or not they were writers and artists or active feminists.)

The woman question was given a central position by his successor, the handsome, charismatic Prosper Enfantin, who proclaimed that the Saint-Simonian age would be marked by the complete emancipation of woman as well as by the rehabilitation of the flesh. According to Enfantin, woman would formulate the new morality of the future. Until woman had spoken, nothing could be finalized. He appealed to woman in her role as prophetess, "the sibyl of the future." In January 1831, women were being invited to join with priests, scholars, industrialists, in the general transformation of society.

It was over the subject of marriage that Saint-Amand Bazard, twin

Father with Enfantin, fearing lest the latter's audacious theories might ultimately enslave women, withdrew in November 1831. At the beginning of the following year, in a state of mounting exaltation and near ecstasy, the Saint-Simonians were awaiting the coming of the Mother Messiah to join Enfantin, now sole Father Messiah. Some went so far as to envisage the angelic couple who, after Fourier, would serve the needs of the sexually frustrated or deprived. The Saint-Simonians felt that social regeneration could only be founded on the equality of men and women. In 1833, "Year of the Mother," they would go seeking the Mother Messiah in the Near East. They would appeal to Jewish women, among whom they hoped to find their savior. The suggestion of an androgynous godhead presented a challenge to traditional, paternalist monotheism, a challenge encouraged perhaps by the presence of newly emancipated Jews among the leaders. The notion of an androgynous godhead, though, was propagated also by the crazy Ganneau, founder of Evadaisme and self-styled Mapah (from mamma and papa), who claimed to speak in the name of God the Father and Mother of all.

The passionate and bizarre spiritual-cum-sexual speculations that accompanied the industrial, scientific, and social aims of the Saint-Simonians in the early years of Aurore's artistic beginnings in Paris provide a backdrop to her own work. That some of their doctrines were for a time attractive to gifted men like Sainte-Beuve and Heine indicates how urgent was the quest for new spiritual values in the rapidly changing social context. All the same, with her countrywoman's common sense, which often vied with her rashness, Aurore remained aloof. She could say that she saw in Saint-Simonian preaching only an "impractical error" and could ridicule the "lady pope" who showed off her sky-blue velvet gown and swansdown boa. "I've heard the Saint-Simonians, alas!" she exclaimed.

Nonetheless, the eccentric and ecstatic disciples of Saint-Simon, by their preaching and propaganda, made many people think about existing sexual arrangements, about the code of marriage as it functioned in the husband's favor at the time, about divorce, about traditional family morality and the possibility of replacing it with something less tyrannical and hypocritical. Some of the problems raised by the Saint-Simonians were ones that Aurore had already confronted in her private life and that she would naturally think about when she came to draw on her own experience in her writings. Happiness in the eternal bond of marriage is a lottery, she told a bachelor friend who was contemplating matrimony. Why exchange freedom for chains? Casimir, simply because he was a man, could do exactly as he pleased with his servant mistresses or his property (which was largely hers), and nobody thought any the worse of him. This great freedom should be mutual, Aurore informed her mother. It was this personal sense of woman's equal right to freedom and justice, the legacy of the Revolution, that underlay her attitudes, rather than any theory.

Apart from her prentice journalism under the wing of Latouche, Aurore was hoping to break into the more lucrative field of fiction in collaboration with Jules Sandeau. Latouche's advice was sound, and she heeded it: "Make use of your own resources . . ." he urged. Still, she found that his sharp critical intelligence tended to undermine her self-confidence. From the corpulent young Balzac, who climbed the five flights to her attic on the quai Saint-Michel and never stopped talking about his own work, she dimly hoped for good counsel. He glanced at her papers and observed casually, "Idealize in the sphere of the pretty and the fine, that is woman's work." According to her, this remark betrayed neither sarcasm nor contempt. All the same, Balzac would later reveal in his work a certain prejudice against literary women in general.

The first short stories written by Aurore and Jules together, like *La Prima Donna*, praised by Balzac, appeared under the pseudonym "J. Sand." So did *La Fille d'Albano*, inspired by a painting by Horace Vernet, though Aurore later claimed this tale as her own. *La Fille d'Albano* is less interesting for its artistic promise than for the insight it provides into Aurore's state of mind at the beginning of 1831 and into the quality of her imagination. It concerns a talented girl painter, Laurence, who, urged by her brother, flees on the eve of her marriage to the conventional young man she loves, significantly named Aurélien, to embark upon the artist's life in Italy. Laurence's brother tempts her with the attractions of the bohemian life—artists' suppers, nocturnal wanderings. "The intoxication of the artist! The fiery exaltation of a sublime ecstasy, the burning sensation of intellectual pleasure! The orgy of genius, the penetration of celestial fire!" The images of fire and heat recall the meditation on the volcano in her early *Histoire du rêveur*, a meditation that reveals what Gaston Bachelard has called her Empedocles complex, the fascination of destruction by fire, the urge to live dangerously even if it means being consumed in living.

The heroine's brother continues: "Genius has no sex. The woman born to perpetuate the species and the artist who shares in the life of an entire world are creatures completely distinct." The conflict in Aurore herself between art with Jules Sandeau in a garret overlooking the Seine and her love for the children she had left behind is here simplified by being set before marriage has occurred, and is resolved by the unequivocal choice of art. It is interesting, too, that in this brief tale about a girl pulled in different directions by her womanly nature and her talent, the claims of art take precedence and no mention is made of mere professional considerations. The ideal value of art and the sacred mission of the artist had become widely accepted by the early years of the century, and Aurore herself clearly subscribed to them, claiming from the first a woman's right to figure among the lofty band. All the same, throughout her life, she would fluctuate disconcertingly between the rival demands of writing as a trade and as an art.

Another sketch of Aurore's, composed in the summer of 1831, shows the concern for documentation that was never to leave her. This piece, unpublished in her lifetime, was *Une Conspiration en 1537*, written in the popular dramatic shape of a "historic scene," and intended less for the stage than for periodical publication. Aurore's episode, drawn from the Italian chronicler Varchi, deals with the assassination of the debauched Duke of Florence by Lorenzo de' Medici. The tyrannicide is purified by his protractedly bloody deed—a sign of her republican sympathies. Later, Aurore was to make a present of this prentice sketch to Alfred de Musset, who thought a number of her phrases sufficiently telling to be incorporated without alteration in his tragedy *Lorenzaccio*, perhaps the most resonant drama of the period.

Further collaboration with Sandeau resulted in the novel *Rose et Blanche*, published in December 1831 as the work of "J. Sand." At Nohant in September, Aurore had been working on this book from seven at night to five or six in the morning, including in it reminiscences of her convent years and of the Pyrenees, as well as the portrayal of an unworthy mother (who redeems herself). Its chief interest now lies in the confrontation of two feminine types, the nun and the actress-singer, who were to symbolize divergent strains in her nature.

In October 1831, Aurore was running about Paris requesting puffs for the forthcoming *Rose et Blanche*. Where was Sandeau? By the autumn of that year, the first fine careless rapture was fading fast. In the beginning, Aurore had delighted to watch handsome young Jules as he lolled about in his shabby artist's jacket and dreamed of ambitious projects, never to be fulfilled. That summer, though, the cost of furnishing the fifth-floor flat on the quai Saint-Michel had made a considerable dent in her funds. She had been obliged to borrow money from her friends. Enough of an aristocrat to think that tradespeople could wait, she was anxious to erase debts to friends as quickly as possible, with Jules's help.

His natural indolence contrasted with her unflagging energy and resource. She nagged him to get to work for his own good. He had not envisaged that his dream of the artist's life would turn into a veritable treadmill. Moreover, he was given to disconcerting, uncontrollable bouts of melancholy and depression. These could be very catching. Aurore spent some years helping to keep Jules. She paid for his exemption from military service; she sent him money in the three-month periods when they were apart; and later she was to rent a flat for him.

Still, the underlying cause of the growing doubts she would barely admit to herself were probably sexual in nature. After working on *Une Conspiration en 1537* with its bloody death scene, Aurore had a nightmare. Jules was being crucified and actually begging to be bludgeoned to death so as not to suffer. Apparently, Jules himself often spoke of stabbing her. This sounds like some sadomasochistic game where the parties, in imagination or reality, alternately changed roles in their quest for dominance and submission.

Aurore in love constantly felt the need to confide in a third party the details of their "wild ecstasies"; there was something both narcissistic and exhibitionist in her desire to be "seen" to be loved and sexually fulfilled. When Jules paid a surprise visit to Nohant to see her, Gustave Papet stood guard outside in the garden all night. It may seem surprising that the lovers did not wake Casimir, Hippolyte, the children, the maid and the dog, considering the noise they must have made, according to her highly colored account of their reunion (after misunderstandings and rows). "I overwhelm him [Jules] with reproaches, abuse, contumely, dirt, kicks and blows," she told Emile Regnault. "Then he turns angry, tells me to go to hell and that very night he was there, in my room, in my arms, happy, beaten, kissed, bitten, grunting, crying, laughing. . . . It was a frenzy of delight such as I don't think we have ever experienced. . . . I am black and blue from bites and blows. I can't stand up. . . ." The use of teeth was to figure largely in Aurore's endearments. She had come a long way from the dialogue of souls with Aurélien de Sèze, and perhaps this ostentatious display of violent passion was one way of proving to herself that she was frenetically happy at last.

Having found platonic love unsatisfactory, Aurore tried to throw herself into the opposite extreme with Sandeau, into a violently passionate physical relationship. But it was difficult to keep the affair at a constant pitch of frenzy. From her candid if truncated allusions to their conduct in bed in her letters to Regnault, it would appear that she cooled before Sandeau. To explain her attitude (to herself as much as to Regnault), she began to use a medical argument of the time, to be found in Balzac, that excess (like abstinence) is ultimately fatal. She even referred to herself, after Balzac's novel, published in August 1831, as Sandeau's "peau de chagrin," or "wild ass's skin," the symbolic talisman of life, which shrank with the fulfillment of each desire. As Balzac's old Jewish antique dealer tells the young gambler, Raphaël de Valentin, "It is your excessive desires, your intemperate habits, your delights which kill you. . . . For perhaps sickness is only violent pleasure. Who knows at what stage sensual pleasure becomes sickness and where sickness is still sensual pleasure?"

Gradually, Aurore realized that the passion for Jules to which she had, as she sometimes felt, "sacrificed" her children, her reputation, and her home, was not bringing her the unadulterated happiness she yearned for, that instead she was once again falling into spleen, melancholy, and disgust. At first, she blamed herself. "I bore him," she confided in Regnault. In the months ahead, there would be more violent rows and frentic reconciliations with Jules, "my life, my strength and my hope," but by the autumn and winter of 1831–1832 the relationship was becoming ever more strained.

If only they could live as a family, without agonizing separations, perhaps the situation might improve. She would bring little Solange with her to Paris. At three and a half Solange was—in Aurore's view—far too small to ask awkward questions about her mother's bohemian existence, where student friends might be found spending the night on the floor. Jules welcomed the idea, though the budding medico Regnault, despite his casual affairs, professed to be shocked.

Aurore arrived with Solange in the capital at the beginning of April 1832, shortly after the outbreak of the terrible cholera epidemic that was to claim many thousands of lives in Paris alone—an epidemic whose advance had been feared and anticipated. From her balcony, Aurore could see the grim convoys of corpses being carried in farm carts and even furniture vans to the morgue across the river. Two months later, she witnessed with mounting horror some of the bloody street fighting during the insurrection of June 5–6 that almost overthrew the monarchy of Louis-Philippe. Little Solange was terrified.

What impression these public upheavals together with her mother's private style of life made upon the small child, who was passed from the supervision of Boucoiran to that of Sandeau, Regnault, or the porter's wife, may readily be imagined. Aurore saw herself as a caring mother who could competently do as she wished with her children. Caring she was in large theory, which did not always strictly accord with daily practice. Maurice, continuing his schooling at Nohant under Boucoiran, was older, of a more docile and malleable temperament than Solange. Aurore's reunions with her son were, so she maintained, like lovers' meetings. His plump and amusing sister, with her imperious ways and her inexplicable whims, resembled more closely their grandmother, Sophie. At times Aurore slapped Solange, at times she spoiled her, thus completely and unconsciously repeating the pattern of Sophie's conduct toward herself as a child.

The presence of Solange, despite Jules's fondness for the little girl, did nothing to cement the growing cracks in his relations with Aurore. These were soon to be widened further by Aurore's latest literary undertaking. In February 1832, Aurore had begun to write a novel at the corner cupboard desk in her room at Nohant. This was to be *Indiana*, which she conceived quite clearly in the beginning as a work of straightforward realism. The subject, she told Regnault, "is as simple, natural, real as you could wish. . . ." Here was nothing romantic or frenetic but "ordinary life, bourgeois verisimilitude."

The book was to deal with the intimate feelings and thoughts of her characters, and indeed, she feared lest it might be considered dull. "And yet, what is more interesting than the story of the human heart when that story is true? The question is, to make it true, that is the difficult thing. . . ." As for her heroine, "she is the typical woman, weak and strong . . . an incredible mixture of weakness and energy, greatness and pettiness, a being always composed of two opposing natures, now sublime, now wretched, skilled in deceiving, easily deceived." In describing her intentions and her concept of the heroine as representing the divided nature of woman in general, Aurore was plainly drawing upon her own memories, her own experience in the role of the weak "little woman" she had formerly enacted for the benefit of Casimir and Aurélien and in that of the bold strategist who had dared to make a bid for freedom and happiness.

Indiana, though, carries psychological undertones of which its writer may not have been fully aware. It frequently lingers complacently over poetic images that veer between passivity and physical or mental cruelty, between suicide by water or the Ophelia complex on the one hand and whips, chains and prisons on the other. Thus it dimly echoes Aurore's stormy erotic relations with Sandeau on one level, while symbolizing her irreconcilable need to be sexually dominated as well as to be free of all domination.

In the opening scene, Indiana's elderly parvenu husband, Colonel Delmare, a Napoleonic veteran, bullies her beloved bitch Ophélia, at once conveying his cruel insensitivity to his frail young wife's feelings. A Spanish creole, Indiana appears as submissive yet brave and proud. She comes from the island of Bourbon, afterward known as Réunion (whose exotic scenery Aurore derived largely from the written recollections of her jocose, republican admirer, the La Châtre–born botanist, Jules Néraud, some eight years her senior, nicknamed "the Madagascan" on account of his youthful travels in the tropics). Indiana falls in love with a magnetic Lovelace and conservative political climber, Raymon de Ramière, who had already taken her naïve, passionate creole maid, Noun, as his mistress. On one occasion, he sleeps with Noun in Indiana's bedroom, when she is adorned in Indiana's apparel. The pregnant Noun, discovering that it is Indiana whom Raymon really desires, drowns herself.

However, when Indiana ultimately leaves her husband for Raymon, he repulses her. He prefers to make a socially acceptable marriage. In despair, Indiana contemplates suicide with her taciturn English cousin, Sir Ralph Brown, the ever-loyal protector and father figure who has long secretly loved her. They are mysteriously saved from death in a poetic dénouement that denies the original, purely realistic intention of the book. The happy ending is the book's major weakness, revealing as it does Aurore's secret need for union with the lost father as well as her understandable inability as yet, in art, either to resolve her private problem as a woman or to let it stand unresolved.

In *Indiana* the author's attitude to the place of woman in society is obliquely conveyed through the careful accumulation of detail. Marriage as depicted in the book is an unhappy affair. Above all, the delicate Indiana is yoked to an uncomprehending tyrant who invokes the law and who, when exasperated, indulges in acts of brutality. On the contrary, the final free union of Ralph and Indiana in their island retreat looks idyllic. The reader is left to draw his own conclusions. Unlike women, men can get away with any misdeed. It is the woman who pays. As for a girl of the lower orders, like Noun, she can expect the worst.

The suffering, humiliation, and abandonment of credulous Indiana, repeatedly the dupe of the man she loves, are affecting. Though she is ready to sacrifice her reputation to Raymon, she is foolish enough to expect him to make equal sacrifices for her (an effort which, as Mme de Staël suggested, no man was prepared to make). Heroically, Indiana defies her husband and the law:

> I know that I am the slave and you the lord. The law of the land has made you my master. . . . You have the right of the stronger party, and society confirms you in it; but over my will, sir, you are powerless. . . . Seek out, then, some law, dungeon, instrument of torture which may give you command over that! . . .

And she adds: ". . . you are not morally my master and . . . I depend upon myself alone on this earth." There is also a moment when Indiana defies Raymon, rejecting received religion that serves established society and worships "the god of men" rather than the divine creator of all human beings.

The political setting of the book, during the last years of the Resoration and the July Revolution and after, fulfills the function of juxtaposing the egotistic conservatism of Raymon and the republicanism of Ralph, who is in romantic revolt against existing society. The hatred of injustice, the struggle against it, the thirst for freedom and for equality of responsibility between the sexes, the dream of a better life for everybody, symbolized by Indiana and Ralph when they buy back and free as many sick black slaves as they can—all these elements placed the book firmly in the radical side.

When *Indiana* was published in May 1832, its impact was immediate. "Our literature saw the rise of a masterpiece," wrote Delphine de Girardin, "and the name of *Indiana* resounded throughout France, despite the cholera epidemic and the riots which were contending for our leisure moments at that time." Critics and readers could not fail to be impressed by the author's fresh lyrical gift and insight into the human heart, by several scenes of imaginative erotic power that they did not normally associate with women writers they knew. Balzac saw that the book was resolutely modern in intention. His estranged guide, Latouche, at first glance muttered "pastiche of Balzac," but after spending the night reading the whole, he bowed in admiration:

> . . . everything is fine, subject, order of events, poetry, intimate and admirable understanding of the human heart; the simplicity, brilliance and firmness of style place you, in one bound, at the forefront of contemporary writers; no woman alive can force you to submit to the impertinence of a comparison. Believe your old grouch of a comrade, you are destined to know a success like Lamartine's. Balzac and Mérimée are buried under *Indiana*.

Latouche's touching pride in his pupil's achievement may pardon some exaggeration. He did not, however, suggest that she had "buried" Mme de Staël.

One perspicacious critic, the greatest of the age, noted exponent of the biographical method of literary criticism, was unlikely to overlook the work's shortcomings and awkward passages. This was Sainte-Beuve, who praised the naturalness of the characters, though, as well as the picture of current manners. The character of the worldly, pleasure-loving Raymon, whose passions and conduct were so at variance with his high principles and fine talk, particularly impressed Sainte-Beuve, as it did his contemporaries. A man would never have been capable of perceiving so much, wrote Sainte-Beuve, "nor have dared to say it." What Aurore had succeeded in doing was to portray from the woman's point of view the sexual caddishness of the admired lady-killer of her day.

Indiana appeared under the pseudonym "G. Sand," with the author impersonating a masculine narrator, and with a timid preface. These devices could not mar the courageous aspects of the work. Aurore spelled her new name as Georges Sand and did not adopt the English style of the Christian name until later, when she may have been secretly thinking either of the famous actress, Mlle George, Napoleon's mistress, whom she had seen perform in La Châtre in 1826, or of George Gordon, Lord Byron.

The pseudonym she chose proved highly significant in itself. Her immediate predecessors among women writers had written under their single or married names. Through the pretense of being a masculine author, Aurore was claiming equality with her men colleagues. In this role-playing she wanted to be judged on their level, not solely as a woman author subject to condescension. Moreover, the name she chose, while it had a foreign ring, lacked aristocratic associations. Unlike Mme de Staël, she was not bothered about losing her rank of baroness. Unlike the parvenu Balzac, with his fondness for titled mistresses, she did not invent an intrusive "de." Women writers who came after her understood the point she was making, and many from "Daniel Stern" to

"Currer Bell" or "George Eliot" would assume masculine names after her example.

With the adoption of the new name, something strange happened. At first, Aurore had been slightly frightened by the success of *Indiana*, which brought her instant fame. She would now have to live up to the praise that was being showered upon her. Foolish admirers and people with hard-luck stories besieged her door; publishers hastened to sign the new prodigy. The Saint-Simonians were reputed to be offering her the title of "lady pope" because they thought her novel was "in accordance with their ideas"—however unwittingly so, in Aurore's opinion. "In Paris, Mme Dudevant is dead. But Georges Sand is known to be alive and kicking." The words were written in jest to her friend in La Châtre, Laure Decerfz, daughter of the late Mme Dupin's doctor, but there was truth in them.

A curtain seemed to descend upon Aurore's past life. Aurore Dudevant began to fade from the scene. Instead, Mme George Sand, the composite name she had conquered for herself, took charge. For with the new name came a new identity and a new personality. Like other talented people of widely divergent origin who suffer from some private childhood pain, Aurore was going to create herself. Such self-invented personalities are precarious.

CHAPTER
9

The Perils of Fame

Is she not an extraordinary woman? That says everything; she is left
to her own resources. . . . She leads a singular existence, like the
pariahs of India . . . an object of curiosity, perhaps of envy, and
really deserving only pity.
Mme de Staël
De la Littérature

As for me, I have occasionally envied more passionate and brilliant
talents, and fame more resounding . . . but when I wondered whether
I would be glad to possess these at the price they cost, I quickly resigned myself to doing without them, as I resign myself to doing without
a piece of material which I consider too expensive, without complaining
about not having it, because I do not want to pay the price."
Mme Amable Tastu, letter to Sainte-Beuve, February [?] 1835

AME, which Aurore had often
said she did not want, took
her by surprise. But fame was
one thing; personal relations
were another. In the colossal
success of "G. Sand," Jules had
no part. While Aurore was
working hard on her next
novel, *Valentine*, at Nohant in
August 1832, Jules was supposed to be at work ("which
he doesn't much care for") elsewhere. She became deeply depressed
and unhappy as a crisis developed in their association. After all, Jules
was finding himself in a secondary position, hurtful to his masculine
literary vanity. He was being treated as a child, and children rebel.
Doubtless, too, his youthful eye was roving.

Aurore, revisiting the scenes around Nohant that had witnessed their early happiness, confided in her notebook:

> Everything passes, and it is folly to become attached to places where one has been happy. Happiness fades, places change, and the heart grows older. . . . For others, lazy habit and lukewarm forgiveness, but between us, if there were any grave injury, there could be no going back. The more one has loved the being to whom one has given oneself utterly, the more one must loathe him, when the poison of ingratitude has entered his heart.

In a poem addressed to Hoffmann's mad musician, Kreisler, she envied those who were able to live and to love. For her, the two words were virtually synonymous. She was truly afraid that if she did not love somebody, she would become ossified.

With "despair in her heart," Aurore made a sudden journey to Paris to confront Sandeau. There was a violent row, followed by a shaky reconciliation. She moved into Latouche's leafy apartment, 19 quai Malaquais (her mentor having retired to the country), while Sandeau went to live in a flat in the rue de l'Université that she rented for him. Officially, they had not yet broken with each other, though the break could not be far off.

How could she have expected their ill-sorted union to endure? Here, she was as much the dupe of her desire as her heroine Indiana. In a short story, *Melchior*, where the sailor hero, believing the ship is about to sink, takes his virginal beloved to bed, with disastrous consequences, Aurore wrote:

> Education develops in us, from adolescence, a burning curiosity and often even mistaken emotional needs. From a literature whose aim seems to be to poeticize desire and excite love, our precocious imaginations have drawn, perhaps to excess, the dream of grand attachments. Thus, in demanding of life its unknown joys, we have merely enacted on the stage of reality a bitter parody; we have merely gleaned shame and suffering where we arrived full of vigor, guided as well as deluded by the traditions of poetic ages, of lost loves.

The failure of reality to live up to the inordinate demands of the imagination became an underlying theme of hers, as of her generation's.

This theme is probed in one of Aurore's most powerfully evocative early short stories or prose poems, *La Marquise*, composed with verve, where an eighteenth-century noblewoman falls in love with a gifted actor, named Lélio after Hoffmann's character. Lélio returns her passion, but the marquise, whose experience has confirmed her distaste for the animal side of sexuality, cries, "Oh! do not let us risk this dreadful test!" They sacrifice their physical desires to their imagination, where esteem and respect will never be destroyed.

These two short works, *Melchior* and *La Marquise*, form, as it were, panels in a diptych of disillusion where sexual love is concerned. Aurore's second novel of the year, *Valentine*, confirms the sense of a setback. The dream love of the youthful high-souled but lowly born Bénédict for the noble, devout young heiress Valentine undergoes intense strain when he penetrates her room (where she lies in drugged sleep on her wedding night) and exclaims that he has "possessed" her "in his mind." Neglected by her odious, materialistic husband, who has never consummated the marriage, Valentine finally yields to Bénédict, but suffers torments of conscience afterward. Their union is doomed.

The novel is set in the countryside around Nohant, which Aurore for the first time designated as "la Vallée Noire," from the deep blue, almost black tint of the wooded hills under rain. Thus she created her own personal idyllic landscape out of what is really nothing more than pleasant farming country, forestalling Hardy, Proust, or Faulkner. What struck readers above all, however, was the treatment of the current moral and financial abuses of marriage, from the (then rather titillating) point of view of a woman disguised as a masculine writer. Bénédict's outraged cry, "Marriage, society, institutions, hatred upon you, hatred unto death!" would be echoed many years later in Gide's notorious outburst, "Families, I hate you!"

Valentine, a work of considerable charm and psychological insight, despite its far-fetched plot mechanisms, confirmed the literary reputation of George Sand. The rising critic Gustave Planche brought her his article that contrasted the poetry of *Indiana* and *Valentine* with the didacticism of Mme de Staël's fiction, finding George's to be superior. In his early days Planche was a good-looking though already short-sighted fellow, with a Greek profile and chestnut curls, anxious to be of service. She was also introduced at last to a far more subtle and elusive figure, very self-conscious about his ugly appearance, Charles-Augustin Sainte-Beuve, whose friendship she requested "without misinterpretation." Characteristic of her slight grip on reality was her confirmed belief that the waspish Sainte-Beuve possessed an "angelic soul." Planche and Sainte-Beuve had one thing in common: They were already troubled by George's fecundity. Sainte-Beuve remarked to a friend that "with a little more *restraint*, she will give us fine things." Planche advised her to write less, and warned her about the possibility of exhausting her talent. This was advice she never heeded. Writing had already become a consoling drug to relieve private disillusion.

Sainte-Beuve would evaluate the general state of mind during this period in his essay on the philosopher Théodore Jouffroy, noting how people thought that they were about to reach the brow of the hill, from whence they would survey a bright landscape. Instead, they discovered that they still had much farther to go and that the road ahead would be difficult and muddy. So Aurore had come to Paris full of high hopes for personal happiness and freedom; but by the end of December 1832 George Sand, despite her fame, knew that the way ahead looked dark. She was twenty-eight; she had tried marriage, platonic love, passion in a bohemian garret: All had failed. Given the circumstances of her age, what role was left to her as a woman?

Later, George Sand would look back on 1833 as the unhappiest year of her life. It was certainly the strangest. The winter season reached its peak in the frenzied gaiety of Carnival, wilder even than that of the previous year, when two young bloods, Roger de Beauvoir and the Comte d'Alton-Shée (Sainte-Beuve's cousin), had smuggled a naked dancer into the ball at the Odéon. There was uninhibited dancing and amorous intrigue at balls where only the ladies wore masks. A few more carnival seasons like that of 1833, wrote Sainte-Beuve slyly, would do more for female emancipation than any doctrine.

People tried to erase from their minds the gruesome scenes of the cholera epidemic, which had affected all classes (indeed, Aurore herself had suffered a mild attack of the disease). The favorite path of escape from morbid reflections, from private ills and public uncertainties, was to indulge in a life of pleasure or dissipation. In the capital, extreme poverty added more girls and even young children to the thousands of prostitutes whose different categories would be enumerated by Balzac as though by a naturalist. George herself did not entirely escape the moral contagion that accompanied the plague.

Two remarkable women held up a mirror wherein she could see her own image more clearly. One was the novelist Hortense Allart, who had achieved a certain literary reputation without acquiring a place in the front rank. When George Sand met her, she was the mistress of Henry Bulwer Lytton (brother of the novelist), having passed from being the Comte de Sampayo's and then Chateaubriand's for a few years. She would also later briefly become the mistress of Sainte-Beuve—among others. Hortense Allart deeply admired and secretly envied the author of *Indiana*, ambivalent feelings of which the latter was well aware. George Sand remained wary of this handsome, intelligent, liberated, and as yet unmarried colleague who had something in common with herself but for whom she privately expressed distaste. To her, Hortense Allart appeared as the person she herself did not want to be: "a scribbler" who talked politics, "a woman of letters . . . pedantic . . . mannish, a *woman writer*. . . ." Any masculine opponent of women with literary ambitions could have said no worse. Indeed, these were the very words some were applying to *her*.

The other woman artist she encountered, widely regarded as the greatest tragic actress of the day, seemed the reverse of Hortense Allart. More than six years George's senior, Marie Dorval was at the peak of her career after her triumph as the self-sacrificing courtesan in Victor Hugo's *Marion de Lorme* and as the erring wife, Adèle d'Hervey, in Alexandre Dumas's *Antony*. The novelist sent the actress a fan letter (now lost). Fan letters usually tell more about the sender than the recipient, really being addressed to the imagined personage one would secretly like to be. Deeply touched, Marie Dorval burst in upon the newly established novelist and fell into her arms.

That impulsive action was characteristic of Marie. Her contemporaries frequently praised her acting for its naturalness—the impression all great actors who impose a fresh theatrical style are able to create in the spectator's mind. To one critic, she seemed inspired, "ecstasy in person." Another praised her spontaneity. In Théophile Gautier's opinion, Pierre Bocage as the brooding Byronic lover in Dumas's *Antony* and Marie Dorval as the weak woman he destroys performed with amazing, lifelike intensity. Gautier admired the truth of Marie's gestures, her vehement cries from the heart.

A radiant beauty, Marie was also a womanly woman. Her features were soft. She had great melting blue eyes, a sensuous mouth, and she wore her hair in a mass of beribboned curls. Femininity, naturalness, spontaneity, as well as true, unthinking, selfless passion—these were the qualities George admired in the actress and yearned for herself. Sometimes, she spoke of Marie in a novelist's way, as a phenomenon worthy of study. On a more revealing occasion, however, she alluded to her new friend as a woman with a "complete" nature.

Very soon they were on intimate terms, chatting and confiding in each other after the performance in the empty theater or by George's fireside. Marie Dorval's life had been, and would continue to be, stormy. She was the illegitimate daughter of two strolling players, virtually self-taught, twice married, with three daughters (one by the composer Piccini). Among her numerous lovers were Alexandre Dumas and later, Jules Sandeau, as well as many lesser known passing fancies. Since 1831, her acknowledged lover was the jaundiced nobleman Alfred de Vigny, who could never resign himself to the way his discarded predecessors continued to attend her salon. George told Marie how her own mother had once been a small-part actress (with all *that* implied)—information conveyed by Marie with typically thoughtless rapidity to the astounded poet. Perhaps part of the fascination Marie exerted upon George was the result of the novelist's curiosity about her own mother's past. This warm-hearted artist, woman of easy virtue, and fond mother was what Sophie, now always quick to complain and criticize, should have been like.

Before the performance, Marie used to admit a privileged few to watch her preparatory toilet. Vigny loved this ritual: "A really inspired actress is charming when seen at her toilet before the performance. She looks at herself in the mirror, puts on her rouge, takes it off . . . tries out her voice . . ." George, with her musical ear, did not find Marie's rolled *r*'s and hoarse tones particularly beautiful, but there was something catching about her emphatic, actressy way of speaking in private, and the novelist could not help imitating it unconsciously.

The word went round the the small circles of the Parisian literary world—and eventually reached Casimir—that they were lesbians. Gustave Planche risked George's ire by warning her of associating with Marie, because the actress was suspected of a lesbian relationship with her colleague, Juliette Drouet, soon to be the lifelong inamorata of Victor Hugo. George made Planche swear never to raise the subject again. Another literary lady, Mme Louise Swanton Belloc, author of a work on Byron, was reputed to indulge in Sapphic practices with a woman of letters, Mlle de Montgolfier, if Stendhal is to be believed. Journalist and theater director Arsène Houssaye (himself a lady-killer and boon companion of rich dandies like Roger de Beauvoir) later conveyed this gossip about George and Marie and others unnamed to posterity. Though in general far from reliable, Houssaye did know Dorval extremely well when she was Sandeau's mistress and when all three were neighbors in the rue du Bac. Houssaye may well have gleaned something from them in an unguarded moment. He also hinted darkly at lesbian relations between the author of *Indiana* and the beautiful, eccentric fighter for Italian unity, Princess Cristina di Belgiojoso, who had settled in Paris not long after Aurore.

The testimony of Marie's current lover, Alfred de Vigny (who confided his suspicions to the private diary where he also recorded his sexual prowess), though plausible in virtue of his intimacy with the actress, may be regarded as unreliable in a different sense. The "costive swan" was a poet gifted with feminine sensibility, as he himself owned. His sense of his own masculinity was fragile. For him, women were frivolous and weak, destined for submission to men, and those who encroached in any way upon what he regarded as the masculine role, by talking politics, for instance, deserved a whipping. He was obsessed with the idea of women with masculine pretensions, among whom he included the bold heroines of the Fronde so much admired by Aurore as a girl. And from his early verses, written at eighteen, on the Sapphic theme, to his conviction that lesbianism leads to epilepsy—expressed in old age as a warning to his young mistress, a governess whom he liked to keep in Oriental seclusion—Vigny was suspiciously fascinated by this subject.

Marie haunted him in the shape of Eve and Delilah, both destroyers of men. George he envisaged as the biblical Judith, the avenging slayer of the warrior Holofernes. Vigny forbade Marie to communicate with "this Sappho." That did not mean he would deprive himself of the pleasure of flirting on occasion with a woman whose great dark eyes reminded him of the mystics or of Renaissance paintings, even if the lower part of her face seemed unattractive. His attitude to women was complex and contradictory.

The correspondence between George and Marie is incomplete and often cannot be accurately dated. Its gushing tone, characteristic of the emotionalism of the age, sometimes recalls the passionate protestations of love Mme de Staël addressed to Juliette Récamier. One or two actressy phrases penned by Dorval's would-be "cavalier" may give pause but can scarcely be regarded as serious evidence of anything compromising: "Monday morning or evening, in the theater or in your bed, I simply must come and kiss you, my lady, or I shall do something crazy!" wrote George to Marie.

The lyrical dream passage in George's diary, entitled "To the Nameless Angel" (first addressed "To the Angel Lélio"), certainly conveys a distaste for the crudity of masculine caresses. Yet this passage closely relates to moments in the novel *Lélia*, especially one where man in his brutality replaces the ethereal being, the angel of dream desire. This angelic lover may have long dark tresses but, as Freud pointed out, dreams can be of a bisexual nature; the homosexual impulses of the dream are not necessarily translated into actuality. If, as has been suggested, George's feeling for Marie is expressed in *La Marquise* through the heroine's adoration of the actor Lélio, the whole tendency of that short story moves toward nonconsummation. The most suggestive homoerotic passage George wrote occurs in *Lélia*, where the courtesan Pulchérie recalls her adolescent awakening to a masculine quality in her sister.

The problem is hardly capable of proof, though the lines on Pulchérie's awakening certainly reveal an awareness of, and interest in, the Sapphic theme. Nor can the possibility of lesbianism be entirely dismissed. George was always curious about everything. At this period in her life, she had lost her way, she had no belief in anything, no guidelines, nobody at hand to whom she could turn for advice. She was not incapable of trying something to see what it was like.

Yet there was another way in which Marie exerted a spell upon her, so that as George watched the actress she felt as if she were looking into her own soul. The novelist's conduct in the months ahead bears witness to the extent of Marie's impact. To George, Marie appeared to be without restraint, a woman who accepted her nature and her passions without intellectualizing them, and who did not make great demands upon her lovers. When George thought of her own demanding character, which led to her disillusion with the men she had loved and who had all failed her, she was appalled by her own egoism. In contrast with herself, Marie the artist-courtesan was nothing less than "sublime."

Even if Marie did not actually advise George during their nocturnal chats to "become a courtesan"—as Pulchérie, who is modeled upon the actress, counseled her despairing sister, Lélia—the recipe for feminine spontaneity and "completeness" seemed clear enough. Aurore had long shown interest in the courtesan as the opposite of the nun. There was the episode of the apprentice courtesan in *Rose et Blanche*. On several occasions she had tried to pump Sandeau and Regnault about Frascati's, a gambling den in the rue de Richelieu frequented by ladies of the town. To experiment now in changing her manners would not be beyond the scope of her imitative talents. One morning, Jules Boucoiran (whose duties as Maurice's tutor at Nohant were at an end, since the boy was about to enter the Collège Henri IV as a boarder) called on her at her Paris flat. Before he passed into the next room to give Solange a reading lesson, he was taken aback to see George calmly slipping on her shift in his presence. Other male callers might be treated to a similar bohemian spectacle, in what seems clearly an ingenuous attempt to copy Dorval's pretheater toilet. George began to issue would-be casual invitations to eminent gentlemen to call, or to bring their friends. In this manner, she could convince herself that, though déclassée, she was free to make her own society, that she had the power to choose.

The social mores of the day made some allowance for a married woman who lived discreetly with her lover. What society refused to place was such a woman who parted from her lover, as she had previously abandoned her husband. As Balzac was to show in his novel *Béatrix*, the only path for such a woman, however well-born, was to become a virtual courtesan. There was no other recognized place in society for the independent, unattached woman. Society even attributed lovers to her whether they were so in fact or not, just as it assumed the worst of two women who were on intimate terms. To be "far out," as Aurore and her young friends wished to be, meant that one ran serious risk of drowning.

It looks rather as if fame and freedom went to her head. She spoke haughtily of the "social position" that she had created to suit herself, whatever others might say about her. This position was indeed singular. Sandeau and Planche were variously in tow. Casimir came occasionally to Paris, dined with his wife, spied on her in a desultory way through the servants, but seemed largely content to allow her to go her own way so long as she left him alone to go his. When appeals were made, he was rarely in a hurry to disburse funds.

Still, she now had, in addition to her basic annual allowance from him, the receipts from her stories and journalism. On sending *Melchior* to the *Revue de Paris* in the summer of 1832, she had hoped to receive the same fee as most of her fellow contributors, but in vain. She fully expected to earn from *La Marquise* as much as a colleague like Eugène Sue, the future popular author of *Les Mystères de Paris*. When her expectations were deceived, she moved to the *Revue des deux mondes*. It had not taken her long to raise, in private, the question of equal pay— for herself, rather than as a matter of principle. She was ready, though, to advise a struggling author, Antoinette Dupin, how to soothe editors and how to make sure of being paid.

The final break with Jules occurred in the spring of 1833, after further violent scenes of jealous recrimination. Perhaps even blows were exchanged. Both were agreed that their liaison had become a living hell. Jules attempted to poison himself with an overdose of morphine, and on recovery was packed off to Italy. George professed herself deeply wounded by the (unnamed) discoveries she had made about his behavior. Even toward the end of her life she still spoke of the ingrate with contempt and disgust.

She was now on her own in the unique position she had won for herself. The presence of Solange was a great comfort. Casimir had brought Maurice to start school at the Collège Henri IV. At least she had her children close by and could work on her novel, *Lélia*, with Gustave Planche as her literary adviser. But she was approaching her twenty-ninth birthday. At thirty a woman was supposed to be finished. There was no little desperation in her effort to change herself into a natural creature *à la* Dorval.

One illusion lingered: that there existed somewhere a literary society of high-minded kindred spirits. In her imagination, Balzac and Sainte-Beuve seemed obvious candidates for this elite. For some months, too, she and Prosper Mérimée, a friend of Planche's, had been circling around each other. In company with Goethe, she admired Mérimée's plays, purportedly written by a Spanish actress named Clara Gazul. For the frontispiece, Mérimée had himself portrayed as Clara, wearing a mantilla—a form of travesty that could not but appeal to George. "When shall I see you, and when shall I see *Clara Gazul?*" she had inquired of Mérimée's publisher, through whom they were finally introduced. Meanwhile, she had asked Sainte-Beuve to introduce her to Alfred de Musset, then changed her mind. "He is very much the dandy, we shouldn't suit, and I was curious rather than keen to see him. I think it is rash to satisfy all one's feelings of curiosity . . ." Instead, Sainte-Beuve should bring Alexandre Dumas, whose work she admired. Did she not know that the author of *Antony* was a notorious satyr? All that seemed to bother her was the dread of making a bad first impression, due to her incurable social timidity.

While these additional invitations were being issued, Mérimée was paying assiduous court to this interesting female, of a type he had never encountered before. And he had encountered many. A year older than George, he was a member of the dissipated set that embraced Stendhal, the painter Eugène Delacroix, as well as Alfred de Musset. These brilliant rakehells liked to wine and dine together; then, often the worse for drink, they would proceed to some house of ill-fame that boasted a fresh supply of Jewish prostitutes, or to some wild party where chorus girls from the Opéra were prepared to engage in foursomes. In this circle, some betrayed their latent homosexuality by sharing the same woman, or by passing on to their friends a discarded mistress. Mérimée was persuaded by Pauline, a creole in the Opéra chorus, to abstain from raping her, for their greater mutual satisfaction; and having found her to his taste, he passed her to his English friend, Sutton Sharpe. The brutal treatment of prostitutes (alternately despised and sentimentalized in literature) contrasted with the devotion displayed toward adored ladies of a higher rank and with protestations of delicate sensibility. Like Stendhal, the sensitive, stylish Mérimée was rarely without some obscene phrase on his lips when communing with his intimates.

Of striking appearance marred only by a curiously squared-off nose, Mérimée affected the superior aloofness of the English dandy. George, fascinated by his sardonic expression, keen intellect, and experienced talk, imagined he possessed some key to love and living that had so far eluded her. He sought to convince her that she could find satisfaction in a purely sexual relationship. Their mutual curiosity fused. She decided to try the experiment. A disrobing scene of the sort George now believed irresistible cooled Mérimée's ardor and, in bed, the experiment failed. In her frustration, George bit his shoulder, as she had recently made the frustrated Bénédict bite Valentine's. According to one version that the young Henry James later heard in Paris, Mérimée was further disconcerted when, at first light, he watched George in a dressing gown, her hair tied in a red scarf, as she knelt to make the fire before sitting down to write. If this tale is true, she was trying to balance two contradictory images of herself: spontaneous lover and indefatigable writer.

Instead of some surprising new sensation, Don Juan had encountered the sentiment and submission he already knew so well in other women, and thoroughly despised. It was his scathing assessment that George had engaged in "debauchery" out of curiosity rather than from temperament. In her turn, George gave Marie Dorval some idea of his physical equipment and its shortcomings—information Marie passed to her ex-lover Dumas, who gleefully elaborated upon it to others. George also confided to her trusted actress friend Mérimée's brutal comment on her performance: "He treated me like a whore. . . . He said, 'You have the manners of a whore without her assets, and the arrogance of a marquise without her charm.' " This comment, which Marie duly communicated to Vigny, evokes not only George's attempted pose of naturalness but also her (not unnatural) failure to carry it off with aplomb.

George, in thrall to Marie, apparently bore her no grudge for her betrayal. To do so would have been to admit to herself that she was taking a perilous path. But the result of the affair with Mérimée, which lasted a few weeks, was humiliation and bitter self-contempt—doubtless increased when he declined to respond to a further (surprising) invitation. Sainte-Beuve, whom she had made her new (if reluctant) confessor, offered to introduce her to "a skillful psychologist," the philosopher Théodore Jouffroy. George remarked that so academic a theorist as Jouffroy would be incapable of understanding her own ventures into the forbidden. The image she used was that of cannibalism. She told Sainte-Beuve:

> I tried to overcome my nature. . . . I was stricken with . . . that weariness which induces vertigo and which causes one, after having denied everything, to question everything once more. . . . A girl of fifteen would have known better than to behave as I did at thirty [she was, in fact, still twenty-eight at the time of the Mérimée episode]: I committed the most signal folly of my life, I became P.M.'s mistress. . . . If P.M. had understood me perhaps he would have loved me, and then he would have dominated me, and if I could be dominated by a man I should be saved, because my freedom is consuming and killing me.

To Sainte-Beuve she confided her dread of living alone. Her candor was part self-justification and part cry for help.

During the lengthy decline of the liaison with Sandeau, the encounter with Marie Dorval, and the weeks of diplomacy leading up to the débâcle with Mérimée, George had been at work on her novel *Lélia*. She consulted Sainte-Beuve, though Planche's hand is evident in the plan and the treatment of the characters as types. Quite different in manner from her earlier tales, *Lélia* is a work of considerable power, operatic in character, being set in a form that has no current novelistic equivalent, that of the symbolic prose poem.

The proud heroine, Lélia, a poetess and thinker with spiritual yearnings, a free and superior woman, "soars" above the world in which she lives. But she has no role to play in a world where roles are all important. Indeed, the word "role,", together with the impression that people are play-acting, often recurs in George Sand's early work. Old religious certainties have been replaced by new forms of idolatry, love of God by love of man and self. The atmosphere in which Lélia moves is that of existential boredom, spleen, despair, and dread at the approaching end of the civilized world, an ambience common to the literature of the eighteen thirties.

It is not the extravagant plot but the situation of the heroine that commands attention. With Lélia, George projected the romantic Byronic heroine to set beside the Byronic hero. She laid claim as a woman to the modern field of sensibility explored by the exceptional man, frustrated in existing society. Instead of man, it is woman who symbolizes modern humanity. In addition, Lélia incarnates the misery and enslavement of modern woman, the pain of the feminine condition in an uncomprehending, brutal world. Whether as lover, as courtesan, as wife and mother, woman is forced into some form of prostitution.

There could be no Byronic heroine without a Byronic secret. Once, in conversation with Sainte-Beuve, George remarked that even the wisest person has some shameful secret to conceal. The critic, irritated by the way she kept insisting that he was her superior, observed that such private shame renders all human beings equal. As George recorded their talks, however, it was Sainte-Beuve who impressed upon her the literary value of having a great secret in life, some mysterious crime or hidden sorrow, like the "alleged crime of Byron," which endowed the poet with a magic halo. In Byron's case, there were heavy hints of incest covering repressed homosexuality. In Lélia's case, it was impotence in love, which may conceivably have fulfilled the same function. When George read passages from *Lélia* to Sainte-Beuve, the latter owned that he felt afraid of the novelist. Her daemon, her creative imagination had outstripped actuality, George told him. "And don't take my satanic manner too seriously. I assure you it is *a pose* I've adopted."

The passage in *Lélia* that attracted most notice was the heroine's daring confession of sexual frustration. The subject was *à la mode*. The theme of masculine sexual impotence had been treated by the Duchesse de Duras in *Olivier ou le Secret*, a tale that was circulated privately but never published; by George Sand's mentor, Latouche, in *Olivier*; and by Stendhal in *Armance*. Balzac had depicted a frigid woman, Fœdora, in *La Peau de chagrin* and had speculated upon the causes of her frigidity, suggesting among them a traumatic experience due to masculine indelicacy. George took up this theme from the feminine standpoint. Lélia confesses in convincing detail that no man has ever succeeded in satisfying her. Each one has been selfishly intent on his own pleasure, has used her and remained indifferent to her own agony of frustration. Sexual reality has never equaled her dream of orgasmic ecstasy.

This confession was at once taken to be George's, and thenceforward she was known as Lélia. George's experience, however, her early bliss in marriage, her first wild ecstasies with Jules, do not quite tally with this confession. Had Aurore's letters to Stéphane and Jules survived, they might have told a different story from Lélia's. The heroine's tale of sexual woe is, in fact, a sort of blind. The confession suggests nothing so much as the fear of being incapable of love, expressed as the actuality. It also appears as a device for attracting the attention of men who feel they could do better. What it does represent, above all, is an indictment of masculine insensitivity to the just claims of woman. Thus *Lélia* utters a plea for the recognition of sexual equality far in advance of its day (and not always admitted in ours).

Because of her unfortunate experience with men, Lélia resists Sténio, the young poet who loves her. She appears as an *allumeuse*, a coquette who dominates Sténio, but as soon as he shows signs of dominating her in the sex war, she cruelly casts him aside. Since she believes he is giving sexual possession more importance than it deserves, she allows her sister and *alter ego*, the courtesan Pulchérie, to take her place in bed. Shattered by this deceit, Sténio embarks upon a life of drink and debauchery in the style of the gilded youth of the day and ends by denouncing the Don Juan in man who treats woman as a thing, before drowning himself.

Lélia has her liberty. But is she any happier with it? "Admit it, you are not happy," cries Sténio. Her lonely position on the heights gives her vertigo—words echoed by George to Sainte-Beuve. Lélia yearns for some kind of Stoic wisdom of the sort Aurore had admired in Montaigne and as expressed in the person of Trenmor, a compulsive gambler who has expiated his misdeeds in years of suffering. But before Lélia can attain to peace and wisdom like his, she is strangled by Magnus, the mad Irish priest who vainly loves her. Through this wildly frenetic dénouement, George obliquely conveyed her inability to extricate herself from the morass into which her curiosity and her pride had led her.

With the publication of *Lélia* in July, George set about obtaining puffs from established figures. Among these was the popular poet Béranger, who would call her, in private, "the Queen of our new literary generation," a royal title that stuck. He and Hortense Allart would henceforward refer to her as "the Queen." The aging Chateaubriand replied to George: "You will live . . . and you will be the French Lord Byron." Chateaubriand would not be alone in perceiving a link with the poet of *Don Juan*.

The novel caused a sensation. Hostile articles appeared in the press of all shades of opinion. While recognizing that the scandal assured the success of *Lélia*, George was soon asking her friends in the journalistic world to rally to her defense. Immorality was the main charge, though much equivocal fun was had with the enigma of the author's personality: whether "he," "she," or hermaphrodite. One critic considered the novel "dangerous" because of its display of unbelief and egoism. Another affected to see in *Lélia* similarities with a work by the Marquis de Sade that he said he did not dare to name.

The chivalric but clumsy Planche, likewise attacked in the diatribes of this second impudent scribe, challenged him to a duel, much to George's annoyance. The affair of honor took place in the Bois de Boulogne without injury to either party. But coming two months after Planche's abortive challenge to Dumas, who had retailed insulting innuendoes about the pedantic critic's relations with George, it increased her notoriety as a dangerous woman.

By the autumn of 1833, Sainte-Beuve had at last produced a judicious essay on *Lélia*, setting the "lyrical and philosophical work," the "novel-poem," in the context of recent writings by women and the general movement for the amelioration of "the feminine condition" stimulated by Saint-Simonism. He deplored the omission of any solution to the problems raised by Lélia's despairing inability to believe or to love, as well as a lack of the social precision and realistic detail to be found in the author's earlier novels. All the same, he was astonished at the varied gifts displayed by a woman who had so recently made her literary debut.

Some of the women supporters of Saint-Simonism would be particularly impressed by the novel. In the following year, in *Le Livre des actes*, one of them contributed an unsigned article alluding to George in laudatory terms: "Among women there arose one alone, strong and sublime. . . . *Lélia* is a great work . . ." When thanking Marie Talon, a leading disciple of Enfantin, for sending her this article, George politely expressed doubts about the aspect of the Saint-Simonist doctrine that concerned women. For the central problem of morality was still under debate. She herself held no doctrine, made no personal profession of faith; she was simply a novelist. One day, perhaps, she might be ready to define her position more clearly.

As for *Lélia*, it was "a cry of pain. . . ." It offered no moral code. "You yourself have understood it better," she told Marie Talon, "since you have seen in it only a woman who deserves commiseration. . . ." Let women keep to the old moral code and await their delivery, not from their own revolt but from the acts of men who had seen the light. Given her own conduct, her declarations of respect for established morality and ideal marriage may seem odd. It was as if she were issuing a warning against the moral cost of taking the path that she herself—an exceptional case (in her view)—had followed. Her imaginative instinct outran her power of conscious reasoning. *Lélia* was, in fact, one of those books that stimulated and changed the consciousness of its readers, irrespective of their sex, without insisting on any particular course of action.

Hortense Allart was right when she said George did not have any fixed ideas, only flashes of inspiration. She, too, had sought to attach George to the cause of women's liberation. "I had counted on you to help to improve their fate, for it is up to women to do so," declared Hortense, echoing Fourier, and adding, "I myself don't pay any more attention than you do to the virtue demanded of them, but I would take a good deal of notice of some feasible form of virtue. . . ." George loudly protested her inferiority and her ignorance vis-à-vis this erudite colleague whom she regarded as a charmless blue-stocking. She stressed her own misanthropy: "Beyond two or three people, the world does not exist for me." During this period, George was far less interested in political and social change than she had been up to the insurrection of June 1832.

The bitter misanthropy of *Lélia* astounded the friends who had known its author before she became George Sand. "I am still Aurore of Nohant-Vicq . . ." she assured Charles Duvernet. That was not entirely true. As for Jules Néraud "the Madagascan" (who had first met her when, as a girl, she had purloined one of the dahlias he had introduced into Berry, and who later fell in love with her), he could not imagine how the châtelaine of Nohant who had enjoyed puns, studying butterflies, sewing, and jam-making could have written a book so preoccupied with metaphysical doubt and gloom.

What would Néraud have said if he could have seen his idol responding to the handsome Neapolitan poet-in-exile Alessandro Poerio with the words: "As a woman who is bored I am rather fond of anything that arouses my curiosity. . . ." What would the uncomplicated botanist have thought, could he have seen her as she casually changed her clothes in Poerio's presence, or if he could have read her invitation to the gallant Italian: "What has become of you, Monsieur, and why haven't I seen you again? Have I displeased or bored you?" Perhaps Néraud would have been even more surprised than by *Lélia*, had he known that when she wrote that invitation to Poerio she was, in all likelihood, already the mistress of the dissolute young prodigy Alfred de Musset.

CHAPTER
10

In Byron's "Morea"

Slow sinks, more lovely ere his race be run,
Along Morea's hills the setting sun;
Not as in Northern climes, obscurely bright,
But one unclouded blaze of living light!

Byron
The Curse of Minerva and *The Corsair*

. . . debauchery is certainly an art like poetry; it requires strong
spirits; . . . we want to reach the very bottom without knowing why.

Honoré de Balzac,
La Peau de chagrin

OR the past few months, George had been trying to prove to herself that anything men could do, she was perfectly entitled to attempt. Why should they alone enjoy freedom, command their happiness, take the initiative? She would be France's Lord Byron, in life as well as literature. True, so far, her freedom was "killing" her, but possibly that was because she had not yet risked enough, or because she still had to find out more.

When she countermanded her invitation to Sainte-Beuve to introduce Alfred de Musset, she already knew the young poet from his early verses, and by reputation, as a Byronic dandy. The word "dandy" did not imply one merely concerned with the English cut of his clothes, but a man opposed to vulgar commonplace, in revolt against increasing social conformity, prompt to scandalize by his manners, morals, or conduct. She may well have supposed a certain similarity in their defiant stance, in their disarray at their inability to find a religious faith. But how much did she really know about this deeply divided and tormented spirit?

Mérimée could have told her a good deal, although it is unlikely that he did so, for he was outspoken only with his intimates and far less courageous in his published writings than his friend Stendhal, whose fondness for "the bitter truth" he tried to moderate. Privately, Mérimée gave Stendhal a vivid account of a riotous night spent in Musset's company in September 1831, when the poet was twenty. Musset, during dinner at a restaurant with Mérimée and Sutton Sharpe, was all affectation until he became drunk on champagne. He then proposed that the company should proceed elsewhere to witness the "spectacle" of his copulating with a prostitute by the light of twenty-five candles. The others readily agreed to this charming proposal, but although Musset was encouraged by two skilled whores, he was too drunk to provide the show he had offered.

The poet longed to be "seen" as the most vicious and depraved young whoremonger and gambler of his age. This was his revenge upon the post-Napoleonic era that failed to give his generation any scope for spiritual idealism or high deeds. Hours in the dissecting room during his short-lived medical studies made him obsessed with the skull beneath the skin. He modeled himself upon Lovelace, Valmont, and Byron's Don Juan, and, like Byron, he knew the Marquis de Sade's melancholy, perverted logic. When not yet seventeen, he had told a friend that he sought to torment women to death, while awaiting the predestined She; and, moreover, wished to extinguish any remaining traces of inner nobility in punch, beer, and possibly opium. His early writings include a free translation or travesty of De Quincey's *The Confessions of an English Opium-Eater*, with additions of his own. A pornographic work, *Gamiani or Two Nights of Excess*, where the narrator witnesses the lesbian activities of a "Fœdora," the countess Gamiani, and joins in, is widely attributed to Musset.

The cause of his flaunted precocious debauchery, encouraged by a wealthy boon companion, Alfred Tattet (who provided him with horses, whores, and the privacy of his *garçonnière*), was unlikely to be the one the poet loudly proclaimed. According to Musset, the origin of his ride to the abyss was the deceit and faithlessness of his first mistress. The true stimulus lay deeper, in some personality defect or physical inadequacy, or possibly in some early traumatic sexual initiation—horror at the fleshly struggle with the prostitute whom "every father pays for his son at puberty," as he put it. In a passage cut from his autobiographical novel, *La Confession d'un enfant du siècle*, Musset used the image of an innocent child, in flight from murderous brigands, who begs his father to save him, only to be slain by his father, himself a brigand like the rest.

This revealing passage was followed by another, no less telling, in which St. Antony is tempted by a female demon who cleverly assumes the appearance of Christ, concealing herself in the saint's last refuge, the statue of the Savior. Musset's loathing and disgust for women could be indulged to the full with prostitutes, who were unlikely to protest. Secretly, he feared women, his dread of their power to emasculate being obliquely conveyed in his poem "Le Saule" through the image of the Judith of Cristofana Allori, the Florentine painter who depicted his own features in the bleeding head of Holofernes. It was partly this fear and hatred of women that had set Musset on his Byronic course of self-defilement and self-destruction by all available means. He fulfilled his youthful ambition of tormenting women, then savored his repentance and suffering, the very stimulus of his creative urge. For him, woman had to be either idol or whore.

At a dinner given in June 1833 for the contributors of the *Revue des deux mondes*, Musset found himself seated next to a small, quiet, olive-skinned woman, with great eyes, who was wearing a tiny dagger at her waist. So this was the enigmatic creature all Paris was talking about: He, she, hermaphrodite—or maybe a "Fœdora"? His curiosity was now thoroughly aroused. His friend and one-time brothel companion, Sainte-Beuve, could have told him something about the author of *Lélia*, since George had read to the critic passages from the book before its publication. The issue of the *Revue des deux mondes* of May 15 contained fragments of the novel, including the provocative scene where the heroine invites and then repulses the poet Sténio. The taste for pleasure in pain seemed to mirror Musset's own. The same issue of the magazine carried Musset's drama *Les Caprices de Marianne*, where he projected his inner divisions through the luckless dreamer Cœlio and the dissipated Octave, who spurns the woman who loves him.

George, taken with Alfred's golden youthful good looks, his elegant manners, his quick intelligence, and the charming, casual lightness of wit that failed to conceal deep dissatisfaction, saw principally the dazzling poet of "Namouna," who was set on a suicidal course. She could not fail to be fascinated by this embodiment of the Byronic ethos, eternally fascinating to women. Still, she tried to remain on her guard. They discussed literature. She expressed a desire to read a poem he was currently engaged on, and to satisfy her "whim" he at once sent her a fragment of "Rolla"—"Too late have I come into a world too old"— the tale of the suicide of a dissolute youth in the arms of a whore.

Quickly, he followed this gift with stanzas addressed in an extremely familiar tone to George herself, a series of pressing questions about her experiences and her motives in writing the passionate scene between Noun and Raymon in Indiana's bedroom. George thanked him without actually answering any of his urgent queries, remarking upon a supposed hidden relationship in sorrow between some of their invented characters, including Hassan in "Namouna" and Raymon. Musset's poetic portrayal of the Don Juan type was far superior to her own attempt with Raymon, she told him. Where his writings had the freshness of youth, hers were already marked by the years, by her unhappy experiences. She made much of the difference in age: Musset was twenty-two, she was almost twenty-nine when she invited him to visit her "anchorite's cell," an odd name for the recently much-frequented apartment on the quai Malaquais. For Musset's benefit, George played the part of a world-weary recluse. She knew Alfred did not share her ideals about love, rooted in the lofty disquisitions of Rousseau's *La Nouvelle Héloïse*, and she thought him quite incapable of any serious relationship with a woman.

They embarked upon a literary friendship, reading Goethe's *Götz von Berlichingen* together, and understanding each other at a word or a glance. She gave him her early sketch of the conspiracy of Lorenzo de' Medici that was to form the basis of *Lorenzaccio*. They discussed her sick heart, and talked about foreign travel. On reading *Lélia* when it appeared in July, Alfred expressed his admiration, but reassured her: He would not be asking her to go to bed with him. "You know me well enough by now to be sure that the absurd question—'will you or won't you?'—will not be addressed by me to you. The Baltic lies between us in that regard—you can only give the love of the mind—and I cannot return it (always supposing that you didn't simply send me packing if I took it into my head to ask for it). . . ." What he could be to her, however, was "a sort of comrade" without special rights or privileges, thus avoiding jealous quarrels. She idolized friendship between the sexes. So it was agreed. He sat on cushions on the floor of her living room as they talked, amid the smoke of their cigarettes.

This phase lasted some weeks, but Musset could not keep it up, perhaps had never intended to do so. Suddenly, there was a change of tone: "I am in love with you. I have been from the very first day I came to see you. . . . I know what you think of me. . . ." But, though he said he feared he might lose her friendship by his declaration, he trusted in her goodness of heart. George was touched, but still did not trust him. With his keen imaginative insight, he pressed harder: ". . . I should like you to know me better, to see that there is none of the roué's strategy or conceit in my conduct toward you. . . ." She had observed only his face as Octave the cynical debauchee, not his face as Cœlio the sensitive, suffering, faithful lover. He was buried alive; he was a prisoner, in need of compassion, not contempt. And, with a heavy hint of suicide, he concluded: "Farewell, George, I love you like a child."

As Alfred guessed, George could not resist his tears, the appeal to compassion and maternal feelings. The maternal role, when properly fulfilled, was one feminine part that enjoyed universal unqualified esteem, its sole equivalent being the function of nurse. In envisaging his beloved as a combination of mother, sister, friend, Musset was not alone. Balzac also perceived his mistress, Mme de Berny, in a similar multiple role. Having won the day, Musset hurried off to take a perfumed bath and record his triumph in verse.

According to George herself, she became Musset's mistress out of "friendship," not love—meaning, perhaps also, sympathy and pity. "Love" came afterward. She had not expected to find it, "especially there," an allusion to Musset's lurid self-advertisement as a rake. In the early days of their liaison, he was showing her his charming, tender, good-natured aspect, which she found irresistible. Nor could she help feeling flattered at being chosen by so gifted a young man. She did not know how long their union could last, but she let it be known she was happy. Happy, despite discordant moments and a disturbing incident that occurred during the lovers' stay at Fontainebleau, where they had gone to escape the oppressive heat of Paris.

After dinner at the Hôtel Britannique on the day of their arrival, they set out together (George in blouse and trousers) to walk by moonlight to the rocks of Franchard, celebrated by Senancour. Alfred left her for a while in the darkness. Suddenly, she heard a wild cry. She found him, face down, quivering with terror. He had seen a hideous drunken man who resembled him like a brother. It was a hallucination, probably induced by drink or opium, a form of delirium from which he was to suffer at intervals throughout his life.

While George was at Fontainebleau with Musset, Gustave Planche was looking after Maurice and Solange, taking them to see the mime Deburau, and sending bulletins about their welfare. The critical scandal over *Lélia* was about to break. Planche received his dismissal, but nonetheless fought the duel over George's literary honor in which Musset, who was never one for duels, did not rush to participate. Nearly everybody in Parisian literary circles believed that Planche had been George's lover. Her maid reported to Casimir that, one morning, she had seen little Solange climb into bed with George and Planche. It seems unlikely that Musset would not have heard rumors about Planche (whom he detested) from such inveterate gossips as François Buloz, canny editor of the *Revue des deux mondes,* or Sainte-Beuve, one of that powerful literary and political journal's principal collaborators.

To Sainte-Beuve, George repeatedly emphasized that she was not sleeping with two men on the same day. She was extremely anxious to clear up any misunderstanding on this point; but her words about Planche's previous position in her life were ambiguous. "I do not know if my bold behavior will please you," she told Sainte-Beuve. "Perhaps you think a woman should hide her emotional attachments. But . . . I am in a thoroughly exceptional position and . . . obliged henceforward to elucidate my private life in public." Earlier, though, George had simultaneously professed love, albeit of different kinds, for Aurélien and Casimir. For several years she had balanced Stéphane and Aurélien. One of the contemporaries she most resembles in energy and love of life, Balzac, was not above engaging in two love affairs at once. But women were supposed to be too modest to talk about such things.

The new lovers began seriously to discuss the possibility of spending the winter in Italy, where they could escape from Parisian scandal-mongering. They pored happily over maps and devised itineraries. A gifted draftsman, Musset tenderly sketched George as she stood fanning herself, or as she sat on the floor smoking her narghile, or walked in the park with Maurice and Solange tugging at her arms. George gave dinner parties where, to mystify the guests, Musset appeared as the Norman serving maid, while Deburau the mime, disguised as a phlegmatic British diplomat, demonstrated the precarious European balance of power by spinning a plate on the tip of a knife. It was at this time that she incurred a considerable bill for wines.

In November, George was working on a colorful Hoffmannesque novella of fantasy, later published as *Le Secrétaire intime.* Here, she expressed her view of her own situation. The young private secretary of the title, engaged by the talented, mysterious Princess Quintilia Cavalcanti (based on George herself with a touch, too, of the Princess di Belgiojoso), cannot decide about the character of his employer. Is she a queen or a courtesan, an angel or another perverse Catherine II, an enigma or two different women at once? A sister of mercy, says she, "that was the finest role, and I muffed it." Sometimes she strikes him as "a shameless actress . . . playing all roles in turn for her own satisfaction. . . ." This young man stands in the position of the public and the critics vis-à-vis the novelist of *Lélia*, veering between admiration and suspicion.

The Princess Quintilia tells him:

> I have long been in an exceptional situation. . . . I am often misunderstood. . . . Doubtless one day it [the world] will understand me, and if not, I don't care, I shall have cleared a path for other women. Other women will succeed, will dare to be candid; and without discarding the tenderness of their sex, will assume the firmness of yours.

Heady stuff, which would spread rapidly through the drawing rooms of Europe and beyond. The secretary finally discovers that the princess is not at all the depraved creature he suspected but has long been secretly married to a poor student of natural history, details of whose biography bear some relation to Stéphane's. They have contrived to remain "lovers although married." Alas, cries the chastened secretary, "I should have guessed aright the riddle of your character!"

At the end of November, George announced to Casimir her intended departure for Italy, because of rheumatism. The problem was what to do about the children. Someone would have to visit Maurice at school, take him out on free days, and look after him during the Christmas holidays. Her capricious mother seemed preferable to Casimir's frigid stepmother for this obligation. As for Solange, George herself would be bringing her daughter to Nohant on her way south. With a change of itinerary, however, four-year-old Solange was delivered to Nohant by the disgruntled maid. IOUs were left with the wine and fuel merchants, to be paid by Casimir in the event of George's demise. The expenses of the expedition would be met by an advance of five thousand francs, one fifth of which would be dispatched to her in January by François Buloz, who serialized her novels in his influential journal. Thus committed, George could not have envisaged the expedition as anything but a working holiday, toward whose expenses Alfred, too, was expected to contribute by literary labors.

The lovers made the journey to Marseilles by riverboat, traveling from Lyons to Avignon in the company of Henri Beyle, who was returning to his post as consul at Civitavecchia. What the ironic author of *Le Rouge et le noir*, who had heard in detail about Musset's abortive sexual exploit from Mérimée, must have thought about the poet's odd liaison with the egregious Mme Dudevant may readily be imagined. George was not averse to scatalogical humor of the sort favored by Musset, but Beyle shocked her—no doubt deliberately—by his taste for obscenities and by the crude way he teased a nun who discoursed on the physical beauties of a figure of Christ in a church at Avignon. Somewhat inebriated, he had danced round the table at a village inn, and Musset, who sketched him, doubtless did not let him drink alone. George was not sorry to see the analyst of "passion in the head," creator of the haughty, cerebral Mathilde de La Mole, take the overland route to Italy.

Differences of temperament between the two strong-willed travelers began to appear. Moreover, not long after their ship docked at Genoa, George began to feel feverish. She saw the city of the Doria with its gardens and somber palaces through a lowering haze. Nothing could be more depressing than to lie indisposed in a foreign hotel room and to find that one's companion shows no great solicitude for one's welfare. Musset had not come to Italy in order to play nurse to a sick woman. He went out alone at night. More seriously, he deceived her with a dancer—that knife-thrust through their contract, as she would call it. That was not all: He drank heavily in a way that reminded her only too well of the nightly carousing of Casimir and Hippolyte at Nohant. The cooling lovers proceeded by sea to Leghorn; and then by carriage to Pisa and Florence, where once again fever took hold of George. From Florence, she wrote to Casimir, unable to conceal her apathy and disappointment.

It was the night of December 31 when they glided along the Grand Canal in a gondola, with the lights of the Piazetta reflected in the dark waters. Venice in winter can be desolate, but for George and Alfred it was the city of Casanova, and especially of Byron. Some sixteen years before, the poet-in-exile had kept his bevy of squabbling Venetian mistresses and his bizarre menagerie in the Palazzo Mocenigo. Did he not boast to an old crony of enjoying "at least" two hundred women during his stay in Venice?

Alfred was eager to follow in the footsteps of the poet of "Childe Harold." However, after visiting the Accademia and the ancient Jewish cemetery on the Lido, with its overgrown tombs, the scene of Byron's rides, George felt so ill that she had to take to her bed in the Hotel Danieli. She spent a fortnight in her hotel room, by herself, suffering migraine, brooding on her fate.

Invoking the luminous city of despairing prisoners and debauchees as if she feared the potency of its secret music, she wrote in her private notebook: "Venice . . . do not call to me with your myriad voices, do not intoxicate me with your myriad powers of seduction . . . I am young . . . I could have been happy . . . I deserved to be loved; . . . I am alone, without friend, hope or love. . . ." Instead of companionship, she was experiencing the loneliness she dreaded so profoundly.

On January 10, Musset crossed the lagoon alone to visit the Armenian monastery on San Lazzaro where Byron had lingered to study with the monks. By now, Alfred was thoroughly bored with his sickly traveling companion. Bluntly, he compared her performance unfavorably with that of prostitutes; told the dreamy, stupid "nun" that she did not give him any pleasure in bed; in short, that he had made a mistake: He did not love her. Besides, he feared he might be suffering from venereal disease. The poet had found a new friend in the French consul, with whom he had resumed his life of pleasure. Loving is the main thing, what does the mistress matter? What matters the bottle, so long as we have our Bacchic frenzy? the poet once inquired, in lines dedicated to Alfred Tattet. George and the creator of "Rolla" quarrelled, broke with each other, and the door was locked between their rooms in the Danieli.

By the middle of January, she was convalescing, and soon, to the sensuous sounds of Carnival revelry beneath her first-floor window overlooking the Riva degli Schiavoni, she began writing *Leone Leoni*. This short novel, written at speed, remarkable for its vivid narrative, full of surprises, won the admiration of Henry James who, as late as 1899, could still refer to it as "the wonderful *Leone Leoni*." The American novelist must have been drawn to its powerful account of the fascination of corruption and evil.

The story presents a deliberate reversal of Prévost's *Manon Lescaut*, where a decent young man dotes upon and is ruined by a charming but perverse girl. In George's tale, Juliette, the innocent daughter of a respected Belgian jeweller, elopes with Leone Leoni, an immensely talented but dissipated Italian dandy, gambler, and confidence trickster. Juliette seems a fool, as well as being "sublime" in her devotion. The reader is usually several steps ahead of her in her blind trust of her lover. Nothwithstanding his varying passion for her, Leoni makes her his accomplice, persuades her to share his bed with another (a privilege he is disinclined to accord to her when he suspects her, wrongly, of having a lover), even tries to prostitute her, then abandons her. In spite of Leoni's crimes, Juliette leaves her respectable suitor in order to be reunited, however briefly, with her "master," the scoundrel she loves. Drawn to him as if by a magnetic force, Juliette admits she cannot break the shackles that bind her to Leoni as if they were galley slaves. Nonetheless, she adds, "God's hand" has riveted their fetters. These contrasting images suggest not only George's masochistic fantasy but her divided feelings about the nature of her liaison with Musset, now that she was abandoned by him, like her heroine, in Venice.

George's convalescence proved short-lived. She fell ill with dysentery, and so did Alfred. How their enemies in Paris would rejoice! She could hear them saying, "They went to Italy to enjoy themselves, and they've got diarrhea!" Worse was to come.

Alfred now succumbed to a mysterious and alarming illness. He became delirious, wept constantly, trembled lest he was about to die or go mad. George hastily penned a note in Italian to Dr. Pietro Pagello, who had already come to the Danieli once in order to bleed her. She proposed excessive brain work, wine, women, and gambling as possible causes of the poet's startling nervous breakdown. The young doctor, gazing admiringly at the outspoken if melancholy Frenchwoman, diagnosed an attack of enteric fever complicated by delirium tremens. On the night of February 7, Alfred, in a paroxysm lasting six hours, ran naked around the room; two strong men failed to hold him down. His screams and convulsions terrified her—"my God, my God, what a sight!" There was a moment when, trying to kiss her, he almost strangled her. He would not let go. (An echo of this scene can be found in the description of the sick Leoni's crazed behavior toward the end of George's novel.)

Not only was George afraid lest Alfred might breathe his last, she also had other, more mundane worries. Musset had been lavish with money. The bill for doctors and medicine, added to that for rooms in an expensive hotel, had to be met. The outstanding sum of one thousand francs, promised by Buloz, failed to arrive, and would in any case be insufficient for the return journey. She pleaded with the editor not to leave her without money. It was difficult to put her mind to literature in the miserable situation in which she found herself, she told Buloz. Alfred appears to have had nothing to contribute to the common fund;

he was obsessed with a gambling debt of three hundred and sixty francs that he had contracted with some "rather vulgar people" in Paris and that might eventually involve him in a duel. George felt desperate. She thought of finding another publisher, drew up a specimen contract. She wrote to a royalist friend, the Vicomte Sosthènes de La Rochefoucauld, asking him to lend her a thousand francs. When this sum arrived, it momentarily relieved the pressure on the distraught novelist.

George nursed Alfred with a devotion he himself later publicly acknowledged. She watched constantly by his bedside, scarcely taking time to sleep, fully dressed, on the sofa, or to go out for air. Inevitably, George could not fail to recall the long hours she had spent as a girl nursing her sick grandmother. The odor of illness and reminder of death quickened her irrepressible urge to live, already stimulated by the very ambience of Venice.

Young Dr. Pagello called often; his glances became even more admiring. Born at Castelfranco Veneto, birthplace of the painter Giorgione, Pietro Pagello came of cultivated parents. Himself a fan of Byron, at twenty-six he associated with poets, artists, Carbonari. George discussed with the good-looking, intelligent, though scarcely brilliant doctor not only the condition of the patient but literature also.

One evening, as she sat writing by Alfred's bedside, she began to pen one of the most remarkable pages ever composed by a woman. She handed it to the doctor, and when he inquired for whom it was meant, she scribbled, "To stupid Pagello." The page was headed "In Morea." Was it the dream passage from some novel she was planning? (Ill-disposed people liked to say that she wrote her novels on letter paper. She would not be the only novelist to make double use of letters in novels and life—Balzac was a notable culprit.) Or was the heading a reminiscence of Byron's twice-used lines on sunset over Morea, with their romantic suggestion of the greater intensity of life and greater freedom to be experienced in southern climes? In a series of urgent rhetorical questions, reminiscent of those Musset had addressed to her in his stanzas on *Indiana*, and thus of tit-for-tat, George queried Pagello's attitude to her as a woman.

She began, in a tone as familiar as Musset's to her, with an allusion to the different climates in which she and Pagello had been bred, adding:

> Your ardent gaze, your violent embrace, your audacious desires tempt and frighten me. . . . I look at you with amazement, desire, agitation. . . . Will

you be a support to me or a master? . . . Perhaps you have been brought up to believe women have no soul. . . . Shall I be your companion or your slave? Do you desire me or love me? . . . Do you know what I am, and are you concerned at not knowing? . . . am I merely for you a woman like those who run to fat in the harem? . . . Do the pleasures of love leave you like a beast gasping for breath . . . ? You, at least, will not deceive me, you will not utter empty promises and vain oaths. . . . Perhaps I shall not find in you what I have sought fruitlessly in others, but I can always think you have it. . . .

It cannot be said that George actually "saw" Pagello, so seductive with his dapper moustache and winning smile, when she spoke of his virile breast, leonine gaze, and proud brow in rhetorical triads and in the romantic vocabulary of Victor Hugo's Doña Sol in *Hernani*. What she glimpsed was a dream creation of youthful vigor, the lure of a hitherto unknown experience with somebody who might even fulfill her secret fantasy by locking her up; someone who knew comparatively little about her, her writings and her notoriety.

In her allusion to the young Venetian doctor's "violent embrace and audacious desires," George evokes the way in which Pagello pursued and won her. A handsome foreign woman, alone and unprotected, was obvious prey. She confided afterward to her diary how his strategy of mingled humility and boldness aroused her senses. "That Italian—you know my God if his first word did not wring from me a cry of horror! Why did I yield, why, why? Do I know?" Why indeed? Was it impulse, curiosity, physical attraction, revenge of a proud woman on Alfred for his contumely and betrayal—perhaps a mixture of all these?

Lying in bed, between sleep and waking, the percipient Alfred grew more suspicious. He caught the little caressing glances that passed between George and the doctor. "You are a whore," he exclaimed. "My only regret is that I didn't put twenty francs on your mantelpiece the day I had you for the first time."

One morning, when he was feeling stronger and could walk into the adjoining room, Alfred noticed only one teacup on the tray and deduced that George and the doctor must have been drinking out of the same cup. "Supposing we did," retorted George. "You no longer have the right to worry about such things!" "I do have the right, since I am still considered to be your lover." Alfred may have privately resigned his claim from the moment the communicating door was closed at the beginning of January, but Don Juan could not bear the thought of being made to look as ridiculous as a cuckold.

The same evening, he found George sitting on her bed, writing a letter. "What are you doing?" "I am reading," said George, and blew out the candle. "You are reading, you say, without a book. Admit it, you foul prostitute, you are writing to your lover!" he raged. George screamed, and made as if to escape into the street. Alfred surmised that she intended to run for the doctor and to have the poet of "Rolla" certified insane (his perennial fear) on the ground that he had tried to kill her: "You won't leave. . . . If you do, I shall smack an epitaph on your tomb that will make those who read it blench." Skilled at torturing himself, Alfred had an unerring eye for the weak spot, the literary vanity and the inordinate pride of the woman he sought to wound. She cried so much that she felt pains in the stomach. "I don't love you any more," Alfred repeated coldly. "Now is the time for you to take your poison or drown yourself."

At the beginning of March, Musset's smart boon companion, Alfred Tattet, arrived in Venice. He had left his wife behind and was traveling with his current mistress, the actress Virginie Déjazet. Tattet could not help noticing how pale George was, worn out by her long vigils by Musset's bedside. She was working eleven or even thirteen hours a night on her novel *André* (the rustic tale of a charming girl who makes artificial flowers in La Châtre and who is "ruined" by the eponymous hero, a weak reed). George's regret was that she did not have any time for reading. How she yearned for a period free from monetary pressures when she would be able to stoke her inner furnace with foreign masterpieces! All the same, the habit of work, instilled by her grandmother, was a great cure-all.

Not without an ulterior motive, Tattet tried to cheer her. He took her to the elegant opera house, La Fenice, for the first time, to hear Mme Pasta. Of an evening, they sat talking in the handsome Café Florian, in St. Mark's Square. As they lingered together on one of the bridges, with only the cries of approaching gondoliers to break the silence, he questioned her and she confided in him. However veiled her candor, Tattet must have had some idea of the triangle, which was further illuminated by his talks with Pagello. The young doctor turned out to be a fellow after Tattet's own heart, who could not resist telling his new French friend about his amorous conquests. Once out of Venice, Tattet included in a letter to George a mysterious allusion to Pagello and a certain Italian lady named Antonietta. When George translated it for Pagello, she noticed that the doctor reddened. So Pagello was not quite the noble being of whose heart she had thought herself unworthy.

Small wonder that she could write: ". . . I hope there is a God who sees me and knows me, for no man has understood me. . . ." She did not understand herself.

Musset's jealous surveillance, his cold fury and subsequent self-abasement, ended by leaving George with "a sort of scorn for his weakness and injustice." The humiliated poet left for Paris at the end of March, accompanied by George as far as Mestre, his traveling expenses partly subsidized by his ex-mistress. They had parted amicably enough, with a kiss and with Alfred's reassurance that "nothing impure" would remain in his memory of her. George then visited with Pagello some of the cities of the Brenta to the north of Venice, pressing as far as Asolo, but they had to turn back before reaching the high Alps for lack of funds. The industrious novelist had only seven centimes when she returned to Venice.

Spring in Venice was delightful. Pagello proved an assiduous companion in showing her the city, resplendent in its incomparable light. She loved the gradations of color at sunset, from cerise to cobalt. The sounds of Venice, the popular songs, the serenades by gondola, enchanted her. A poet in his leisure moments, Pagello introduced her to his cultivated friends. In conversation with them, she consumed a great deal of coffee, smoked Virginian cigarettes or pipes, discussed poetry, music, and resistance to the Austrian yoke. In rented rooms, amid the animated sounds of the Venetian populace, she finished *André* and worked solidly on the tale *Métella*, her novel *Jacques*, and the *Lettres d'un voyageur*. In Venice and its environs she found material to last for the rest of her life. George was among the first writers of the century to put the lively popular culture of Venice on the literary map.

Her doctor lover, outwardly rather prosaic, was also, she discovered, a Venetian Don Juan, with several women in tow. Besides Antonietta Fusinato, possibly more than Pagello's cousin, there was the musical Giulia Puppati, said to be his illegitimate half-sister, an enthusiast for George's novels. According to malicious local gossip, Giulia and George were both supposed to be the mistresses of Pietro Pagello and his brother Roberto. In addition, one of the doctor's former mistresses, Arpalice Manin, refused to accept her dismissal and tried to tear out her faithless lover's hair. "I'll murder you, you bitch!" cried the doctor. The jealous Arpalice would also threaten to finish George with a knife. How very like the Venetian home life of Byron—if on a more modest scale—it all was! George accepted the situation with a vivacious air of worldly gaiety. She seemed to be floating in a weird limbo between proper forms of existence. The impassioned uproar could be attributed to the Adriatic climate, after all.

Living in Venice was cheap in comparison to living in Paris, her basic needs were few, but still she must have some money to live. The promised sums from Buloz, including remuneration for the manuscripts she had sent him, still had not arrived. George had known money pressures in Paris, but now, for the first time, she experienced poverty and discovered that it could be humiliating. She would never forget it. Nor would she ever really forgive Buloz and his associate for leaving her in distress. While she sewed curtains and chair-covers, it was Pagello (who was not rich) who pawned his belongings to pay for rooms in the Ca' Mezzani and later by the Barcaroli bridge. In order to settle her immediate bills, she was obliged to borrow money from one of Pagello's friends. Eventually, she had to cut down on food. Musset, to whom in her letters she dropped heavy hints about her plight, maintained that he was out of funds. If she had not encountered by chance an old friend, the traveling businessman J.-S. Blavoyer, with whom she had become acquainted at Mont-Dore in 1827, she would have been virtually destitute. Not until June 20 did she receive the money order forwarded from Paris that had been mislaid at the poste restante.

Another pressing worry during these months was the lack of any news about the children. Maurice failed to write. No letters came from Boucoiran. She begged Musset to visit Maurice at school, but the poet eluded the obligation with a fatuous compliment about being reminded of her dark eyes.

From his last moments in Venice, the poet of "Rolla" in his wounded pride had been trying to recover the position he had originally lost through his own indifference. Now, with his pen, he was in his own country of the mind, and so was George in hers when she replied to him. Once they were apart, they moved onto a higher plane, that of "noble souls," of esteem, friendship, comradeship. Both translated their feelings into fraternal, sisterly, maternal affection. We were committing incest, wrote Alfred. You are right, our embrace was incest, but we did not know it, replied George. They agreed that, in leaving Venice, he had performed a magnanimous act of Cornelian self-sacrifice. According to him, they were two lofty minds, two wounded eagles. . . . If so, they could not help beating their wings for posterity.

On May 15, 1834, the *Revue des deux mondes* published the first of

George's *Lettres d'un voyageur*. These "traveler's letters," of which there would be twelve in all, extending over the next two and a half years, purported to be written by a man of indeterminate age, now young, now elderly. The letter form gave George the freedom she needed to range over many topics: impressions of foreign scenes and people; reflections on life, love, friendship, faith, literature, music, politics; her doubts and quests, and those personal, introspective themes that had engaged her interest since girlhood. What endowed these letters with much of their charm was the multifarious personality of the author and the variety of mood and tone, ranging from gay self-mockery to melancholy self-justification. Some readers were stimulated by her probings to see themselves in the lineaments of her self-portrait.

These "traveler's letters" carried George's eager curiosity about life and current issues to a public far beyond the frontiers of France, and stimulated a fashion for the genre. Liszt would imitate the form in his music criticism, and he regarded the work as "the most original book in contemporary literature," one that most successfully revealed George's individuality. Many years later, Mary Ann Evans (the future George Eliot) could be found reading the *Lettres d'un voyageur* "with great delight," stirred by passages of "deep meaning" and "human wisdom." As for Musset, whom George exhorted to abjure dissipation and devote himself to his genius, he thought the first of the three letters addressed to him "sublime." Even Mérimée, hostile to lyrical flights, admired some pages of the work.

When it came to climbing creative literary peaks, Pagello was outclassed. Nobody needs me and my overflowing energy now, George complained. While she lauded the doctor's angelic kindness and solicitude, she observed that he had never read *Lélia*, and would not understand it if he did. For Musset, Pagello was his better part, a pure being (this, after he must have had an inkling of the doctor's love life, might lead one to suspect no little irony).

Indeed, Musset's letters to George were a triumph of eloquence and subtle diplomacy, a credit to the admirer of Valmont and Lovelace. He admitted that he had forfeited his claim: "Even if all my suspicions were correct, tell me, in what did you deceive me? . . . had I any right? . . ." Mingling flattery, wooing ("I still love you passionately, George . . ."), and threats of suicide, he also aimed some cruel darts. Thus, he talked about his return to his former mode of life, his participation in a foursome with his old crony, the Comte d'Alton-Shée. Reminding her (now on the brink of thirty) that he was still young, he told her he intended to look for a young woman, preferably endowed with intelligence and "the heart of a virgin." He had begun work on a novel based on their affair, asked her for his letters, and promised that he would not mention how she had become involved in "a new liaison before bringing the first to a conclusion." Despite all his high-flown protestations of discretion and of loyalty to her, he had already given their joint publisher, Buloz, a well-known gossip, a pretty realistic account of their altercations in Venice, without mincing any of the harsh words he had addressed to her.

During the last few weeks that George spent in Venice with Pagello she was oppressed by the summer heat. But she no longer had any money worries. Besides, she had heard from Maurice and, dropping the much-advertised project of a solitary visit to Constantinople, she aimed to be back in Paris for her son's school prize-giving day. Sometimes, life seemed unbearable, and then:

> Some chance piece of good fortune occurs, a letter from a friend, cheering news of my children, less than that even, an honest urge to work, a refreshing shower of rain that soothes my nerves, and then I'm as gay as a lark. . . . To say one has a character is to boast. What should I say of mine when one day I work out everything by careful reasoning, and the next day, nothing?—when on one occasion I kill love with reasoning, and on others I take to loving so well that I'm as blind as Cupid in person . . . ? I am capable of extreme stupidity and folly, and I constantly have to laugh at myself to myself.

As for true love, which she always thought she was experiencing each time, it required a union of heart, mind, and body, a union so rare as to occur once in a thousand years.

To Boucoiran, now living in Paris, whom she had made general factotum, she sent instructions to have her flat ready, to see that the curtains were cleaned and a charlady available. Shortly before her departure, in a notable understatement, she confided to Boucoiran: "This journey has taken me a lot further than I expected. . . ."

CHAPTER
11

A Woman of Thirty

I shall soon be thirty, and at that age a woman embarks upon dreadful inner lamentations. If I am still beautiful, I shall perceive the limits of feminine life; afterwards, what will become of me?"
Louise in Honoré de Balzac
Mémoires de deux jeunes mariées

If men appear less false, that is because the law grants them greater latitude, and considers engaging in the male what is criminal in the female.
Charles Fourier
Théorie des quatre mouvements

HIRTY!—the age when women were supposed to reach their passionate peak, after which nothing was left but a slow, chilly descent to the grave, with only a sense of duty for comfort. The looming approach of that female climacteric had provided one impetus for George's desperate conduct during the last few years, especially since the break with Jules Sandeau. Now, her long-feared thirtieth birthday had come and gone in Venice in July, apparently without any obvious change in outward circumstances or inner life. The action was to be delayed a while, but when it came, it would erupt into the most violent crisis of her existence.

The moment for returning to Paris had arrived. Pagello (persuaded by a letter from Musset) resolved to leave his patients in order that his mistress should not make the long journey home unescorted. They left Venice on July 24, 1834, traveling through Verona, Milan, Lake Maggiore, and sightseeing on the way. George donned a cap, blue blouse, and duck trousers for the mountains. Still writing at every opportunity, she finished her novel *Jacques* at the foot of a glacier on the Great Saint Bernard.

Evidently, Pagello did not share her enthusiastic response to alpine scenery, of whose sublimity she had dreamed since girlhood. "The Italians appreciate nothing of the beauties of Switzerland and the Tyrol," she was to confide to a private notebook. That "Eldorado of the poetry of the Lake School" leaves them unmoved. If an Italian sees a pupil of Turner's seated on a rock, lost in study of the mists or the nuances of sunset reflected on snow or in water, she added, he turns aside with a pitying smile.

For his part the young doctor, more mindful of the health of the exposed artist than of the romantic esthetic, could not help noticing that George seemed somehow less affectionate toward him. "As we journeyed on, our relations became more wary and more cool. I felt in agony, but made a great effort to conceal it. George Sand grew rather melancholy, and far more independent of me. Sadly, I saw in her an actress who was pretty accustomed to ecapades of this sort. . . ." The fact was that, with Venice an ever-receding dream, George was drawing closer to a reality she had overlooked. The evil-smelling stage-coach they entered at the French frontier was carrying her, with this compromising Venetian companion, toward Paris, the malicious literary gossips, her colleagues, her family, and her eloquent correspondent, Musset.

George and her Venetian escort arrived in the stifling capital on August 14, three months after the infamous massacre of workmen and their families in the rue Transnonain, an attempt to stifle the incipient trade union movement. She settled in her apartment on the quai Malaquais, while Pagello stayed discreetly in cheap rooms in the rue des Petits-Augustins. Only her reunion with Maurice was blissful. A few days later, Musset called on her. Tears came as she stood by the half-open window. It was Pagello's turn to feel the sting of jealous suspicions. "If anyone has every reason to throw himself in the Seine, it is I," he wrote to his father. With Musset ardently pressing to see her, the situation she had created in her quest for freedom and independence was impossible. The "appalling crisis of the sixth lustrum," as she called the female climacteric, struck her in all its melancholy force. As Musset left with pained nobility for Baden and the gaming tables, she set out for Nohant in the company of her mother and her son, bequeathing Pagello to the good offices of the ever helpful Jules Boucoiran.

More than eighteen months had passed since the traveler had set foot in her country mansion, where Casimir, mayor of Nohant-Vicq, now ruled supreme. Those months had been filled with her sudden fame, her new identity, her earnest attempts to imitate Marie Dorval's passionate "spontaneity," her bold risk-taking, and her constant disillusion. At Nohant, she revisited the scenes where her old self, the dreamy, melancholy yet spirited granddaughter of Marie-Aurore de Saxe, once galloped free; where high-minded young Mme Aurore Dudevant had enacted the little wife before her revolt. It was the moment for taking solemn farewell of her youth, and doubtless of life itself, since true and lasting love (the symbol of life) had proved so elusive. Bitter stock-taking began: ". . . my life is hateful, ruined, impossible, and I want to be done with it before long," she said.

Invitations were issued to all the Berrichon friends she had not seen for such a while. The day after she arrived, Gustave Papet, Alphonse Fleury, Charles Duvernet, as well as the good-humored lawyer of La Châtre, Alexis Duteil, called on her. The following day they came to dine, together with her old friend, Laure Decerfz, now Mme Fleury, and the ever faithful Jules Néraud. From Châteauroux hastened the twenty-eight-year-old lawyer, François Rollinat, whom she had first met in 1832 and for whom she felt a particular sympathy and regard—which he returned. George had partly modeled on him, with his intense, grave expression, the character of Trenmor in *Lélia*, symbol of serenity achieved through suffering and self-abnegation, for Rollinat had admirably taken upon himself the labor of supporting his numerous brothers and sisters.

With her Pylades (as she liked to call him) she went for long walks through the narrow, leafy lanes, or "traînes," of the Valée Noire, and at night under the stars they strolled in silence or exchanged confidences in the wooded garden at Nohant. She regarded him as her equal; she needed a Pylades, another Fannelly de Brisac, and he fitted the mold. There existed between them, she felt, a mysterious affinity of the rare sort that had once united in perfect amity Montaigne and La Boétie. Such pure friendship between soulmates seemed more estimable than love and would endure, untroubled, until Rollinat's death.

To François Rollinat and Jules Néraud, sympathetic and devoted listeners, she tried in her spleen and misery to lay bare her soul. Her adventurous life and erroneous ideas had done for her. Néraud suggested that her powerful maternal instinct would preserve her from suicide. To that instinct her attitude was candidly ambivalent. As she owned, if she had sometimes blessed the chain that bound her to her children, she had also on occasion cursed it. What a heroic destiny might have been hers, if only she had not been born a woman! Why did universal disgust and boredom possess her after such joys as she had known? Was there something wrong with her? To the insistent demand for "love, happiness, life, youth" came the echo: "too late." Happiness had eluded her. The dream of sharing a lifelong companionship in art with Jules Sandeau or Alfred de Musset had proved yet another illusion.

As she walked with her mother and her straightforward friend Rollinat over the fields, Solange perched on her shoulder and Maurice running ahead with a playmate and the dog, she remembered the days before she had left Nohant for the literary life with Jules Sandeau. The last few years filled with hard experiences, with busy activity and emotional upheaval, momentarily faded, almost as if lived by another. If she were to go on living, some kind of faith, some renewal of willpower would be necessary.

In September, *Jacques*, one of the novels she had written for the most part in Venice, was published. Despite improbabilities of plot and the device of letters (less faded then than now) to express changing viewpoints, this work stands as a landmark in the cultural history of the nineteenth century. It is the tale of the last passion of an exceptional soul, Jacques, a middle-aged eccentric who has much in common with the novelist—he shares her proud distaste for being thanked for acts of charity and her desperate "need to love" that temporarily obscures the blemishes of the beloved.

A man with a full past where women are concerned, Jacques falls deeply in love with Fernande, an inexperienced young girl, and marries her, although he has no high opinion of matrimony. In a celebrated diatribe, Jacques proclaims:

> . . . I am not reconciled with society, and marriage remains, in my opinion, one of the most barbarous institutions it has devised. I have no doubt that marriage will be abolished, if mankind makes some progress toward justice and reason; a more humane tie, no less sacred, will replace it, and will contrive to protect the existence of children born of a man and a woman, without curbing the freedom of either one or the other. But men are too

gross and women too cowardly to ask for a more lofty law than the iron law which governs them: heavy chains are required for beings without scruple and virtue. The improvements, of which some magnanimous souls dream, are not to be realized in this age; such spirits forget that they are a hundred years in advance of their contemporaries, and that, before changing the law, man must be changed.

Jacques does not define the "more humane tie" that is to replace marriage. With a glance at contemporary utopians, he envisages the reform of marital abuses only in a distant future. His prophetic suggestions may have been implemented by some in our own day, without, however, the saving emphasis on virtue inevitable in a disciple of Rousseau.

George's hero, believing the wifely vows of fidelity and obedience to be absurd and base, promises Fernande lifelong respect and fatherly or brotherly affection in his old age. Should she cease to care for him, he assures her that he will withdraw. In theory, then, Jacques intends to be the ideal, sensitive husband of a type George had never encountered in her society. A rare masculine elite, deeply dissatisfied with the current position and treatment of woman, was to be entranced by this extraordinary model.

Daily life in proximity between two beings ill-assorted in age, upbringing, experience, and expectations brings inevitable tension and misunderstanding. Young Fernande, in her weakness by no means Jacques's equal, finds herself attracted to a dandy, significantly named Octave, like one of Musset's two selves. She has borne her husband twins, and for over a year has had no intercourse with him. Such abstinence was due to the common belief that sexual arousal affected the nursing mother's milk. As Jacques approached Fernande at last, he observed that she was pretending to be asleep, "hoping, the poor creature, to elude my importunity in this manner." He kissed her on the brow and thought he perceived "a shudder of fear and aversion." Realizing that his wife no longer loves him, he resolves never to enter her room again.

Fernande cannot resist Octave and becomes pregnant by him. (The twins, conveniently, die.) Nobody can govern love, declares Jacques, nobody is to blame. What renders a woman base is lying. Adultery, in his definition, applies not to the time a woman grants her lover, but to the night she spends in her husband's arms afterwards, with her body damp from another's sweat. After publicly defending his wife's reputation, Jacques fulfills his promise and discreetly "disappears" to commit suicide in the Tyrol. Only the remarkable Sylvia, possibly his half-sister, can fully appreciate the depth of Jacques's sacrifice. (She is the lofty offspring of a despicable mother who abandoned her and who is stigmatized—not entirely honestly— for having had two lovers at the same time.) In a farewell letter to Sylvia, Jacques acknowledges that he is not one of those who can divert their energies into action for the common good. For him, the loss of the ability to love reveals the abyss underlying everyday existence. He is to be counted among the "useless men" of a type that would find a good many counterparts elsewhere, and especially under the tsars. In this conclusion, Jacques is expressing the author's sense that there may exist, for some, a different course from that of despair and self-annihilation.

Jacques made a deep impression on George's contemporaries. For some of her readers, interest lay in her casuistry, in the sanction accorded to the passion of Fernande and Octave, although these characters are at times portrayed as spirits inferior in vision and courage to Sylvia and Jacques. For others, like Matthew Arnold, the attraction was to be the hero's belief in one essential virtue: self-sacrifice. With the future George Eliot, admiration would concentrate on George Sand's psychological analysis of the gradual decline of a marriage. In Russia, the novel inspired both Druzhinin and Dostoevsky. The bizarre middle-aged Russian critic Botkin was so stirred by the book that, when he found his young working-class French bride did not share his esteem for it, he broke with her.

In France, Cuvier's stepdaughter, Sophie Duvaucel, informed Stendhal in Civitavecchia that *Jacques* was being much praised in the capital. Not long after, the author of *Le Rouge et le noir*, who had not received his due, remarked caustically to Sainte-Beuve: "If we both live long enough we shall see works in the Sand manner being sold at two sous a volume like the *fashionable* novels of Colman in London, and nobody will want them." It was her fluid style rather than her subject matter that Stendhal detested. But controversy in France, where discussion of the moral and financial abuses of contemporary marriage was widespread, turned upon her matrimonial views. The critic Jules Janin (ironically, an indefatigable woman-chaser) scourged Sand's disrespect for maternal authority, family, and society. In *Jacques*, the author had moved outside past, present, and future society, he thundered. (With unconscious hypocrisy, the most ardent defenders of the Family were to include such frequent violators of the strict "family code" as Hugo and Balzac.)

George's hint at the end of *Jacques* that there might conceivably exist a more useful path for the gifted soul, unites with the suggestions conveyed in the third of her traveler's letters, with its sympathy for the controversial Breton priest, Lamennais. The author of *Les Paroles d'un croyant*, whose thirst for certainty touched so many questing spirits, would continue to occupy George's thoughts. On an excursion she organized for her friends and their wives in September to visit the imposing château of Valençay (home of the aged diplomat and statesman, Talleyrand, devious servant of many varied regimes) she talked about Lamennais with the sturdy Rollinat. She also discussed there, with her Pylades, the Saint-Simonians led by Enfantin who had traveled to Egypt, while expressing her fears lest social improvement might only be accomplished through violence and destruction.

With her Berrichon friends, George had been reflecting on Sainte-Beuve's confessional novel *Volupté* and its protagonist's attitudinizing about his recourse to prostitutes. As she smoked to concentrate her mind, surrounded by her friends stretched out on the grass at Nohant, Rollinat read aloud the tale of Amaury in his slow, deep voice. George had not forgotten how Sainte-Beuve had complained about the absence of uplift at the end of *Lélia*. For all her genuine admiration of Sainte-Beuve's novel, George could not see the source of the work's final and, as she thought, unearned note of serenity. Amaury might take holy orders and devote himself to others, but his creator was not a priest. She knew well enough that *Lélia* was a "useless book," and criticized it with acumen. Clearly, she had continued to meditate upon her own creation and its shortcomings. "Oh! If only I myself could do so, I should raise my head and should no longer feel heart-broken, but I search in vain for a religion—God, love, friendship, the public weal? . . ." If only she could delineate a positive, righteous, contemporary human being, as distinct from a frustrated Lélia or Jacques! The quest for some valuable task, for some worthwhile direction of her energies was dimly beginning to take shape.

While George was trying to restore her peace of mind by renewed contact with her roots, Pagello was left to converse with physicians in Paris or listen to honey-tongued Lamartine in the Chambre des Députés. With Casimir's permission, George had invited the Venetian to spend "eight or ten days" at Nohant, but the wounded doctor sagaciously declined. The impecunious Pagello had brought with him four paintings that he hoped to sell. George pretended she had sold them in La Châtre and sent him the money. (In all, he received two thousand francs from her.) When she returned to Paris at the beginning of October, however, their reunion could not have been warm.

Shortly afterward, Musset arrived in the capital. Pagello had had enough. Before his departure for Venice, he doubtless gave Alfred Tattet more precise details about the dates of his liaison with George, since in his farewell letter to Musset's bosom friend he urged him to keep quiet. This he must have known was unlikely. "Did he not do me all the ill he could?" George wrote of Pagello in her diary, forgetting that she had not treated him very well.

The second act of the drama between George and Musset was about to begin, with Pagello's humiliating departure. "Trust me, George, God knows I shall never harm you," Musset had assured her. No sooner were the lovers reunited than new quarrels broke out. These were soon public knowledge in literary circles, for Sainte-Beuve passed on the information that Lélia and Rolla were engaged in mutual recriminations, followed by moments of reconciliation, and then freshly inflicted torments.

The superficial reason for these painful upheavals lay in the somewhat academic question of chronology. Alfred would insist on raking the ashes of the past—what exactly had been going on, and when, while he lay sick in the Danieli. She, strong at least on the issue of his breach of contract and on the closed door between their rooms, repudiated the poet's right to probe. The deeper reason for the torture, however, lay in Musset's tragic inner drive to self-destruction. Suffering inflicted and endured was his element.

The question turns on whether Musset *knew* that George became Pagello's mistress before his own departure from Venice. By the way he repeatedly reviled her as a whore, not only there but on his return to Paris when he confided in Buloz (who took notes), it might be assumed that he had a pretty good idea. True, he could not know for certain. That certainty could now only be conveyed to him by Tattet, armed with Pagello's ultimate revelations. Tattet himself had doubtless long since drawn his own conclusions from what he had heard in Venice. The spectacle of these three libertines, Musset, Pagello, and Tattet, variously engaged in the post-mortem of George's conduct, does not lack a certain irony.

George sought for consolation from atrocious scenes with Musset in her old dream of an elite of artists, poets, musicians, ideally to include Berlioz, Meyerbeer, Delacroix, Liszt. It was through Musset that the young Hungarian virtuoso, whose showmanship could set his audience atremble, came to dine. Then only twenty-three, slight, delicate-looking, but with a powerful head crowned with long, silky locks, the plebeian Franz Liszt nursed his bitter grievances against an aristocracy that had made him feel his place as a social inferior and bohemian outcast. Since her abandonment as a girl by her aristocratic relatives, the Villeneuves, George, too, had no reason to like the aristocracy. Liszt had read voraciously, though without discipline. He admired George's novels, especially *Lélia*, whose protagonist he placed with René and Childe Harold. Moreover, he had frequented the meetings of the Saint-Simonians in the rue Taitbout and had even communed with abbé de Lamennais. An immediate flash of sympathy passed between Liszt and George, to be registered by the suspicious Musset. She began to talk of going to consult Lamennais at his home at La Chênaie.

Around this time, through Liszt, she met Heinrich Heine. Witty, sharp-tongued, the nearly thirty-seven-year-old German-Jewish lyric poet and journalist had been living in Paris since the spring of 1831, having chosen to settle there partly out of enthusiasm for Saint-Simonism, an enthusiasm that had since become somewhat muted. Nonetheless, deeply concerned as he was with the question of social amelioration, Heine—like Liszt—could in conversation reinforce the vague inclinations toward social renewal that were already beginning to stir anew in George's mind, where they had lain virtually dormant since her break with Jules Sandeau.

The endless recriminations between Alfred and George continued unabated, until, less than three weeks after their impassioned reunion, the poet ended their association. He had exacted revenge for his humiliating dismissal in Venice not only on Pagello but on the woman who, when the poet had abandoned her to pursue his own pleasures, had ventured to console herself. Having refused to listen to Tattet late in October, when it did not suit him to do so, Alfred broke off relations with George early in November, on the pretext that he had just learned from Tattet how she had become the Venetian's mistress before his own departure.

George lost her head. So, at thirty, this was the end of her daring quest for personal happiness, for love and life. Platonic love for Aurélien, though incomplete, had been the best. She even forgot her children; it seemed there really was nothing left for her but death. The horror of being alone, the dread of "eternal solitude" that had seized her just before her encounter with Musset seventeen months before and again during Carnival at the Danieli took command once again. She would do anything, grovel, beg forgiveness, if only she could find a way to win Alfred back. The poet did not deign to answer her wild, desperate notes. Nor would he admit her. She sent him a skull, and a swath of her dark hair. He had succeeded in reducing her to a character in one of his poems or plays.

With roughly shorn head, she had to pose for an artist she had long wished to meet: the elegant, swarthy Eugène Delacroix, whose studio on the quai Voltaire was situated only a stone's throw from her apartment. This portrait had been commissioned by Buloz for reproduction in the *Revue des deux mondes*. The great colorist recorded with visionary power the beauty ravaged by weeping, the large, upraised, sorrowing eyes, as of a repentant and aspiring Magdalene (though one unusually clothed in a frock coat). While she smoked his cigarettes, she told the painter (thought to be Talleyrand's illegitimate son) about her sufferings. She asked him for advice, as she had already sought Sainte-Beuve's help. With his commanding, leonine gaze, Delacroix, one-time brothel companion of Musset, advised her to give way to her grief. He himself had found that eventually grief would wear itself out.

On more than one occasion she went to the Théâtre des Italiens, in a vain attempt to forget. Seated in the pit, dressed as a youth, bored by Gabussi's opera *Ernani*, she could hear people whispering, "It's George Sand." "Where? Where is she? Oh!" A few days earlier, at a friend's, she had encountered Jules Sandeau to whom, as to her one-time ally Planche, she attributed much of the scandalous tittle-tattle about her that had circulated while she was in Italy. Jules tried to explain, and they took leave amicably enough, for "it is dreadful for two people to bear a grudge when they have loved each other," wrote George, thinking of Alfred. Jules asked, and was granted, permission to see Solange, whom she had just placed in a Paris boarding school run by two English ladies, the Misses Martin. George could not cope with the capricious six-year-old.

Contrary to her custom, George appeared loquacious, recounting her woes to Buloz, to Marie Dorval, to all and sundry. Liszt told her one evening that God alone deserved to be loved. Discreetly keeping quiet about his passion for Marie d'Agoult, he said he would never succumb to earthly love. "That little Christian is certainly lucky," noted George. As for Heine, speaking from varied personal experience of Parisian prostitutes, he told her cynically that the head and the sexual instinct played a greater part in love than the heart. Her colleague, Hortense Allart, literary *femme galante,* advised diplomatic ruse where men were concerned. None of these acquaintances, with the sole exception of Sainte-Beuve, gave her the slightest comfort.

Before leaving Paris in a state of collapse for Nohant, George signed with Buloz the contract for an edition of her complete works and for her memoirs—the subject that had haunted her since girlhood. These memoirs (which in fact would not be started for many years) were to be published posthumously. For she was going to kill herself, after writing her autobiography to provide a dowry for Solange. Buloz appears to have believed that she meant to carry out her suicide plan.

At Nohant, a repentant note arrived from Alfred. George sent him a leaf from the garden, and he sent her a lock of his hair. She did not want to see him ever again. Among her friends were those who recalled how different she had once been from her present self. One of them happened to remark on this to Sainte-Beuve, who wrote advising her to try to return to the simpler state of mind of her pre-Parisian period.

Meanwhile, Casimir was far from pleased to welcome his errant wife, who, by her presence, kept disturbing his solitary rule of the estate. He himself was feeling thoroughly depressed, owing to his mismanagement of affairs and his accumulation of debts. There were noisy scenes here, too. Once, when she accidentally spilled some champagne at the table, he scolded her before their assembled guests, as if she were a servant.

This kind of incident set George thinking: Here she was, working all hours of the night to provide for the children, while Casimir in his incompetence was depleting the family assets. To whom, after all, did Nohant really belong? Was she to be humiliated, treated like an unwanted domestic, in her own home? Something would have to be done about Casimir.

No sooner did George return to Paris than the contrite Alfred presented himself at her door. In spite of everything, she could not refuse him when he pleaded, even though she now envisaged their union as a form of recurrent illness. January 1835 thus saw the two lovers reunited in the third act. To Tattet, George sent an invitation to dine: ". . . Alfred is my lover again. . . ." Others invited during that month included Heine, who playfully addressed her in a tone of gallant flattery. It was not Heine, however, but Liszt who, professing for George a deep spiritual affinity, contrived to arouse Musset's jealousy. She was obliged to ask the fascinating pianist, who was so enthusiastic about the artist's mission to the masses, to refrain from calling.

In her pride, George felt the full humiliating force of Musset's "forgiveness," and she yearned to escape from the net of endless suspicion and recrimination. "All of this, you know, is a game we are playing," she told Musset, a game where the stakes were their own selves. In her novel *Jacques*, she had given to Octave one of her theatrical metaphors: ". . . after all, life is a play, where the actors are not taken in; . . . after the tirades and the sensational scenes, each wipes off his make-up, removes his costume, and proceeds to eat or sleep." The underlying reality for George at this time was not only the state of her family finances and her own position with regard to them. It was also her desire to recover Nohant from Casimir.

For, in the midst of renewed quarrels with Musset, interspersed with moments of respite, visits to the theater and opera during a brilliant season that included the Paris première of Bellini's *I Puritani*, George was involved in negotiating a separation from Casimir. The agreement was signed amicably (as she thought) by both parties in Paris on February 15, 1835. The mansion of Nohant and the estate were to go to George, while Casimir was to enjoy the revenue from the Parisian property, the Hôtel de Narbonne. George would keep Solange and pay for her education, while Casimir would have charge of Maurice and pay for his son's. Her mother's annual allowance would be George's responsibility. This was the settlement that, without granting her everything she wanted, since Maurice was assigned to her husband, would at least restore her to her family home and prevent Casimir from making further inroads into the estate by his incompetence and ill luck.

The day before the signing of this separation agreement, which was to be short-lived, George was present with Musset at a performance of Vigny's play *Chatterton*, that somber call for bread for the poet neglected by society. She was deeply moved by the play, and full of admiration for Marie Dorval in the role of the compassionate Kitty Bell. All the distractions of Paris, though, could not conceal from her the fact that she and Alfred were indeed chained together like the galley slaves she had described in *Leone Leoni*. Both highly susceptible creatures of considerable willpower, they doubtless loved each other in their fashion, but clashed endlessly. Musset's conception of woman as goddess or prostitute, his distaste for any admixture of heaven and earth, as he once put it, found no room for the untidy human complexity of his mistress. His expectations did not extend to a fallible woman who kept asserting an inviolate inner purity. Moreover, while she affected an almost regal unceremoniousness, he prided himself on his place in the nobility and could make his "inferiors" feel the weight of his "name" and his "position in society." Libertarian in a general sense, Musset did not warm to the messiahs who were springing up everywhere.

As George grew ever more interested in the concern of Lamennais for the well-being of "the people," in the social and political reforms discussed by Heine, or the Saint-Simonian views of Liszt concerning the role of the artist in the cause of social amelioration, she found that Alfred did not share her spirit of inquiry or her sympathy for the new ideas. In a wordy prose poem, supposedy recited in Hebrew in ancient Caesarea by a bold prophetess named Myrza, George hinted at the role she envisaged for the inspired woman artist: "For, listen to the Jews: they say that woman has brought as dowry sin and death, but they also say that on the last day she will crush the head of the serpent, the spirit of evil." (These words harmonize with those of the Saint-Simonians who had left to look for the Woman Messiah in the Near East.) The people refuse to stone Myrza, despite her reputation for immorality. Virtue is always beautiful, whatever voice utters it, declares an old priest. Bravely, she sets out, all alone, for a hermitage. George, too, was expecting soon to find herself alone.

One day, Musset, in his jealous and threatening rage, went too far, upbraiding her in the presence of Maurice and Solange. "My own children! my children, my children! . . ." Perhaps George, masked, overheard her lover discussing their liaison with others at the Opéra ball. Shortly afterward, she laid her plans. On March 6, without telling Alfred, she booked her place in the coach for Châteauroux. With her surreptitious departure, she had broken with him for good. The violent third act of their liaison had lasted two months, more than twice as long as the second act.

Once at Nohant, George plunged into work on a new novel. To Boucoiran in Paris there came urgent requests for her hookah, for volumes of Greek drama, Shakespeare, Plato, the Koran. She was going to embark on the serious reading she had often talked about, to reflect upon some more purposeful course of life, suited to a woman of her years.

To her friends Alphonse and Laure Fleury in the autumn of the previous year she had observed, half humorously, that human liberties were pretty "fictitious" and that it would be difficult enough to make a man free, let alone a woman. Now, a month after she fled to Nohant, she was analyzing her behavior for Sainte-Beuve. Her insatiable pride had been her ruin, she told him. In a life of "brazen heroism," as she conceived it, living only for herself and putting only herself at risk, she declared: "I have always exposed and sacrificed myself like a free creature, aloof, useless to others, mistress of herself to the point of suicide. . . ." The sophistry of men and of books was to blame for her present low state. If only she had confined herself to the moral precepts of Benjamin Franklin (known to her largely through *Poor Richard's Almanac*), whom she had long admired and whose portrait hung above her bed. But there was no going back. One thing was sure (George would confide to another friend), never again would she yield up her freedom.

If George wanted to claim independence of the sort enjoyed by men, a freedom embodied in the interconnected rights proclaimed by the French Revolution of 1789, then just like Mary Wollstonecraft before her, she went about it in a way that compromised the cause of female advancement. Perhaps there was no other way to rebel against the existing system of society and its canting manners and double standard for men and women. To a woman in quest of equality, her male contemporaries failed to set a very good example. George had much to suffer at their hands, locked as her lovers were in their own expectations of woman, and she made them suffer in her turn. Moved by strong physical desires and by an even more powerful imaginative drive, George, like many of her contemporaries of both sexes, filled the void caused by spiritual nihilism with a dream of ideal passionate love. It was perhaps this dream of love, rather than passion alone, that governed her. Yet how difficult it was for her, even with her urge for self-understanding, to distinguish between the false and the true, between the contraries depicted by Stendhal as passion in the head and passion in the heart.

In her wildest delirium, when she was displaying her misery in the Parisian theaters and crying aloud to every new acquaintance as well as to her old friends, she gives the impression of being a creature in the grip of passion in the head who has mistaken it for the genuine article. Yet desperation at failure, her submission to each new humiliation, her clinging to the faintest hope of keeping Alfred by her, her perennial dread of being left all alone to decline into old age—these were real enough.

When she could look back with some tranquility on this critical period of her life, she told Marie d'Agoult: "For a long while, I believed passion was my ideal. I was mistaken, or else I chose badly." Even more revealing was a later remark of hers to Delacroix: "I know you will not laugh at me, you who understand me through and through and who know what desperate efforts I made to convince myself that I had a grand passion." By then, she had found a direction for her immense energies, an aim that the humiliating outcome of her liaison with Musset, the climax of numerous earlier disappointments, had compelled her to seek.

PART IV

The Road
to Independence

CHAPTER
12

~~~~~~

Woman's Fate

. . . people think it very natural and pardonable to trifle with what is
most sacred when dealing with women: women do not count in the
social or the moral order. I solemnly vow—and this is the first glimmer
of courage and ambition in my life!—that I shall raise woman from her
abject position, both through my self and my writings, God will help
me! . . . let female slavery also have its Spartacus. That shall I be, or
perish in the attempt.

George Sand, letter to Frédéric Girerd, 1837

Y LIFE as a woman is over,"
George informed a noted
young Saint-Simonian journalist, Adolphe Guéroult, in April
1835. She had started to write
"My love life," but had
changed her mind. Since she
had "some small reputation
and a kind of influence, neither
sought nor deserved," she
might try to put these to good
use. When George wrote those words she had just encountered one of
the most eloquent, forceful, and ambitious republican personalities of
the moment and had become involved with him in a fierce struggle for
domination, whose outcome was as yet undecided.

The image of a woman in whom all passion was virtually spent as
she turned to a more active life became, however, the one George now
felt determined to promote. Her motive was not far to seek. Too many
details of her private life had become public property. Besides, discre-

[161]

tion would be needed if, as she now suspected, there might be serious trouble with Casimir.

By 1835–1836, her literary position was established, and her influence, of which she spoke so modestly, already considerable. When Sainte-Beuve drew up his eminent guest list for an imaginary dinner, she figured on it as the only woman. In his long essay on Mme de Staël, published in May 1835, he went so far as to describe George as more of an artist (though less of a thinker) than her illustrious predecessor, and affirmed that the creator of *Lélia* was unanimously considered the most eminent authoress since Napoleon's liberal adversary. Such was the critic's temperament, though, that public praise for contemporaries tended to be balanced by acerbity elsewhere. Eventually, his feline digs and indiscretions would constitute in George's eyes a betrayal that was to lead to their estrangement for many years.

In fact, George's literary reputation was of a distinctly mixed character. If her work was admired by bolder and more advanced spirits, or by those dreaming of liberation, it was nonetheless an object of scandal to women of conventional outlook. Liszt sent a copy of *Lélia* to his aristocratic, married "Beatrice," Marie d'Agoult. "Read this amazing book at one go, but read it when alone," he advised, "and if your health allows, at night; above all, do not show it to the Marquise, since for her as for so many others (less pure and sincere than she) it is nothing but a profoundly immoral, scandalous and even disgusting book. All our Parisian she-dragons of refined and forbidding virtue have uttered cries of horror." Some of Sand's feminine readers could thus enjoy the thrill of their own secret daring and their defiance of convention.

From Sand's novels, such questing feminine readers could draw the conclusion that, in certain instances, women were superior to men in intellect and moral capacity. This tendency of hers served to rehabilitate women in their own eyes, giving them a sense of confidence in their worth and dignity as women. Unfortunately, though, according to George, women's immense potentialities went largely unrecognized, and were indeed incapable of realization in the existing state of society, with its oppressive hierarchies and harsh materialism. In her account of vulgar rural wedding customs in *Valentine*, or of the premarital freedom enjoyed by the *grisettes*, or easy-going working girls, of La Châtre in *André*, George could be quite realistic about the condition of women in the provinces, as well as critical of the disabilities and abuses from which they frequently suffered. This urge to voice a social conscience was common to a number of the lesser-known novelists, both men and women, who were writing after the July Revolution, and whose tales promoted opposition to privilege, materialism, marriage, family tyranny, the enslavement not only of blacks but of workers and women. George, in particular, included details that would encourage later women writers to venture to discuss such delicate matters as illegitimacy, unmarried motherhood, and prostitution—and to be considered "coarse" and "masculine" in consequence.

While part of George's reputation was the result of literary adventurousness and merit, part was also evidently due to notoriety. To what extent was that notoriety deliberately sought? Her literary lovers, her wearing of frock coat and trousers (though largely for practical reasons), her smoking of cigarettes and cigars in public—all these aroused intense curiosity and occasioned scurrilous remarks. The trousered, masculine image, imposed upon the image of extreme femininity that preceded her Parisian advent in 1831, hints at inner division as well as at deliberation. It appears to contradict, too, the femininity to which George strongly laid claim. In fact, though, the lovers, the trousers, and the cigarettes were all feminine weapons. The lovers offered, as in the case of Catherine II of Russia, with whom George's role-conscious contemporaries so liked to compare her, a proof of femininity despite gifts of intellect and command. The trousers and cigars were a form of self-advertisement as well as a means of breaking the feminine stereotype.

It was not long before she found imitators. As a frustrated wife with literary ambitions, Marie d'Agoult donned her husband's frock coat and trousers and, gazing at herself appreciatively in the cheval mirror, exclaimed: "That's what I needed, trousers and a riding-whip!" In Geneva in the autumn of 1835, a lady in male attire seen dining in a hotel was assumed to be the author of *Lélia*. At about the same time, two women Saint-Simonians, wearing something close to masculine costume, astonished the citizens of Cairo. The following year, an ambitious provincial literary lady, Mme Caroline Marbouty, dressed as a man, would accompany Balzac to Italy, to be greeted there as George Sand. Mme Marbouty (an author who had temporarily consoled Jules Sandeau after the break with George) confided to her mother that masculine dress allowed her certain delightful and unusual liberties. That George Sand's example was being followed in the mid-eighteen thirties would suggest a state of dissatisfaction and ferment among thinking women as well as a desire for some new dispensation.

The Road to Independence

As for the new Saint-Simonian feminine dispensation with "rehabilitation by the flesh" offered (so conveniently for himself) by Enfantin, surrounded by his adoring female disciples, George roundly condemned it when speaking to Liszt. She still did not care for Enfantin, despite Liszt's advocacy, and liked even less the personality cult fostered by the Father. The Saint-Simonian position on women was, in fact, extremely confused. Some of the leaders, like Olinde Rodrigues, continued to express traditional views on morality. For strong-minded and impassioned women militants like Pauline Roland, however, any suggestion that the Father should marry the mother of his son was anathema. That Cornelian soul, having understood that the Father's spouse was to be the Mother of Humanity, observed crossly: "They are all perfectly insufferable with their outmoded notions about virtue."

On this score, George differed from a single-minded feminist like Pauline Roland. Despite her own egregious example, George held fast in theory to the principle of moral virtue. She had at times the gift of looking at her own adventurous behavior with a certain remarkable detachment, almost as if she were speaking about another, or even as though her generalizations did not apply to herself. The moral revolution that should have raised women to equality with men had been thwarted, she would tell her friend François Rollinat, as she reflected on women in love in 1835. Women, enslaved, could not be blamed for throwing off the yoke of chastity, but they could not be esteemed for it either. They damaged their cause by a disorderly life. Moreover, no free union in her experience remained untroubled or lasting.

George was aiming to discourage her Pylades from becoming too deeply involved with a young married woman. For them to set up house together with reasonable hope of success required money, which he did not have, George reminded him. If, on the other hand, he and his beloved slept together and the woman became pregnant, the wretched creature would still have to share her bed with her husband (Rollinat's friend)—a fate that aroused George's exclamation of disgust (conceivably inspired by personal experience). Do not let your feelings degenerate into irresistible physical needs, advised George. Passionate extramarital affairs might furnish a theme for Balzac, Scribe, and George Sand, she told him, but "these are not the people to be regarded as judges where wisdom and reason are concerned." At a time when her influence was becoming marked, she could make a clear distinction between her own heady literature and the social realities of the day. As for "the condition of woman," it was now in a period of "transition" (to use a Saint-Simonian term). Yet such was the growing desire for equity among both men and women that justice would ultimately prevail. She herself appeared to be in no pressing hurry.

While George had been involved in her disastrous marriage and eventful love affairs and was inclined to envisage the woman question in terms of human dignity, sexual equality, equal moral responsibility, and high-minded fair play, vast numbers of her fellow countrymen and -women were engaged in a harsh struggle for existence. That they seemed so far not to have impinged greatly upon her consciousness may be due in part to egocentric vision and in part to the fact that she hated the town, and mostly lived—either in actuality or in spirit—in what was then a fairly remote and relatively prosperous agricultural region.

Throughout George's life, France would remain primarily an agricultural country, but since 1815 there had been a steady migration of unskilled rural workers into the large cities, like Lyons and Paris. The slow progress of industrialization in France, as compared with England, merely protracted the suffering caused by the industrial revolution. Crowded together in unsanitary conditions, yet cheek by jowl with the wealthy, the workers and their families in the towns often knew misery and degradation. It was not only the menfolk who labored in the workshops and factories, but women and children also. Even before the depression and the sharp decline in wages, a Parisian working woman would earn seventy-five centimes for an eleven-hour day, when a four-pound loaf of bread cost eighty-five centimes. In the mid-eighteen thirties, the average wage of a male textile worker was two francs a day, for a woman one franc, and forty-five centimes for a child.

The distance between such struggling unfortunates and members of the higher levels of society was immense, even where a woman like George, who constantly experienced monetary difficulties, was concerned. In the years when a working family could just subsist on between 760 and 860 francs a year, George would be arguing with her recalcitrant publisher, Buloz (whom she treated at times as if he were a tightfisted grocer disinclined to give credit), urging him to pay her 300 francs a sheet as he did his male contributors, instead of the 200 francs a sheet he assigned to her.

Serious discontent among the textile workers in Lyons had erupted into revolt in 1831 and again in April 1834, after wages were reduced. From Lyons, the revolt had spread to other cities and to Paris, culminating in the massacre of workers and their families in the rue Transnonain. A year later, in April 1835, the defeated ringleaders who had wanted to "Live working or die fighting" were brought from all over France to stand trial in Paris. The government had decided to hold a sort of massive "show trial," transforming the Chamber of Peers into a Court of Peers, a procedure whose legality was much questioned. The accused had rallied to their defense many leading lawyers, writers, and thinkers, some of whom wished to seize the opportunity to make political capital out of the trial. Prominent among the latter was a republican lawyer of growing reputation, Louis-Chrysostome Michel, known as Michel de Bourges.

It was early in April 1835, on a visit to Bourges for a consultation about her domestic affairs, that George first met Michel through her lawyer friend, Gabriel Planet, who collaborated with him on his republican journal. From seven o'clock in the evening until four in the morning, as George, Planet, and Alphonse Fleury walked the deserted, cobbled streets of the dignified city—with its blue-grey slate roofs and gables, its jewelled cathedral windows and turreted palace of Jacques Cœur—Michel dazzled them with his marathon eloquence. The chance to convert the author of *Lélia* to his republican doctrines seemed too good to miss. His words fell on fertile ground, for George had earlier sympathized with the republican sentiments of Jules Sandeau's student circle. But it was Michel who for the first time made politics so exciting that she wished to participate.

In search of a faith and a cause, an escape from egoism, in Michel she glimpsed a man of trenchant ideas, fanatically convinced of their rightness. Here was a being whom she fully expected to play an important part in any future upheaval. He indulged in the threatening "guillotinomania"—often attractive to women of a somewhat sado-masochistic turn—that Heine had noted among French republicans. "I have made the acquaintance of Michel who has promised to have me guillotined . . . when the republic is set up," she told a friend facetiously. She suspected Michel's fanaticism, but she was fascinated by it. Like an antidote to the poetic strain in her, ever responsive to nuance, Michel appeared as that refreshing novelty: a man of decision.

A strong and dominating personality, Michel was also a self-made man, representative of the new, educated peasant class epitomized in literature by Stendhal's Julien Sorel. His life story as he recounted it to her must have sounded like something out of a novel, and would soon be transposed into her fiction. The posthumous son of a Provençal woodcutter murdered by royalist soldiers in 1797, he had been brought up by his widowed peasant mother and his grandfather to dream of nothing but vengeance. Taught by the local priest who fostered his gifts, he had discovered his true vocation as a volunteer in the army, while defending one of his comrades before a court martial. As a result, he had taken up the law, subsidizing his studies by working as a tutor. While still a law student, he had joined the secret society of the Carbonari and had become acquainted with that arch-conspirator, Buonarroti, the leading disciple of "Gracchus" Babeuf. Having set up as a lawyer in Bourges, he married a wealthy widow and took to sporting fine linen. He distinguished himself there during the July Revolution and rapidly made his name as an aggressive political lawyer and demagogue.

When George met Michel he was thirty-eight, his hair was thinning, and he looked stern and pedantic with his penetrating eyes hidden behind metal-rimmed spectacles. He was, moreover, highly strung and subject to gloomy hallucinations. It was not his outer person so much as his magnetic personality and above all, his voice, that captivated her. She would build him into a father figure, her loyal friend and support, for public consumption, stressing that he looked prematurely aged. No sooner had she returned to Nohant than Michel bombarded her with almost daily letters in a barely decipherable hand. She decided to follow him to Paris to attend the mammoth trial, due to open there on May 5.

The trial, one of the most sensational episodes of Louis-Philippe's reign, was also to be the highpoint of Michel's public career. On the instant George found herself, through him, at the center of political excitement. Through him she would see or come into contact with a number of the heterogeneous celebrities and future celebrities—Ledru-Rollin, Pierre Leroux, Jean Reynaud, Raspail, Carnot, Blanqui, Barbès—who had temporarily shelved their differences and had converged on Paris to give their support to the accused. Heated discussions on principle were taking place among them—how vital it all was! She would meet also some of the militant women relatives of the defendants, like Mme Julie Baune, wife of one of the leaders of the revolt in Lyons, who could give her a new perspective on the feminine condition in the lower orders and with whom she would remain on terms of friendship.

Among the eminent writers who had come to Paris especially for the trial was the renowned abbé de Lamennais, one-time defender of the papacy who had defied the Pope for failing to fulfill the Church's divine democratic mission. He arrived expecting the immediate advent of the universal republic, sourly noted Sainte-Beuve, a disillusioned admirer. George first met the controversial Lamennais, a frail, diminutive figure of immense personal charm, at a dinner given by Liszt, where Heine was present together with Puzzi, as Liszt's fourteen-year-old pupil Hermann Cohen (later to be baptized) was known. The guests included, too, a converted Jew turned Catholic apologist, the Baron d'Eckstein; Pierre-Simon Ballanche, author of the influential mystic *Orphée*; the Saint-Simonian, Emile Barrault, who had penned the rapturous appeal to Jewish women; and two famous singers, Cornélie Falcon and Adolphe Nourrit. Coyly, George afterward maintained that she contributed little to the conversation, daring only to commune with Puzzi and the cat. A few days later, Lamennais, dressed as ever in a grey frock coat and accompanied by Liszt and Puzzi, graciously called on her in her blue-curtained apartment on the quai Malaquais.

News of the surprising association between the "sanguinary priest" and the "dissolute woman" soon made the rounds. It would particularly stimulate Sainte-Beuve's bile, since he felt that Lamennais was neglecting his true spiritual mission for vain notoriety, which the polemicist now shared with the author of *Lélia*. The celebrated former priest already appeared to the discerning as an equivocal character. Once engaged in the slave trade, Lamennais was reputed (by the gossiping popular poet Béranger) to have been a swashbuckler and lady-killer before reluctantly taking orders at the age of thirty-four. As for Lamennais and Sand, Sainte-Beuve would acidly remark, they were the fashionable gods of the hour: ". . . one fine day, the entire audience . . . will start shouting right in the middle of the play in which we shall all be taking part, right in the middle of this tragical-comical-social farce or *Robert Macaire* writ large, and the two great fashionable actors will come forward holding hands and bowing deeply. . . . How I loathe such roles as *agitator*, *tragedian*, *gladiator*, whatever you like to call them! She at least is a *singer* and she sings, that's fine; but as for you, priest, man of wisdom, what have you become?" In Sainte-Beuve's view, all the new apostles, including Lamennais, who thought themselves to be priests, philosophers, and politicians, were really writers and artists.

George, too, could not help seeing Michel, with his gift for emotive imagery, as a kind of unknowing artist. It was on the very subject of art that she soon clashed with the aggressive lawyer. Several disputes later blended in her potent memory of one spring night in Paris. Returning on a fine May evening from the Théâtre Français, deep in discussion with Planet and Michel, she began to question the tribune about the social problem. They had paused on the Carrousel bridge, looking toward the lights of the royal palace of the Tuileries, where festivities were in progress. George's attention having wandered, she was surprised from her reverie by the word "Babouvism." Michel was elaborating what she, with her vague notion of a share in happiness for all, considered the "outmoded" system of authoritarian communism of Babeuf and Buonarroti. Their desperate methods were unsuited to modern civilization, she told her new would-be guide.

"Civilization!" repeated Michel, furiously striking the balustrade of the bridge with his cane. "That is all you artists can think about!" Before the present corrupt form of society could be renewed, the Seine would have to run red with blood, he assured her, the accursed Tuileries be reduced to ashes, and the entire city laid bare for the poor to plow and build thereon. Warming to his apocalyptic theme, he discoursed on the corruption of cities and the enervating effect of the arts. Only after everything had been put to the sword or the torch would the golden age arise, as if by magic, upon the smoking ruins of the old world. Michel grew even more annoyed when George not only complimented him on his imagery but proceeded to defend the cause of civilization and art.

His attack on art and artists thus led her to reflect upon her own writings and to measure how far she herself fell short of the lofty ideal of pure artistic devotion—represented for her by Liszt's friend, Berlioz—the ideal that she now thrust before Michel. True, circumstances, the need to earn a living to support herself and the children, had obliged her to treat her art as a mere job. In her role as male traveler, she confessed in oddly erotic metaphor: "I violated my muse when she refused to yield; she avenged herself by cold caresses and gloomy revelations." A writer condemned to work in haste in order to pay his creditors or feed his family could not but feel humiliated when he observed those colleagues who took time to reflect, to correct and polish their writings. As for journeymen like herself, she added, they produced rough, shapeless work, sometimes full of energy, but always overhasty and incomplete.

Was this in fact George's misfortune as a writer, that with all her talents she was forced to work too fast and with insufficient care? Or was she prone to exaggerate the pressure at times so as to circumvent criticism? Was she, in short, one of those writers who need some intense external pressure in order to fuel their creative energies? At the moment of ever-growing fame, her modesty, self-scrutiny, candor, and regret are nonetheless (intentionally) disarming.

The noisy quarrel with Michel did not prevent her from falling under the spell of his bloodthirsty Babouvist rhetoric, in a way that would for some years affect the tone of her writing, both private and public. Their April encounter in Bourges, commemorated by a ring, was shortly afterward followed by physical consummation. His desire hypnotized her: "I submitted to your love . . . in ecstasy," she was to remind him nearly two years later. The temper of their relations is possibly symbolized by the fierce struggle of the heroine, Fiamma, bloodied in her attempt to seize hold of a kite, which has been wounded by the hero and which he finally subdues, in her novel *Simon*, inspired by her association with Michel. That he held some special, earthy sexual power over her seems indubitable. There were times when he treated her like a "pasha." On one occasion, he went out after locking her in the room (as she had once dreamed of being locked up by Pagello). He dominated her as she had long wished—or thought she wished—to be dominated in her secret fantasy.

This was also the glamorous moment when, "like a Caius Gracchus," he was dominating the Court of Peers with his fierce, nervous eloquence, his startling improvisations, his electric gaze. Michel passionately took to task those of his colleagues who wished to keep the trial on a strictly legal basis. He stood with those who desired to make some spectacular gesture of sympathy for the accused. To this end, he enlisted George's help. It was she who sketched the draft of the famous open letter to the accused, which he made far more aggressive and which consequently failed to gain the unanimous agreement of their supporters.

On May 20, Michel defiantly challenged the competence of the Court in a brilliant address. That day, George succeeded in gaining admittance by the recognized device of wearing male attire, and could be seen ardently spurring on her friends. Women, largely treated as minors by the law, were not permitted to attend the sessions. Even the wives of the accused were not allowed in court: the Grand Referendary of the Chamber, the Duc Decazes, advised Mme Baune to don masculine dress if she wished so desperately to follow her husband's defense.

Michel earned a sentence of one month's imprisonment and a fine of ten thousand francs, thus adding his name to those of the trial's political martyrs. He was, however, permitted to serve his sentence during the law vacation. When George returned to Nohant in mid-June, (leaving the children in their respective schools in Paris), Michel, suffering from nervous exhaustion after his labors, joined her at her country home. George paid scant regard to Casimir, who returned from a funeral in La Châtre and retired to bed with a temperature. Her contempt for her husband could not have been made more manifest.

At the beginning of July she traveled back to Paris by way of Bourges. This was the period of her "deserted cottage," as she liked to call it in her writings, giving the impression that her solitary abode for concentrated literary endeavour was a rustic one by the Loire, in Bourges, or "in China," when actually it was a ground-floor apartment in the mansion on quai Malaquais, where decorators had temporarily stopped work. Here, Michel shared her supposedly solitary retreat, whose address she revealed to very few. Even her beloved son Maurice did not know that his mother was in Paris.

It was during the summer of 1835 that she began to draft *Simon* (published in installments early in the following year), whose eponymous republican hero, educated son of a peasant massacred by royalists, owes much to Michel. She had already addressed the sixth of her traveler's letters to Everard, the fictional name she gave to Michel, adding to his celebrity and making his political stance, as well as her response to it, known to a wider public. *Simon*, which she mistakenly expected to equal the success of *André*, cannot be counted as one of her best romances. The author seems too close to her inspiration, and what she gains in spontaneity she loses in detachment.

The young hero's republican politics are shared by the heroine, Fiamma, since she is Venetian-born. Nobly, she encourages Simon to sublimate his passion for her and to rise through his gift for oratory. Fiamma herself yearns to participate in guerrilla warfare and to play an active role in the cause of Italian emancipation, but "this odious feminine garb . . . obliges me to remain inactive, and utter sterile wishes. . . ." Her real father being not, as all suppose, the unpleasantly materialistc Comte de Fougères but a dead Italian peasant partisan leader, the way is ultimately clear to her union with the plebeian Simon. What the book does convey, apart from a sense of the glamor of the partisan, is a feeling of humane generosity. It is one of the ancestors of the modern committed political novel, with all that implies of encouragement to like-minded persecuted liberals and radicals scattered across Europe, as well as of limitation. Clearly, in George's view, high-souled women dreaming of an "active role" were to play at least an important moral part in the broad movement for social renovation, carrying a flaming torch, like the aptly named Fiamma.

At the beginning of August, George left her "deserted cottage" to return brieflly to Nohant. Casimir was away and, unbeknown to him,

Michel came secretly to stay for four or five days and nights among the wild strawberry plants beneath the sweet-smelling acacias. The house was supposed to be closed, and it was only some time later that her husband learned from the servants how Michel had been privately doing the honors in the master's absence. Casimir was not pleased.

George went back to Paris again early in September. After the abortive attempt on Louis-Philippe's life by the Corsican terrorist Fieschi on July 28, which had left nineteen dead and twenty wounded, the government had increased its surveillance of known radicals. The author of *Lélia* began to fancy herself in the role of a political exile or martyr, and made no secret of her disgust for the "September law" that restricted civil liberties and the freedom of the press. Her apartment on the quai Malaquais, frequented by Michel and his associates, had become known to the police as an "anarchist committee room," she told her half-brother Hippolyte with a certain satisfaction.

The time had arrived for Michel to serve the sentence he had incurred during the mammoth trial. But he was laid low by fever. A doctor sent by the Chamber of Peers to examine the sick man at the abode of "la dame Dudevant" confirmed that the tribune was too ill to enter the prison of Sainte-Pélagie. It was George who penned Michel's letter to the Peers, requesting that he serve his sentence close to his family in Bourges. In consequence, Michael spent most of the month of October in prison in that city.

Meanwhile, George had become enrolled as a humble "drummer-boy" in the republican cause, as a modest but ardent campaigner for a more just and egalitarian society. In her eyes, justice for women naturally formed part of this general movement. She told Emmanuel Arago, a young man whom she had first met at Balzac's in the rue Cassini some three years before and who would later become known under the Second and the Third Republic, that she wished to work solidly and seriously with a social and political aim. She would soon be reminding her schoolboy son, Maurice, of "all those unfortunates who work twelve hours a day to earn ten sous! When you think of it, tears come to your eyes and sweetmeats taste bitter." With her new insights, the lack of a useful social conclusion to *Lélia* was now bothering her more than ever.

Such concern serves as a reminder that her new awareness of contemporary social distress and her new hopes for amelioration did not spring out of a vacuum, nor were they merely the consequence of her encounter with Michel de Bourges, who served to define their direction.

On the contrary, these hopes were deeply rooted in a willed reaction against skepticism and a pessimistic assessment of personal and human realities.

Some of these less worthy aspects of human nature were about to be fully displayed in a bitter, long-drawn-out struggle with her husband for the control of her children, her property, and her rights. She was on the eve of the gravest battle of her life.

The Recourse to Law

It is man, then, whom I accuse before you, O Nazarene! . . . it is all those I have loved in vain whom I come to denounce to your justice; avenge me, or see that I forget them and that I enter upon the indifference of age.   Léa in George Sand's
Le Dieu inconnu

FTER having signed an agreement with his wife on February 15, 1835, for a separation to come into effect in the autumn, Casimir began to have second thoughts. He did not see why he, the lord and master, should yield the house and lands of Nohant and all the privileges of squiredom, in exchange for the income from the Parisian property, the Hôtel de Narbonne—no matter if that income were to help settle his debts of twenty-two thousand francs. He resented his wife's presence at Nohant, her friends, her ways, her intellectual superiority, the fact that she wrote books. George perceived that he was not going to keep his word—an awareness that accounts in some degree for her indifference to his feelings, since he cared so little for hers. To an old family retainer who had obliged her, Casimir insisted: "Another time, when Madame gives you orders, you will kindly inform her that I am the master here." One evening, after a day's hunting with friends, his bottled anger exploded.

The Dudevants were taking coffee after dinner with their guests, who included Alphonse Fleury, Gustave Papet, Alexis Duteil, Joseph Bourgoing and his wife Rozanne, in the drawing room at Nohant. Young Maurice, aged twelve, was hanging around Casimir and getting on his father's nerves. Casimir reprimanded him several times, finally blaming his son's faults on his mother's influence. This was to touch George on a delicate point: the sacred nature of her maternal feelings. These feelings had always been strong. Circumstances were about to shape them into a veritable cult.

She told Maurice to go to his room: "You see how you are upsetting your father, and he does not know . . ." She stopped herself. Casimir finished the sentence for her: "Your father does not know what he is saying," and he added: "You want to make me look a thorough nitwit." George told her husband that she thought he was rather tipsy. "Maybe," he said, "but you can shut your mouth." He then ordered her to leave the room. "I shall do no such thing," George replied. "You forget that this is my home quite as much as yours." At this, Casimir coarsely retorted: "Get out, or I'll slap your face." Friends seized hold of him to prevent him from striking her, but he broke away and rushed into the next room to find his gun. Somehow they managed to calm him. As he sat down, white-faced, at the table, George stood by the fireplace, staring at his distorted features.

This scene occurred on October 19, 1835. Two days later, as Casimir took the children back to their respective schools in Paris, George hastened with Gustave Papet to Châteauroux to consult François Rollinat about the prospects for a legal separation. Always careful, her dearest friend favored the idea, but he warned her about the unpleasantness she would inevitably incur. Together, they traveled posthaste to consult Michel, who was still languishing in prison in Bourges. Michel advised on the course to be taken.

First, George should seek asylum with the Duteils in La Châtre. She should then file suit for a legal separation from her husband. This she did, in the hope that Casimir would agree to a settlement out of court. To this end, he was offered five thousand francs a year if he refrained from going to law.

The risk George was taking was considerable, even though the future reward of her peace, her independence, her control of her children and her property seemed great. The magistrates of La Châtre were thought to be unsympathetic to appeals for separation. Any detailed revelations about her numerous affairs would be far more damaging to her, as a wife and mother, than Casimir's escapades with the servant girls, which merely enhanced his provincial reputation for virility, could be to him. She might face public ignominy, as well as the loss of her children. Women did not lightly seek the protection of the law.

Legal separation was, however, the only possibility open to an injured wife. Divorce did not exist. A law permitting divorce had been enacted in 1792. Modified under Napoleon, it was abrogated in 1816, during the Restoration. Attempts were made, without success, to restore it in the reign of Louis-Philippe, when the question of divorce was much discussed as a moral and political issue. In the eyes of the law, a girl came first under her father's protection, then under her husband's. Only when these natural protectors failed her could she appeal to the law to take their place. George's case would be that Casimir had protected her inadequately. It had suited him to leave her free and to be free himself: She possessed a letter he had written to her to this effect in December 1831. In actuality, such private marital arrangements that allowed mutual freedom were far from uncommon, since marriage was then largely a matter of convenience and business. Leaving aside his desire to keep control of the property, one reason why Casimir had not raised a hue and cry over his wife's love affairs was doubtless his dread of the stigma and ridicule attached to the name of cuckold.

So long as husband and wife were not legally separated, Casimir could burst into her apartment on the quai Malaquais at any time. He could even sell the attractive furniture she had collected with her literary earnings. George could never suppress the fear that he might break in upon her—with disastrous consequences for herself. She would from time to time send urgent instructions to trusted servants or helpers like Jules Boucoiran, to remove Musset's clothes from the cupboards or to conceal in a place of safety compromising letters and her large private diary, titled in English, *Sketches and Hints*.

For the laws treated men and women with gross inequality. An errant wife could be sent to prison for adultery for at least three months or anything up to two years. In view of the general laxity of manners, it might be supposed that such a law was more honored in the breach than in the observance. Nonetheless, nearly ten years later, in July 1845, when the wife of the painter Auguste Biard was discovered *flagrante delicto* with Victor Hugo, it was not the poet who suffered ignominy but the unfortunate Mme Biard whom the police hurried to prison. Indeed, under article 324 of the penal code, a husband who killed his wife on finding her in bed with her lover was usually acquitted.

[176]

The only misdeed for which a husband might be penalized was that of sleeping with his mistress in the conjugal home. Here, Casimir might well be challenged, since at Nohant he had intercourse with Solange's nurse, Pepita, and later also with Claire, Mme Hippolyte Chatiron's maid, who had borne him a son. The worst that could happen to Casimir, though, was not imprisonment but a fine ranging from a hundred to two thousand francs.

There began for George a period of uncertainty, waiting, and legal delay. The home of Alexis Duteil and his wife in La Châtre, where she had sought asylum, stood in one of the old town's narrow, cobbled streets, opposite a noisy country inn. Despite the upheaval, in accordance with her custom, she worked from midnight to dawn, "like an ox of Berry," composing a political novel, *Engelwald* (later destroyed). She would need money to pay the expenses of her lawsuit.

Meanwhile, she was also writing long letters to explain her case to her mother (to whom she recommended prudence, should Casimir call); to her friends; to those who, like members of the Roëttiers du Plessis circle or Jules Boucoiran, could serve as material witnesses. Some, like Boucoiran, would give her invaluable support; others proved a bitter disappointment, including servants who were afraid of backing the wrong horse. The worst blow was struck by her half-brother, Hippolyte, whom she failed to win to her cause by appeals to family ties and self-interest. Boon drinking companion of Casimir, whose mistresses he sometimes shared, he was too closely implicated with her husband. Besides, the lawsuit stimulated his hidden resentment at the injustice of fate in giving preference to his half-sister, and his secret envy and bitterness. He was to play an odious role, collecting low tittle-tattle in the Parisian cafés and flattering Casimir's weakness and obstinacy.

George herself, aiming to demonstrate her bourgeois conventionality, adopted an air of modest virtue in public. She refrained from publishing anything that might offend the right-thinking reader. For the district magistrates she professed utter contempt in private, alleging that one had sold his wife to the highest bidder, while another was "brutalized by masturbation." As for the locals, they "think I am on my kness in sackcloth and ashes, weeping over my sins like Mary Magdalene. The awakening will be dreadful," wrote George with forced gaiety to Marie d'Agoult, who had left her aristocratic husband and young daughter six months before to live with Liszt in Geneva. The author of *Jacques* was prepared to do anything to win her case.

Her tactics (or rather, Michel's) appeared to be working. Casimir having decided not to plead, the court ruled on February 16, 1836, in her favor. George took possession of Nohant, the home of her "ancestors," the burial place of her father and grandmother, for as yet nothing was heard from her about her mother's plebeian family. Alone at night in the eighteenth-century house, she savored the moment as she walked slowly through the candlelit ground-floor rooms. That her victory would be short-lived she well knew. Hippolyte lost no time in informing her that Casimir had changed his mind and intended to lodge an appeal.

Toward the middle of March, George visited Châteauroux, where Michel de Bourges was appearing in court. She was in the habit of meeting him, under an assumed name, in the towns nearby where his legal affairs took him. Michel may well have visited Nohant surreptitiously during the winter. To her friends, George maintained the fiction that her relationship with her lawyer Michel was one of a disciple's warm filial or platonic devotion to an "elderly" peasant mentor. Accustomed to impose her fictional inventions upon her readers, George came to carry fiction into actuality. If the "lie" was the foundation of novelistic art, it also represented what could or should have been in real life, a way of imprinting dream on reality. Yet, while the lie had become second nature in the tireless dreamer and mythmaker, it served also as a game of skill as well as a token of contempt for those taken in by it.

Inevitably, her secret encounters with Michel were fairly rare. The ambitious lawyer had his wealthy wife and his legal practice to consider. He spared George what time he chose from his business and political affairs. With her demanding nature, that was hardly likely to be enough. She would gradually realize that he was not going to give up everything for her when she became free.

The lawsuit contributed to reinforce the low opinion of human nature that George had acquired at the time of her grandmother's death. When she visited Paris in the spring of 1836, her contempt for Casimir and Hippolyte, her frustration with Michel, spilled over into her treatment of those she met, like the young Emmanuel Arago, who was obviously in love with her. Indeed, George could not help despising most of her lovers (the embittered Stéphane was a partial exception, of whom she would later grandly write that he was "neither despised nor despicable"). Aurélien did not escape, pilloried as Raymon in *Indiana*. Jules Sandeau certainly incurred her scorn. So did Musset, despite the fact that his recently published masochistic, fictional account of their affair, *La Confession d'un enfant du siècle*, whose appearance she had dreaded, spared her the worst. The book made her cry. She wrote to Musset that she had loved him a great deal, that she "forgave" him for everything— a sure and superior token of her contempt. It seemed to her that none of these men—not even Michel—was capable of plumbing the depths of her love. They followed her mother, who had failed to respond adequately when Aurore was a lonely little girl.

As soon as George arrived in Paris, she spent an evening with Charles Didier, the shy, Swiss-born political writer to whom she had been introduced by Hortense Allart in February 1833. George had occasion during the winter to reread his novel *Rome souterraine*, where the Carbonari are shown working for the people and the emancipation of Italy, a book whose republicanism she could now appreciate more thoroughly. Letters had passed between them. Just over a year younger than George, Didier was thirty, a man of distinguished bearing, whose prematurely white hair led George to call him "my white bear." The large chip on his shoulder was due to his unhappy childhood as the unrecognized natural son of a bourgeois father and low-born mother. Of melancholy temperament, Didier was a doubter by nature. He lacked confidence in his ability and never knew solid literary success; and he distrusted other people, being as suspicious in his assessments as George was recklessly impulsive and quick to poeticize her friends (subject to depoeticizing them later). He was to die by his own hand.

Ever since he had first met George, Didier was fascinated by her. He observed, pitied, puzzled over her. Can she be capable of passion? he asked himself. Sainte-Beuve had shocked him with an account of her "depravity" at the time of the Mérimée episode. Now here he was actually having supper with her, together with Emmanuel Arago and Charles d'Aragon, another of her young admirers. "Incredible night," Didier confided to his diary. "We did not leave her until 5 in the morning. It was daylight. Arago was tipsy. . . . There I lay with my head resting on the cushions of the divan, while she, in sad and not too imperious a mood, sat ruffling my hair and calling me her old philosopher."

The next evening, Didier brought three bottles of champagne to the quai Malaquais apartment. All the guests became rather fuddled at supper. "George was all smiles and gaiety. I don't like her vulgar side, but I forgive it . . ." he noted pompously, despite or because of the way his arms were entwined with hers. A number of evenings of a similar sort followed at the end of March and beginning of April, supper parties that suggest George was both celebrating and trying to drown her disillusion with Michel and her fears about the future.

While Didier was spending so many hours with George and trying to decide what he really thought about her, Casimir filed a virulent and defamatory appeal. It portrayed George as a low prostitute who even instilled her taste for debauchery into her daughter. That Casimir could so defile the child seemed unnatural. The worst had happened.

It is in this context that her association with Didier grew more intimate. On the fine April morning when she learned of Casimir's defamatory suit, George strolled with Didier in the Jardin des Plantes. She felt ill on their return to his apartment in the rue du Regard which he shared with his Genevan friend, Dr. David Richard, a disciple of Lamennais. Didier managed to make her feel better by magnetism, in which Richard firmly believed. It was Richard who gave her lessons in the fashionable study of phrenology. Didier suspected that his doctor friend was "a little in love with her," and felt rather jealous. On occasion, George and Didier spent the night at each other's homes without, apparently, taking the final step.

In his diary, Didier noted how often Michel's name was mentioned: "She speaks to me a great deal about Michel and tells me of the purely intellectual nature of their relations. She swears to me that she has not had a lover since her break with Musset. . . . She was beautiful and charming." This downright lie of George's might be attributed partly to her upset at the crisis in her legal affairs, partly to her reaction against Didier's jealous suspicions—if she had not already lied to him once before (in August 1833) when she told him that she had stayed alone at Fontainebleau, although in fact she had been there with Musset. She was now exacting vengeance on Casimir and Michel through Didier, as she had formerly exacted vengeance on Musset through Pagello. Just as she had once made use of Pagello, so she now made use of Didier. She needed gentle affection and tenderness, and she took it. She needed someone with whom she could dreamily hold hands, like Didier, to counteract the tough authoritarianism of Michel or Casimir's loathing. To scheme and lie to men was no better than they deserved.

The luckless Didier wanted to believe her.

> I study her, I watch her, lost in anxiety, confusion and doubt. This complex creature is unintelligible to me in more ways than one, and I fear her reckless changeable nature. I keep on studying her. I do not understand her. Is she straightforward? Is she acting a part? Is her heart dead? Insoluble problems.

So spoke a suspicious observer. Having given up her apartment on the quai Malaquais, George moved temporarily into the rooms Didier shared with David Richard, causing much clacking of tongues. Didier made up a bed for George in his study and withdrew, under strain. Her books, papers, and furniture, which she was still afraid Casimir might seize, were deposited elsewhere.

Nothing concentrated George's mind upon female disabilities so intently as the vagaries of men and the anomalies of the legal system. Why should it be assumed that a woman had less sense of responsibility than a man? Why should she be expected to sign documents without reading them? One day, she would no longer be a "female slave." She encouraged Marie d'Agoult to compose a work—"boldly and modestly" —on women's fate and rights.

Through her admirer Charles d'Aragon, an opportunity arose for George to express her own ideas on the subject in an important review of the augmented autobiography of the Comtesse Merlin (the first part of which had been published anonymously in 1831). Born in Havana, Mme Merlin was an intelligent creole beauty who, in describing her early upbringing in Cuba, protested against corsets, convents, and Negro slavery. In her review, George foresaw the time when women might have access to the arts and sciences, as well as philosophy. Men of intelligence could not but desire "the intellectual emancipation of women"; mediocrities alone feared it. George was writing at a period when the law on universal primary education, enacted by Guizot in 1833, did not include girls.

Inevitably, declared George, men appeared as yet intellectually superior to women. For her, the greatest women in literature and learning without exception in past and present were merely "second-class men." The weakness of writings by women did not prove women's intellectual inferiority but their educational disability. There should eventually be equality in education. Although eschewing the demand for political rights—for which, in her opinion, women were not yet ready— George stressed the psychological importance of writings by women in leading the way toward an improvement in woman's fate.

While concerning herself chiefly with female education and the position and treatment of the woman author, George fell behind some of her contemporaries on the political front. A far-seeing statesman and writer, Salvandy, had urged more active participation by women in public affairs in his preface to a novel *Natalie*, published in 1833.

Three years later, the bizarre but brave Flora Tristan, having returned from her humiliating attempt to recover her Peruvian inheritance, was advocating a combination of feminism and internationalism. By that time, too, *La Gazette des Femmes* was demanding women's right to vote and a place in the professions (albeit for the middle-class). George feared lest excessive demands might prejudice the attainment of modest objectives.

Her moderate stance, which, it must be added, did not seem all that moderate to the conventional-minded majority, may appear better attuned to the slow reformist movement of the age than the more advanced feminist position of the Saint-Simonian Claire Demar or the Fourierist Flora Tristan, neither of whom was as widely known as George or carried as much weight. Could George have used her fame to try to impose female emancipation? It was Fourier's contention that women writers like Mme de Staël had not done as much as they could in that direction. (Indeed, none of the leading women poets and novelists—Elizabeth Barrett Browning, the Brontës, George Eliot—would be militant feminists.) That George considered her reasonable essay to be of some importance is shown by her proud injunction to her publisher, Buloz: "Do not change a syllable." Hitherto, she had often been casual about corrections and alterations to her work.

A moralizing essay on her novels by the critic Désiré Nisard, who accused her of attacking marriage, bothered George in the context of the lawsuit. In her reply to Nisard, included among the traveler's letters, George the opportunist insisted that, as a poet, she had no great aims as a social reformer. With the humility that was the twin of her pride, she protested that any misunderstandings about her intentions were due to her literary inadequacy. It was the abuses and follies of marriage rather than the institution itself that she had condemned in her novels. She waxed sardonic, however, about any suggestion that mismatched women should suffer in silence. Why did not Nisard reprove masculine debauchery and violence and prescribe Christian chastity for the husband as well as for the wife? The double standard of her day in judging the conduct of the sexes always aroused her ire. She felt that she still had much to say on the question of female disabilities and women's quest for justice.

While George was in Paris, flirting with Didier and the rest, Casimir had resumed residence at Nohant. His bitter sense of humiliation, his rusty knowledge of the law, the promptings of his stepmother, Baroness

Dudevant, and of Hippolyte, led him to go too far. By associating seven-year-old Solange with her mother's misdemeanors, Casimir proved how little he cared about the girl. When drunk or in an ill humor, he would call the child names that reflected upon the legitimacy of her birth. It was certainly ill-advised to suggest that his wife was little better than a depraved courtesan and, at the same time, to urge her return to the conjugal abode. If she were so corrupt, it was he who should have asked for a separation. There were a number of precedents where the husband's case *against* separation, based on accusations of the wife's misconduct, had been dismissed. The lawyers found Casimir's tone unprecedented, and refused to read his text in court. Michel's line of defense was "admirable," thought George. Meanwhile, Casimir went about telling everyone that Michel was his wife's lover, vowing to kill him, and doing nothing about it. George could no longer recognize the man she had married and whom she had once thought so kindly, decent, and sensible.

It was thus against a background of publicity and scandal that the court of La Châtre upheld in May the separation order it had granted to George three months earlier. George had been deeply worried lest she might lose the children and had even contemplated absconding with them to the United States if the case had gone against her. Despite her victory, damage was done. News of his literary mother's goings-on had reached Maurice and his schoolfellows in Paris. They taunted their comrade, now nearly thirteen years old. "If you only knew what school is like, I believe you wouldn't want me to stay here," wrote Maurice pitifully to his mother. ". . . when I think what they call you, I couldn't say the word to you because it is too vile—p . . . —there, I've told you in spite of myself. . . ." Moreover, Casimir's stepmother visited the boy and tried to bribe him away from his mother. All Maurice yearned for was reconciliation between his parents. The strain was to tell upon the boy's health.

George wrote her son uplifting and self-justificatory letters that succeeded in blaming Casimir without appearing to do so:

Wasn't it he who placed you in school? Have I ever tried to remove you without his consent? Have I ever suggested to you the thought of disobeying him in anything whatsoever? What is wrong with him? And why does he want to take my son away from me? . . . He well knows that if there is a slight preference, it is always in the mother's favor. Nature wills it so. Women are fated to suffer. God condemns them to bear children and to give birth in fearful pain. But God, who is good, compensates them with a

[183]

more intense and tender love for their children, who respond to it with a secret, God-given instinct.

As for Maurice's malicious school fellows, he should ignore them: "Show your utter scorn for boys who dare to speak ill of a mother to her son. Let the display of this scorn be your sole response." A contemptuous silence remained as ever her own ambiguous response to imputations against her character and conduct.

George's worries were by no means at an end. Casimir was still ensconced at Nohant, intending to appeal against the decision to the Royal Court at Bourges. She now stayed in the quiet home of her friends Joseph and Rozanne Bourgoing, which was situated on the old rampart, close by the medieval tower in La Châtre. George's room, with its white wood table, straw-bottomed chairs, and red-curtained bed, overlooked the garden terrace, with the valley of the Indre beyond. "I am vegetating," she said. Birds, insects, stars, provided an absorbing interest. At night, she strolled alone in the rose-scented garden, or rode out by herself from dusk to midnight. Then she stayed up, writing, planning additions to her novel *Lélia* in the light of her new opinions, raising her eyes from the page to watch the subtly varied merging of night into day. These delicate visual impressions passed into the second version of *Lélia*.

It was a moment for reflection. The need to collect evidence for the lawsuit had brought her into contact with some of the intimates of former years. Letters passed between George and Zoé Leroy, the confidante of Cauterets and Bordeaux: "Passion no longer plays any part in my life . . . to-day I am a *nun* in every sense of the word"—a nun, because she was living quietly in contemplation, like an Essene. George never asked herself why she had behaved as she did. "I chose to do it!" she boldly informed Zoé, the moderately independent woman. "Call me *George* in the masculine," urged the author of *Lélia*. She could no longer bear to be addressed as Aurore—the difference between her former and her present self was too great. Letters passed, too, between George and Aurélien de Sèze, now married. At her request, he sent back her journal in the form of letters, to be used if necessary in court, asking her to return it to him afterward. (Michel was to quote only from her long letter of "confession" to Casimir, written in November 1825, which won her much sympathy.) Aurélien's tone was correct but chivalrous—very different from what she had heard from others since.

The "nun's" relations with Didier had soured. She accused the touchy and critical fellow of treating her as "a sort of platonic whore." He had declined to hasten to her defense, on the ground that he was not her lover, when she was attacked (along with Balzac and others) for sexual frankness. This attack occurred in an article in the *Quarterly Review*, which was translated and reprinted in France. The British critic, impervious to her originality, accused her of going far beyond her master Rousseau in portraying what he called "the actual scene of guilt." (It was left to the estranged Sainte-Beuve to defend her as a writer "second to no man in talent," while also taking her to task for venturing to find Mme de Staël boring.) George was outraged at Didier's "betrayal":

> Proud Mme de Staël with all her court at Coppet was insulted as much as I in the periodicals and she didn't owe her triumph over them to Benjamin Constant. As for me with my country companions from the Vallée Noire, if I ever have a name I shall owe it to myself alone, no friend will give it to me, no literary journalist will take it from me. . . .

A true friend would not wonder whether he would "look silly when standing up for me because he hasn't slept with me."

In contrast, if she so wished, Michel would leave everything for her, she told Didier, playing one man against the other. Didier never received this caustic dressing-down. Unable to face a break, he had hurried to La Châtre. George and her "white bear" were reconciled. There followed five days alone together in Nohant (Casimir being absent)—walks in the narrow lanes that Didier had read about in *Valentine*, rides through the countryside, moonlit June nights spent on the terrace in conversation, with her head on his breast. "I should have been completely happy if the name of M[ichel] had not been uttered; but it was, and cast a shadow . . ." noted Didier. All the same, he decided that George was "essentially kind." She was inserting a scene about the Carbonari, in accordance with his own republican views (and hers), into the revised version of *Lélia*. Besides, "M[ichel] is very jealous of me; he speaks of this in all his letters"—information that George alone could have conveyed to Didier.

For the moment, George felt exasperated with Michel, who was clearly never out of her mind. She told her friend, Marie d'Agoult, that she was sick of "great men"—they were "unkind, importunate, capricious, tyrannical, galling, mistrustful." Didier meant little to her; he simply happened briefly to be on hand at a moment of intense worry and frustrated physical energy.

As the summer progressed, she used to leave the house to go walking at three in the morning. Sometimes, she lost her way in the leafy lanes, running after insects. Deep in her dreams, she trudged miles in the heat and cooled off several times by plunging fully dressed into the river Indre. It was as if through these *"Essenian* walks" she were seeking renewal in communion with nature, trying to reshape herself in accordance with new conditions and responsibilities.

On the eve of the court hearing, George wrote on the wall of the house where she was staying in Bourges a solemn entreaty for divine protection against human persecution and iniquity. She had already invoked the protection of her grandmother, transmuted into a symbol of passionate motherhood. The Royal Court held session in the fifteenth-century palace of Jacques Cœur, outside whose quaint portal she and Michel had paused on their first perambulation of the city. Michel's address was "truly sublime," declared George, who appeared demurely dressed in a simple white gown and flowered shawl. The assistant public prosecutor nonetheless distributed blame to both parties. The Bourges court, being divided, postponed its decision, but Casimir saw things were going against him and withdrew.

Two days later, on July 29, he and George signed the agreement that put an end to the lawsuit (though there would be further litigation in the years ahead). The terms were much as before the legal tussle. Casimir was to have the usufruct of the Hôtel de Narbonne and to pay for Maurice's education. "I keep Nohant and my daughter," George told her mother, while reassuring Sophie about the payment of her annual allowance. Papet had brought Solange from Paris, on Michel's insistence, before the hearing, and on July 31, 1836, George and her daughter took possession of Nohant. With Maurice's arrival for the school holidays in mid-August, George's family was reunited.

"Free at last!" wrote George, as she had written once before, in January 1831, on leaving Casimir for Paris and Sandeau. Once again, freedom had limitations. The lawsuit had consumed a great deal of money. She was urgently in need of funds, and therefore remained under heavy pressure to write in quantity. Her responsibilities concerning the children seemed greater.

Motherhood became her dominant theme. Her children were her only love, she proclaimed to Marie d'Agoult. For her, the joys of motherhood were the only true and lasting thing for women. George had managed somehow—by luck or contraception—to escape the frequent pregnancies of Marie d'Agoult or Hortense Allart. Not surprisingly, such emancipated ladies did not share her maternal raptures. Marie d'Agoult would confide to her diary, when staying at Nohant in 1837 and with George obviously in mind:

> Let women believe that they are sublime because they suckle their offspring as the bitch does; that they are self-sacrificing when they are selfish; let them repeat how maternal love exceeds all others, while they clutch at it as a last resort. . . .

As for Hortense Allart, she wanted Marie d'Agoult to use the illegitimacy of her children by Liszt to further the cause of female emancipation. In her view, along with freedom of the press and of the individual, an additional freedom should be granted: that of childbirth.

After George's cult of the sacred mission of motherhood, a counterbalance to criticism of her "depravity," George had discovered, in her midnight rides and reflections, the virtue of goodness. Kindness, gentleness, generosity—these were the feminine values she would henceforward exalt in contrast to the cruelty and tyranny of men. These values were to be superimposed upon a character notable for its self-will, its harshness when crossed, its regal pride and scorn. As she was to observe later: ". . . we each have two beings to master: the one we are and the one we should like to be"—hence the curious oscillations and disconcerting contradictions in her behavior and attitudes.

CHAPTER

14

The Female "Spartacus"

T HERE was only one way to celebrate her new freedom: a holiday. Accepting a long-standing invitation from Liszt and Marie d'Agoult in Geneva, George—still obsessed with Michel de Bourges—hastily collected together her fine cotton men's shirts, her trousers, her velvet frock coat, her grey silk flowered dress, lace and veil, as well as a supply of her favorite cigarettes and two newfangled chemical lighters. Comfortable slippers for swollen feet were thoughtfully included in the baggage. Much of the wardrobe suited a high-spirited bohemian youth, the role George had determined upon when she, Maurice, and Solange—"the Piffoëls"—set off on August 28, 1836, with her own childhood playmate, the maid Ursule, to join "the Fellows" in Switzerland. A twenty-two-year old aristocrat, Gustave de Gévaudan, encountered by chance at Autun, chose to escort the novelist to Switzerland, and thus aroused the violent jealousy of Michel.

On arriving in Geneva, George found that the Fellows had left for Chamonix. Although she had been introduced to Marie d'Agoult and had been corresponding with her, their lively meeting at the inn at Chamonix provided the first real opportunity for the two alert women to become acquainted. In theory, Marie resembled one of the novelist's noble heroines who sacrificed all for passion. By the time George caught up with the Fellows in Chamonix, however, the relationship between the roving young virtuoso and his not-so-young mistress was already under some strain. Willowy, fair, elegant, Marie contrasted with gypsy-looking, unceremonious George, a mere four feet ten inches, who made sport of everything.

Marie played the princess, and George played up to her, calling her Princess Arabella. The Comtesse d'Agoult would later confess that George's earthy facetiousness disconcerted her. Unlike the author of *Indiana*, Marie was neither high-spirited nor an enthusiast by nature. Moreover, she had reason to feel uncertain of herself: Her origins were almost as divergent as George's. As an impoverished émigré officer in Frankfurt, her father, the Vicomte de Flavigny, had married the widowed daughter of Simon Moritz Bethmann, member of a wealthy banking family of Jewish origin. Marie, educated partly in her birthplace, Frankfurt, and partly in Touraine, kept quiet about her Jewish antecedents. George knew perfectly well, though, that Arabella was, on her mother's side, as little of a princess as she herself.

In her traveler's letters, George left an exuberant account of the excursions made on mule-back by the party, which included the energetic Solange, a somewhat subdued Maurice, the ubiquitous Puzzi, and a rather humorless, if learned, Swiss artillery major, Adolphe Pictet, whom George liked to tease. An admirer of Hegel and Schelling, Pictet failed to convert George to German philosophy and metaphysics. All intuition and imagination, she cared little for abstract speculation and analysis. One day, when they stood gazing at La Mer de Glace, George —who in *Jacques* had already associated glaciers with extinction—exclaimed to Liszt: ". . . I don't like death. . . . A volcanic eruption with its burning lava should clear this wilderness and restore it to life by destruction. Life! Life! Franz! Long live life!" The urge to live remained her dominating passion.

Exhilarated by the bracing mountain air, by the discussions on humanitarian action, on art and illusion, and by Liszt's playing of part of Mozart's *Dies Irae* on the organ of the church of St. Nicolas in Fribourg, nonetheless George was very conscious of her single state in the light of Franz's ostentatious display of devotion to Marie. It was early in October when George broke her return journey in Lyons, where she had arranged to meet Michel de Bourges. Meekly, she stayed on there at the inn for five days, while the children grew ever more bored and funds declined. To her intense disappointment and anger, the erratic demagogue failed to appear.

"Michel, you are crazy!" she wrote to him on reaching Nohant and finding his letter, which she characterized as that of an old banker to his kept mistress. Nothing whatsoever had passed between herself and her useful young traveling companion Gévaudan—or Liszt, to whom she gave sisterly kisses "in front of his mistress." Michel, with his conventional masculine outlook, thought boorish conduct perfectly natural for the strong like himself in their treatment of the so-called weaker sex. She could not accept so insulting an attitude toward her as a woman. During her stay in the mountains (she confessed to Michel):

> I suffered a great deal from my chastity, I make no secret of it to you, I had very enervating dreams. . . . I often sat down apart and alone, my heart full of love and my knees all a-quiver with sensual feeling. . . . I am still young, even though I tell other men that I have the calm of old age, my blood is on fire and, before scenes of intoxicating beauty, love stirs within me like the sap of life within the universe.

What did Michel make of this remarkable confession of feminine sexual need? Very little, it would seem.

Naturally, she had kept her secret from Franz and Marie:

> The others think I am Lélia in every sense of the term and that, when I turn pale, it is because I have walked too much, and the opportunity would not have been lacking for my relief, I can assure you. There were many men younger than you around me. . . . What preserved me from this blot, slight in itself, but ineradicable for those who love, was not what women call their virtue, I don't know the meaning of that word. . . . It is of you I dream when I awake bathed in sweat. . . . That a man like you should judge and treat in such a way a woman like me is pitiable.

Underlying her despair at Michel's authoritarian treatment of her as a woman was the perennial "horror of loneliness." If he did not change his attitude, she would have to reconcile herself to loneliness or to some less demanding emotional tie. Perhaps she was thinking of Charles Didier. In the meanwhile, all she could do was to work in order to deaden her disgust.

It will be recalled that in April 1836 George had given up her quai Malaquais apartment and now lacked a Parisian pied-à-terre. The Fellows, who returned to Paris in October, invited George to take rooms in the Hôtel de France, where they were staying. There, she would find in Marie's salon Victor Schoelcher, the noted abolitionist; the messianic

Polish poet, Adam Mickiewicz; and, besides Heine and Lamennais, Liszt's respected colleague Frédéric Chopin. Here, too, George would soon add to her intimate circle Charlotte Marliani (a Frenchwoman married to the Spanish consul), and the rough-hewn socialist philosopher Pierre Leroux, who was to leave an indelible mark on her writings.

The gatherings at the Hôtel de France were a dazzling amalgam of those who frequented both society and its rejects, and those who constituted the elite of art, music, literature and social reform. Its tone could be raffish. Didier called on George there, noting that the "bohemian" element in her seemed uppermost. She looked beautiful, he wrote in his diary, and men were paying court to her. Charming when she so wished, on occasion she revealed toward himself what Didier called a strain of harshness and ferocity. The touchy Genevan loathed the tone of raillery she sometimes adopted toward him. There were bitter scenes of recrimination between them. Once Didier went into Marie's salon and wept on her carpet. He may not have known that George had recently talked amicably with Jules Sandeau; but he certainly knew and disapproved of her meeting with Alfred de Musset, with whom she was trying to negotiate the return of her letters. George expressed surprise at Alfred's "narrow outlook." Indeed, at this time he published anonymously a satire on the "humanitarians" among whom she counted herself.

Outwardly leading a brilliant social life—attending a soirée at Chopin's elegant apartment; dining with Marie, Liszt, and Chopin at Mme Marliani's; or seeing so much of Lamennais that tongues wagged— George was inwardly tormented by spleen. She appeared at a select concert at Chopin's on December 13, dressed to kill in a white- and- crimson Turkish costume. From midnight onward, though, Didier was alone with her in her room and, much to his astonishment, he witnessed her collapse into doubt and despair.

The reasons for her gloom were various. Foremost was the bitter struggle to hang on to Michel de Bourges, in spite of his despotism. On the more mundane level, she was short of cash. That same day she had written a savagely mocking note to her publisher, Buloz:

"Buloz!" "Eh?" "Buloz!!" "Eh?" "Bloody Buloz!!!" "What?" "Money!" "I can't hear you." "500 francs!" "What are you saying?" "Devil take you. You promised me 6,000 francs in a few days, and I'm asking you for 500 francs tomorrow." "I never said a word about that . . ." "Oh! so you're not deaf then?"

A little later, she was telling the offended Buloz that she would not die if he made her out to be grasping. Let him realize that she was no longer the George of former days to be led like an infant.

More pressing than her worries about money was her distress at her son's feeble health. The holiday in the mountains had apparently done little to restore him. The thirteen-year-old boy loathed having to go back to the school where his fellow pupils had made him suffer so harshly during the months of his parents' legal battle. George longed to remove him from the school and have his education completed by a private tutor at Nohant. Casimir was opposed to this idea. He himself had experienced a tough upbringing as a child and in the army. He did not want his son to grow into a weakling. Disinclined to believe the doctors who advised Maurice's removal, Casimir finally yielded when he saw for himself his son's disturbed condition. That Christmas the roads south were blocked by snow, but at the first thaw, early in January 1837, George left for Nohant with Maurice, calling briefly at Bourges on the way to see Michel. Eight-year-old Solange remained in Paris in the boarding school run by the Misses Martin, who declared themselves dissatisfied with her conduct and progress.

Although George had won her own way where removing Maurice from school was concerned, she could not stop worrying about his continued lack of spirits. A rising twenty-three-year-old political journalist, Eugène Pelletan, was invited to become Maurice's tutor, "as an artist at an artist's." Pelletan's tenure of office would prove relatively short-lived. It ended ignominiously with George's opening of one of his letters to a friend, where he complained that she treated him like a child, that he intended to take "a *grisette* to cure myself of women," and work as much harm as he could. These were the words of a vain, humiliated young man. He would later join the bloods who—like Roger de Beauvoir —liked to boast of having been George's lovers, a boast that cannot be proved. All the same, Pelletan would eventually be found among the considerable number of associates upon whom George could call to run her errands.

Sharing her thoughts along with Maurice throughout the first half of 1837 was the indomitable Michel. She loved them both equally, she assured her recalcitrant lover. The two days she had passed with the quarrelsome lawyer in Bourges on her return to Nohant in January had been spent nonetheless in weeping and humiliation. George observed that her tears and reproaches appeared to bore him. He seemed impervious to her worries about her son. Instead, he played variations on the shortcomings of women in general and herself in particular. His power over her struck her as singular:

> I told you the story of my life as if you had the right to know it . . . the power to change it. And you did change it. . . . No other man had exerted an intellectual influence over me; my spirit, always free and wild, had refused to be directed. I had remained myself, doubting everything, accepting only what sprang from myself. . . . You came, you taught me, and yet you were not the upright man I had dreamed of. Sometimes it even seems to me that you are the spirit of evil, when I see in you such depths of cold cruelty and egregious tyranny toward me. . . .

They stood riveted together in thought and action forever, even though their misunderstandings and differences were proving an endless source of pain.

In the midst of the continuing crisis with Michel, Marie d'Agoult arrived early in February at Nohant for a long stay. The two women had plenty of time to examine each other at close quarters. In the evenings, they read Plato, Shakespeare, Molière, the naturalist Geoffroy Saint-Hilaire (with whom George corresponded), and "talked nonsense." Marie's doubts about her relationship with Liszt were growing. The young musician came to join her briefly at the end of the month, outwardly as devoted and attentive as ever, his manner in obvious contrast with Michel's boorish conduct toward George. Still, Marie could write to a confidant: "And yet, is this love [of Liszt's] and mine anything but the sublime lie between two beings who would like to give each other the happiness which neither of them any longer believes possible for himself?" George could not help half envying their liaison while half perceiving its precarious nature.

While Marie was staying at Nohant, George was busy each night writing into the small hours. She was working on a historical novel, *Mauprat*, and also on a didactic work in letter form, the *Lettres à Marcie*. Both of these were largely inspired by her sense of the incompatible expectations of men and women, by the clash between Michel de Bourges and herself on woman's role.

The *Lettres à Marcie* appeared in *Le Monde* in installments from February 12 onward. Lamennais, newly appointed the paper's editor, welcomed the collaboration of the famous novelist who not long since had asked him to become her spiritual director. The third letter, however, was so heavily cut by Lamennais that it read as a paean to the submissive woman. George wrote to try to clarify the position with the former priest: "I do not even know if the present fate of woman has aroused your concern, amid so many religious and political preoccupations in your very full intellectual life," she proposed delicately. Although she herself had long been writing on the theme, she felt that she had never really put her thoughts in proper order.

Since she had begun the *Lettres à Marcie*, though, she wanted to enlarge the work's scope on questions relating to women. "I should like to discuss therein all duties of marriage, motherhood, etc. . . ." Explaining her intentions to Lamennais and suggesting that he allow her complete freedom, she told him that she wished to advocate divorce. So solemn a step as divorce should not be lightly undertaken, naturally, but there was no other way for exceptional spirits (such as herself, Marie, and Liszt, understood). As for herself, she added in a vigorous aside, "I should prefer to spend the rest of my life in prison rather than remarry." Her experience in these matters was broader than his own, she ventured to tell her "master."

To this appeal for a free hand Lamennais responded without enthusiasm. He did not want anything on divorce. What he required was some entertaining narrative. Despite this interchange, where George seems to have expected from Lamennais a tolerance that was beyond him, the fourth and fifth letters continued to appear. However, with the bold sixth letter, published on March 27, the series came to an abrupt end. Lamennais (whom the malicious would accuse of "so-called Greek inclinations") later observed that women are incapable of reasoning. Such were "the gracious monkish compliments" with which he thanked George for her generous contribution, noted Sainte-Beuve, who was sufficiently impressed with the fourth letter to find in it "the most admirable pages since Rousseau."

The *Lettres à Marcie* aroused a furore. Jokes in rather bad taste about the collaboration between the impotent Lélia and the celibate Believer made the rounds, but a favorite game in the salons was to name the letter one preferred. The mere fact that an intelligent and gifted woman was prepared to discuss, in public, the doubts and difficulties that oppressed her, proved sufficient to arouse controversy in 1837. The letters were addressed to a lonely, intelligent spinster, typical of those to be found in the French provinces, and who were beginning to write to George about their limited prospects. "Marcie" could easily have been George's melancholy childhood friend, Félicie Molliet, whom she (wrongly) thought to be her half-sister—unmarried, unattractive to men, high-principled. Such a woman did not seek pleasures and material liberty so much as intellectual and spiritual liberty, in a society that acted "as if, with steamships and the marvels of industry, the solution had been found for all the problems of the mind, the satisfaction of all the needs of the soul."

Once again, as in her essay on Mme Merlin's autobiography, George opposed political action for women, though now in a broader context. There were more urgent miseries to be relieved: "Amid such real and deep *poverty*, what interest do you expect proud complaints of cold intelligence to arouse? The people go hungry. . . ." Bread for the people must come first. All men must be made free, for the enslaved could not grant freedom to others.

All the same, woman is man's equal before God, although her role differs from his. She is fully entitled to the moral respect and the intellectual equality that men have denied her. The masculine conspiracy to deprive woman of the sense of her own worth, so as to dominate her by brute force, is also forcefully denounced in the *Lettres à Marcie*, where the Church is seen acting as an instrument for the subjugation of woman.

In April, the second work to derive from her altercations with Michel de Bourges, her novel *Mauprat*, began serial publication in the *Revue des deux mondes*. Sometimes regarded by George as an onerous task, nonetheless this novel of adventures set in the years immediately before the French Revolution would prove one of her most attractive and enduring works. The structure of flashbacks, the portrayal of the mysterious and terrible eyrie of the Mauprat outlaws, are thought to have been in Emily Brontë's mind when she came to write *Wuthering Heights*. George drew on local relics and legends of the feudal past: the ruined castles and their violent lords who once terrorized the inhabitants of Berry.

Her hero, the young orphaned Bernard de Mauprat, who is carried off and brutalized by his wild, depraved uncles, yearns only to possess his seventeen-year-old cousin, Edmée, brought as booty to their castle. All instinct and desire, he does not realize that Edmée secretly loves him. In her feminine pride she wishes to raise him to a nobler understanding of the relations between the sexes. He undergoes a series of trials, which include service with Washington during the American War of Independence. Suitably enlightened at last, Bernard marries Edmée and survives her. Devoted to his wife's memory, he offers poetic proof that man, however brutal in upbringing and outlook, can be brought to a properly balanced, civilized relation with a woman—in a way that Michel, apparently, could not.

Of *Mauprat*, Berlioz wrote to Liszt: "It is of immense interest, and besides, what fantastic vitality of style! If ever Mme Sand writes a play, nobody will fall asleep, you can take my word for it." The composer of the *Symphonie Fantastique* may not have been entirely impartial, for he was hoping that George would write a play with a role in mime for his "obsession," the Irish actress, Harriet Smithson, now his wife, whose talents did not extend to performing in French. Marie d'Agoult, who had joined Liszt in Paris for a few weeks, acted as intermediary for George in this and other matters, such as negotiations with Lamennais and Musset. George worked on the dramatic project for Harriet, but it came to nothing. However, it did help to turn George's thoughts toward writing for the theater, which was reputed to be highly lucrative.

During Marie d'Agoult's absence in Paris, Michel may well have visited Nohant on April 7—April, the month of their first meeting two years before. A few days afterward, George paid a twenty-four-hour visit to Bourges. "I love you more than ever," she told him, treasuring her moment of happiness. Her bliss was interrupted by the news that Solange had caught smallpox. The child was brought home from school in Paris. Fortunately, Solange had only a mild form of the disease and, with the aid of vaccine, would not be marked. Marie-Louise, one of François Rollinat's sisters (all of whom were governesses) was engaged to look after the difficult girl.

Meanwhile, George continued to ply the absent Michel with long, passionate letters. For the moment, she ceased to accuse him of various infidelities. She no longer hinted at the way he had tried to debase her one day by showing her his "conjugal bed." Instead, she endlessly poured forth her doubts, her sexual submission: "And what of you, you jackal? There are days when you hate me. . . . I want to bite, but where is the flesh that lures my teeth?" She would confess to him that she had far too much to do: "I hate my profession yet it alone helps me out of life's difficulties. There's only you, my old lion, whose burning breath and sharp nails revive my energy. . . . Come, come. . . ." In great, long lyrical sweeps, she wrote of the nightingales at Nohant, discoursed poetically on the constellations, and reflected on Byron's great poem, "Darkness," with its desolate account of the destruction of the universe. To these rhetorical outpourings, the bored Michel replied ever more sparingly in his indecipherable hand.

At the beginning of May, when Marie d'Agoult returned to Nohant accompanied by Liszt, they witnessed the struggle in George, who had just come home after another brief visit to Bourges. This struggle was soon to be exacerbated by an insensitive note from Michel. He complained about the way she was adding to his domestic battles. Women were not proper adversaries for one who aimed to combat tyrants. To dispute with women was beneath him. George was outraged at this declaration of her inferiority as a woman. His behavior urged her to become the female "Spartacus." If women are not equal with men in love, then a liaison is no less of a yoke than marriage, she told him bitterly.

All the same, she hurried once again to Bourges early in June. This short encounter marked the beginning of the end of her liaison with Michel. In her diary, sardonically entitled *Daily Conversations with the most learned and accomplished Doctor Piffoël, professor of botany and psychology,* she wrote on June 11 (the day after their disappointing reunion) an ironic parody of the Ave Maria: "Hail, Piffoël, full of grace . . . chosen among all women dupes . . ." Two days afterward she elaborated on her disillusion:

> Must one prove one's devotion at all times . . . ? Must one even sacrifice one's love of art? Must one accept repugnant faults, vices even . . . ? Must one rush, sweating, on an icy night, to satisfy a whim . . . ? No, Piffoël, doctor of psychology, you are a prize fool.

Man thinks such devotion is owing to him "simply through having issued from his mother's womb." Let a man find a woman who can do without him, he turns angry—and his anger "is punished by a smile, a word of farewell, an eternal oblivion."

So petered out, in shame and self-disgust, the last "great passion" of George's life. It consumed more than two years of her existence, and with it died her hope of a lifelong association with one she had thought a great man of action. They would still meet occasionally during the next ten years, but the spell was broken. The memory of his effort to dominate her would color her feminist pages. Never again would George allow a man to rule her.

That summer, one consolation for George, with her deep love of music, was the playing of Liszt. His piano stood in "Arabella's room" on the ground floor, just beneath her own. She could hear him trying out passages. One evening, when she and her friends were sitting on the terrace, Franz played Schubert. The tall "Princess," wearing a white veil, moved ethereally through the moonlit garden, like an embodiment of the music. In descriptive passages of great beauty, George poeticized in her diary the presence of her intimates.

On June 15, the querulous and confused Didier arrived at Nohant to an embarrassed welcome. He had the impression that George wished to avoid private conversation with him. He was shown her diary (or part of it), though, and his vanity was hurt when he found its pages full of Michel, Liszt, and Marie, to say nothing of a wounded warbler that had inspired reflections on the exploitation of woman. The entry that upset Didier most, however, ran: "Up to the 20th. —Nothing." "*I* arrived on the 15th," he confided to his own diary.

Didier left for a few days in July, returning to find, besides her rocklike friend François Rollinat, a bearded twenty-four-year-old dramatist from Mauritius, Félicien Mallefille, Maurice's new tutor. Also present was the celebrated actor Pierre Bocage (whom she had originally encountered in the circle, at a first night in February 1833). Observing the warmth between George and Bocage, Didier decided to leave. He disdained to have a mere actor as his rival. Before his departure, however, he had a long chat with Marie. According to the (scarcely loyal) opinion of the "Princess," George was on the moral downgrade.

Four days after the Fellows themselves left Nohant toward the end of July, George set out to spend a holiday at Fontainebleau. She was registered as Mme Gratio at the Hôtel Britannique, where she had stayed with Musset four years earlier. This time, her companion for a few days among the rocks of Franchard was Bocage. Now in his late thirties, Bocage cut a dashing figure. Originally by trade a weaver, he shared George's radical views. Although their liaison did not last long—he was about to leave on a tour of Belgium—Bocage would afterward stage and appear in some of her plays. From Fontainebleau, George could write to a friend that "my life has reached the final stage of disenchantment."

A month earlier, George had learned that her mother was seriously ill. The news had shaken her: ". . . poor woman, I did not realize I loved her so." Over the years, George had visited Sophie from time to time in the rue du Faubourg-Poissonnière, sometimes welcome, sometimes not. From Fontainebleau George hastened frequently to Paris. With the aid of her half-sister, Caroline, she tried to cheer Sophie's last days. The sight of her mother, suffering from an incurable liver disease, disturbed George deeply. To add to her worries at this cruel moment, she received a warning from Hippolyte that Casimir was planning to abduct Maurice. George arranged for her son's new tutor, Mallefille, to bring the boy from Nohant to Fontainebleau.

On August 19, Sophie died. George was not there. She arrived to give her mother "a last kiss she did not feel." The funeral took place two days later, with Casimir in attendance. George privately penned the obituary of her mother, once to be easily fobbed off with cheap compliments: "Her last words were: 'Comb my hair.' Poor, dear little woman: shrewd, intelligent, artistic, quick-tempered, generous, a bit crazy, cruel in small matters yet kind in important ones. She made me suffer much and my greatest ills came from her." As for Caroline, although there was no close feeling between the sisters, George tried to help her financially: "I can say I no longer have any family. I have not been happy in that regard. . . ." Before the end, was there in fact a new understanding and reconciliation between Sophie and her daughter, as the latter liked to imply? Later, when George had her mother's body moved to Nohant, the tomb was not placed next to those of George's father and grandmother, where there was then room for it. Sophie's memorial stands forever apart, in token perhaps of those great "ills" that her daughter could never quite forget.

After the death of Sophie, which could not but stimulate George's urge to live, the subdued novelist returned to Fontainebleau. She and Maurice went riding alone through the forest, or they took a picnic and spent the day collecting flowers and butterflies. At night, George continued to write. *Les Maîtres mosaïstes*, a tale of the persecution and vindication of true artists, set in Renaissance Venice, was already appearing in serial form. She was planning another Venetian story for the end of the year. This was to be *La Dernière Aldini*, about a proud plebeian singer called Lélio (originally the gondolier Nello) who was loved by a noble widow—and then later by her daughter—but who declined to marry either. The far-fetched tale seems to reflect obliquely upon any alliance between plebeian artist and aristocrat (and hence upon Liszt and Marie). The Fellows would not care for it. George maintained that the book was just a potboiler. It has moments of charm, however, and the theme of the artist's lofty view of himself and of his role in society made a great appeal, at a time when musicians in particular might be received but were subject to humiliation.

It was when George was about to return to Nohant with Maurice in mid-September that she heard the extraordinary news. Casimir had descended on Nohant and, after a struggle with Mlle Rollinat, had carried off the screaming Solange to Guillery. It seemed an incredible act of revenge against George for engaging in litigation to stop his allowance from the moment that he came into his inheritance, on the death of his stepmother. Casimir knew George was tired and distressed by her mother's death. Moreover, he had never shown much affection for Solange. George rushed to Paris. Maurice was deposited with her friend, Charlotte Marliani. Frantic, George used the telegraph, she ran to the police, she besieged the ministries and, armed with the requisite papers, she set out for Nérac in the company of Mallefille, a lawyer's clerk, and Bocage's manservant. After three days and nights of concentrated activity and traveling by post-chaise, she arrived at Nérac, where she enlisted the aid of the young sous-préfet (the future Baron Haussmann, creator of modern Paris). There was a sour exchange between Casimir and George on the doorstep of Guillery as Solange was handed to her mother.

Guillery, from whence she had written her lofty thoughts to Aurélien de Sèze so long ago, inspired her with an impulse to revisit the Pyrenees. With Mallefille and Solange (as intrepid on horseback as her mother), she pressed on as far as the Marboré (the Cirque de Gavarnie). By the beginning of October, George was back in Nohant, while Mallefille left to bring Maurice home from Paris. Sometime toward the end of the year, the obliging Mallefille was promoted to lover, providing a more gentle kind of affection than the strong-minded Michel.

In her diary that autumn, George reflected upon all that had happened in recent months, her mother's death, the abduction of Solange, adding bitterly: "You saw Franchard again, and with whom?" (So much for Bocage.) "You saw the Marboré again, and with what?" (So much for the good-natured Mallefille.) "I can't stop. The lesson of this farce you like to call my life is the same as that of the legend of the Wandering Jew. I am forbidden to die or to rest." She was thoroughly demoralized. To a doctor friend, she wrote: "Have you found a remedy for the pains of the spirit . . . ?" The faithful Rollinat, who saw her at the turn of the year, was disturbed by her exhausted state and her persistent low spirits.

Maurice's poor health continued to worry her during the winter of 1838. George herself suffered from severe rheumatism that affected her right arm to such a degree that she could not use a pen. She had to dictate everything to Mallefille. She dreamed of one day earning enough money to travel south with Maurice for the winter.

On February 19, 1838, Honoré de Balzac, who was staying with friends near Issoudun, some twenty-seven miles distant, wrote to inquire if he might call at Nohant. Immensely energetic and hard-working, Balzac had taken Jules Sandeau's part in 1833; he had engaged the indolent fellow as his secretary-collaborator; and had come to rue the day he gave the winning Jules his friendship and trust. During the intervening years, George had occasionally met the author of *La Peau de chagrin*. She had refused to become involved in Buloz's quarrel with her colleague; Balzac might be a detestable stylist, but she would never do anything against him.

As for Balzac, with his passionate interest in human fauna, he remained curious about this gifted woman who failed to fit into any obvious category. Besides, he wanted to obtain her double autograph as Aurore Dudevant and George Sand for his beloved correspondent, Eve Hanska, the intriguing Polish-born lady who had written to him out of the blue, like so many of his admiring female readers. In her first letter to Balzac, Mme Hanska, middle-aged wife of an elderly Ukrainian nobleman, urged the novelist to portray women in a nobler light.

The author of *Physiologie du mariage* (who would sometimes compare himself to the faithful Ralph in *Indiana* when writing to Mme Hanska, now his mistress) arrived at Nohant at half-past seven on the evening of February 24. He found George in red trousers, yellow slippers and dressing gown, smoking an after-dinner cigar by her fireside. He registered George's double chin, her nicotine-stained fingers. To his amazement, Balzac discovered that her timetable resembled his own; though whereas George went to bed at six in the morning and rose at noon, he liked to go to bed at six in the evening and rise at midnight. On successive days, the two novelists talked from late afternoon to early the following morning, getting to know each other better than ever before.

Doubtless to avoid arousing Mme Hanska's jealousy, Balzac emphasized the masculine element in George (which, indeed, counterbalanced the feminine element in himself). "I chatted with a fellow writer. She has lofty virtues, of the sort that society misconstrues." Their discussions turned on his project for a play (which George encouraged), but above all on the question of marriage and free love. Here, George's views startled him:

For, as she said with immense pride (I shouldn't have ventured to think it where I am concerned), "Since we are preparing a revolution as regards the way people will live in the future, I am struck as much by the disadvantages of the one as of the other."

While reiterating his notion of freedom for girls before marriage, but fidelity after it, Balzac liked to feel that he had convinced George of the need for the institution of matrimony.

Ostentatiously conservative, he was as complex a creature as George. A few years earlier, he had humorously suggested to Liszt that a man could not be complete without seven women: one for the home; one for the heart; one for the mind; a fourth to act as servant; a fifth to serve one's whims; a sixth to be loathed; a seventh to be perennially pursued but never possessed. Mme Caroline Marbouty, who had accompanied him to Italy as pseudo-George Sand in 1836, observed that he needed the act of love merely as physical relief; otherwise his entire life was devoted to his work. While protesting unswerving constancy to the suspicious Mme Hanska, the remote mistress who would eventually marry him shortly before his death, Balzac possessed a string of (often titled) mistresses. In theory, though—and without logic—he found it difficult to accept equal freedom for married women.

To Balzac, George appeared inherently "chaste"—as indeed, paradoxically, she was in one part of her rich character. If she praised virtue one day and scorned it the next, she remained true to the sensation of the moment. In Balzac's view, George was a remarkably good mother, though he disapproved of the way she dressed Solange in boy's clothes and he thought Maurice feeble and precocious for his age. What particularly impressed him about George, apart from her contempt for the public, was her self-criticism: "She knows and says of herself exactly what I think of her without my saying it: that she lacks power of conception, the gift for constructing plans, the ability to attain to the truth, the art of pathos, but that, without knowing the French language properly, she has *style*; this is true." It may be doubted whether Balzac had as profound a respect for George's talent as she would show for his. While recognizing his clumsiness, she would be among the first to proclaim his originality and greatness, in an essay published a few years after his death, partly from syphilis, at fifty-one. (Here, George proved her acumen as a critic. In contrast, Sainte-Beuve maintained that Balzac was inferior to Sand as a writer, while Flaubert considered the creator of *La Comédie humaine* essentially "second-rate.")

At one stage, hostess and guest confided in each other their disillusion

with Sandeau. She told Balzac how she had also been the dupe of Marie
Dorval (a revealing admission, this, in the light of the actress's influence
on George's wild gallop to freedom in 1833 and their continuing friendship), and more recently, the dupe of Lamennais, of Liszt and Marie
d'Agoult, among others. Balzac took away with him from Nohant not
just the taste for smoking latakia or Turkish tobacco in a hookah, as
a stimulant to work, but also the theme of the galley slaves of love as
represented by Franz and Marie. This literary gift, which George felt
she herself could scarcely use, would form the *donnée* of the novel
Béatrix, to be counted among Balzac's most subtle works, where George
figures as Félicité des Touches, otherwise Camille Maupin, the brilliant
and equivocal writer who becomes one of the recurring figures of *La
Comédie humaine*. The two novelists' conversation on love and marriage
would also inspire Balzac's strange *Mémoires de deux jeunes mariées*,
dedicated to George.

When Balzac visited Nohant, he found George at a major turning
point in her life. With his sharp eye, he saw that Mallefille was her
"inferior" and that she would not find lasting contentment in that
quarter. Didier, Bocage, Mallefille—these were temporary companions,
offering refuge from the profound loneliness of the author's existence
in the study. To Balzac, her intellectual equal, she revealed her simplicity
as a hard-working writer like himself as well as a proud awareness of
her revolutionary significance. It was at once true and a splendid performance that regained her Balzac's friendship. Disillusioned by free
love as she had been by platonic love or marriage, George was yearning
for some more stable form of companionship. When she found it with
a musician of genius, she would enter upon the period of her controversial maturity as a writer and of her extended fame.

PART V

Queen and Mother

Aphrodite-Athene

How good you are and how beneficent is your friendship. . . . You must live and triumph. Queen, Queen, Queen!

Pierre Leroux, letter to George Sand, October 1837 [?]

. . . for as long as you wish, you will always be our queen, everyone here accepts your queenship.

François Buloz, letter to George Sand, August 9, 1839

I N THE spring of 1838, approaching her thirty-fourth birthday, George could look stunning. A young artist, Auguste Charpentier, who came to Nohant to paint her portrait, was lost in admiration of her beauty and graciousness. To him, she appeared twenty-eight at most. In stature, she might seem too short. Her features were not faultless, either: the double chin noted by Balzac; the markedly aquiline nose that inspired her choice of the nickname Piffoël; the rather pendulous lower lip and, according to Heine, the not entirely attractive though good-humored smile. Eyewitnesses agreed, however, on the total grand and unforgettable impression left by the head itself. It was not just the long, smooth, dark hair, the large, expressionless eyes. Nor was it solely her voice, soft and low, and her unaffected way of speaking. Rather, her attraction lay in the enigmatic fascination of her multiform personality.

This was the woman, elegantly dressed in a simple black gown relieved by a large cameo, whom the twenty-eight-year-old Frédéric Chopin saw in the Parisian salon of her friend, the warm-hearted chatter-box Charlotte Marliani. George had come to Paris to pursue her lawsuit against Casimir, now lord of Guillery, for the recovery of the Hôtel de Narbonne and its income. Dissatisfied by the brief sexual relationships of the previous year, inwardly uncommitted to the dull though helpful Mallefille, she was looking for a change in her style of life to suit the change in her intellectual outlook. For she was now deep in the study of the socio-religious philosophy of Pierre Leroux, whose ideas she would propagate unceasingly for many years. Regarding herself as the mere handmaid of Leroux, she was largely responsible for popularizing the theories of the metaphysician and socialist.

As for Chopin, George had known him socially at least since the autumn of 1836, when she took rooms in the Hôtel de France along with Liszt and Marie d'Agoult. Chopin's first impression of her was unfavorable. He reported to his family in Warsaw (in a letter of which this is the sole extract to survive) that he had met "a great celebrity," Mme Dudevant, known as George Sand, and found her antipathetic. This impression did not last long. When Marie d'Agoult was staying at Nohant in 1837, George repeatedly invited various notable Polish members of her guest's circle: the long-suffering poet in exile, Adam Mickiewicz; another friend of Chopin's, Albert Grzymala, a freemason who speculated on the stock exchange; and Chopin himself. According to Liszt, Chopin was quite keen to visit Nohant. Indeed, Chopin told Anton Wodzinski, brother of the girl to whom he was secretly en-gaged, that he was thinking of accepting George Sand's invitation. Nothing came of it, however, because Chopin could not make up his mind.

It was Liszt who had urged George to see Chopin when she visited Paris. She promised to shake "Sopin's" hand in the absurdly childish private language in which Piffoël and the Fellows indulged. Her genuine sympathy for martyred Poland went back to September 1831, when she expressed shock at the capture of Warsaw by the Russians. At Nohant, she and Casimir entertained Polish exiles who had settled in some num-bers in the district. George actively tried to help at least one painter among them.

Since September 1831, Chopin had been living in Paris, though not precisely as a political exile. He left Warsaw before the uprising, a sheltered only son and musical prodigy, gently pushed out of the be-loved family nest in order to make his way in the world. To Poland, transfigured in his music, he would never return. Strangely, he thus imitated, in reverse, the journey made by his French father, Nicolas Chopin, son of peasant wine-growers of Lorraine. Chopin's father left Marainville before the French Revolution for Poland, and did not again set foot in his native land. (During the long years that the composer lived in France, he never visited his two aunts in Marainville, perhaps did not even know of their existence.) Chopin senior, a Voltairean, married somewhat above his station a devoutly Catholic Polish girl, the poor relative of a well-born family. He had risen to become tutor to the sons of the Polish aristocracy, in whose company young Frédéric was educated. The pianist's princely air, his perfect manners, his elegance, partly derived from this upbringing among the scions of the nobility.

At first, Chopin experienced a difficult struggle in Paris, until he was introduced by Prince Valentin Radziwill to the Rothschilds. With success in society, which brought him many pupils, the young dandy was able to indulge his expensive tastes in apparel and perfumes, and to furnish his dove-grey-papered rooms with chairs covered in white silk. He unwisely neglected to follow his thrifty peasant-born father's reiterated advice to put something aside for a rainy day. Fragile in health—only his coughing was permanent, Marie d'Agoult once remarked unkindly—Chopin loved late nights in Parisian society, which were so damaging to his well-being. With his originally straight fair hair carefully curled, his vulnerable blue-grey eyes (noted by Liszt), he dazzled small gatherings of connoisseurs in the salons not only with the poetry of his compositions but also with his talent for mimicry (his repertory of stereotypes including a phlegmatic Englishman and a greasy Jew). So experienced a judge as Bocage could say that the pianist should have been an actor. Here, in the lively and sometimes hurtful wit that covered a deep melancholy as well as in the poetic and improvisatory quality of his imagination, Chopin shared something with George's interior self.

Where he differed from George, with her constantly varied confession in letters, diaries, and novels, was in his reticent, even secretive nature. He did not like people to know too much about him, partly from superstition and partly because he was well aware of the fragile foundation on which his aristocratic elegance rested. Unlike George, too, he could be moody. His thoughts easily turned to gloom and he always feared the worst. When he had visited, alone, the deserted St. Stephen's cathedral in Vienna, over seven years before, it was not from piety (he inherited from his father a taste for Voltaire), but to contemplate the tombs, overcome by an inner "lugubrious harmony" and the sense of his own solitude. In the revealing corpse-haunted journal he wrote at Stuttgart at the time of the fall of Warsaw, he envisioned the agony of his father and mother, the violent death of his dearest friends, the rape of his sisters and of Constantia Gladkowska, the young singer he worshipped from afar. In his frustration, he invoked a cruel vengeance. Despite his delicacy, there existed in him a mine of buried aggression that exploded at times in scathing remarks about Polish exiles, Jews, his editors, anyone whom he fancied had crossed him, as well as in his revolutionary compositions.

In experience, Chopin was a mere child in comparison with George. As a youth, he had had a crush on his school friend, Titus Woyciechowski. Chopin long kept Titus's letters next to his heart. As a youth, too, he may have paid the regulation visit to prostitutes, the supposed prophylactic against the dread madness allegedly induced by masturbation. Writing to a compatriot, he alluded to "the souvenir" of Theresa and his subsequent affliction, which deterred him from associating with Parisian prostitutes, in whose blatant presence, as in the public warnings against venereal disease, he evinced considerable interest on his arrival in the capital. When, on two separate occasions, he reported being (wrongly) taken for a seducer, he may well have been indulging in the youthful masculine bravado he thought *de rigueur*. He had an eye for a pretty woman; he liked to flirt. But his true ideal was the "pure young girl": the singer, Constantia Gladkowska, and later, his childhood playmate, Maria Wodzinska. When his engagement to Maria, kept secret on the insistence of her mother, was gradually allowed to lapse in a particularly chilling and humiliating way for Chopin, he did nothing about it (just as he had done nothing actively to win Constantia).

Eight months had passed since Chopin's secret betrothal to Maria Wodzinska had faded for good by the time of his return from London in the summer of 1837. He was a wounded and disillusioned young man. The sympathetic interest of George, whom he met often in the spring of 1838, helped to soothe his hurt. They both loved the theater and the opera. She thought music the greatest of the arts, and she was an intent listener. Something more than sympathy grew between them. Given Chopin's character, the initiative lay with her. A warm note—"A certain party dotes on you. George" (to which Marie Dorval added "So do I") would be found in Chopin's album after his death. It was George who imprinted the first kiss.

Still, Chopin hesitated. He would never be a man of decision; he was far too much of a worrier. Besides, a liaison was unknown territory for him. From Nohant George wrote a lengthy letter to Albert Grzymala, which some have found particularly shocking. She took Grzymala, a man of the world, into her confidence, as formerly she had confided in Casimir (for Aurélien), in Regnault (for Sandeau), in Sainte-Beuve (for Mérimée and Musset). This pattern may be seen as the need to analyze and explain her emotions for a father confessor, to adopt an estimable role—a mixture of perfect candor and something less than candor.

George was not sure of her ground; hence her maneuvering. Chopin had plainly betrayed his feeling for her, but, characteristically, had otherwise not shown his hand. If Chopin remained attached to his Polish beloved, George did not want to come between them. The young composer seemed to her to be too frail to withstand emotional upheavals. Besides, on her side there was Mallefille, a "perfect" creature, though malleable as wax (whose caresses admittedly now embarrassed her). Since she could not settle permanently in Paris because of Maurice's indifferent health, perhaps she and Chopin might fuse briefly from time to time. She would be his "Italy," a place one yearned for and loved to visit, but where one did not stay for long. In short, although she wanted him, she felt that in many respects she did not know him at all. "I have only seen the aspect of his being lit by sunlight," she observed perspicaciously.

As for physical consummation, it might be a woman's deepest and most enigmatic secret, but she had no theories about it. She longed to discover some theory to accord with her instincts and emotions, though in vain. "I've changed my views twenty times." In all the varieties of love she had experienced (the love of wife, sister, mother, nun, poet), she had been perfectly sincere at the moment: "My being entered into these various phases, like the sun. . . ." Superficially, she might appear mad or hypocritical, she owned, yet in reality she was a seeker after truth, beauty, perfection, "weak in judgment, often absurd, always in good faith. . . . That is my life, dear friend, and you see it's not up to much." Her keen probing of the self is often marred not only by self-justification but by self-approval. The desire for truth, which she certainly possessed, made a strange and incompatible bedfellow for her irresistible urge to idealize.

What seems particularly modern in the letter to Grzymala is the frank defense of sexual love from the woman's viewpoint. She had received the impression that, although Chopin wanted her, he was holding back partly because he did not wish to "sully" their love with physical union. Such an attitude was repugnant to her. What wretched woman had given him so poor an idea of physical love? "So he has had a mistress unworthy of him?" She disliked the very term "physical love." It gave a false idea of something holy: "the divine mystery, the most serious act in life. . . ." Moreover, for "lofty spirits" there was no such thing as a purely fleshly love.

Whatever advice Grzymala may have imparted to George and Frédéric respectively on studying this singular letter, they became lovers sometime in June, after her return to Paris. In July, Delacroix, a friend to both, began to paint a joint portrait of the lovers. (A vandal later cut the unfinished canvas in two, though a preparatory pencil sketch remains.) Chopin is seated at the piano, while George, half in shadow, listens to him in rapt delight, almost as if she could shape the sounds with her fingers. Just as Delacroix has captured the inner tormented soul of Chopin, so he has caught the secret soul of the contradictory George Sand, whose simple essence is dreaming and musicality.

Both Liszt and Heine were agreed that she was supremely a listener. And Heine once remarked:

> Rather is she taciturn from pride, because she does not think you worthy of the favor of her being generous with her wit, or even because of egoism, seeking to absorb within herself the best of your words, in order to let them fructify in her soul and employ them later in her writings.

Musset had pointed out to Heine this characteristic of hers—of not giving anything away in conversation "from avarice" and of always drawing something from it: "She has a great advantage over us there," Musset told Heine. "With an amiable and sometimes odd smile, she listens, when others speak. . . ." Delacroix portrayed George the listener, counterpart of the woman so voluble in her writings.

By September, George could report to Delacroix that she had spent three ecstatic, cloudless months with Frédéric: "You think it cannot last . . . ? If I consult my memory and my reason, it certainly cannot. If I consult the state of my heart and my poetry, it seems to me it cannot end." Mallefille, unaware, had been dispatched with Maurice to spend a holiday in Normandy.

George was living "like a poet" as "Mme Dupin" in a confined attic in the rue Laffitte, whose walls shook with the rumble of every passing omnibus. She was working "like a galley slave" on a Faustian drama, *Les Sept Cordes de la lyre* (having interrupted her spiritual thriller, *Spiridion*, to do so). In her symbolic drama, which juxtaposes the limitations of reason with the mysterious insights of poetic vision, it is the heroine who, in a state of trance, becomes the seer bewailing the sufferings caused by the new industrial society. The ecstatic rhetoric of *Les Sept Cordes de la lyre* would meet with incomprehension.

This work is among the earliest of her writings to betray the strongly marked influence of her friend and mentor, Pierre Leroux, the "guiding star" who, at thirty-nine, had actively entered her life roughly at the same time as Chopin, toward the end of 1836. Two years before, Sainte-Beuve had recommended the writings of the former carbonaro as a cure for her scepticism, but she could not understand them. By the autumn of 1837, however, she had fallen under the spell of Leroux's philosophy, so rich in poetry, as Marie d'Agoult put it. Despite the common element of poetry, superficially no two men could have been less alike than Chopin and Leroux. A rough diamond, stocky, untidy, with tousled hair and intelligent eyes, Leroux was a family man with numerous children and dependents, poor, plebeian, and proud of it. He wore no gloves, while Chopin could scarcely be parted from his. Leroux's curiosity was insatiable—he wrote on literature, aesthetics, history, religion, metaphysics, psychology—whereas Chopin, though interested in new scientific discoveries, cared deeply for little outside music.

Originally, Leroux had made his name as a journalist. His early writings, critical of the moral state of society, deeply stirred a number of poets and writers. The young Sainte-Beuve had become associated with him on the influential journal, *Le Globe*, which Leroux had helped to found. Differing from Enfantin on the question of marriage, Leroux left the Saint-Simonian movement at the time of the schism of Bazard in 1831. His aim was to produce a synthesis of existing knowledge, and to this end he worked with Jean Reynaud on the production of a New Encyclopedia. It was through Pierre Leroux that the word "socialism" entered general use, in an article published in 1834. Not only was he a stimulating literary critic, he held enlightened views on women. But what really attracted George to his writings was the positive quality, the element of continuity in his view that every man is Humanity; above all, the propagation of a new religion based on creative progress, humanitarianism, and reconciliation. It was as if she had discovered a key to the universe of the future. George was not the only writer to consider

Leroux, with his humanitarian gospel, a new Plato and a new Christ. He fulfilled a spiritual need at a time when there was an upsurge of hope in social regeneration.

Leroux himself flattered George's passionate desire to be good and to do good, treating her as his lady bountiful. In addition, he gave her a new and not entirely fortunate literary ambition. As he wrote in 1834: Art is both expression of the present and prophecy of the future, striving, like the rest of human knowledge, toward a single goal. But art that fails to reach for this goal "rapidly perishes." In short, he convinced her of the inferiority of any art that was indifferent to social good. She began to look askance upon the fresh stories of her youth. When Buloz complained about the "mysticism" of *Les Sept Cordes de la lyre*, she would respond with spirit. She did not want to keep on writing the same type of book. She hoped to have escaped for good from the exhausted genre represented by her popular novel *André* or by the erotic tales of Balzac, into something new and rather more profound.

To Leroux, George entrusted the task of dealing with Mallefille who, enlightened at last about her defection, was creating jealous scenes and threatening to do violence to herself or Frédéric. George felt she had no need to reproach herself. Mallefille was to be informed that women "do not belong to man by right of brute force." Still, the situation was unpleasant. Besides, after the jealous André-François Chazal shot and wounded his wife, Flora Tristan, rumors were current that George Sand had been assassinated by her husband. It would be politic to get away.

With her head full of Leroux's theories, she began to formulate the long-treasured plan of a winter working holiday in a Mediterranean country. A warm climate had been prescribed for Maurice as well as for Frédéric. Italy was the obvious choice, but the Spaniards she had encountered in Charlotte Marliani's salon sang the praises of Majorca. Besides Manuel Marliani, the Spanish consul himself, there was Mendizábal, the liberal statesman (both of them natives of Cadiz). Mendizábal, a man of huge stature and florid complexion, was of Jewish ancestry—the Spanish caricaturists liked to portray him with a tail. As Prime Minister he had recently implemented a policy that nationalized church property. He was thus far from popular with the devout. Any letters of recommendation from the Spanish statesman could prove an embarrassment on Majorca. Moreover, no one seems to have pointed out beforehand to the innocent travelers that, since 1833,

Spain had been engaged in civil war; that bands of Carlist partisans were roaming Catalonia; that war refugees had converged on Majorca and had overextended the island's limited services. (Indeed, even the mainland itself rarely saw visitors—so far only a few English and French painters and writers had ventured there.)

Discreetly, George set out beforehand with Maurice, Solange, a chambermaid, three trunks and numerous packages. Chopin traveled separately, with Mendizábal (who was returning to Madrid), to join George's party at Perpignan. The Marquis Astolphe de Custine, patron of the arts, author, and a well-known homosexual, much attracted to Chopin, commented acidly on the composer's departure, to Sophie Gay: "The poor fellow does not see that this woman has the love of a vampire! He is following her to Spain. . . . He didn't dare tell me where he was going: he talked only of his need for a sunny climate and rest. Rest with a ghoul for Corinne!" In contrast, a few years later Adam Mickiewicz would confide to a fellow poet, Mme Juste Olivier, that Chopin was George Sand's "evil genius, her moral vampire, her cross. . . ." From divergent viewpoints, both Custine and Mickiewicz charitably envisaged each partner as potential death to the other.

On November 1, the party embarked at Port-Vendres for Barcelona, where they spent a few days before crossing to Palma. The old city of Palma, dominated by its cathedral, with its Moorish Almudaina, its sunlit port, its palms and pomegranates, delighted the exuberant visitors. What gradually began to please them less, as working artists, was the difficulty of finding suitably quiet, spacious accommodation where George could complete *Spiridion* (for which Buloz was pressing her) and Chopin finish his Preludes. The type of inn that Palma then boasted was unsuited to their requirements.

After much haggling, George rented a country house, So'n Vent, a few miles outside Palma, at Establiments. At first, all went well. But though pleasantly warm in the daytime, the house was cold at night and had no fireplace. It was tricky to manage the brazier, which smoked. That year, the rains came early. Chopin, who had been well enough to take long walks with Maurice, caught a severe cold and began coughing badly.

George had not expected to have to spend her hard-earned cash to purchase saucepans, sheets, furniture, to set up a household from scratch. As she put it ironically to Charlotte Marliani, for luxuries like chamber-pots you have to send to Barcelona. The lack of common necessities would not have bothered her unduly were it not for Chopin and the children. Chopin could not face the food, cooked in lard or in the un-refined olive oil that was in general use in Spain until relatively recently.

Consequently, George found herself doing much of the cooking. She had to help her chambermaid, who complained about excessive work. At the same time, she was giving the children lessons, educating Maurice particularly in "Leroux's gospel." Each evening, she had to read grammar, philosophy, history, in order to prepare for the next day's lessons. Each night, she worked at *Spiridion* or at the second version of *Lélia*. In addition, she nursed Chopin, wracked with severe bouts of coughing.

The Majorcan doctors who examined Chopin diagnosed tuberculosis. However primitive Majorca might seem in other respects, in medicine the inhabitants had profited from the learning of Moors and Jews, and believed the disease to be contagious, whereas in northern Europe ignorance prevailed. The Majorcans were thus reluctant to have any contact with Chopin. George, strong in her early training under Deschartres and Stéphane, was thoroughly outraged at what she considered Majorcan barbarism and inhumanity. This sense of outrage was increased when the proprietor of So'n Vent told them to leave his house forthwith.

For a few days, George and her dependents took brief refuge with the French vice-consul in Palma. On December 15 they set out for the village of Valldemosa, on the mountainous north side of the island. George had rented a cell, consisting of three spacious rooms, in the Charterhouse of Valldemosa, whose monks had been dispossessed a few years earlier. On the eve of their departure, she confided to Charlotte Marliani that the trip had proved in many ways "a frightful fiasco."

Nonetheless, both George and Frédéric were truly delighted with the poetic site, worthy of Byron. From the terrace of the Charterhouse, where each cell had its own private flower garden and tiled Moorish water tank, they overlooked a bosky valley between slopes of vines, cypresses, and orange trees. The sea, though not far off, was hidden by the mountains. In a certain light, one sometimes had the illusion that one could see it, a sliver on the horizon. A tall, solitary palm tree below the terrace would figure in *Spiridion*, which George was trying to finish. The long, deserted arcades of the great cloister, the quiet cemetery, blended with reminiscences of her English convent to inspire the ambience of that curious novel.

With the rains, the path up to the Charterhouse turned to a morass. The wind lamented through the desolate cloister. Chopin had good moments, when he could compose at his "pitiful" rented piano, but there were others when he was extremely low. George's rheumatism returned with the chilly damp. She went on as before, however, looking after Chopin, cooking, cleaning, writing, teaching the children. This last task proved more arduous than she had expected. If Maurice continued to show aptitude for drawing and absorbed history or philosophy with relative docility, Solange, though quick, was lazy and often rebellious. George was pursued by financial worries, about the sale of a farm, Côte-Noire, established on the estate by Casimir, and the repairs to the Hôtel de Narbonne, which had since reverted to her under the final property settlement with her husband in July. To the repentant Hippolyte, now anxious to please his half-sister by looking after these affairs of hers, she found time to send lengthy and detailed letters of advice. Her present style of life could not continue, she felt. She was tired after more than six years of virtually uninterrupted writing. Now she had added teaching to her daily burden. ". . . I must be made of iron to stand up to what I do," she told Hippolyte.

What made things so much more difficult for her at Valldemosa was the general unhelpfulness and even hostility of the villagers. They were not used to foreigners, let alone those with advanced views. The inhabitants were upset to find that neither George and her family nor Chopin attended mass. Her daughter ran about dressed in blouse and trousers. These heathens, Moslems, or worse still, Jews, could therefore be charged high prices for fish, eggs, vegetables. In mid-January 1839, an inveterate Italian-Polish traveler, an acquaintance of Chopin's, Carlo Dembowski (the son of Stendhal's beloved, Métilde Dembowska), called bringing letters and newspapers for George. To Dembowski the parish priest confided that, according to the Charterhouse apothecary, the French lady actually rolled her own cigarettes, slept by day, and smoked and wrote all night. What could this odd creature possibly be doing in Majorca in midwinter?

These simple folk would have been even more shocked had they known what she was writing in her cell each night. For it was nothing less than an attempt to replace Catholicism with a new faith, one without need of victims, hellfire, and eternal punishment. The founder of this religion, a seventeenth-century Jew named Hebronius, had been converted to Lutheranism and later to Catholicism. Still dissatisfied as a monk, in his tireless quest for truth he had ultimately created a new gospel, buried with him in the tomb. As Spiridion, he appeared in spirit to the rare seekers he hoped to enlighten.

Hebronius-Spiridion, who may seem a purely literary invention, could easily have been modeled on someone like Gustave d'Eichtal (so typical of the lost, newly emancipated Jews). D'Eichtal wrote to Enfantin: "I was born a Jew, and had faith in Judaism. At fourteen, I converted to Catholicism and had the most ardent Catholic faith. At nineteen, I embraced the Saint-Simonian faith. . . . Finally, Father, after ten years of incomplete faith, I met you and you converted me to the new religious faith." With her allegorical mystery tale of a quest for spiritual truth, George touched a nerve in many of her contemporaries. The remark of the monk Alexis, that there are no atheists, that their despair is a cry to the veiled Deity, would find an echo in Dostoevsky. As for the one-time seminarist Ernest Renan, future author of a controversial life of Jesus, he would proclaim his indebtedness, asserting that *Spiridion* provided an essential image in his religious dreams.

The presence of the forcibly converted Jews, or *xuetas*, on Majorca intruded upon George's imagination. Her attitude toward Jews was ambivalent. In one respect, they appeared as precursors like Hebronius, or as unfortunate victims of that instrument of Catholic barbarism, the Inquisition (which was not definitively abolished in Spain until as late as 1834). Indeed, until her encounter with Pierre Leroux and with Chopin, George had not manifested much interest in Jews or their historic fate. In her drama *Les Sept Cordes de la lyre*, though, she disguised Mephistopheles as a cunning Jewish peddler. Ironically, as tough in financial negotiations with Casimir or with Buloz—now called "a Jew"— as Chopin could be with his music publishers, George was scathing about Majorcan "Jewish money-grubbing." Such remarks may be attributed partly to her association with Chopin, noted (like Liszt) for prejudice against Jews, and partly to her enthusiasm for Pierre Leroux, for whom "the Jewish spirit" meant "the financial spirit." As an eager disciple of Leroux, George could not remain unscathed by this influential strain in one aspect of early French socialist thought.

Chopin's condition continued to worry her intensely. With the arrival of the piano forwarded by the distinguished music publisher and piano maker, Camille Pleyel, on which a heavy duty had to be paid, Chopin had brightened somewhat. He was able to complete the Preludes and to work on the Polonaise in C minor, as well as the second Ballade in F major and the Scherzo in C sharp minor. However, much as he appreciated the moon rising over the orange trees, the eagles soaring overhead, the scenic beauty, he felt out of his element at Valldemosa. To a friend in Paris he wrote: "Here I am, my hair uncurled, no white gloves, and pale as usual. . . . Silence. . . . You can cry out . . . silence still. In a word, I am writing to you from a very strange place." The isolation influenced his nervous state as much as the damp affected his physical condition.

By the second week of February he was so poorly that the exhausted George determined to leave. After the rough journey through the mountains to Palma in an unsprung conveyance (for, in dread of contagion, nobody would lend them a carriage), Chopin suffered a hemorrhage. He continued to spit blood on the crossing to Barcelona, made in company with a malodorous herd of pigs. A doctor on a French brig harbored at Barcelona managed to stop the bleeding. George swore that if ever she wrote about the Majorcans, it would be with gall—a promise she kept.

In her distress about Chopin, George was eager to return to France. Only there, she felt, would he have proper treatment. After a brief rest, the party embarked for Marseilles, where they were to stay for more than two months. Under the care of Dr. Cauvière, a physician George had met at Mme Marliani's, the sick composer began slowly to improve. According to the good doctor, there was nothing seriously wrong with the invalid. To Charlotte Marliani, George confessed that she was responsible for three children, and that Chopin was not the one who concerned her the least.

Despite the improvement in his health, he still needed constant care. The slightest thing could upset his nerves. He hated to be left alone for a moment. Without the children's company or her readings, he soon grew bored. "My angels," Chopin called George, as though she were in herself more than one. "You know, you would love her even more if you knew her as I do now," he wrote to Grzymala, adding, "I know now what it means to look after someone." By mid-April, he was sufficiently restored to be able to play Schubert on the organ at the funeral service for their friend, the socially committed singer Nourrit (who had killed himself in Naples).

In addition to nursing Chopin, George was working extremely hard. The door was closed to literary beggars and idlers eager to glimpse the celebrated pair. Here, in Marseilles, George composed her long *Essai sur le drame fantastique*, much admired by Chopin for its "grandiose insights," a study of modern spiritual torment as expressed in Goethe's Faust, Byron's Manfred and Mickiewicz's Konrad. The essay included an allusion to the gathering movement for change in Russia and sympathy for Mickiewicz's cry of protest, sentiments that would win friends for George among those struggling for freedom in Eastern Europe.

George also completed a novel of adventures in dramatic form, *Gabriel*, whose protagonist, a sixteenth-century Italian girl brought up as a boy, observes that she does not feel her soul is of either sex. Balzac generously praised this odd and rather tired work as "Shakespearean."

For George was tired. She was still suffering from rheumatism and persistent migraine. Her chief recreation consisted of reading a page or two of Leroux, on whose behalf she found time to engage in active propaganda, initiating Dr. Cauvière into the new faith. She would like to be able to relax a little and preferably not to have to depend on the income from her writings. She was no longer young. Supposing she were to fall ill, or supposing there were a revolution? she asked Hippolyte, to whom she confided: "This trip has not done me any good at all."

Gabriel had been written in order to obtain an advance to finance a short holiday in Italy. On May 3, George embarked with Maurice, Solange, and Chopin for Genoa (last visited with Musset). They enjoyed the palaces, the paintings, the luxuriant vegetation. A friend of Balzac's, the Marquese di Negro, invited them to dine at his splendid villa. Balzac would later describe a visit by "Camille Maupin" to this villa in his masterly tale *Honorine*. According to the acerbic Marie d'Agoult, then residing in Italy, George "did not open her mouth" and Chopin did not play the piano but "coughed frightfully."

A stormy crossing back to Marseilles on May 18 was followed three days later by a slow journey by boat and carriage to Nohant, where the travelers arrived on June 1. For George, Chopin had become an adopted son, another Maurice (who was now, at fifteen, almost a young man). A visitor to Nohant in June observed that George looked after Chopin as she would a child, adding, "I took this sickly looking and even diaphanous being, so slight and thin was he, for a boy of fifteen, a friend of Maurice's." Only Chopin's elegant manners revealed that he was not a mere boy.

Gradually, George had progressed from being the mistress of Chopin to being his mother and nurse. Just like Regnault or Pagello, Grzymala would find himself maneuvered into the role of George's "husband," with the third party as their "child," whose welfare "father" and "mother" must cherish. This recurring pattern may be seen as a secret desire for an ideal marriage, blessed with an understanding (but remote) husband and father (who is at the same time a father figure to herself).

In this ideal marriage, she has the dominating and noble maternal part. She is in theory "wife" to Grzymala, the confidant, and in practice "mother" to Chopin, whom she loves. What part her own long-dead father and her unsatisfactory mother play in the formulation of this pathetic scenario may readily be guessed.

Almost without realizing it, George glided into an association whose timetable would remain virtually unchanged for several years. Summers at Nohant, meals in the open air, the visits of friends, excursions to the Creuse valley—the fresh air and quiet that Chopin needed for survival and for composition. Then to Paris in the winter (since she realized Chopin could not live long out of his element), where the musician could continue to give lessons, or rare concerts, and frequent the salons that were his favored milieu. Without those intervals of repose provided by George, it seems unlikely that Chopin would have given the world many of the masterpieces for which he is celebrated.

CHAPTER
16

Creative Woman and the Workers

. . . if we did not speak out as a woman, we should still have the right to do so as a member of the working class; for, in addition to being indissolubly bound to the working class by the blood in our veins, we perceive in the cause of woman and that of the working class a striking similarity which seems to make them interdependent. The same state of subjection, the same ignorance, the same impotence unite them. . . . we do not separate into distinct causes this great and never-ending cause of the ignorant and the poor. . . .

George Sand
Réponse à diverses objections

FTER winding paths and quicksands, George had reached the high plateau of an orderly existence. She could reflect on the period of "excessive living," the bitter memory of which she longed to extirpate. She could devote herself to her new vision of the disenfranchised working man as an equal who might ultimately contribute to society the potential strength of his class. This vision required from herself, as the creative woman artist, a new emphasis upon her own plebeian connections, an emphasis largely due to her friendship with Pierre Leroux, his family, and associates. For the first time she was to

[222]

expatiate upon her dead mother's humble origins and dubious past, in a remarkable confession to Charles Poncy, the mason-poet of Toulon. "I never forgot that plebeian blood flowed in my veins . . ." she would tell him (not entirely accurately), aiming to inform the public of this fact, should she ever write her memoirs.

When George claimed to be "the daughter of a patrician and a gypsy," she would deliberately overlook the bourgeois element in her richly divergent ancestry, the element represented by the office of her wealthy paternal grandfather, the taxgatherer. For her, as for so many radicals then and since, the bourgeoisie had become the bugbear. All hope lay with a symbolic union between an enlightened gentry and an emancipated proletariat—a union conveniently prefigured in her own person. Upon the hated, selfish bourgeoisie, she poured her pained disgust for her own earlier egoism, now concealed under the new altruism.

The living model for her revised, austere myth of creative and compassionate womanhood soon appeared on the scene. On October 8, 1839, a plain-looking Spanish singer of eighteen made a sensational debut at the Odéon in Paris as Desdemona in Rossini's *Otello*. Daughter of Rossini's first Almaviva and sister to the ill-fated Mme Malibran, whom George had so admired in 1831, Pauline García possessed a moving contralto voice of remarkable range. Théophile Gautier addressed her in a poem as a vocal hermaphrodite. Pauline's natural, expansive mode of singing would remind George of her grandmother's.

However, the author of *Lélia* missed Pauline's opening night, since she and Chopin did not leave Nohant until two days later. When George did hear Pauline, she was as deeply moved as she had been by Marie Dorval. But whereas Marie represented for George the interpretative woman artist and the dangerous embodiment of spontaneity and "completeness," Pauline García stood for youthful purity and the creative woman artist of integrity. George hastened to express her admiration and her understanding of Pauline's significance in an article.

The appearance of Mlle García will register as an outstanding date in the history of art created by women. The genius of this consummate and inspired woman musician marks a progress of intellect not hitherto revealed in the female sex in so decisive a manner. . . . It has often been said and written that women could equal men in performance, but that they could not exceed a certain range of talent in the conception of works of art. . . . But here is a girl of eighteen who writes truly beautiful and powerful music. . . . That seems to us Mlle García's principal title to imperishable fame. . . .

George's opinion of Pauline the composer may well seem excessive, yet her new protégée's compositions were to be admired by Chopin, Liszt, Adolphe Adam, the Marquis de Custine, and many more.

There existed deeper, more private reasons why George would become devoted to Pauline, comparing in her diary her affection for the young singer with the ideal trusting love she had felt for Mother Alicia. Pauline appeared to George as an ideal self, an artist governed by reason and a powerful will, capable of sacrificing everything (including her personal inclinations) for her art. At once George was reminded of her own youth: her faltering beginnings, half-conscious struggles, the way in which, under the spell of Marie Dorval, she had been deflected from unswerving commitment to art in her impulsive (and futile) quest for happiness. She recalled how often she had been obliged to press on in haste to meet a deadline or a debt. Now people could say that she was slipping. Small wonder that George would write to Pauline: "I live in you, you are my youth, my fame and my future."

It was not only Pauline's intelligence, her gifts, her single-minded dedication to art that George admired, but also her simplicity, her kindness to others. These were the very qualities George most esteemed and longed to possess, and those she now believed to be most lacking in her daughter Solange. Pierre Leroux had pointed to egoism as one of the principal ills of modern society. To her deep chagrin, George could not avoid the conclusion that young Solange cared only for herself. Precocious in some ways, Solange first experienced menstruation at just under twelve (when the average age before 1850 lay around fifteen). Although George was concerned for her daughter's welfare, she never showed for Solange the boundless indulgence she displayed for Maurice. Inevitably, the girl, who was no fool, felt the distinction.

The more the disappointed mother struggled to form Solange's character on the lines of her own newly shaped ideals, scolding, sermonizing, punishing, the more recalcitrant her daughter grew. In early childhood, Solange had often been left to maids and obliging friends, or else thoroughly spoiled; now she was to be consigned to the Paris boarding school run by Monsieur and Madame Hérau, and when that establishment seemed to George to provide insufficient discipline, to Monsieur and Madame Bascans' boarding school for young girls. Betraying a singular lack of perception for an intelligent woman, though not, perhaps, for a demanding mother, George held up to Solange the image of the adored Pauline, her "fifille," or darling little girl, her ideal daughter.

In her role as the good mother, George took Pauline under her wing with greater success than she had so far enjoyed in extending help to her idle young nephew, Oscar Cazamajou, son of her half-sister Caroline. When Pauline was being courted by the dissolute Alfred de Musset, George hastened to save her protégée for art by favoring marriage to a sound, cultivated friend of hers, some twenty-one years her "adopted" daughter's senior, who happened to be director of the Italian opera theater in Paris. George had known Louis Viardot as a literary and political journalist, an active opponent of the regime. He would be to Pauline the fatherly guide and protector-cum-impresario that George had needed but never known. After the couple were married in April 1840 (much to Musset's vexation), George could freely advise Pauline on everything concerning the development of her career.

George herself was about to launch upon a new career, that of dramatist. (She had been preceded in this endeavor by Mme de Staël, whose plays, however, were destined only for the private theater at Coppet.) The author of *Jacques* had come to Paris in the autumn of 1839 for rehearsals of her play *Cosima*—which, as it happened, were postponed to the spring—having been "*persuaded, dissuaded* and *re-persuaded*" by Chopin to give the piece to the Théâtre Français. Marie Dorval, though not a member of the company, was engaged at George's insistence for the principal role of the weak, persecuted wife. The supposedly high financial rewards accruing to dramatists were urgently needed.

Although the settlement with Casimir left George with heavy debts that involved her in what she called "forced labor," she had borrowed a further thirty thousand francs in October 1839. This considerable sum was required partly for the decoration and furnishing of her fine apartment at 16 rue Pigalle with the antiques that had become newly fashionable. In her drawing room stood a superb rosewood upright piano and, on the tables, magnificent Chinese vases filled with the flowers she always loved. The walls were hung with paintings by Delacroix and her portrait by Calamatta. In her bedroom, two mattresses lay on the floor, Turkish style. That keen connoisseur of luxury, Balzac, who was among the distinguished guests including Heine and Delacroix, to whom she offered exquisite dinners, left profoundly impressed. Despite this high style suited to Chopin's taste, George maintained that it was far more costly to live at Nohant, where each summer she kept open house for her friends.

In any event, her play *Cosima*—whose odious seducer offers a résumé of her assessment of the conduct of Musset or Michel—did not contribute anything to ease her financial position. According to Heine, the author's political and literary enemies were looking forward to the "immoral" creature's comeuppance and determined in advance to contribute to it. Rumors were circulating among such one-time friends as Marie d'Agoult and Didier that George was pregnant. Too proud to engage a claque, George nonetheless tried to find seats for well-wishers, including the indefatigable Mrs. Frances Trollope, the novelist's mother, who had already written about her with sympathy. All the same, the general hostility of the audience, quick to find any pretext to snigger at supposed indecency, proved too much for Marie Dorval, who went to pieces. After seven performances, the play was withdrawn. George pretended not to mind.

Perhaps no unkind remark among those proffered to intimates by Marie d'Agoult since her stay at Nohant wounded George more than the insinuation that her talent was in decline. Such a decline was what George dreaded, since it would deprive her of her livelihood. She knew of Marie d'Agoult's pointed innuendoes (thanks to the revelations of Charlotte Marliani). An "explanation" between the two estranged women had taken place in November of the previous year, followed by a barbed "reconciliation," which could not disguise the animosity of the one and the distrust and dislike of the other. In fact, George's talent was in process of transformation and renewal. She was about to produce some of her most original and influential works, which reveal her concern for the dignity of the common man and the enduring problems attendant upon its literary expression by those who are not strictly members of the working class.

For more than two years, George had struggled to revise *Lélia* in the light of her changing opinions, and in the second version of the novel she had ended with a curious amalgam. To the courtesan Pulchérie was given a call for revolution, a cry of vengeance against the parasitical oppressor (including the repentant Magdalene herself). This passage plainly epitomizes the private sense of social guilt that dominates George's writings in this period.

The poetic cloudiness of the second *Lélia* gave way to the concrete documentation of *Le Compagnon du Tour de France*, written in August–September 1840. Through Pierre Leroux, George had read Agricol Perdiguier's book on the Compagnonnage and, much taken with it, had invited its modest author to dinner. Perdiguier, a gentle, good-looking, self-educated journeyman joiner, was not much younger than George, who soon busied herself finding sewing tasks for his wife (and later, a place in an old-age home for his parents-in-law).

The fierce customs of the Compagnonnage, or ancient French artisan guild system, recounted to her by Perdiguier, gave George an insight into a strange world. She saw here the possibility of an entirely new literature based on little-known customs of the people. An adolescent apprentice carpenter or mason would spend several years traveling about the country, learning and practicing his trade. As the enrolled member of a particular guild, each with its own secret rites, he would be in honor bound to challenge with due ceremonial and to fight with any member of another guild whom he chanced to encounter. These traditional divisive practices among working men disturbed Perdiguier, who wished to reconcile his fellow workers.

George set her novel during the Restoration, at the time when the young Perdiguier had performed his "tour de France" as an apprentice joiner. This enabled her to offer fairly accurate reportage (through Perdiguier). There had been virtuous proletarians in French literature since 1830, but with her handsome, eloquent, talented, Christlike carpenter, Pierre Huguenin, who loves and is loved by a grave young noblewoman, Yseult de Villepreux, George raised the relation between "virile" worker (harbinger of the future) and woman of position (reluctant embodiment of the past) to the level of myth. It was a myth powerful enough to inspire in various ways George Eliot with her noble carpenter in *Adam Bede* and Henry James with his ingenuous bookbinder in *The Princess Casamassima*; to awaken the appreciation of that carpenter's son, Walt Whitman; to find an oblique reflection in D. H. Lawrence; and to extend to the committed left-wing literature of the nineteen thirties and beyond.

Like much later left-wing literature, the book suffers from being written from the outside. Since George did not know how workers talked among themselves, she had to crave the reader's indulgence as "translator." Some five years afterward, George would observe to Charles Poncy that Pierre Huguenin had not yet come forward in real life. (Perhaps that was why she could never write the promised sequel.) More convincing than the main plot is the earthy, passionate affair between the marquise, Yseult's sister-in-law (by birth a bourgeoise), and Pierre's carpenter friend, Amaury, who abandons a decent working widow for her.

Yet George was surely right to tell Poncy how the idea that led her to conceive the type represented by Pierre Huguenin was a true one. She had much sympathy for the idealizing quality in Schiller and a great deal in common with the ennobling drive of Corneille. La Bruyère's celebrated comparison between Racine and Corneille must have been in her mind when she told Balzac, roughly at the time when she was writing this novel, that "you know how to depict man as he is . . . whereas I feel prompted to depict him as I wish him to be, as I believe he should be." George portrays an artisan gifted with natural intelligence, capable of self-improvement, and deserving of respect. Supposed inferiority of class resembles supposed inferiority of sex, in her view. Her sphere of action is moral—the questioning of the basic assumptions about rich and poor in a hierarchical society. Being unable to resign herself to the misery of others, she asks her readers whether they are able to do so without a sense of guilt.

When her book was written, the modern organization of French workers was in its infancy. That the institution of Compagnonnage was already in decline; that Perdiguier failed in his efforts at reconciliation; that workers' organizations would eventually be founded not among the more articulate rural artisans but among the town laborers; that Flora Tristan would soon be making her "tour de France" to urge the workers to achieve their own emancipation—all this cannot detract from the moral contribution of George's novel (as distinct from its literary demerit as a form of preachment).

The novel's sales were disappointing. Appearing at a time of economic crisis and industrial unrest, the book was not well received by the frightened bourgeoisie or the liberal aristocracy whom she heavily satirized. Nor was it welcomed by the clergy and the conservative devout, who were displeased to be told by Yseult de Villepreux that she had decided "to marry a man of the people in order to become one of the people," just as converts to Christianity accepted baptism, and that the Church had betrayed the egalitarian teachings of Jesus. Many found it distasteful that a mere woman should write on such high matters at all. According to George, the clerical press accused her of going every Sunday to the city gate to study the habits of the workers, whence she supposedly returned, dead drunk, with Pierre Leroux. Rather more heartwarming was a letter from a humble working man, assuring her that she seemed to him to be a veritable angel.

George was only one woman writer among several in France who were in the forefront of the movement to improve the condition of the working class. Pierre Leroux's circle of feminine admirers included such widely different humanitarians as Flora Tristan and Hortense Allart. The link between the cause of women and that of the workers seemed obvious to many, since both were excluded from full equality of rights granted in principle by the French Revolution. George would later write that the two causes were interdependent. Her views were far from airy: In her journalism she was shortly to demand a reduction in hours of work and decent hygienic conditions for the workers in home and workshop.

Women writers were also conspicuous in the struggle to support the fledgling working-class literature. The determined Mme Amable Tastu encouraged the worker poets, on whose behalf George would write numerous articles and prefaces. Among these poets were some working-class women like the seamstress Louise Crombach, an unmarried mother whom George helped financially. In contrast, though, George had little sympathy for many of her middle-class feminine colleagues. For Caroline Marbouty (who so longed to approach her) she suggested a good kick, while referring unambiguously to her and to Louise Colet with their literary lovers as "the fannies of letters." George admitted that Flora Tristan was brave, but found her eccentric, vain, an "actress."

Whatever George's disdain for such militant feminist colleagues as Flora Tristan, her own good intentions toward the proletariat were genuine enough. No matter how hard-pressed George might be for money, her purse remained open for Pierre Leroux and his family or the struggling worker poets, and she would sometimes borrow temporarily from friends in order to meet the needs of her numerous protégés. Yet the role of good mother to the proletarians could not help being that of lady bountiful. The virtuous, far-seeing role that had already become second nature to her, like the need to endow her "good" characters with unadulterated noble and disinterested sentiments, covered her own, more natural human failings and contradictions, which she wished to conceal from prying and hostile eyes.

The handsome, costly antiques and lavish entertainments in her apartment in the rue Pigalle, for instance, balance uneasily with her pained observations about the odious contrasts between luxury and poverty in Paris in the early eighteen forties. A keen-eyed visitor, the poetess Mme Juste Olivier, would observe that George "thinks she is poor." To economize, servants were dismissed at Nohant, a task entrusted to her late mother's companion, Pierret, and, oddly, to Chopin also. Her assessment of her own peasant farmers was far from idealized: She remarked that if given an inch, they would take a yard. Perhaps the sharpest observers of this complex and contradictory creature were those who commented on her desire to appear unaffected and ordinary.

One admirer who had modeled his fictional heroine, Wally, upon George's Lélia, the "Young German" publicist, Karl Gutzkow, would finally gain access to her Parisian apartment with an introduction from a suspect source, Marie d'Agoult. He found George seated at her embroidery, with Solange, in the dim light of a table lamp. Later, she lit "one of those innocent cigarettes where there is more paper than tobacco, more coquetry than emancipation." The conversation was strained. "She did not wish to give anything away. . . . She wanted to appear cold, mistrustful and even irritated. She betrayed to me her fear of betrayal." Gutzkow felt sorry for her, realizing how deep an experience of disillusionment underlay her attitude to strangers. With great penetration, he had hit upon her enduring sense of betrayal, which dated from her mother's abandonment and that of the Villeneuves, though he naturally interpreted it as a result of the calumny and malice to which she had long been subjected and which had increased since her adoption of the proletarian cause.

Some idea of George's courage and distinctiveness may be gauged by the strong reaction of her publishers to the socialist tendency of her novels. If Buloz declined to print *Le Compagnon du Tour de France* in the *Revue des deux mondes*, he certainly would not accept her new novel, *Horace*, without alterations (which she refused to make). He did not want to upset his subscribers with her views on property. "You are no communist, I hope . . ." suggested Buloz gingerly. At least, he had not observed before *Horace* any trace of communism in her writings.

George, speaking through the reflections of her decent carpenter, Pierre Huguenin, wavered between a defense and a criticism of private property. She did not as yet know precisely what the term "communism" implied. In response to her query, Pierre Leroux told her that both of them were "communist" without knowing it. The word "communism" had caught on in France by 1841, but it was sufficiently new for him to define it for her as denoting "a republic under the rule of equality."

The word conveyed, he added, a tendency rather than a doctrine. The various communist sects were divided, some of their writings being, in his opinion, nothing short of madness. As he saw it, communism in

France resembled Chartism in England (that is, a political working-class movement). Personally, he would prefer the word "communionism," to express a social doctrine founded on fraternity. All the same, Leroux hedged, if there was no need for them to accept the title of communist, there was no need to reject it either. (This discussion took place over two years before Marx adopted the term as his own.) George was to call herself a "communist" in the sense then given to the word in France. She understood by it neither system nor violence.

The questing George had been dissatisfied with the political stand of Buloz and his journal for some time. The difference over *Horace* prompted their final break. Experienced as a printer and journalist, Pierre Leroux suggested the creation of a new review to express their republican and reformist opinions, under a triumvirate consisting of George, Louis Viardot, and himself. Encouraged by Chopin, George joined them in founding *La Revue Indépendante* (the title was her own invention). It was in this journal, which would arouse the interest of Arnold Ruge and Karl Marx (then planning their own), that *Horace* and many of her subsequent works would be published, even after the directorship had passed to others.

The novel that so upset Buloz was a courageous work, nowadays unjustly neglected. *Horace* depicts sympathetically the rebellious student milieu that George had known on her arrival in Paris to join Sandeau. The narrator, a medical student, lives in a perfect free union with Eugénie, an adherent of Saint-Simonism, in an attic on the quai Saint-Michel very similar to that once occupied by Aurore and Jules. Among the narrator's friends are two young men in love with the same woman, the humble Marthe. One, a pupil of Delacroix, is the selfless working man Paul Arsène, who has to renounce his artistic vocation to support his ungrateful sisters. The other is Horace Dumontet, a provincial bourgeois egoist, for whose law studies his mother has sacrificed his sister's dowry.

Upon Horace, George has lavished her considerable and underrated talent for comic satire—he was *"affected naturally,"* observes the narrator of her anti-hero. Horace presents a mixture of irresistible charm, laziness, and ambition above his emotional or intellectual station. He is constructed largely out of her recollections of Jules Sandeau, who had recently published a novel about his affair with George, *Marianna*, which Balzac thought ungentlemanly. There are elements in Horace's character, too, of the jealous Michel de Bourges, striking the balustrade with his cane in uncontrollable rage, and of Alfred de Musset's bizarre treatment of women. George's tragicomic anti-hero meets his match in the Vicomtesse de Chailly, with her artificial beauty, artificial intelligence, and artificial nobility, a vitriolic portrait of Marie d'Agoult. This portrait, coming after George's contribution to Balzac's *Béatrix*, provides some justification for Hortense Allart's view that the advocate of simple goodness could be extremely "vindictive."

The self-sacrificing Paul turns to politics. He hears the famous republican tribune, Godefroy Cavaignac, call for free education, universal suffrage, the gradual reform of property. "In 1832, people were not afraid, as they are today, to be thought *communist*, something which has become the bogy of all shades of opinion at the present moment," interposes the narrator (or rather George) loosely. It is the heroic Paul who is wounded in the bloody street fighting of June 1832 (an essential scene that George eludes, although she had been a horrified eyewitness who then called for a plague on all houses). Horace, who has played with the romance of revolution out of vanity, contrives to find himself outside Paris at the fateful moment.

Feminism occupies as large a place as politics in the novel, and not only through the dignified Eugénie, respected by all because respected by her lover. There is also Paul's and Horace's contrasting treatment of the unfortunate Marthe, whose downfall was caused by her need to escape from her drunken father's incestuous lust (George's concession to the actual degradation of numbers of the urban working class). Where Marthe's silent suitor Paul learns to attribute her fall to society, dreaming of "the rehabilitation and emancipation of humanity in the *person of woman*," her vain lover Horace torments her with jealous suspicions—"The Virgin Mary was alone worthy of Monsieur Horace Dumontet!" Horace is horrified when his mistress becomes pregnant. Marthe runs away. She has her revenge by registering the child as "of unknown father," thus depriving Horace of any legal right to the boy, whom Paul nobly adopts as his own.

Horace, the equivocal and absurd anti-hero, embodiment of the phony rebel, proved immediately recognizable. A few years later, the exiled Russian publicist Alexander Herzen could think of no greater insult than to call the German poet Georg Herwegh, who was having a much-publicized Sandian affair with his wife, a *"petit-bourgeois*, like George Sand's Horace. . . ." Something of George's anti-hero has passed, too, into Turgenev's Rudin and Flaubert's Frédéric in *L'Education sentimentale*. George had the original inventive ability and the psychological penetration. What she ultimately lacked was the power to sustain, in a totally disciplined and convincing narrative, the inner clash between her ideal aspirations and her true self.

Before the serialization of *Horace* was completed in *La Revue Indé-pendante*, George began publication of *Consuelo* in the new magazine. With its sequel, *La Comtesse de Rudolstadt*, this vast three-volume historical novel, which Henry James considered her masterpiece, took her two years to complete. It was composed—with obvious enjoyment —by a risky method. As she went along, she consulted friends and acquaintances (Heine, Godefroy Cavaignac, George Henry Lewes), read over forty volumes, took notes, and produced some ten chapters a month virtually without interruption, keeping in mind a large cast of characters and an extremely intricate plot. This output was only slightly reduced when the magazine became bimonthly.

The tale is set in her favorite period, the eighteenth century, blend-ing her love for its composers, both known and less-known (inherited from her grandmother) with her interest (inspired by Leroux) in heretical or mystic underground movements as precursors not only of the French Revolution but of current egalitarian ideas. (As George would suggest, the hidden face of the age of reason was far stranger than her own fictional inventions.) With the modern revival of neglected eighteenth-century music as well as the present mode of the occult, this double aspect may well strike a chord today.

George took full advantage of the wide liberties allowed the historical novelist. Coincidences abound, as they do in a more recent "poetic" novel built on the guiding concern of Providence, Pasternak's *Dr. Zhivago*. Unlike *Horace*, her complex tale does not belong in the "realist" tradition of the nineteenth century but with a more free, even modern strain of psychofantasy, the poetic projection of a woman's secret dreams and yearnings. These are conveyed through the poetic imagery of the garden, or the prison (George's recurrent fantasy), or in the heroine's two loves, one for whom she feels respect but physical re-pulsion, while experiencing uncontrollable physical attraction to the other, who both significantly merge into the same man.

George's heroine, Consuelo, a young Spanish-born singer of un-equaled talent and impeccable virtue, meets with adventures that take her from the *Scuole* of Venice (in the charming opening chapters) to a mysterious castle in Bohemia, once the scene of the bloody Hussite

Wars, and from the court of Maria Theresa in Vienna to that of Frederick the Great in Potsdam. This cherished pupil of Handel's rival, the Neapolitan opera composer and great teacher Nicola Porpora, encounters the youthful Haydn on the way to Vienna and talks unaffectedly with the crowned heads of Europe (of whom she cordially disapproves).

Tolstoy was to call *Consuelo* "a heap of rubbish, crammed full of scientific, philosophical, artistic and moral phrases, a pastry made of sour dough and rancid butter, stuffed with truffles, sturgeon and pineapple"—but then, the author of *Resurrection* did not think much of Shakespeare either. Without placing George's novel on quite so lofty a level—though in spirit it has something in common with *The Winter's Tale*—one cannot help noticing that there is nothing else quite like it in French fiction.

In this rambling fable, Consuelo's adventures form part of her tests and trials as a woman, her long quest for wisdom, her gradual education toward enlightenment. The learned Elizabeth Barrett, who loved the book, would tell Robert Browning, who did not, that it was "a female odyssey." Consuelo is admitted "like a man" into the highest rites of the masonic order of the Invisibles (whereas in George's day women were not received as freemasons). For it is Consuelo who is courageous enough to descend into the cistern to help Albert de Rudolstadt at the risk of her life. She appears as the solitary woman artist of integrity, who suffers obstacles and enmities in her career. Moreover, she stands for woman the consoling angel. In short, Consuelo incarnates the myth of creative and redemptive womanhood, finally expressed in the ballad "The Good Goddess of Poverty," verses of her husband's set to music by herself.

The choice of a singer-composer as heroine is not due solely to the fact that she is modeled on Pauline Viardot (although Consuelo in middle age, the noble gypsy and sermonizing mother, has more in common with George herself). Unlike the woman writer, the woman singer is not accused of masculine intellectualism. That was doubtless one reason why Mme de Staël made Corinne a singer.

In addition, George endows her heroine with an inability to witness suffering without wishing to relieve it. One of the most impressive (and indeed, modern) chapters of the book depicts Consuelo's agonized passage through the torture chambers (of the sort George had seen in Barcelona), symbol not only of man's inhumanity to man but of man's indifference to the pain of others. Ultimately, the much-tried Consuelo and Albert, in harmony with the humble folk, represent both precursors and exemplars of a new humanity—where men and women are free, equal, and humane. Here, for those who represent the future envisaged in George's dream, it is the conclusion rather than the analysis that must appear wanting.

George could advise Charles Poncy, the worker poet, to be pitiless with himself. It was good advice she could not carry out. Yet despite its inordinate length (which she good-humoredly admitted), *Consuelo* proved to be one of the seminal works of the nineteenth century. Many were those who borrowed from it without acknowledgment. Among them, Baudelaire, for instance, would find in its pages on the heretical rehabilitation of Satan a source for his Satanic litanies (while elsewhere expressing disgust at George's denial of hell). In George's crazed visionaries, Dostoevsky could find inspiration for his Prince Myshkin. As for Walt Whitman, he often reread the novel in translation and thought it "truly a masterpiece . . . the noblest, in many respects, in its own field, in all literature. . . ." He would remember Consuelo's words about the open road as the symbol of "an active and varied life." Moreover, the work's final pages would inspire his democratic view of man the poet-visionary as the spokesman of all mankind—"the women not forgetting."

The ending of *Consuelo* is not so much a happy as a hopeful one. The hero and heroine, two souls in one, do not yield. Despite persecution and misfortune, Consuelo and Albert contrive to lead a simple, obscure, good life among the humble, making music in exchange for hospitality, according to the system of barter advocated by Leroux. This was hardly the home life of George and Frédéric.

What Chopin, with his acute self-criticism and perfectionism, thought of George's rambling metaphysical-social-artistic compendium of a romance, witness of her wide-ranging curiosity, may readily be imagined. He differed from Leroux in suggesting cuts. Nor did he share George's views on what she called "the philosophical question of property." Like Delacroix, he held no lofty concept of the artist's mission.

Above all, in recurrent bouts of nervous suffering, Chopin inclined to see everything in dark colors. The constant ups and downs in the health of Chopinet, or Chip-Chip, as she called him affectionately, were reported almost daily to friends. As for herself, she told Delacroix:

Life goes on the same. I banish any excessively dark thoughts with a hearty kick, and when I am sensible, I find life *bearable* because it is *eternal*. You call that my chimera. I call it my faith and my strength. No, nothing dies, nothing is lost, nothing ends, whatever you may say. . . . But you live with beings weaker than yourself, your power of negation dominates them, whereas my power of affirmation would fight against you and would at least divert your thoughts by the struggle.

The obstinate fight to affirm was doubtless reinforced as much by Chopin's skepticism and spleen as by Delacroix's.

CHAPTER 17

No Villain Need Be...

Here is a fitting spot to dig Love's grave. . . .
The wrong is mixed. In tragic life, God wot,
No villain need be! Passions spin the plot:
We are betrayed by what is false within.

George Meredith
Modern Love, XLIII

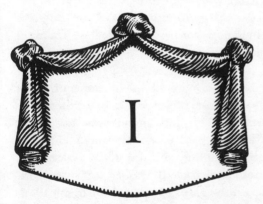

N THE eighteen forties, when George stood at the height of her literary fame, Chopin used to enter the room quietly, take her hand, then keep discreetly in the background. Those who called on George in her new flat overlooking the small inner garden of the Square d'Orléans (where she had moved partly to suit Chopin, who took rooms in the same complex) knew that she was not to be disturbed before four in the afternoon. Her Parisian routine remained unchanged: writing nightly into the small hours, rising late, dinner at the neighboring flat of Charlotte Marliani, where expenses were shared, then conversation and music or a visit to the theater with friends.

These were the years of reconciliation. The tie with her former "father confessor," Sainte-Beuve, had already been warily renewed. There followed a revival of friendship with her irascible one-time literary mentor, Latouche; and with Liszt, now parted from Marie d'Agoult. Then (as a result of a chance meeting) came fresh contact with her aristocratic relative René Vallet de Villeneuve and his family, culminating in a visit to Chenonceaux, their stately home, though she made it clear to an old friend that "they took the first step." The awkward girl, whom they had once cast off, had indeed "arrived."

These were, too, the years of an ever-widening intellectual circle. She corresponded with Bettina von Arnim, passionate friend of Goethe's declining years, on socialism. The "Young Hegelian," Arnold Ruge, introduced to her the arch-romantic anarchist, Mikhail Bakunin, whose favorite author she was—indeed, the Russian devoted to her a veritable cult. The great English Shakespearian actor Macready, who brought his company to Paris to perform *Hamlet* and *Othello*, became a firm friend. A long-haired, youthful poet, Matthew Arnold, would make a never-to-be-forgotten pilgrimage to Nohant. With Bonaparte's nephew, Prince Louis-Napoleon (the future Emperor Napoleon III), she engaged in guarded correspondence. Then a prisoner at Ham, author of a pamphlet on the way to abolish poverty, he expressed "warm sympathy for the woman illustrious for her genius and her magnanimity." Such were but a few of her increasingly numerous contacts in the world of politics, literature, and the theater. For, after working through the night on her novels, George would still have the energy to write articles for the press and to conduct a vast correspondence, perhaps her greatest claim to fame, since in its vivacity it embraces almost every aspect of the life of the day.

Her journalism, especially when she adopted the persona of some humble peasant being forced into the workhouse, could be brilliant. An example of her crusading journalism in this period was her eager publicizing of the Fanchette affair, the case of an unwanted idiot girl of about fifteen turned out of the foundling hospital of La Châtre and deposited by the roadside in another district. It was an age when unwanted youngsters—in mid-nineteenth-century France, over thirty thousand each year—could be callously abandoned. This episode led her to discuss with her old friends Charles Duvernet and Alphonse Fleury the idea of founding a local republican journal. After long negotiations in search of a suitable editor, in which George played a dominating part, *L'Eclaireur de l'Indre* was finally launched, one of the early instances of the creation of a free provincial press.

The letters of support that George managed to obtain for the new paper included one from Lamartine and another from the author of *L'Organisation du travail*, the diminutive Louis Blanc. Firmly believing in the right to work, Louis Blanc propagated the notion that the state should expropriate the capitalists gradually and without violence and should place the instruments of labor within reach of all. It was to the recently founded radical organ, *La Réforme*, with which Louis Blanc was associated, that George contributed at some financial loss her novel *Le Meunier d'Angibault*, where worker hero and aristocratic heroine, scorning wealth, ultimately unite to found a small rural commune. Through *La Réforme*, George had dealings not only with Louis Blanc but with such leading republicans as Etienne Arago (uncle of her friend, Emmanuel) and especially with Ledru-Rollin, dealings that were to prove of capital importance to her later in a new activist role.

The mid-eighteen forties were, for George, a period of intense literary fecundity and experiment. Preceding *Le Meunier d'Angibault* came *Jeanne*, highly (though not unreservedly) esteemed by Balzac, the story of an illiterate peasant girl, as it were a mute, inglorious Joan of Arc. In *Jeanne*, George attempted to incorporate into the novel both the rural legends of Berry and local peasant speech. This endeavor to convey peasant speech failed to satisfy George herself, and only reached artistic fruition in the ever-popular country tales of her maturity, *La Mare au diable* and *François le Champi* (and later still, *La Petite Fadette*). Written in four days, *La Mare au diable* was the result of a conscious desire for simplicity, a reaction not only against the involved, far-fetched plots of some of her contemporaries (like Dumas and Sue), but also against what she herself had once thought necessary to a novel.

Quite consciously, too, George was trying to record local traditions and speech patterns before these were swept away by creeping industrialization and the coming of the railway. In her novel *Le Péché de Monsieur Antoine*, she had presented conflicting attitudes to the new industrialization: the generation gap between a ruthless capitalist and his son who prefers to engage in land reclamation. One would make workers into wage slaves; the other insists upon a society where all men can have the opportunity to become full human beings. The confrontation, sketched in the early days of industrial selfishness and at the height of French speculation in railway shares, still has validity.

Such works promoted reflection, changed attitudes, moved to action readers as far afield as Russia. It is not necessary for works to be "great" in order to do this, a word that could scarcely be applied to *Le Péché de Monsieur Antoine*. But it is not always great literature that is the most potent. Besides, at her simple best, in *La Mare au diable*, for instance, George could convey a grandiose image of the human dignity and worth of all humble creatures, which endures. Her vision would stimulate later writers and artists to probe more searchingly into the life of the peasant.

One of the most curious experiments of this period is the novel *Isidora*, which at one point foreshadows the modern rejection of the "realist" tradition by envisaging the characters less as "real people" than as fictional beings. Deeply enmeshed in George's inner divisions, *Isidora* offers a glimpse into her state of mind in the mid-eighteen forties. Is humanity composed of two entirely separate and distinct beings, men and women? inquires Jacques Laurent, an innocent young philosopher making an abstract study of women and then torn between a middle-aged courtesan, Isidora, originally corrupted by poverty, and a virtuous widow. The union between an austere spirit like Jacques and one damaged by experience like Isidora must prove fragile. Isidora breaks her chain and decides to become reconciled with old age: ". . . it is another woman, another *self* who begins. . . ." Disjointed though it appears, the novel richly reflects George's secret frustration at her union with Chopin.

At the same time, she was steadily cooling toward Leroux. The socialist philosopher had set up a farming colony at Boussac, excluding monetary reward for labor. He also aimed to produce cheap books for educating the masses by means of his invention, a printing press that he never quite managed to perfect. Leroux's head was full of excellent schemes of which he was inclined to tire before they were complete. Friends urged George to stop supplying the philosopher with funds, for his own good. From being a source of living waters, he became "an intellectual sybarite"—worse, no longer a true proletarian but an egoist always expecting other people to make sacrifices. George, together with Charlotte Marliani, had poured considerable sums into this bottomless sack. Must she abandon her family for his? Gradually, George moved closer toward the more concrete ideas of Louis Blanc, advocating in an article in July 1846 the purchase of land in neglected areas by the state for the settlement of impoverished families, to whom it should advance the instruments of work.

Gradually, too, she would come to sympathize with the activist stance of the tireless Italian conspirator Giuseppe Mazzini, in exile in England, with whom she had been in correspondence since 1842. To Mazzini, she was "the leading woman today," "a flag," "the voice of downtrodden womanhood." He served as intermediary between George and her growing number of English and American admirers. Thus it was through Mazzini that the socially conscious Derbyshire-born writer Geraldine

Jewsbury, who liked to smoke in public, asked George for an opinion on her novel *Zoë*, with its heated love scene between the heroine and a priest significantly named Everhard. (Jane Carlyle, for whom Miss Jewsbury professed passionate friendship, thought George Sand herself could not have written some of the best passages in *Zoë*, though decency forbade the work's publication.)

It was through Mazzini, too, that the ill-fated American feminist Margaret Fuller—who had tried to assess the French novelist's significance in *Woman in the Nineteenth Century*—called on George in the Square d'Orléans. After a momentary misunderstanding with a rustic servant, George appeared at the door, dressed in dark violet silk, a figure of simple, ladylike dignity. "She needs no defense, but only to be understood," thought Miss Fuller, "for she has bravely acted out her nature, and always with good intentions." While inclined to see George as the novelist saw herself, Miss Fuller regretted that George kept exploiting her talent without proper care. At the same time, the former editor of *The Dial* visited Chopin, "frail as a snowdrop," in his room. She had been told that George felt only friendship for the exquisite composer, whereas he played the jealous lover. Miss Fuller had not been misinformed.

Already, as early as March 1840, Marie d'Agoult, no friend to Chopin, reported that the composer was sick with jealousy, the tireless tormentor of himself and others. George, she added, though exasperated, feared lest a break might kill him.

An altercation had taken place in the summer of 1841, when George wished to invite to Nohant Anton Wodzinski, who was having an affair with Marie de Rozières, Solange's piano teacher. Mlle de Rozières who, like George, was no longer young, had been introduced to the novelist by Chopin himself. Naturally, it was acutely embarrassing to Chopin to think of finding himself in close proximity to his childhood friend Wodzinski, who not only owed him money but who happened to be the brother of the pianist's one-time ideal betrothed. His fury concentrated upon Marie de Rozières, that indiscreet old maid who deserved a good thrashing, that "insufferable pig who, in an utterly amazing way, has managed to steal into my walled garden, to sniff around and look for truffles right between my rose bushes." The creature's principal crime lay in her self-justification by Sandian principles and her suggestion that she knew all about Chopin's past through the Polish colony in Paris.

Having lived so long in the public eye, defiant of scandal, George never really understood the nature of Chopin's susceptibilities concerning Anton Wodzinski or the depths of his rage at any invasion of his privacy. To her, Marie de Rozières had a perfect right to grasp at happiness. George's feminist principles were at stake. What is rather distasteful, though, is the way she confided in the unfortunate woman, telling her all about Chopin's inexplicable tantrums:

> He wanted to leave, he said I was making him look crazy, jealous, absurd, that I was breaking up his relations with his best friends. . . . In short, as usual, he demands that nobody should suffer from his jealousy except me, and that it should in no wise be reproved by his friends. . . . I have never had and never shall have any peace with him . . .

Then she added, significantly, "I do not want him to think he is the master." After a time, the storm passed when Wodzinski abandoned his mistress to return to Poland. Chopin then accepted Mlle de Rozières as a useful dog's body.

He might be the superb poet of the nocturne but he was also a difficult man, being almost constantly in physical or mental pain. In ordinary social intercourse, where distance could be kept, nobody could be more charming; in private, when displeased, he withdrew into cold sulks or hurtful raillery. He had fixed upon George an exclusive and demanding passion, and his jealousy increased with the years, for the most part apparently without foundation. Clearly, he was pained to see George receive on occasion at Nohant such former lovers as Bocage (about whom she had candidly confessed all, to no avail), or Michel de Bourges (now deemed retrograde). But Chopin's suspicions extended to all and sundry. Consequently, George felt obliged to keep away from Nohant a number of helpful friends whom Chopin could not abide.

Presumably, given the pianist's delicate health, sexual relations between them were rare or nonexistent, and this, too, must have sharpened his pain. Instead, George served as his devoted nurse at all hours of the day and night, sometimes when feeling ill herself. On the death of the composer's father, she invited Chopin's sister Louise and her husband to stay at Nohant. If Chopin returned to Paris before her, she fussed over him, sending urgent instructions to friends to make sure he had enough money or to see that he took his morning chocolate. Grateful as he was, Frédéric could not but feel humiliated by her attachment to him as nurse. She assured his mother that her own life was devoted to him forever.

Her frustration was nonetheless revealed in occasional complaints to intimates. Turned forty, weary of Chopin's unjust accusations, she betook herself to meditate in the little wood at Nohant and sat down to weep alone. She arose strengthened and determined to be reconciled with old age, seeking only the accomplishment of duty, stern daughter of the voice of God. That, however, did not prevent her from engaging in all likelihood in a brief liaison with the ambitious thirty-three-year-old Louis Blanc, to whom she wrote, "My beloved angel . . . I love you." This passing affair was rapidly transformed into an enduring friendship.

Meanwhile, Maurice and Solange were growing up, and George felt increasingly that Chopin's role as jealous lover of a woman in her forties (who, she said, felt more like eighty) made her look absurd. She eventually hit upon the tasteless idea of transposing their relationship into a novel, after the manner of the day. One of her aims must have been to teach Frédéric a lesson. She had already found the courage to tell him a few home truths and to threaten him with a separation, after which (she informed Mlle de Rozières) he had recovered his senses, "and you know how good, kind, deserving of love and esteem he is, when he is not out of his mind." *Lucrezia Floriani* affords a penetrating psychological study of Chopin the man (divorced from Chopin the musician), thinly disguised as Prince Karol de Roswald. It depicts the tormented liaison between the prince and a brilliant, much experienced though burnt-out Italian actress and playwright, Lucrezia Floriani, mother of four children by various fathers, a not unflattering portrait of George herself. The truth of George's insight into the type represented by Prince Karol is borne out by the fact that the young Dostoevsky saw some of his own traits in the prince. Others, like the admiring Liszt and the outraged Hortense Allart, recognized the true model at once, despite George's reiterated and disingenuous denials.

Delacroix, who loved Chopin, arrived for his last visit to Nohant in the summer of 1846, to be treated to a reading from this novel:

> Would you believe that Mme Sand conceived the notion of reading to us both, one evening, the manuscript of her *Floriani*, a novel where Chopin's obstinate devotion and eccentric character are portrayed with transparent veracity? . . . the executioner and the victim equally astounded me. Mme Sand seemed completely at ease, and Chopin never stopped admiring the tale.

At midnight, the two men retired together. Delacroix seized the moment to probe Chopin's reactions: "Was he playing a part for my benefit? No, really, he had not understood. . . ." Chopin's self-control must have been considerable, and George herself was not quite as untroubled as she appeared. She had been sufficiently dissatisfied with the first version of the novel to rewrite it (a rare occurrence for her). Moreover, she asked a lawyer of her acquaintance to "tell me if you despise and detest Lucrezia. It is a study for me, and I am anxious to know the impression of the reader, of certain readers, without being spared."

Chopin's position in the Sand household remained anomalous. He was a permanent guest, and never managed quite to adapt himself to the invidious role. Nor did he easily resign himself to the fact that George declined to accept him as master or to be guided by his judgment in family matters. Young Maurice and his sister, ever more aware, did not always treat Chopin with deference either. (There came a time, however, when Solange would have a crush on the composer, secretly scribbling his initials and crossing out her mother's name.)

Beloved Maurice had been accepted as a pupil by Delacroix in February 1840. According to the painter of the "Death of Sardanapalus," usually sparing of praise, Maurice could go far, if he worked hard. The young man preferred to idle in Paris. His mother grew anxious about his association with dolls and dandies. She well knew how weak and easily influenced he was, and did not spare him (any more than the rest of her circle) her lengthy sermons. Then, at nineteen, Maurice fell deeply in love with Pauline Viardot who, much to his mother's surprise, reciprocated his feeling. Better Pauline than the dancing girls at the masked ball, thought George, but still, her "fifille," a married woman with a small child . . . This would not do.

George wondered how to divert Maurice's attention and, at the same time, to acquire a daughter-in-law who would be indebted to her and whom she could control. Otherwise, she could foresee trouble ahead at Nohant. In 1839, when only sixteen, Maurice had been momentarily attracted to a fifteen-year-old relative, an extremely pretty and docile music student named Augustine Brault, who was unhappy at home. Her mother, Sophie's cousin, a former "kept woman," was trying to sell the girl to the highest bidder. Her father, a tailoring hand who had fallen on hard times and who accepted George's charity, at first welcomed the idea that his daughter should go to live with George at Nohant. The "adoption" of Augustine Brault in 1845 proved to be one of George's major errors. Not only was Chopin passionately opposed to it, but, in trying to manipulate Maurice, George overlooked the jealous nature of Solange.

For a while, Solange, now seventeen, appeared quite pleased to have

Augustine, over three years her senior, as her companion. Soon, however, she looked down on the interloper as a poor relation and grew irritated when Augustine—the model, dutiful, "adopted" daughter—was dressed in finery and treated as her equal. She carried her complaints to Chopin. It seemed as if, never able to assure herself of George's love, she were now being forced to share her pittance, so inferior to Maurice's sum, with a mere outsider.

Solange had read her mother's early sensuous novels of revolt at fourteen. She preferred the proud Edmée of *Mauprat* to the charitable Consuelo, for, as George liked to repeat, her daughter was haughty and "born a princess." The girl privately mocked and rebelled against George's humanitarianism. Passionately fond of riding, she was quite capable of trying to stop her periods if they interfered with her pleasures. In embryo, Solange already belonged with a rising generation of cynical *lionnes*, who smoked larger cigarettes than George's and who had adopted the Sandian teachings about woman's right to independence and self-fulfillment, while discarding the "nobility of soul" with which her mother had clothed them.

Various suitors had been proposed for the girl, in the customary manner. Hippolyte even counseled a rewarding match with George's friend, the well-to-do doctor Gustave Papet, when Solange was a mere twelve years old. The merits and demerits of Louis Blanc as a possible husband were discussed with Latouche. It was by no means unusual for a mother to marry her daughter to an ex-lover (witness Marie Dorval, her daughter Caroline, and the actor René Luguet). However, to Charlotte Marliani, who busied herself with matchmaking, George had sharply observed that she wished Solange to marry late, say at twenty-five, and without outside interference.

In June 1846, George was invited by an enlightened landowner, the Comte de Lancosme-Brèves (to whom she had been introduced the previous summer by her good friend Rollinat), to visit the recently founded horse races at nearby Mézières-en-Brenne. It was the example of Lancosme-Brèves, who had reclaimed derelict land for horse-breeding, that inspired George's article on state aid for similar projects to relieve the ever-increasing distress in the countryside. At Mézières, George the keen horsewoman, accompanied by Solange and Augustine, encountered a well-mannered young squire, Fernand de Preaulx. Though attracted at first to the pretty Augustine, Fernand de Preaulx soon found himself in thrall to Solange.

The willful girl enjoyed having the slender, bearded fellow of twenty-three on a string for a while, but in the end she "said yes," a little coolly, to his pressing suit. George was pleased; Chopin approved. Though lacking in education and hard cash, Fernand de Preaulx was gentle and kind-hearted. Certain members of his family, minor country gentry, who knew of George Sand by reputation as a revolutionary and ungodly writer (some of whose works were on the Index), disapproved of the match. Time passed in the effort to win their consent (as well as that of Casimir). In any case, George saw no need for urgency. The two young people could become better acquainted while Fernand stayed during the winter at Nohant.

On November 11, 1846, Chopin returned to Paris alone, knowing that, for once, George would not be following. He did not know—and neither did she—that he would never again sport with her pet dogs, watch while Delacroix painted in the garden, or ride a jenny to the ruins of Crozant. Maurice, goaded by Frédéric's sharp pinpricks and by the composer's ill-concealed hostility toward Augustine and another "permanent guest," the young painter Eugène Lambert, had talked of leaving home. Torn between her son and her lover, and herself weary of the "pills" the latter had caused her to swallow, George suggested a brief separation. There was no question of a total break, for solicitous notes continued to pass between them.

Various matters contrived to keep George at Nohant, apart from the betrothal of her daughter. The disastrous autumn floods, the ensuing starvation and riots, kept her busy with many local charitable projects. In any case, apart from such acts of God, she loved autumn in the countryside: the dull thud of falling fruit, the mournful cries of migrating cranes, the lengthening evenings when the *chanvreur*, or hemp-dresser, recounted the old wives' tales that had made her blood run cold as a child. Significantly, for quite some while, she and Maurice had discussed the idea of forgoing winters in Paris after Solange's marriage— Parisian winters essential to Chopin's program of lessons—and indeed, in January 1847, George gave notice of leaving her flat in the Square d'Orléans. She contemplated the installation of central heating and double windows at Nohant. The railway, notwithstanding its blight on the landscape, would offer her the means of paying rapid business visits to the capital, if she chose to reside permanently in the country. (The line from Paris to Orléans, opened in 1843, was to be extended to Châteauroux in the autumn of 1847.)

With Chopin's departure came an almost audible sigh of relief. From early December onward, the entire household busied itself with amateur theatricals. George served as dramatist, actor, producer, assistant costume hand and scene painter, prompter and pianist. A new play was composed each evening during dessert, parts were learned during coffee, and the piece improvised up to midnight. Afterward came supper, and bed at two in the morning. The young people, Solange and the awkward Fernand de Preaulx, Maurice and his amusing friend, Eugène Lambert, together with Augustine, joined in the fun in the warm drawing room, while the snow descended outside. These were the last moments of unadulterated pleasure and gaiety that George was to experience for a long time.

Accompanied by her family and by Fernand de Preaulx, George arrived in Paris early in February 1847 for the signing of the marriage contract. Eight months had passed since the first meeting of Fernand and Solange, who dominated him unmercifully. Now, a disturbing presence was about to enter their lives.

In response to an invitation from the sculptor and painter Jean-Baptiste Clésinger, who presented a bronze copy of his Faun and offered to sculpt busts of mother and daughter free of charge, George and Solange posed in his crowded studio. Clésinger had addressed an absurdly flattering letter to the eminent writer nearly a year before, naming a statue "Consuelo." He was soliciting the protection of the world-famous authoress—a calculating form of self-advertisement. George had then been introduced to Clésinger by an old acquaintance of hers, the witty Captain d'Arpentigny, author of a book on palmistry, who told her of readings of her novels in the sculptor's studio. As an art critic, Baudelaire had already praised Clésinger's work, exhibited in the Salon of 1845, and would continue to find merit in it.

No sooner had eighteen-year-old Solange set eyes on the powerfully built, free and easy former cuirassier than all thought of marrying Fernand de Preaulx vanished. When the contract was being drawn up, she sobbed and whispered that she was not ready for marriage. With the sorrowing departure of the unfortunate fiancé, it became clear to George that her capricious daughter had set her heart on Clésinger. She deplored Solange's harshness to Fernand, but could find no fundamental objection to Clésinger, a rising "artist" of thirty-two, perhaps more suitable, in this respect, than a benighted royalist country squire. Captain d'Arpentigny was horrified. He had introduced Clésinger as a sculptor of repute, not as a prospective son-in-law. He hastened to inform George that Clésinger was not merely heavily in debt, but that his character, drinking habits, and private life left much to be desired.

George challenged the sculptor, who coolly denied that he had any debts. To bear witness to his good character, he sent his friends, the landscape painters Jules Dupré and Théodore Rousseau, to call on George. As it happened, George was well acquainted with Théodore Rousseau, whose gifts she highly esteemed. The persecuted artist was a friend of Maurice's. Nearly seven years before, she had contrived to arrange the purchase by the state of his "Avenue of Chestnut Trees" (now in the Louvre). Having conducted what she called a veritable inquiry into Clésinger's affairs, she felt she had no reason to doubt the asseverations of Théodore Rousseau (whom even the suspicious Chopin regarded as an honest fellow), supported by those of Dupré. She concluded that Clésinger might be imprudent and vain—a typical "artist"—but that he was good-hearted. To Chopin she would afterward observe how daring and ambitious the sculptor appeared—attributes that the musician, unlike George (who shared them), did not regard as qualities. Still, to Poncy, she owned that she was very upset.

Why did George disregard Captain d'Arpentigny? Why did she fail to consult any of her old friends, like Manuel Marliani and Emmanuel Arago, or Delacroix and Chopin (both of whom accompanied her to the Luxembourg on April 1). All of them could have enlightened her about the size of the sculptor's debts, his heavy drinking, his brutal treatment of his pregnant mistress. D'Arpentigny she knew to be hypercritical and argumentative. She excluded Chopin because she did not want to give him a master's rights, and besides, he had cried wolf too often about perfectly decent friends of hers. All the same, there is a mystery here, one deeply hidden in her own changeability and self-will, in her fluctuations between good sense and folly, in her illusions about the sanctity of woman's right to passion and about the latitude to be granted to the "artist," in her weariness with Solange's caprice and intractability.

When George returned to Nohant with Solange and Augustine early in April, nothing was settled. A few days later, Clésinger arrived, "like Caesar," demanding a "yes" or a "no" within twenty-four hours. Solange said yes unhesitatingly and defiantly, despite her mother's misgivings. Clésinger's willpower impressed George, who wrote to Maurice, "Not a word to Chopin. It does not concern him. . . ." To Poncy, she confided strangely that this marriage must be concluded "impetuously, as if by surprise." Why? Had Clésinger and Solange become lovers?

George could hint to her literary adviser and future publisher, Pierre-Jules Hetzel, that they threatened to elope if she opposed them. Startled by her daughter's sensual arousal, knowing the strength of Solange's willfulness, and fearing lest the girl might lose her reputation, George consented. Contrary to her earlier wishes, she too became caught up in the rush to conclude the marriage at high speed.

That George was by no means as happy with the outcome as she pretended to be seems perfectly clear. She returned to thoughts of suicide in her diary. She made a will. Chopin, informed of the forthcoming marriage on May 1, took to his bed in Paris with a severe attack of asthma. George well knew how he must have suffered from being kept aloof, but she confided a little in Delacroix, in Grzymala, not in the composer who, as he himself owned, had done all he could to prevent the match. She did not want him to interfere.

George's old friends, much hurt, were not invited to the simple ceremony in the little church at Nohant on May 19. George had to be carried into the church, having pulled a muscle in her leg. Never was marriage less gay, she wrote, thanks to the gloomy presence of Casimir. Instead of the usual costly feast, a thousand francs were distributed to the poor of the parish.

Matrimony is catching. On the way to Guillery to obtain Casimir's consent, Clésinger had urged Maurice to marry Augustine Brault. At once, Casimir threatened to disinherit his son, who lamely dropped the project, saying, "My father objects. . . ." The trouble was that Maurice did not really want to marry, since he was obsessed with Pauline Viardot; but he did not like the idea of Augustine's union with anyone else. Clésinger, meanwhile, had encouraged his friend Théodore Rousseau to propose to Augustine, who accepted him. George assured Rousseau that her "adopted" daughter would eventually receive a dowry of one hundred thousand francs, either from the expected sale of the novelist's collected works or else from a legacy in her will.

When Solange and her husband learned about this future dowry of Augustine's, they were furious. Solange had received as dowry the Hôtel de Narbonne (although part of the mortgage remained to be redeemed). All she understood was that the interloper was to obtain what rightfully belonged to her. Anonymous letters (penned by the Clésingers), insinuating that Augustine had been Maurice's mistress, shook Rousseau. The thirty-five-year-old painter, thoroughly distressed, then began to behave rather like George's Horace. He informed the astonished novelist that, contrary to his own distaste for matrimony, he had agreed to marry Augustine to satisfy George. Consequently, he demanded proof of Augustine's purity or a confession, together with monetary compensation. He professed to be upset by George's "marital policy, which you, least of all, should have contemplated." She made it plain to Rousseau that, if he thought her work opposed to matrimony on principle, he was very much mistaken.

Solange, having contrived to break the luckless Augustine's match with Rousseau, adopted toward her mother what the latter called "a tone suggestive of hatred." Though besieged by creditors, Clésinger continued to live in Paris in extravagant style, keeping a hired carriage and liveried servants. His mother-in-law, her eyes opened, had no intention of paying his debts, as he had thought she would, since he supposed that her fame spelled wealth. Let the pair live simply, as she herself had learned to do.

July 1847 saw George's forty-third birthday. A dreadful scene occurred on the eleventh at Nohant, in the presence of witnesses, between Maurice and Clésinger, egged on by Solange. Somewhat the worse for drink, the sculptor brandished a hammer with which he had been nailing his luggage. George threw herself between her son and her son-in-law, smacked the sculptor's face, and received a blow in the chest from Clésinger's heavy fist. The newlyweds then departed for the inn at La Châtre, where they spread odious scandal, Solange having offered not the slightest token of repentance to her mother. After this, George made another will, leaving Nohant in entirety to Maurice.

Expecting Chopin's imminent arrival, George wrote to the composer her version of what had taken place, telling him that Clésinger had struck her and making a condition that he should not mention the name of her son-in-law or her daughter. Chopin showed this letter (now lost) to Delacroix, who thought it "ghastly," and who added: "Cruel passions, long repressed impatience, are revealed; and, by a contrast that would be droll if the theme were not so grievous, the author occasionally replaces the woman and launches into tirades seemingly borrowed from some novel or philosophical lecture." Delacroix could engage in risqué verbal flirtation with George, but he could not comprehend the profound shock she had received from Solange's ingratitude and lack of feeling. A confirmed bachelor, his opinion of women in general was poor. He would copy into his journal quotations like "Woman is an inferior being, ruled to excess by her internal organs." In his view,

Parisian women had far too much freedom and authority, and should be controlled more effectively.

Meanwhile, George grew anxious at not having heard from Chopin. When his chilly reply finally arrived, it proved a revelation. It showed no concern for what she had endured. He politely refused to accept her condition concerning her daughter—"who cannot be a subject of indifference to me." She realized at once what this letter signified: It meant that, despite the years of supposed exclusive devotion, Chopin preferred Solange to herself. Much that she had previously disregarded now fell into place, especially the shared secrets and antipathies of her lover and her daughter.

George's interpretation of the transfer of Chopin's affections to his old ideal, "the pure young girl," is corroborated by a passage in a letter from the composer to his family in Warsaw, a letter that (after his years of reticence) suddenly reveals his unconscious thoughts. Alluding to Clésinger's notorious "Woman bitten by a Snake"—the sensation of the Salon of 1847—that portrayed the courtesan, Mme Sabatier, not in the throes of deadly snake bite but of orgasm, Chopin wrote that Clésinger would probably display his wife's belly and breasts at the next exhibition. He "will sculpt Solange's little behind in white marble. *That is what he is capable of doing.*" George's friend Emmanuel Arago confirmed her view of Chopin's "bizarre reversal," telling her that it was no news to him and that this type of turnabout was common enough in situations like hers.

The last letter George sent to Chopin was a grim and characteristic refusal to defend herself against her daughter's calumnies, which he cared to heed "and possibly believe." For Solange communicated to him her distorted imaginings, or carefully omitted vital details. George told him: "I take refuge in my role as injured mother. . . . I forgive you. . . ." As an afterthought, she asked him to let her know occasionally how he was. "It is useless ever to revert to the rest." So ended, in tragic misunderstanding, without violent scenes, what she called with only slight exaggeration "nine years of exclusive friendship." Oddly enough, Chopin could observe: "Eight years of a more or less orderly life—that was too much for her." Did he know, then, in his innermost being, that his jealous accusations had been largely unfair?

In George's eyes, Chopin had committed the ultimate sin: He had been failing in trust, like her great-uncle abbé de Beaumont and so many others since her youth. He had betrayed her—however platonically—

to side with her own daughter, who was frenziedly engaged in black-ening George's name while bewailing her mother's lack of affection. George may well have been relieved to be free of Chopin's needling and of the responsibility of looking after him, but as a woman of forty-three she could not help being deeply hurt at his defection. It seemed to Chopin that George, with her intense imagination, was "playing the part of a better and more perfect mother than she is in reality." She had indeed, to her mind, nothing on her conscience in that regard. Per-haps the greatest wound inflicted by Solange was that she publicly damaged George's carefully constructed self-image as the good mother. For there was more than a grain of truth in Solange's view that her mother preferred Maurice—and it was this awareness that had con-tributed to warp the girl's character.

George was to meet Chopin only once more, at the entrance to Charlotte Marliani's apartment in March 1848, when he politely in-formed her that Solange had just given birth to a girl at Guillery and George equally politely inquired after his health. As months passed, his assessment of her grew more bitter with his increasing sickness, and he came to believe the worst that could be spoken of "Lucrezia," whom he would have liked to condemn to hell. Well-meaning friends tried to effect a reconciliation, but in vain. There could be no going back.

After his concert tour of Scotland and England, Chopin would return to Paris in 1849, prematurely aged by suffering, to die in public view in a room crowded with visitors. It was Solange who closed his eyes. Her husband, whom Chopin had once so detested but had helped for her sake, was to sculpt the composer's monument. Naturally, George was distressed by Chopin's death; but she could also say, in a moment of appalling aberration, that she had endured greater mental suffering for his sake during their liaison than he had endured physical suffering during his entire life. Words prevailed.

As yet, however, Chopin's death lay in the future. Private disasters did not interrupt George's literary activity. The second, imaginative life she lived during the night at her desk flowed on. Indeed, the desire to provide Solange with an allowance that would be beyond Clésinger's reach and a dowry for Augustine (who would eventually marry a Polish émigré, Charles de Bertholdi) kept George busy. Two novels were completed by October 1847: *Célio Floriani* (published several years later as *Le Château des désertes*) and *François le Champi*, with its curiosly equivocal transmutation of filial and maternal love into sexual love—

that borderline she so often crossed and recrossed in imagination and in fact. She had also begun work in earnest on the long-standing project of her autobiography, stimulated, as once before, by a mood of suicidal gloom. This was the great undertaking that was intended to restore her fallen fortunes and to save her from despair. It would be interrupted in mid-course by matters of public moment in which she was to play a prominent and distinctive role: the Revolution of 1848.

PART VI

Woman of Action

CHAPTER
18

"Red" Revolutionary

If there is a revolution, why shouldn't Julien Sorel play the part of
Roland, and I that of Madame Roland?
Mathilde de La Mole in Stendhal's
Le Rouge et le noir

Instead of only a few sections of the bourgeoisie all classes of French
society were suddenly hurled into the orbit of political power, forced
to leave the boxes, the stalls, and the gallery, and to act in person
upon the revolutionary stage!   Karl Marx
The Class Struggles in France 1848–1850

A T one o'clock on the afternoon
of February 24, 1848, a young
diarist, looking out from his
balcony in the rue des
Capucines, saw the ironmonger
across the road in the act of
hastily hammering off the word
"Royal" from the shop sign.
The overthrow of Louis-
Philippe swept into power an
uneasy, inexperienced coalition
of liberals, radicals, and socialists. For years they had been voicing
discontent, dreaming of revolution and a just society. Now, after two
days of fighting on the barricades, Louis-Philippe had surprisingly ab-
dicated in favor of his grandson. Among those who went to persuade
the popular liberal spokesman, the lyric poet Lamartine, to oppose
a regency and favor a republic, were two close friends of George's: the
publisher Hetzel (politician as well as writer) and her one-time lover,
the radical actor Bocage.

As it happened, Maurice was in Paris, staying in a fifth-floor attic in the rue de Condé, near the Théâtre de l'Odéon. An excited letter reached George at Nohant. He had been to see the "magnificent" barricades. All Paris was under arms. The red flag was flying everywhere. Once again people were addressing each other as "citizen." He had seen genuine *sans-culottes* adorned with the Phrygian cap. "It's marvelous!" George learned that her colleagues on *La Réforme* now occupied positions of power. The republican lawyer Ledru-Rollin was minister of the interior in the Provisional Government, with responsibility for arranging elections to the Constituent Assembly. Her former short-term lover Louis Blanc headed the government commission in charge of the so-called National Workshops, which had been hurriedly set up to propitiate the workers. It seemed to George that the cause of the humble workmen, about which she had been writing so persuasively for so long, was about to be heard and their wrongs righted at last. The republic of her dreams could soon become a reality. Through the just victory of "the people," endowed with superior though untried qualities, she might perhaps finally assuage all the humiliation she had suffered at the hands of those who despised her plebeian mother.

Accompanied by her old friend Charles Duvernet, George hastened to Paris, arriving in the capital on March 1. Next day, she called on Ledru-Rollin, a well-meaning, stout man with large white hands. Without ado, he provided "Citizeness George Sand" with a pass that gave her access to all members of the Provisional Government. Two days later, she could write to the conservative René Vallet de Villeneuve, "I know *better than anyone* what is going on both inside the government and in the streets." She made it her task to take note of public opinion and mood.

If a lyric poet like Lamartine, whom she knew personally and held in relatively little esteem, could enact a leading role in public affairs, there seemed no reason why she, an eminent novelist, even though a woman, could not play a vital part behind the scenes. After all, women had left a mark during the Revolution of 1789. Quite apart from the prostitute Théroigne de Méricourt who, in blood-red riding habit and with pistols in her belt, had dominated the Paris streets, there was Mme de Staël who wove intrigues to little purpose, or Mme Roland who ruled through her husband (by coincidence, minister of the interior). Manon Roland, as the wife of a minister, had not been obliged to "earn" her position of power in the same way as George, and she paid for her irresponsibility and her self-importance with her head. That was an instructive example to bear in mind.

But, of course, the Second Republic was going to be entirely different from the First. The words "liberty," "fraternity," and "equality" were to be put into practice at last. The tone was set for George when the Provisional Government began by proclaiming universal (manhood) suffrage, the abolition of slavery in the French dominions, together with the abolition of the death penalty for political acts. To the astonishment of many, the victorious populace did not abuse its new freedom. George felt elated by the revolutionary festivals and processions, the planting of trees of liberty. Her private bitterness at Solange's ingratitude and Chopin's defection was rapidly banished by urgent activity. What form did this activity take?

One of the first problems facing the Provisional Government concerned the elections to the Constituent Assembly—Ledru-Rollin's province. How to ensure that the new voters, now including thousands of uneducated men, would return a majority of candidates agreeable to the present rulers? Besides, these new rulers differed among themselves about their aims. As for George, like Louis Blanc, she knew perfectly well what she wanted: a socialist republic.

Among the commissioners newly appointed by Ledru-Rollin to rally provincial support, George discovered, there figured Michel de Bourges, before whom she had all too often abased herself. By defending a government functionary against an opposition journalist, Michel had turned renegade in the eyes of George and her Berrichon friends. With Charles Duvernet, she hurried to the Hôtel de Ville. Louis Blanc came out of a meeting to greet her: "You here as a petitioner? Your proper place is inside, with us." He led her into the Council Chamber, where all rose deferentially. The President of the Council exclaimed: "Dear lady, by the right of genius you should be in my place!" After stating her reasons for opposing the nomination of Michel as commissioner, she withdrew. The appointment of her one-time republican mentor was formally revoked.

Her first revolutionary act thus exemplified the revolutionary fanaticism she felt was needed: the strong-minded substitution of public duty for private affections. There must be no hesitation in "sweeping away everything marked by the bourgeois spirit." George was not the first, and would not be the last, to mistake secret animosity (worthy of

[259]

Mme Roland at her worst when intriguing against Danton) for revolutionary zeal. (Two months later, when Ledru-Rollin dismissed Alfred de Musset from his obscure job as librarian at the Ministry of the Interior, George did not protest.)

In these early days, she was busy recommending her Berrichon friends—Duteil, Fleury, Planet, and Duvernet obtained important posts. On March 4, she stood chatting amiably with Lamartine as she watched, from the Foreign Ministry windows, the funeral procession of those killed on the barricades. The city was thronged with foreign visitors— she had seen among them old friends from Geneva as well as Giuseppe Mazzini (for whom she requested a passport).

A few days later, after having completed a propaganda article, "Yesterday and Today," which envisaged the elimination of the very word "class" from the dictionary of a new humanity, she set off for Nohant, endowed with Ledru-Rollin's full authorization to carry the revolution to Berry. To this end, Maurice was proclaimed mayor of Nohant-Vicq. George was thoroughly enjoying herself—she felt alive, a mere girl of twenty again. Her head was full of ideas for pamphlets, for a newspaper of her own. She wanted each area to elect at least one town worker and one peasant. It was she who suggested to the noted Saint-Simonian Hippolyte Carnot, the minister of education, her plan for sending selected workers to educate their fellows, or rather to "make propaganda" in the provinces. The Provisional Government accepted the scheme, but did nothing about it. Finally, she would convince Ledru-Rollin of its value, though he bungled it by hurting the feelings of the young workers she presented to him.

After organizing a republican ceremony at Nohant, George returned to Paris, accompanied by Victor Borie, one-time editor of *L'Eclaireur de l'Indre,* the provincial paper she had helped to found. Introduced to her by Pierre Leroux some four years before, Victor Borie had since assumed a loyal place among her Nohant circle. At twenty-nine, he was a close friend of Maurice's (now approaching twenty-five), the good-natured butt of mother and son in their private jokes about his broad provincial accent. Sharing George's radical views, he made himself useful to her in practical negotiations and business matters. He became her companion and lover possibly sometime in the summer of 1847 (though whether before or after the defection of Chopin cannot be conclusively established). George settled into Maurice's fifth-floor attic in the rue de Condé, later renting a large room for Borie on the third floor. Every morning between eleven and one, and again in the evening from six to eight, George could be found at Pinson's modest restaurant in the nearby rue de l'Ancienne-Comédie. Pinson's, an establishment she had advertized in *Horace*, having frequented it in the impecunious period of her journalistic debut, served as her political headquarters.

Meanwhile, the Provisional Government Council had authorized Ledru-Rollin to arrange for the eminent authoress to contribute articles to the *Bulletin de la République* (a series of large broadsheets aimed at enlightening the masses, and posted in public places all over the country). From mid-March to the end of April, George contributed possibly ten articles, all unsigned, for which she received no payment. The earliest of them, her admonition "To the Rich," had been previously published in La Châtre, so the author's identity soon became common knowledge. In this article, George played down the widespread fear of communism based, in her view, upon a misapprehension. She herself, though a self-styled communist, had never met any of those communist fanatics who were supposed to be intent on destroying property and family by fire and sword. Some (like herself) belonged to no sect, but regarded communism as the faith of the future, as true Christianity. This somewhat incautious attempt to calm the fears of the bourgeoisie produced the opposite effect and confirmed George's reputation as a dangerous "red" revolutionary.

So George acted as unpaid secretary for propaganda, accused of being on the Provisional Government's payroll. She would prove a gift to the caricaturists, as Ledru-Rollin's female *éminence grise*, in quest of the leading role; as "The Political Old-Woman-Who-Lived-in-a-Shoe of 1848," whip in hand, while little men ran feverishly in and out of her voluminous skirt.

Animosity, experienced since her girlhood, meant little to her; indeed, she scorned and thrived on it. Above all, she told Maurice with deep satisfaction how busy she was, just "like a statesman," writing two government circulars in one day, and delightfully in great demand on all sides. Her low-priced weekly, *La Cause du peuple*, largely written by herself, would soon be appearing, though it only ran to three issues. After it folded, she would contribute to *La Vraie République*, edited by Théophile Thoré, an ardent radical (later well-known as a discerning art critic).

Members of the Provisional Government came to call on her in her "hovel," the attic in the rue de Condé, where she held what might be regarded as a modest version of Mme Roland's political salon. She herself called on various ministers, staying as late as one or two o'clock in the morning, while on occasion her obliging escort, Victor Borie, cooled his heels in the antechamber.

In addition to her role as unpaid secretary for propaganda, George also assumed that of unpaid secretary for the arts. She obtained an official commission for her son-in-law, Clésinger (while keeping Solange —whose baby lived only a few days—at arm's length). Rather grandly, she privately offered the directorship of the Opéra to Pauline Viardot's husband or brother. It was George who organized a free performance at the Théâtre de la République (formerly the Théâtre Français), for which she wrote a short play entitled *Le Roi attend,* where Molière falls asleep while awaiting Louis XIV and dreams of the advent of the Republic. The warm reception accorded to this pastiche provided some consolation for the failure there of her play *Cosima,* which, despite disclaimers, had rankled for eight years. George had urged Ledru-Rollin to commission a patriotic cantata from Pauline, whom she hoped would create a revolution in art to parallel the political revolution. Unfortunately, her friend was too ill to sing the cantata herself, but the celebrated actress Rachel repeated her fiery recitation of the Marseillaise, "sublime in pose, gesture and expression." George duly reviewed the whole performance, stressing the virtue of the popular audience in the first issue of her weekly, *La Cause du peuple.*

In short, George made herself useful to the Provisional Government, while also trying to be of use to her friends. Afterward, when differences arose, Ledru-Rollin let it be known that she had thrown her weight about. In the beginning, though, he and his colleagues had been pleased enough to have so forceful a pen at their disposal. Yet there could be no question of offering a woman, even one so devoted, energetic, and famous, any official post.

The Revolution of 1848 brought to the fore once again questions raised and unresolved by the Revolution of 1789, including the problem and status of women. Under the new Republic, several serious attempts would be made, chiefly by Saint-Simonians and Fourierists, to improve woman's lot. The Saint-Simonian minister of education, Hippolyte Carnot, favored measures for female instruction. The Jewish-born minister of justice, Adolphe Crémieux, would attempt to reestablish divorce, though in vain. One of the leading Jewish Saint-Simonians, Olinde Rodrigues, in his project for a new constitution, was to proclaim the civil and political equality of both sexes. Fourier's chief disciple, Victor Considérant, demanded votes for women. This demand was simply the logical extension of the institution of universal manhood suffrage.

Among the mushrooming revolutionary clubs, whose members met in empty shops and churches, were several run by women. None of them appealed to George—least of all the *Club des Vésuviennes*, consisting of prostitutes who presented petitions to the Provisional Government in the name of total freedom. More noteworthy, however, was the *Club des Femmes*, formed by Saint-Simonian women under the leadership of Eugénie Niboyet. According to Flaubert's amused friend Maxime Du Camp, its members condemned man, demanded trial marriage and divorce, and wanted a woman's children to be left to their "fathers". These were the women cruelly caricatured by Daumier as "The Lady Divorcers." (Some national guards, not to be deprived of their fun— Maxime Du Camp, a member of the national guard himself, relates— carried off a few unfortunate women to an ill-lit corridor and whipped them.) Another source gives the club's aims as the vote, equality before the law, equal education, the right to work, the removal of sex discrimination.

George's passionate English imitator, the novelist Geraldine Jewsbury, besotted with the Saint-Simonian Charles Lambert, came to Paris with friends to see what was going on and attended a session of the *Club des Femmes*. So did Matthew Arnold's friend, poet Arthur Hugh Clough, another admirer of George's, much put out by the odious behavior of men in the audience, who roared at any hint of double entendre. Eugénie Niboyet, however, by contriving to keep her patience, won Clough's respect.

It was Eugénie Niboyet who, on April 6, proposed the perfect embodiment of the Saint-Simonian man-woman symbol, George Sand, as the first woman candidate for the Constituent Assembly (a proposal seconded by the *Club des Jacobins* a few days later). The gesture was, in reality, an empty one, since officially women could neither stand nor vote. George herself, in the twelfth *Bulletin de la République* of April 6, having eloquently protested against the sufferings of exploited working women, had observed that such poor, uneducated women would have gained nothing from the presence of their talented sisters in public posts. This conviction, together with her enduring suspicion of Saint-Simonian feminist policy, led her forcefully to reject the proposal. She hoped nobody would waste a vote on her; haughtily denied acquaintance with the ladies of the club; and coldly pointed out that an article in their journal, *La Voix des femmes*, signed G.S., was not hers.

Evidently, this snub to Eugénie Niboyet and her friends bothered George. Feeling that she had not expressed her views adequately, she began to draft a long and involved public statement to the electoral committee. Some of what she had to say was already present in the article on Mme Merlin and the *Lettres à Marcie* of many years before. Women will participate in politics in the future, she opined, although society must be changed first. They should not try to act politically to bring about this radical change, because—given existing social customs and laws, the miconceived popular association of female emancipation with Saint-Simonian or Fourierist promiscuity, and the general debasement of women (comparable to that of female slaves)—they could not do so honorably or without suffering insult. Doubtless, she had in mind some of the wilder scenes in the clubs. As she expressed it, ". . . my age and perhaps some services rendered to the cause of my sex by my numerous writings, give me the right to remonstrate."

What women should seek, as a first step to female emancipation, was civil equality and property rights. These would be among the first matters to receive attention in a socialist republic. Enlightened men will support the cause of civil equality, of equal rights and dignity within the family, declared George, whereas few will take seriously the idea of women as political candidates. This draft letter remained in her drawer, presumably because she felt dissastisfied with it.

In short, George advised women to act with prudence. Public opinion must be won over first. Her aim was to strive for goals she regarded as attainable in the society of her day. Such feasible reforms might be hindered by extreme and unrealizable demands. Besides, there was no point in adding uneducated women to the uneducated men on the enlarged electoral register, she was to add in a later article. George would not appreciate the symbolic value either of the forty votes cast for her (unauthorized) candidacy in May 1849 or of the historic act of the secretary of *La Voix des femmes*, the Saint-Simonian Jeanne Deroin, who dared to stand for the Assembly.

Perhaps because the socialists were the principal supporters of the feminist cause, George was misled into believing that socialism would ultimately solve the woman question. Equally, she was misled by her profound contempt for the majority of women, represented in her own mind by the image of the "little woman," the role she herself had so fervently enacted during the early years of her marriage. The memory of that period in her life, source of secret self-contempt, distorted her appreciation of political action for women. Yet there was one sense in which she was not mistaken: To aim primarily for the vote was indeed to put the cart before the horse, as she suggested. After women finally obtained the right to vote—almost a hundred years later in France in 1945—the question of full civil equality and full human dignity remained there and elsewhere, and to some degree still remains, outstanding.

It is ironic, though, that while George continued to oppose political action for women in general, she herself was deeply involved in the preelectoral preparations for the Constituent Assembly. Not only did she engage in extensive journalistic propaganda, she also served as agent for the Provisional Government. Afterward, she would claim that she was not at all interested in politics as such, like the erudite Hortense Allart, and that she had not participated in electoral maneuvers "unsuited to my sex." The evidence tells a different story about her clandestine activities.

By mid-April, George had other matters on her mind, matters more vital, in her view, than the subordinate question of female suffrage. In secret discussions in her attic flat, at the Ministry of the Interior, in the clubs, she had become a party to the various intrigues that were afoot to thwart a possible electoral victory of the moderates or conservatives, the forces of reaction, by means of a coup d'état like the notorious one of 18th Fructidor 1797 (coup d'état carried out on September 4, 1797, by the Directoire when it felt threatened by the election results. Troops entered the two chambers and arrested representatives). When writing to Maurice, she had gaily envisaged *"chucking* out of the window" successful candidates of reactionary hue. She told Maurice, moreover, that the people's will would triumph *"inside* or *outside"* the Assembly —scarcely the words of a keen advocate of parliamentary democracy.

According to Marie d'Agoult (writing under the pseudonym Daniel Stern), her former friend was "one of the most active agents of the conspiracy," though she added, incorrectly, "less in the interest of Ledru-Rollin than of Louis Blanc." For there was more than one conspiracy. Both these leaders were engaged in combined as well as separate plots. Believing that such action would save the (true) Republic, George favored the combined conspiracy of Ledru-Rollin and Louis Blanc, even though she now found the former to be tainted by class pride, while the latter appeared to her as would-be dictator. Besides, Ledru-Rollin also had the support of her new friend, Armand Barbès.

When in March she first met the pale, hollow-eyed, bearded Barbès, he had just been released by the Republic—along with his fellow conspirator, the sinister-looking Auguste Blanqui. (They had spent nearly nine years in prison for their part in the abortive uprising of 1839.) Even the opponents of Barbès had to admit that he was completely disinterested—the liberal-conservative political thinker Alexis de Tocqueville would call him a combination of demagogue, madman, and knight. Such a chivalric figure, marked by suffering nobly borne, could not but appeal to George, who regarded him as nothing less than heroic—a word scarcely to be applied to Ledru-Rollin, Louis Blanc, or the ineffective Pierre Leroux.

On April 15, in an unsigned article in the sixteenth *Bulletin de la République*—an article for which she later claimed responsibility—George showed her hand. If "social truth" did not triumph in the forthcoming elections, if these were merely the expression of a particular class (that is, the reactionary bourgeoisie), then the people would have only one means of saving the (true, socialist) Republic: to resort to the barricades a second time. Heaven forbid that such an extreme measure should have to be taken! This prayer could not conceal the drift of the preceding words, which were construed as a form of incitement.

When, on the following day, members of the extremist revolutionary clubs attempted a coup d'état (which was rapidly quashed), some of the responsibility for it was ascribed to George. For many months she would not be able to live down those words, which caused her name to be execrated by her opponents. To some, she appeared as the reincarnation of the firebrand Théroigne de Méricourt (minus pistols), while Ledru-Rollin served as the bastard Danton and Louis Blanc as the bastard Robespierre. Such comparisons with the larger-than-life revolutionaries of the previous century merely reinforced the sense of black farce. The events of April 16, some of which she witnessed since she joined the procession of workers to the Hôtel de Ville, left her disillusioned with the character of most of the leaders (not least, "that wretch, Blanqui"). Her dismay increased with bourgeois shouts of "Death to the Communists!" which, in company with Victor Borie, she heard in the streets that same evening.

Some slight relief was provided when, on the overcast morning of April 20, George stood as of right with the leaders of the Provisional

Government at the Arc de Triomphe, from whence she viewed the entire Festival of Fraternity. The bayonets adorned with lilac, the excited crowds, and later on, the torchlit processions, thrilled her. All the same, the result of the elections, held three days later, fell far short of her original hopes, since the new electorate chose largely to vote for the old guard.

Despite the tense situation, one of her numerous visiting English admirers and an acquaintance of long-standing, the member of Parliament and celebrity hunter Richard Monckton Milnes, decided to give a literary luncheon for her. The ill-assorted guests included the English journalist F. O. Ward, together with Charlotte Marliani, Victor Considérant, Alfred de Vigny, Alexis de Tocqueville. In his sublime ignorance, Monckton Milnes had also invited Prosper Mérimée who, not having seen George for many years since their fiasco, for a moment wondered who the good-looking middle-aged lady was. He thought her appearance had considerably improved. She did not address him, but they could not help casting sidelong glances at each other.

George found herself seated next to the forty-two-year-old Norman aristocrat, Alexis de Tocqueville, newly elected to the Constituent Assembly. The author of *De la Démocratie en Amérique* had never met her before, being mightily prejudiced against her, since he loathed women writers in general and especially those who did not confine themselves to the weaknesses of their sex (a remark that suggests he had not read her novels with close attention). She soon charmed him, however, and he had to admit that she possessed something of the naturalness of the great. Like so many others, he was struck by her simplicity of manner and speech, though he noticed a certain affectation of simplicity in her dress, adding the cryptic phrase (more revealing of his attitude than hers) that if she had been more elaborately dressed she would have seemed to him even more simple.

For a whole hour, they discussed politics. "Besides, Mme Sand was then a kind of politician . . ." noted Tocqueville (afterward Minister of Foreign Affairs), much impressed. For the first time, he was conversing with a person who was prepared to tell him—perhaps not very discreetly—something of what was going on among his political opponents. "Mme Sand gave me a very detailed and lively account of the condition of the Parisian workers, their organization, numbers, arms, preparations, thoughts, passions, their fixed and dread purposes." George, who had listened attentively to the workers in the streets and in the open-air clubs, and who knew their leaders well, clearly seized the opportunity to expound her view of the dangerous state of affairs in conversation—contrary to her normal custom with strangers.

At first, Tocqueville thought her picture overdrawn, but events, as he later owned, were to prove his informant correct. "Try to convince your friends, sir, that they should avoid forcing the workers into the streets by arousing their fear or anger; just as I should like to instill patience into mine, for, believe me, once fighting starts, you will all lose your lives." These words may seem at first to contradict the stirring rhetoric of the sixteenth Bulletin and George's earlier expressions of revolutionary zeal. They do not contradict, however, the moderate tenor of some of her propaganda, which aimed at class reconciliation. What Tocqueville took for her own fear at the workers' triumph and her compassion for the possible fate of himself and his party (no doubt real enough) might also be interpreted as an act of policy, an attempt to frighten her opponents into a conciliatory attitude.

On May 15, eleven days after this revealing encounter with Tocqueville, George walked for three hours alongside the huge procession that slowly wound toward the doors of the National Assembly, where a petition was to be presented for aid to martyred Poland. On reaching the doors, she learned that a group led by Barbès and Blanqui, for whom the demonstration for Poland served as a pretext, had pushed forward into the chamber. In the ensuing uproar, the hot-headed Barbès announced the dissolution of the Assembly and proclaimed a new government, to include Louis Blanc, Pierre Leroux, Etienne Cabet, and Théophile Thoré. Many years later, Barbès was to tell George that her name would certainly have figured on this list had he not become dazed in the general din. This assertion may be taken with a grain of salt, since he had kept his wits sufficiently to name the others. However, no sooner had Barbès announced a new provisional government than he and his friends were arrested in the name of the old one.

George, meanwhile, had remained with the main body of the procession outside the doors, apparently in ignorance of the plan. Yet she had been in close contact with Barbès, and only the day before she had tried to calm him. Was she quite as unaware as she later liked to appear? Would she have remained aloof had the coup proved successful? Fearing a visit from the police, George destroyed her papers. Word reached her that she was about to be arrested. Her friends advised her to go to Italy. In haste, she left Paris for Nohant on the evening of May 17.

There followed a long period of denial and self-justification—including the denial that she had left Paris because she feared arrest. Although George admitted that she had passed through the rue de Bourgogne on May 15, she insisted that she had not harangued the crowd from a café there—certainly an action contrary to character. She told Ledru-Rollin that "what I loathe most is to look as if I am performing a part for the sole pleasure of thrusting myself forward. . . ." Besides, she maintained, having no connection with the ill-advised abortive coup of May 15, she had nothing to fear from an inquiry.

From Nohant, she continued to contribute to Théophile Thoré's *La Vraie République* brave articles in defense of the policies, character, and conduct of her friends Louis Blanc and Armand Barbès. (She was also to write to Karl Marx to refute allegations, published by him, that she possessed documentary evidence about the treachery of another friend of hers, Bakunin.)

Thus it was that George found herself at Nohant when the strange and virtually leaderless Parisian uprising of workers erupted on June 23, prompted by the closing of the National Workshops. Facing hunger, many had determined to fight and, according to Tocqueville, in this desperate insurrection the women played as great a part as the men and were the last to surrender. So George did not witness the fearsome atrocities committed by some of the insurgents, horrors matched only by the terrible repression that followed at the hands of General Cavaignac.

After the June days, she could not deny the existence of class struggle over the question of bread and work for the poor. She had dreamed of a social transformation without civil war, she told Mazzini, and this yearning for class harmony provided one forceful theme of her political journalism. All the same, a deep hostility to the haves provided another. The urge to be rid of those who did not share her views could scarcely be reconciled with sweetness and light. Whether she was aware of this inner contradiction seems unlikely. It was but another aspect of the deeper split between her outward noble, compassionate persona and the private, less noble, more common impulses that this persona served to conceal—from herself as much as from others.

The collapse of her ideals in the horror of the June days left her sick with pain and disgust. Not only her hopes for her country, but her private affairs lay in ruins.

Like most aspects of business endeavor, publishing had suffered as a result of the upheaval and the financial crisis brought about by the Revolution. At this low point, George had to try to raise funds to prevent the sale of the Hôtel de Narbonne. These efforts to salvage Solange's dowry, quite unappreciated by her daughter, would be in vain, and the property would be sold when the market was at its lowest. Living quietly in her retreat at Nohant, the disillusioned George would return to her interrupted autobiography and find consolation in writing a charming rustic novel, *La Petite Fadette*, dedicated to Barbès, about the vindication of a misjudged peasant girl.

For, with the total defeat and dispersion of her party, George had become an easy target for her opponents in the press and elsewhere, who did not spare her private life and morals. There were even numerous threats by some locals to raze Nohant to the ground. On occasion, local people jeered at her, or worse still, threatened her with that old French revolutionary measure: hanging from a lamp post. And these were the very unfortunates who had never wanted for alms if they called at her door, those whom she had cared for since she was a girl. It was a period of intense bitterness—with the misguided workers, with the baseness of human nature in general—a bitterness she strove to overcome. She could not avoid reproaching herself for being able to live in comparative ease at Nohant with Maurice and Victor Borie, while others had paid for their convictions with their life or their freedom.

As for the equivocal Ledru-Rollin, she thought that he should not have stayed in office after Barbès was imprisoned. Besides, Ledru-Rollin had been far from chivalrous in failing to come to her defense in the matter of the sixteenth Bulletin. He had allowed her—a woman whose name should never have been revealed—to become a scapegoat. She had taken to using her womanhood as a kind of shield in battles against her attackers, stressing that she was "a *woman* who had never departed from her woman's role, either in politics or literature."

Further reflections on womanhood were occasioned by the visit to Nohant of one of her translators, Eliza Ashurst, an English spinster of thirty-five, introduced by Mazzini. As the daughter of an active liberal and feminist, Eliza, like her three sisters, was an ardent admirer of the creator of *Indiana*. The latter soon reached the conclusion that her novels had turned her visitor's head. To George's dismay, Eliza rattled on about man and woman, as if they were totally different creatures, instead of concerning herself with the concept of "the human being." It was as human beings, as souls in quest of spiritual perfection, that both men and women were to be seen. When Eliza questioned the author of *Lélia* about her view of Mazzini's feminism, George grew irritated. She told Eliza firmly that Mazzini's concern was with "humanity, which embraces the two sexes from a loftier standpoint than that of individual passions."

Eliza's attitude, which struck the mature George as hysterical, enabled the novelist to carry her own ideas a step further, toward the proclamation of the supremacy of the human being's spirit over his or her attributes. However, her declaration of faith to Eliza, repeated to Mazzini, did run counter to George's remark in an article of May 7 in *La Vraie République*, where she took socialist and feminist women to task and told them that equality must not be mistaken for similitude. It would not do to expect consistency from George Sand: She was all-too-human for that.

Nearly three years later, George was to express her enduring doubts about the destiny of women in a letter to her colleague Hortense Allart:

> I have suffered like you, my dear Hortense, for all our difficulties as women are related. . . . we make ourselves unhappy without being able to do otherwise. Do you think it will ever change, and that improved education, more outlets for action, a more important place for our sex, will alter our instincts, our capacity for suffering, our jealousy, our pitiful limitations? I am not too sure, since women like ourselves, artists who can live almost as men do, remain women in spite of everything. . . .

For a moment, George offered a glimpse into the fundamental short-comings of the human condition (irrespective of sex), which reforms in attitude and legislation might do much to relieve but could scarcely eradicate.

George had contributed to the Republic as journalist, as propagandist, as dramatist and sponsor of the arts, as political agent and participator in high-level discussions and clandestine intrigues, as reporter and witness. All this activity of hers had been crammed into the short space of some two and a half months. Then it was all over. By her example as a woman engaged in political action (indeed, as the only woman to appear semi-officially at public functions alongside ministers of the Provisional Government), George Sand had embodied the cause for which the Saint-Simonian and Fourierist women were fighting, regardless of the discouraging and even sardonic words she addressed to them. They themselves were not mistaken about the true significance of her role.

However, she had taken considerable risks in ardently committing herself to what proved to be the losing side of the "red republicans." She would have plenty of time to brood over the disaster and, by imperceptible degrees, to maneuver her forces in an attempt to restore her position in the years of trial ahead.

The Age of Discretion

... a woman on her knees ... This woman has white hair ...
George Sand, draft letter to Prince Louis-Napoleon Bonaparte,
May 1852

The greatest grievance which the Emperor Napoleon has against me,
is the respect which I have always entertained for real liberty.
Mme de Staël
Ten Years Exile

OR three years after the election of that shrewd and unscrupulous adventurer, Prince Louis-Napoleon, to the presidency of the Republic on December 10, 1848, George lay low. She was crudely guyed on the stage as "Madame Consuelo" in *Les Femmes saucialistes*, or ridiculed by Louis Reybaud in a chapter entitled "The Misfortunes of an Egeria." The cause she had espoused so boldly was to suffer a series of shattering blows, not only in France but throughout Europe. Unkindest cut of all, the "people," whose virtuous instinct and whose sovereignty she had so loudly proclaimed, chose to vote, en masse, for Bonaparte's nephew, the mere shadow of a great name.

She drew the conclusion that the "people" were still children, to be pitied rather than despised for their lack of political education. So she was able ultimately to resign herself to a situation largely brought about, in her view, by the shortcomings of the "people" and of her political friends. Apart from occasional business visits, she would keep well away from Paris, where a reactionary regime was engaged in sending the defeated insurgents of June to exile or to the penal colony. Nor did she abandon prudence to visit the court at Bourges that condemned her friend Barbès to life imprisonment.

Her mood of deep prostration would be reinforced during these years by the death of her alcoholic half-brother, Hippolyte (with whom she had remained unreconciled after Solange's marriage); of her adored Marie Dorval; of the estranged Chopin; of her confidante, Charlotte Marliani. Besides, George herself was experiencing "a physical crisis," the menopause—"the most difficult age in the physical life of women," as she would later allude to it—with its accompanying stomach pains and severe migraines, to be followed by wearisome hot flushes. She made no secret of these intimate details in her letters to masculine as well as feminine friends.

It was during this period that George began to turn her attention to writing seriously for the theater. To her friend, the actor Bocage, newly appointed director of the Théâtre de l'Odéon, she offered the play she had constructed out of her rustic novel *François le Champi*. Having determined not to attend rehearsals, she gave him a free hand to cut, though not to add, to the dialogue, since Berrichon speech was her speciality, besides being a novelty on the stage. *François le Champi* proved a resounding success. That there was a taste for simple rustic themes in the theater may be deduced from the fact that some rivals produced an unauthorized dramatization of *La Petite Fadette*.

Meanwhile, at Nohant, "our snuff-box theater," as she would later call it, ceased to be a mere country-house diversion. It provided the opportunity for her to test her plays in advance, and to make alterations where necessary. Maurice and the young artist friends who kept him company at Nohant, Eugène Lambert and Léon Villevieille, not only painted the scenery but performed the roles, along with local friends, visitors or passing actors like Sully-Lévy, a new protégé. In addition to the main stage, there was also the tiny, free-style marionette theater, dependent on audience participation, with its one hundred and twenty-five dolls costumed by George and manipulated by Maurice to brilliant effect.

With the radical Bocage, George planned to create a consoling, moralizing theater for the masses. Unfortunately, Bocage's imprudent celebration of the anniversary of the Second Republic offended the authorities and lost him his directorship of the Odéon. George supported him loyally nonetheless. Her play about the rehabilitation of an unmarried mother, *Claudie*, in which Bocage returned successfully to the boards at the Porte-Saint-Martin theater, moved many to tears. The increasingly active censors, noting "socialist tendencies" in the play, had insisted on the removal of the words "wicked rich people." In George's opinion, they were furious because, despite political upheavals, she had somehow managed to continue to produce works of "art" that could still put the public "on my side." *Claudie* did meet with considerable political opposition from the upper crust. Like so many later dramatists, George was obliged to admit that the popular audience, for whom she was primarily writing, failed her. "One cannot be maintained by the people to whom one speaks and for whom one works," she told Bocage sadly.

Writing plays not only gratified her lifelong passion for the stage, whose magic she tellingly evoked in many of her stories and novels, it also opened for her an entirely fresh and exciting field. That it was a genre for which she had only limited natural gifts may be readily granted. Yet although Delacroix, with his discriminating literary taste, could patronize her drama in the privacy of his journal, she was to enjoy—amid difficulties and flops—several notable triumphs. (Indeed, the critic Baron Ernest Sellière could still remember, when over fifty in 1920, how he had enjoyed revivals of her plays in his youth.)

Perhaps some of her most arresting work during this period, however, is to be found in the prefaces she composed for the novels reprinted in the illustrated edition published by Hetzel. In these prefaces —which may well have served as model for those of Henry James—she noted the place and circumstance of composition, her state of mind at the time, her intentions. These prefaces often differ considerably from earlier ones, modifying her original, more daring views. Taken all together, the prefaces form an intriguing literary document, offering an insight into her ever-changing outlook, her desire for self-understanding as well as self-explanation and self-justification.

In her retreat at Nohant, George found in Maurice both support and consolation. As she would say revealingly, he was "rather like *the daughter of the house.*" Discussing George with Delacroix, Chopin had remarked, some months before his death, that the only thing to touch her deeply would be either the loss of Maurice or if her son were to go to the dogs. Ostensibly, she had written off Solange, who remained nonetheless a source of secret chagrin.

For Solange had not even troubled to inform her mother of the birth of a second daughter, Jeanne-Gabrielle, at Guillery. (No doubt, the young wife grimly recalled George's reluctance to leave the Ministry of the Interior to hasten to her side on the death of her first child.) Solange's position had changed. Now that the ambitious Clésinger was busy with commissions, his handsome wife could hold a literary and artistic salon in Paris, frequented by eminent poets like Victor Hugo and Théophile Gautier; the theater director Arsène Houssaye; the powerful newspaper editor Emile de Girardin; the well-connected sculptor and aging dandy, Comte Alfred d'Orsay, whose "invisible inexpressibles" or close-fitting flesh-colored trousers had once shocked Jane Carlyle.

Eventually, the Clésingers, alternately fond and squabbling, seemed ready to patch the quarrel with George. Maurice having visited his sister in Paris after a long break, a guarded reconciliation was effected. George, who had come to Paris briefly to see her play *Claudie*, returned to Nohant with Solange and little Jeanne-Gabrielle, or Nini as she was affectionately called. It was the first time that Solange had set foot in her birthplace since the appalling scenes of the summer of 1847. Thenceforward, Solange would descend from time to time on her mother, fussing about accommodation for her English groom, flirting outrageously with Léon Villevieille (who consequently received his dismissal from his hostess). In vain, George tried to foster her bored daughter's latent literary talent, which foundered in self-pity.

As for George's private life, it had reached a quiet haven. Her young companion, the journalist Victor Borie, having been charged and convicted of an infringement of the press laws, had fled to Belgium at the end of 1849 in order to avoid a year's imprisonment and payment of a heavy fine. Despite his usefulness, his faults of character had become increasingly apparent to her before his hasty departure. It seems unlikely that he had counted for much in her life.

Borie's place was briefly taken by a friend of Bakunin's, a classical scholar and keen musician, the amiable thirty-seven-year-old Hermann Müller-Strübing. George met him at Pauline Viardot's and invited him to Nohant. Müller-Strübing had spent seven years in prison in Germany for his revolutionary activities and had fled to France after his part in the uprising of 1848. Tall, fair, of athletic build, he made George think that she had found the strong, fatherly protector she imagined she wanted. This impression proved extremely short-lived, she confided to Hetzel, her new father confessor after the defection of Grzymala. The easy-going Müller-Strübing remained at Nohant, making himself useful, later moving nearby to become tutor to the children of Charles Duvernet.

Müller-Strübing had originally traveled to Nohant with one of Maurice's friends, the engraver Alexandre Manceau. At thirty-two, of humble birth and poorly educated, Manceau was experienced with women. For a woman of forty-five, whom the menopause often left with aches, constipation, migraines, he proved an assiduous companion, eager to anticipate her wishes, to bring her slippers, plump her pillows; and he was immensely proud of the role he suddenly assumed in the great woman's life. He took command of the theater at Nohant, where he became the leading actor. Orderly and industrious, he copied George's manuscripts and letters, arranged her files, and kept the accounts, saving her a great deal of time and trouble. These services were often performed at the expense of his own work, as she well knew.

Not without faults, Alexandre Manceau could be aggressive and calculating, but he had one overriding virtue in her eyes: Unlike any of his numerous predecessors, he was unswervingly devoted to her service. When they were together, he behaved like "a tender cat" or "a faithful dog." She grew attached to him with all his shortcomings and absurdities, "and there is an astonishing tranquility in my love, despite the difference in our ages," she told Hetzel, almost as if she were unable to believe her good fortune.

Her "marriage" to Manceau, for it developed into a virtual marriage where he played to a considerable extent the dexterous woman's part as subservient helpmeet, was to last fifteen years, until the engraver's untimely death in 1865. Their relationship was perhaps partly responsible for her more mellow views on the institution of matrimony expressed in the novels of her later years.

If George had attained tranquility in her companionship with Manceau, public affairs were far from tranquil. Revolutionary uprisings in Dresden, Baden, Hungary, and Italy had been suppressed. The Roman Republic, under the leadership of her admired friend Mazzini, had been defeated by a French expeditionary force. In France, a feeble attempt at revolution inspired by Ledru-Rollin had provided a further pretext for repression. George felt disgust for the vain and power-hungry men who, she believed, had jeopardized the republican cause by their imprudent thirst for action. Any hopes for a united front among the political exiles in London were dashed when, in 1850, the activist Mazzini formed an alliance with Ledru-Rollin (whom she now considered an opportunist, "a *woman* in the worst sense of the word"), in opposition to Louis Blanc, still loyal to his socialist principles. This alliance was one of the main causes of her final discouragement with politics. "I abstain," she told Mazzini, sadly but firmly.

Throughout 1851, George wrote nothing on politics. Everybody was expecting trouble in the following year, when Prince Louis-Napoleon's term of office as president was due to expire. To her "adopted" daughter, Augustine de Bertholdi (whose husband held an obscure government post in the provinces, and who was longing to move), George confided: "Whatever the result of the crisis, we shall have connections on one side or another to counsel how to proceed. . . ."

In mid-November 1851, George came to Paris to supervise final rehearsals and attend the premiere of her play *Le Mariage de Victorine* at the Gymnase. This picture of bourgeois manners proved a huge but short-lived success. The play was killed by the coup d'état of December 2. Nobody knew quite what was happening. Prince Louis-Napoleon who, as president, had sworn to uphold the constitution, dissolved the Assembly and restored universal suffrage. What did those contradictory measures signify? Barricades were hastily erected, bitter street battles were raging when, on December 4, George hastily departed by train for Nohant, together with Manceau, Solange, and Nini. "If I were a man, I shouldn't go away; but the children must be saved, that is a woman's chief duty, a mother's chief need. And then, what could I do here except get myself killed?" she wrote in her diary. Comte d'Orsay congratulated her: "You did right to leave, and to decide that you would no longer lend your great name to petty people."

Those republicans who had not already fled the country were being arrested, soon to be condemned to imprisonment or deportation to Algeria or French Guiana. Many of them—including her Berrichon friends—were small fry who had actually done nothing. George, remembering her part in the events of 1848, felt scared. Perhaps her turn might be next. Once again, she thought of fleeing to the United States. The local prefect issued an order for her to appear (enforceable through arrest), but it was not put into effect. Solange (with her powerful new connections like the equivocal liberal, Emile de Girardin, and Comte d'Orsay, both supporters of Louis-Napoleon) obtained a travel permit for her mother. Presumably through Alfred d'Orsay, Solange learned that neither the prince president nor his illegitimate half-brother, Morny (who had largely engineered the coup), intended to take any action against the celebrated novelist.

When George thought of the coup d'état she came close to self-criticism: "It is no longer a question of teaching without foreseeing the consequences. . . . One must see reality, study men as they are. . . ." As for the "unhappy people," she addressed them in her diary: "You wanted what is happening to you: an emperor. . . . Submit to his ephemeral reign. . . . Refuse to fight. . . ." In the December plebiscite, a huge majority endorsed the coup. To Hetzel, who had fled the country, George wrote: "France in its entirety consents to the violation of the Constitution. . . ." Perhaps Louis-Napoleon, that unknown quantity, would alone be strong enough to provide work and education for the underprivileged. She advised Hetzel and all her friends to follow her own course and to declare that, without abjuring their republican and socialist principles, they would abstain from active political opposition. Her attitude cannot be regarded as anything but defeatism, at the moment when Victor Hugo went proudly into exile to thunder his resistance to Napoleon the Little.

George had decided that this was not the woman's role, although Mme de Staël had vigorously opposed Napoleon the First during her long exile. To George's mind, the womanly part was to stay behind to plead for the victims, to try to save them from deportation or execution, to mitigate as best she might the suffering of their wives and families. She chose the role of Volumnia the mother before Coriolanus. In one way, this was a noble humanitarian role that, by a sleight-of-hand, elevated George from potential victim to lofty intercessor. In another way, it also enabled her to treat with the regime.

As early as November 1849, she had envisaged the role of intercessor in an article appealing to the president and his supporters to prevent transportation to the penal colony, which spelled death for many political prisoners. This appeal had fallen on deaf ears. Some months before, she had even written a letter, to be shown, in practice if not in theory, to the president, on behalf of Augustine's husband (who feared losing his job). She then went so far as to invite her intermediary to inform Louis-Napoleon of her "displeasure."

Now, in January 1852, immediately after the coup d'état, she was determined to solicit an audience of the prince president. She wrote to him from Nohant, clearly stating her position: "Prince . . . I am not Mme de Staël. I have neither her genius nor the pride she displayed in fighting against the double force of genius and power. . . ." Rather, George appealed for clemency to one who, through magnanimity, could rise above everything—like Corneille's Auguste—while she readily abased herself, through womanly devotion and sacrifice, as a scapegoat for others. It was, indeed, a form of humiliation that fed her pride. "Amnesty, amnesty, soon, prince!" she cried.

On January 24, George left for Paris with Maurice. They stayed in her modest rooms at 3 rue Racine (where Manceau had his studio on another floor). George felt comfortable there, having furnished her pied-à-terre with a blue carpet and a few antique pieces. The prince president received her on January 29. He was a gambler who believed in his star. Insignificant to look at—he was about five feet tall—he had neither the handsome profile nor the forcefulness of his uncle, the first consul. Since Louis-Napoleon had risen through being all things to all men, many observers, including George, had assumed that he was an ambitious blockhead. George herself had once privately called him "a cad" and had declared herself unmoved by the flattering way he had addressed her in his letters years before, when he was a prisoner at Ham with a reputation for being progressive.

After the novelist had described to the prince president the suffering caused by the proscriptions instituted by his agents against many humble and innocent people—for George assumed that he must be ignorant of such acts of personal vengeance—she saw "a real tear" in his lusterless eye. He suddenly stretched out his hands to her, saying that he was not to blame. As the petitioner was about to withdraw, he again took her hands in his and promised to do whatever she asked for any friends she wished to name. What George wanted, however, was not individual acts of clemency but a general amnesty. And this was just what she would not be granted. Afterward, she had an interview with the minister of the interior, Persigny, in the very office where she had once spent many hours in the spring of 1848. She had met Persigny years earlier, and he greeted her amicably, called the local prefect a stupid brute, and promised freedom for several friends of hers.

The president received George at a second audience on February 6, granting remission (that is, exile instead of deportation to French Guiana) for Marc Dufraisse, a leading republican journalist and al- ministrator; for Jean-Louis Greppo, disciple of the anarcho-socialist philosopher, Pierre-Joseph Proudhon; for Luc Desages, Pierre Leroux's son-in-law. She found the prince so "perfectly chivalrous" that he won her esteem. Nonetheless, for all Louis-Napoleon's promises and his apparent good intentions, the proscriptions continued. Surprisingly, her tone changed to one of sympathy for the strange, unhappy man: "Oh! how I pity him!" Louis-Napoleon, having adopted the mistaken notion that "the end justifies the means," had become a dupe and a victim of base hangers-on. Again she solicited an audience, but this time her request was not granted until several months later, long after she had returned to Nohant.

During George's weeks in Paris, although she was often in acute pain from a liver complaint, she went on writing, negotiating for her plays with various theater directors and actors, attending rehearsals. Dramatic quarrels between Solange and her husband provided additional harassment. Still, George was not going to allow ill health, the change of life, or family worries to interfere with her activity. She visited friends in prison; she hurried from police headquarters to the Ministry of the Interior or the Ministry of Justice; she submitted pleas and pressed for interviews.

In the beginning, she had some success. Four soldiers condemned to death were pardoned when she intervened on their behalf with the prince president. But her efforts to secure the release of Pauline Roland, only a year younger than herself and mother of three children, were frustrated. Not long since, that indefatigable fighter for a socialist federation of teachers of both sexes, together with the feminist and trades unionist Jeanne Deroin, had written from prison to congratulate their American sisters on the Seneca Falls declaration of woman's rights. Now, Pauline Roland was to be deported to Algeria (whence she would return, broken, to France, to die in December 1852).

Inevitably, George's solicitations had led to connections. Solange's protector, Comte d'Orsay, served as kindly intermediary, and it was through him that George was able to enlist the aid of the president's gifted cousin, Prince Napoleon, familiarly known as Plon-Plon. The "red prince," as he was called, loudly proclaimed his republican and anti-clerical views. (Indeed, it was he who, immediately after the coup of December 1851, had offered Victor Hugo asylum.) Early in February, Plon-Plon, looking remarkably like his uncle, the first Napoleon, came to lunch with George in her rooms in the rue Racine. Manceau kept the visitor's cigar butt as a souvenir. George's companion warmed even more to Plon-Plon when he procured for the engraver's father a job as concierge at the Senate. However, the republican prince apparently did not exert himself to obtain a decoration for Manceau's father, solicited by George (who, in the course of her more grave requests, did not forget to ask her military connections for promotion for her nephew Oscar, then serving as a spahi in Algeria). In Plon-Plon, George acquired an extremely powerful friend, close to her son in age. Notwithstanding Maurice's revolutionary ardor in February 1848, the one-time mayor of Nohant was to betray bonapartist sympathies, which, after all, George herself had shared in her youth.

Numerous Berrichon prisoners for whom she interceded, as well as many poor working people to whom she restored breadwinners, expressed their deep gratitude for her saintly succor. But, much to her surprise and anger, some of the objects of her intercession were not always grateful. Her old friend Alphonse Fleury proudly asked her not to trouble to intervene on his behalf. (This was the stance of Victor Hugo himself, who publicly requested that no steps be taken to obtain his recall from exile.) Others even ventured to complain about her attitude. Marc Dufraisse, for whom she had secured exile in place of transportation, wrote to her from Brussels:

> Your deeds, in these days of proscription, will in my opinion signal one of the finest pages in your life. Doubtless, I should have preferred you to attack perjury, the violation of right and law, thus through your womanly courage making men blush for their cowardice. You do not desire such fame . . . perhaps it is better to be yourself, interceding for France, for the victims, for your friends, rather than to reenact Mme de Staël, even though surpassing her, and to exacerbate a vindictive, rancorous nature. . . . But I suspect you do not have a very low opinion of that man [the president]. . . . I do not like to hear you say he is chivalrous, and I like it even less that you think it.

This letter left George deeply hurt.

The chorus of opposition swelled. From London came a letter from Louis Blanc: "You do not have the right to ask pardon! By your entreaties you are compromising us." George replied that she was acting simply as a woman whose law was compassion. Though moved by her words, Louis Blanc maintained that her action was a political mistake, since it gave Louis-Napoleon the magnanimous role and left the impression that she submitted to the victor. (Later, Mazzini, too, would criticize her attitude of resignation when, in his opinion, she should have been protesting against an immoral state of affairs.) Certainly, the regime was not slow to profit from her actions and to publicize Louis-Napoleon's acts of clemency granted to the socialist "woman of genius."

The great historian of revolution, Jules Michelet, who visited George early in March 1852, saw the fecund author at a low ebb and involved in a new liaison "scarcely worthy of her." He was not alone in having a poor opinion of Alexandre Manceau. The aging historian could not help contrasting George's precarious mode of life with the purity of his own marriage (a "purity" rooted in his voyeuristic obsession with the blood of his young second wife's periods). Michelet recorded his discussion with George in his diary:

> I found Mme Sand, as always, dignified, simple, good. . . . Still, her goodness is not always appreciated. Why? Because it partly derives from a kind of sceptical ease in accepting everything. . . . She did not much conceal that she felt there was little distinction between contemporary victors and vanquished, with their common cry that "the end justifies the means." *"And what about justice, madame? Is that nothing separating the two camps?"*

cried the historian, whose inner being rose in revolt at her neutral attitude. George's bitterness at the chorus of criticism from eminent friends turned to disgust and scorn. To Hetzel she announced her "resignation from politics."

It was in this mood of wounded pride that she welcomed one of her most passionate English admirers, Elizabeth Barrett Browning, who was staying in the Champs Elysées with her husband, Robert, rather less of an enthusiast. Armed with a letter from Mazzini, obtained through the good offices of Carlyle, the delicate, ringleted Mrs. Browning was determined, despite all obstacles, to see the busy author of *Consuelo* (to whom she had earlier addressed two bizarre sonnets). Even bitter cold did not prevent the invalid poetess from setting out in a closed carriage, wrapped in furs, and wearing a respirator, for, as she told her remonstrating husband, "if I lost seeing her I should with difficulty get over it."

On arriving at the small flat in the rue Racine, Mrs. Browning stooped to kiss George's hand, but the novelist quickly stopped her and kissed her on the lips. George was dressed very simply, in a grey serge gown with a plain linen collarette—rather as she appears, full of face, in the celebrated drawing by Thomas Couture, tenderly engraved by Manceau. The observant Mrs. Browning, reporting to various friends, registered not only the noble eyes but the nose "of a somewhat Jewish character," the rare smile about the mouth ("not good"). The visitor was struck, too, by the low, unemphatic voice in which George gave advice to various young men or spoke of the grave situation and her friends' distress. "But you could not help seeing (both Robert and I saw it) that in all she said, even in her kindness and pity, there was an undercurrent of scorn. . . . Her very freedom from affectation and consciousness had a touch of disdain." On learning that George was suffering from a weak chest and had just been bled for it, Mrs. Browning took her respirator from her muff to show it to her hostess: ". . . you should have seen the disdain with which she looked at my respirator," Mrs. Browning told her brother, George Barrett. " 'Oh'—said she—'life wouldn't be worth the trouble of such precautions'. . . ."

The second time Elizabeth Barrett Browning visited George, the novelist was sitting "like a priestess" in a circle of eight or nine men, warming her feet at the fire amid deferential silence. Robert Browning later observed caustically that "if any other mistress of a house had behaved so, he would have walked out of the room." His exhausted hostess was in fact preoccupied, not only with the fate of her friends, but with rehearsals for her new play *Les Vacances de Pandolphe*, to whose first performance she invited her distinguished guests. What the poet and failed dramatist particularly disliked was the company she kept, a mixture of "the ragged Red diluted with the lower theatrical," from which George sat so apart and alone in her melancholy scorn. Both husband and wife felt that they could not penetrate her mask. "Perhaps she doesn't care for anybody by this time—who knows?" Mrs. Browning reflected afterward. (Two years later, they would both exclaim in unison, "Love . . . she never loved anyone but herself." This was maybe the deepest of their insights into George's elusive character.)

The two women discussed Louis-Napoleon, whom George called "honest." Mrs. Browning, with her "immoral sympathy for power," warmly admired the president. She had been in Paris during the coup d'état, which she thought grand from a poetic and dramatic standpoint, insisting that there had been no bloodshed, presumably because she had not seen any herself. (All the same, she disapproved of deportations and censorship.) Thus Mrs. Browning had little sympathy for those who maintained that George's conduct was "a proof that she could not resist the influence of power and was a bad republican." The Brownings, however, did not see eye to eye on the subject of the prince president, and it may be deduced that here, too, Robert Browning (who, during this visit, met George some six times in all), proved less of an admirer of the neutral position of the author of *Consuelo* than his wife.

Without realizing it, George had changed. She still called herself a republican, a socialist, or a communist in the manner of a Christian of the year A.D. 50. Still, a Christian of that era was awaiting in a state of exaltation the imminent Second Coming. George had no such hopes any longer: Only through atonement and expiation would the new world of her earlier dreams come into being in some extremely remote future. Sorrowfully, Mazzini would later remark that her writings had displayed not the inspiration of a priestess but the evolution of an artistic talent. He had, perhaps, expected too much of a novelist. George had reverted to her attitude at the time of the Parisian street battles of 1832: an essentially apolitical, humanitarian stance. She stood as the defender of human dignity against those who hasten in political upheavals to reduce the human being to a mere thing. Nobly, she stressed humane reasons that are "eternal and eternally misunderstood."

Perhaps Delacroix, no enemy of the new regime, was right when he said that the contemporary writer wanted to give the reader "a high idea of the author, and above all, of his kindness of heart." Whatever George's hidden motives may have been—fear, disillusion, self-disgust, the desire for expiation, pride, disdain, expediency—the noble principle she publicly upheld was indeed that of the good mother to all the children of men. Unfortunately, her own "bad" mother was no longer alive to absorb the lesson.

PART VII

Sphinx

CHAPTER
20

Woman of Letters

I have seen Mme Sand . . . a sort of Sphinx, almost without expression.
Mme Victor Hugo, letter to her sons, March 1860

. . . the figure of the greatest of all women of letters, of Letters in truth most exactly . . .
Henry James
"George Sand" (1914)

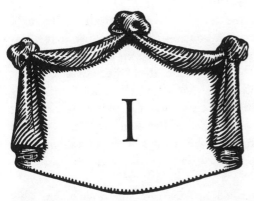

I T WAS not just George who had changed. Almost everything seemed to change under the Second Empire, proclaimed on December 2, 1852. The visage of the capital, familiar to contemporaries of Balzac, would be transformed by Baron Haussmann. Wide, handsome boulevards would be cut through picturesque but ramshackle districts. Often a pretentious façade replaced old houses, where once the well-to-do and the indigent had lived on different floors. "Paris is no longer my Paris," cried Charles Didier. "Everything in it—people and things—awakens my distaste. . . . No longer is it the city of free thought and free speech." In an era of rapid industrial expansion, the speculator and the arriviste rose to the top. This atmosphere of speculation was a side of contemporary life that George particularly detested.

To the casual eye, she had grown ever more like a provincial lady.

The mansion at Nohant had been modernized and made comfortable (central heating having been finally installed in 1850). She took a keen interest in gardening, while returning to the botanizing of her youth, adding to these hobbies natural history and geology, the collecting of butterflies and minerals that so fascinated Maurice. With her docile companion, Manceau, she knew the quiet contentment of readings by the fireside, of discussions on the latest books, followed by a game of dominoes or bezique. From time to time, some new novel would arouse her enthusiasm. Such was Harriet Beecher Stowe's *Uncle Tom's Cabin*, the rage of the hour. Moved by the work of "this good biblical creature," George contributed an article on it to Emile de Girardin's *La Presse*.

For, manifestly, George was still no ordinary middle-aged provincial lady engaged in country pursuits. A performance of her play *Le Pressoir*, a glittering success, was attended by the Emperor and his frigidly beautiful, devout Spanish empress, who was seen to shed tears. Plon-Plon could call on George with Rachel, his mistress of the moment. Then he was off to the Crimea, where he signally failed to distinguish himself. George supported the Crimean War. Patriotism took precedence over opposition to a dictatorial regime, which, nonetheless, she felt, would lead to inevitable upheavals.

As a novelist, George continued to be extremely prolific, although, as she herself once owned, "Conscientiousness replaces absent inspiration. . . ." Elements from her experiences with Chopin or Solange would recur in *Les Maîtres sonneurs*, the most elaborate of her rustic tales, in *Mont-Revêche*, *La Filleule* (and later, *Mademoiselle Merquem*). The theme of the foundling or illegitimate child and the unmarried mother remained a perpetual obsession, a reminder of her own precarious origins as well as of contemporary manners. (She herself took under her wing the local prostitute's son, who afterward became involved with a homosexual gardener.)

Her current preoccupations tended to pass into her novels, her new heroes often being noble, hardworking geologists or entomologists. These she contrasted with irresponsible poets or dreamers who drifted into destructive love affairs (as in *Valvèdre*, which would include a well-meaning but embarrassing attempt to revise her attitude to Jews through the wealthy and exceedingly generous businessman Moserwald). While relying rather too much on convenient devices like eavesdropping, George could still count on her narrative grip in handling triple plots, her lively dialogue, her ability to charm, her psychological penetration, but she had lost the freshness or the commitment of her earlier novels without any gain in depth. Besides, she could rarely dispense with a final note of redemption or rehabilitation.

Tastes, however, were changing. She would find herself in the thick of the battle between so-called idealists and realists (a battle she ultimately lost). After the upsurge of utopian hopes and dreams, frustrated in 1848, came a sober concentration upon "scientific" evidence, upon material facts, with an ever-increasing emphasis on the unpleasant or grisly detail and without any moralizing intention. In Taine's startling phrase, "Vice and virtue are products like vitriol and sugar." The crude positivist philosophy of Auguste Comte (with his firm belief in the inferiority of women that he upheld against John Stuart Mill's objections) dominated the minds of the age. Thanks to George's interest in natural history, the destructive ideas of Charles Darwin concerning spontaneous creation, the animal origins of mankind, and the survival of the fittest were already being discussed at Nohant in the autumn of 1853, even before the publication of his major work.

George's curiosity about new movements in thought and literature was such that she readily engaged in 1854 in correspondence with the young provincial novelist Champfleury, the leading if mediocre exponent of the new "realism" associated with his friend, the painter Gustave Courbet. She declared that it was a style, not a school. Nor was she against it on principle. Like all styles, it had to be judged by the quality of the artist's vision. Besides, "the truth has two facets (if not a hundred thousand)," she told Champfleury. In effect, she disliked any literary theory that was limiting, as she made clear in an essay entitled "Realism," published three years later, where she discussed the work of Champfleury and Flaubert. While praising the masterly, innovative talent of the author of *Madame Bovary*, George noted that he "wanted the woman who scorns real life to be unbalanced and despicable," her surroundings dull and ugly. Flaubert had written of Emma Bovary that "she read Balzac and George Sand, seeking in their works some imaginary satisfaction for her private desires." No doubt he himself had once done the same. Obliquely, his novel challenged George's outlook.

By the time that Flaubert came to write *Madame Bovary*, George Sand stood, almost a symbolic figure, casting a shadow across a quarter of a century during which she had propagated, besides the value of idealism, the notion of the moral superiority of the remarkable but misunderstood woman. From his London exile, the Russian publicist Alexander Herzen could consult George about his marital misfortunes, considering her the highest authority in feminine matters as well as the embodiment of the revolutionary idea of woman. After the dogma of the Immaculate Conception, promulgated in 1854, there was bound to be a strong reaction against the exaltation of woman.

George personified not merely the successful woman of letters but powerful womanhood in its challenge to men, and not least to those of homosexual inclinations, like Flaubert. He had admired her work, particularly *Jacques*, in his youth. But he could say even then that woman is a vulgar animal around whom man has constructed too high-flown an ideal. Later, he would assert that one of the chief causes of the degeneration of the nineteenth century was the poetic exaltation of woman.

Flaubert's hostile feelings about woman in general were shared by many of his contemporaries, by Alexandre Dumas the younger, by the inseparable Goncourt brothers who liked to observe in passing in their journal that woman is vicious and stupid, that the female mind is irredeemably inferior. For such as these, Pierre-Joseph Proudhon's influential polemical writings on woman and marriage helped to soothe their deepest fears about the threat of female sexuality and female intelligence to their entrenched position of masculine privilege. No mean wielder of paradoxes, Proudhon, the self-educated son of a cooper and a cook, would allot only two roles to woman: prostitute or wife-and-mother. He set out to "prove" woman's total physical, intellectual, and moral inferiority to man. His polemic was to include a savage attack on women writers, whom he naturally disliked as a species, from Mme Roland and Mme de Staël to Daniel Stern (Marie d'Agoult) and George Sand. Indeed, Proudhon anticipated Nietzsche, that high priest of the cult of virility, when he spoke of the dominant feminine element in literature as a symptom of morbidity, a sure sign of a people's decadence.

The age was marked by signal coarseness toward women. Flaubert boasted of copulating in his youth, in full view, with the ugliest prostitute he could find in the brothel, while keeping a cigar in his mouth. Whether he actually did so seems less important than that he could expect the exploit to entertain his literary confrères. As for Plon-Plon, he disposed of his current mistress, George's friend the actress Sylvanie Arnould-Plessy, in a particularly offensive way. He arranged for her to come upon her successor, the courtesan Anna Deslions, who was bathing nude in the marble pool of his Pompeian villa amid a circle of admiring men. George knew well enough what Plon-Plon was like, since she had refused to allow a pretty woman like her beloved Augustine to solicit a favor of him personally, not wishing to resemble a bawd. She had asked Plon-Plon to treat Sylvanie with kindness, when the inevitable hour of separation arrived. However, despite her sympathy for her actress friend, George remonstrated but did not quarrel with the influential if caddish prince.

Such was the era of the notorious "grandes horizontales," the courtesans like "La Païva" or "Cora Pearl," who flaunted their expensive charms in the Bois or at the theater. As the Goncourt journal has it: "The prostitute is a businessman and a power. She is enthroned, she reigns . . . she munches marrons glacés in her box, right beside your wife. . . ." A later mistress of Plon-Plon's, the cultivated courtesan Jane de Tourbey, was to serve as hostess to his salon, a role he would not think of entrusting to his devout but dull Italian wife. At Jane de Tourbey's dinner table, Théophile Gautier and Flaubert would vie coarsely with each other on the theme of beating or being beaten by women. Pleasure of all varieties was available to those who could afford it during the Second Empire, which glittered with an endless succession of brilliant parties, balls, and festivities.

At the same time, hypocrisy was as blatant as pleasure. Unmarried women could journey to England, announce their (fictitious) marriage to an Englishman, and, following his equally imaginary demise, return home a year later as interesting "widows." This was the age that could prosecute Flaubert's *Madame Bovary* and Baudelaire's *Les Fleurs du Mal* for offending against public morals and religion. The clerical policies of the Second Empire—with the Church in control of education and with religion employed as a means of keeping the lower orders, women, or the opposition in check—aroused the fury not only of the republicans but of all who favored the free interchange of ideas. George herself turned violently anti-clerical. The collaboration of Church and State in suppressing freedom of thought and speech reminded her of the worst abuses of the Restoration.

As the taste for revelling grew more notorious, George became more "moral," struggling to keep alight the idea of good like a candle in a naughty world. She seemed to forget all about her adventurous past, her years of bohemian revolt when she had longed to be "far out." She forgot the times when she had characterized herself as proud or hard. Instead, she inclined to project herself ever more consistently as an irreproachable creature of inexhaustible benevolence. To this self-created image, Solange's conduct would contribute not a little. For, with the Second Empire, the bored, amoral Solange would find her true milieu. Already, tempted by the sound of gaiety and galloping horses, the young wife had toyed with the idea of what she called a life of vice and pleasure, receiving from her mother a sharp and lengthy lecture including an allusion to the perfect dignity of Solange's upbringing. It was rather like the kind of lecture that the reformed Sophie used to give George when she was young.

In the summer of 1852 the tribunal had entrusted little Nini to Solange when she left Clésinger. Nini's ways delighted George, who loved to look after her bright granddaughter at Nohant. Nothing gave her greater pleasure than to make an elaborate "Trianon," or doll-sized landscape garden, for the child, with a mossy grotto and cascade, just like those Sophie had shaped for her when she was small. George was reliving her own moments of childhood bliss when, in May 1854, Clésinger discovered compromising letters between Solange and her lover, Gaston de Villeneuve, René's grandson. As a result, Clésinger in a fury took Nini away from Nohant, placing her in a Parisian boarding school. The child was fated never to return to her grandmother's home.

Although custody of Nini was granted to George in December 1854 by the court that decreed the legal separation of the Clésingers, the novelist had cause to fear the response of her erratic son-in-law. His lawyer (who had been Casimir's at the time of the Dudevants' separation) prevaricated, doing nothing to expedite the handing over of the child to her grandmother. While George worried at Nohant, Manceau, deputed to make inquiries, was told at the boarding school that Nini had caught scarlet fever. The thoughtless Clésinger, moreover, had been allowed to take the girl out for the day in thin clothing in the December chill and had then gone away hunting. Only when it was already too late did the school call for Solange. Five-year-old Nini died in her mother's arms on January 13, 1855. George was as distraught as her daughter, blaming the boarding school for negligence, Clésinger's lawyer for personal animosity: "The worst of it is, they've killed her for me . . ." she cried.

George wept for days. Eventually, it consoled her a little to compose a fragment entitled "After the death of Jeanne Clésinger," in which she expressed her long-held belief in the immortality of the soul, in the idea that we shall meet the beloved departed in another world, though in another form. Such notions, with which she had often tried to console others, were confirmed by Jean Reynaud's *Ciel et Terre*, a book she had been reading with enthusiasm only recently.

Meanwhile, Solange, in the weeks of strain before her daughter's untimely death, had been "converted" by a fashionable Jesuit preacher through the offices of her lover, Gaston de Villeneuve. At Nohant, she was reconciled with Augustine. "Solange believes she has become devout," George had noted acidly, doubtless stimulated in her anti-clericalism and her particular dislike of the Jesuits by this unlikely turnabout. The death of her second child would set the embittered Solange upon her pleasure-loving course with a succession of rich lovers—much to her mother's distaste. Filthy lucre had never entered into *her* love affairs.

Disturbed by George's low state, Maurice and Manceau persuaded her to accompany them to Italy. Traveling via Genoa, where she met several French political exiles including Louis Blanc, George arrived in Rome. Her response to the grandiose eternal city was violently hostile. In its beggars, its decay, its lack of free expression, she found the consequences of clerical rule and a clear warning to her own countrymen— a warning to be conveyed in her controversial novel *La Daniella*. On the return journey, she stayed in Florence, briefly meeting Elizabeth Barrett Browning there. Superficially, this holiday may have helped to distract her mind from her loss. Six years later, though, she was still mourning the tragic death of Nini.

The tragedy had occurred during the serial publication of George's outstanding work, her autobiography (which appeared in Emile de Girardin's *La Presse* from October 1854 to August 1855) and haunts its final pages. Unlike her late novels, her *Histoire de ma vie* represents an original achievement, despite its obvious faults and lack of proportion. As a wag suggested, the long first part of the book consists of her life before she was born. Yet her publication of her father's letters underlines her own quest for him and for a defined identity. The book is the culmination of a project, inspired by Montaigne, sketched many years before, repeatedly attempted in other forms (in letters, in diaries, in autobiographical writings, in stories and novels): the urge to know and to understand herself as a woman, as a human being, within the social context of her age.

As long ago as January 1838, George wrote: ". . . the passion for truth . . . is the greatest passion in my life." In her autobiography, she declared: ". . . I want to be true." There is no reason to suppose that she did not mean what she said at that moment, in her desire for authenticity. At the same time, she could not resist tampering with the documents, removing a phrase here, adding one there, smoothing the awkward but spontaneous style of others, inventing dialogues. Nor was she above suppressing the truth, in her passages concerning Stéphane de Grandsagne, or "Claudius" (who died in 1845), or suggesting the false, in her presentation of Michel de Bourges solely as irascible paternalistic mentor.

As a writer and a woman, she liked to charm, and charm does not always fit with strict veracity. Many years earlier, George had written to her young son: ". . . one must make oneself loved if one wishes to be loved for a long while. Everybody loves children. . . . But as they grow up and become capable of thinking, people no longer love them unless they set about making themselves really lovable." Her own mother's withdrawal had made George as a girl fear not being loved. It had also made her feel the need to work at making herself lovable. This tendency had never left her.

Hence, along with a genuine wish for true self-understanding, there existed the desire to re-create herself, to promote the self-image of the moment, a talent that had become second nature through her experience as a novelist. When she was writing her autobiography over a period of some eight years, she saw herself as a frank, sober, straightforward person of simple tastes, one who easily forgave injuries and who was really the victim of other people's passions. To her mind, she differed from most women of her day, whose instinct for duplicity was fostered by their pitiful education. (If she knew about feminine ruse, it was because she shared it while despising it.) This self-portrait made a nice contrast with the frivolous fashion-conscious women of the Second Empire, to whom the Empress Eugénie, in George's later view, set so bad an example. George's vanity lay in another direction: in the wish to be thought simple, high-minded, and good.

What she left out of her story was all the scandal about Sandeau or Musset and the rest that her contemporaries were eagerly expecting. She had no intention of writing confessions, after Jean-Jacques Rousseau, whose vanity lay in owning to his worst actions. Nor did she seek to strike poses and drape herself in grandeur, like Chateaubriand. Her purpose was not to relate her life in its entirety but to inquire into the origins of her intellectual and moral life. She concentrated upon her memories, impressions, reflections, her changing beliefs: in short, upon the way in which she saw her development as a person and as a writer. Here lay her true originality. A number of French women had written memoirs, but they had not set out with the clear and deliberate aim of probing their own nature or tracing their own growth. Delacroix recognized George's achievement when he called the book her monument, telling her that there was nothing else like it in the genre. (However, he had noted in his diary that the poor dear woman felt obliged to praise all her colleagues so as not to be thought envious.)

Besides offering a narrative of selected moments in her life, the book provides a varied assortment of her current opinions, rather in the wandering manner of Montaigne: on her noninstitutional religious beliefs; on the treatment of servants; on ideal friendship as personified in her relations with Rollinat; on women, usually highly strung, to whom in general she preferred the company of men. Gifted women should not despise sewing or household tasks (often regarded as degrading forms of female slavery), for these occupations could serve as a counterbalance to intellectual pursuits or mental agitation. Her remarks on the sexes aroused anew the admiration of Elizabeth Barrett Browning:

> How magnificent . . . is . . . the volume which concludes with the views upon the *sexes*! After all, and through all, if her hands are ever so defiled, that woman has a clean soul. . . . I read this book so eagerly and earnestly that I seem to burn it up before me. Really there are great things in it. And I hear people talking it over coldly, pulling it leaf from leaf! Robert quite joins me at last. He is intensely interested, and full of admiration.

Robert Browning would not be alone in being won over by the work.

One of the most impressive tributes came many years later from those malicious gossips, the brothers Goncourt, who had hitherto cared little for George's talent. They now admitted that they had been unjust:

> We have read the twenty volumes of the *Histoire de ma vie*. Amid the hotch-potch of a speculative publication, there are admirable pictures, invaluable information about the development of a writer's imagination, portraits of arresting characters, scenes depicted with simplicity, like the eighteenth-century style death of her grandmother and her delicate heroism, her mother's death as a true Parisian, which wring from one admiration and tears! It is a great document—unfortunately verbose—of psychology and analysis, where Mme Sand's gift for truth, the observation of others and of herself, her illustrative memory, cause astonishment and surprise.

Their assessment does justice to the rare qualities of a work that deserves to be better known.

George received many letters on the publication of her autobiography, letters from women, priests, soldiers, workers, long-lost convent friends. It may have helped to inspire, too, a missive from an unlikely source.

The poet and dandy Charles Baudelaire, then on the brink of notoriety, wrote to ask George to secure a part in her forthcoming play, *Maître Favilla*, for his elusive mistress, the actress Marie Daubrun. His tone was self-deprecating and deferential in the extreme. He spoke of his admiration for George, his long hesitation before deciding to send his letter. The playwright informed the diplomatic poet that she would do what she could for Marie Daubrun (who had earlier appeared in *Claudie*). When George was unsuccessful, Baudelaire scribbled on her reply: "Mme Sand deceived me and failed to keep her promise." Years afterward, the friend of Proudhon would pen some savage comments on the novelist, or, as he charitably called her, "this latrine." George, the self-publicized mother figure, presumably suffered at second hand from Baudelaire's complex and distorted feelings for his own mother.

Criticism of George's autobiography turned upon her treatment of her mother. Liszt professed to be shocked at her excessive candor. Hortense Allart observed: "Posterity will know of her mother only what she relates. . . ." (In fact, posterity knows a good deal more.) The animosity of some of her critics would make George think again. She would realize that the self-portrait displayed in the autobiography had been insufficient to impose without demur the image she desired.

Something of that image was forcefully conveyed a few months later, however, to the celebrated author of *David Copperfield*, then residing in Paris, who dined with George and Maurice at the Viardots' on January 10, 1856. It was the first time that Charles Dickens had met the fifty-one-year-old authoress, whom he knew by repute rather than by her work. "I suppose it to be impossible to imagine anybody more unlike my preconceptions than the illustrious Sand," wrote Dickens.

> Just the kind of woman in appearance whom you might suppose to be the Queen's monthly nurse. Chubby, matronly, swarthy, black-eyed. Nothing of the blue-stocking about her, except a little final way of settling all your opinions with hers, which I take to have been acquired in the country, where she lives, and in the domination of a small circle. A singularly ordinary woman in appearance and manner.

She was adapting *As You Like It* to Parisian taste, owning to Dickens that to do so was to ruin Shakespeare. He went to see her version, and left after the second act.

The autobiography had inevitably led George back to her letters. These, essential evidence for any full story of her life, had been on her mind for some time, as her concern with posterity's verdict grew. It was by an amazing coincidence that she had recovered her letters to Chopin a few years before. The composer's sister, Louise, had decided to take them home to Poland after his death, but, fearing lest they might be seized by the police, she had deposited them with a friend who lived in the Silesian frontier town of Mystowitz. There, Alexandre Dumas the younger, in pursuit of his dazzling Russian mistress, Countess Nesselrode, and forced to cool his heels in the frontier town, had discovered the letters, neatly preserved and tenderly tied together. He had read and even copied some of them, moved by the lively intimate details, in already yellowing ink.

It was his earnest desire to be able to return these touching relics "in hommage to Mme Sand." The younger Dumas hastened to inform his father, who told George of his son's discovery. From Mystowitz, young Dumas wrote to George that he would contrive to obtain the letters for her, with or without Louise's permission. Moreover, he would naturally send his copies as well. When George finally received the letters, she found on rereading them that they were full of her complaints to Chopin about Solange. Presumably, she then consigned the majority to the flames, together with most of Chopin's letters to herself. Upon this holocaust to her maternal image would be founded her enduring maternal relationship with Dumas *fils*.

The obliging rescuer was about a year younger than Maurice and then in his late twenties, a good-looking man-about-town with just a faintly exotic hint of his West Indian ancestry. His greatest dramatic successes, including the play based on his novel, *La Dame aux camélias*, were still before him. The illegitimate son of the womanizing Dumas and an uneducated dressmaker, he had been acknowledged by his father at the age of six, but not before he had suffered from his mother's humiliation and defeat. Removed from his mother's care, tormented at boarding school as a bastard, largely "brought up" in the company of his father's various mistresses, he ended with a deeply scarred personality. The elder Dumas, moreover, had introduced his adolescent son to prostitutes and to the *demi-monde*. Both father and son were to be seen together at places of pleasure.

Consequently, the son acquired a precocious understanding of women of easy virtue. Later, he liked to allot savage punishments to them in his rhetorical, rigidly constructed, apparently outspoken dramas that reinforced conventional morality. In any case, he believed all women were whores, except mothers (who, in achieving motherhood, had ceased to be mere women). Also exempt were eminent ladies like Plon-Plon's sister, Princess Mathilde, whose literary and artistic salon he was to frequent, and George Sand. He would tell George that she had raised herself so high as to be above comment and without equal. (And he would say much the same to Princess Mathilde.) Such compliments are equivocal in the extreme.

"Dearest mamma" and her "adopted" son were soon to be found exchanging confidences. He would tell George how, after a long struggle, he had succeeded in subduing his second Russian mistress, Princess Nadejda Naryshkine (whom he eventually married), so that she was finally down. George would listen calmly to his attacks on women, challenging him only mildly and with good humor when he proposed that husbands should kill erring wives. Their disagreements about woman's inferiority did not disturb their friendship, since his disparagement did not extend to her. He would give her advice, helping her to adapt for the stage her novel *Le Marquis de Villemer*, an agreeable tale about the love of a poor but high-minded lady's companion for her employer's well-born son—one of George's greatest dramatic successes. Her views on the unmarried mother would suggest to him the theme of his play *Les Idées de Madame Aubray*. Yet if her opinions stimulated his imagination, some of his opinions subtly began to color hers.

Far more troubling to George than the letters to Chopin, recovered by Dumas *fils*, was the question of her correspondence with Alfred de Musset. With posterity in mind, he had been trying in vain for years to have his letters restored to him. Fearing the use that might be made of them in George's much-bruited autobiography, he had inquired about them again in the autumn of 1853. The entire correspondence, though, remained in the safe-keeping of her trusted friend Gustave Papet. Apparently, Musset was still much concerned about the letters during his last illness. Over the years, he had published poems that enshrined his enduring memory of their days together. Still, the prematurely aged poet had also confided to his brother Paul and to his mistress, the poetess Louise Colet, some of the less rarefied aspects of his affair with George.

Where Musset was concerned, the noble intercessor and supreme mother figure really had something to bother about. She had a skeleton in her cupboard—Pietro Pagello, still living in Italy—and reminder of the fact that, for whatever motive, she had been involved with two men at once in Venice in 1834, one of whom already belonged to the national heritage. (As Dumas *fils* was to write ironically, any well-bred woman allowed at least a decent interval between liaisons.) The compromising episode haunted her. In 1841, when she was writing *Horace*, she had arranged for the long-suffering heroine, Marthe, to get rid of the eponymous anti-hero and any claims he might make upon their child by *pretending* to have had two lovers at once. That fictional virtuous lie tells a great deal.

Clearly, the George of 1834, the bold, inquiring, vengeful adventuress, did not tally with the candid, benevolent George of her autobiography and her present quiet mode of life with Alexandre Manceau. When critics pried into her private life, she had once informed Hetzel that she had nothing to blush for: *"nothing, nothing,* from *a* to *z*—That I've had lovers? So what? . . ."* Never had she committed an indelicate, egotistic, or base action, she insisted. The deep need to continue to maintain this improbably magnanimous front amid the general riotous living of the Second Empire is not without piquancy.

In May 1857, Alfred de Musset died at the age of forty-six. The moment seemed propitious for publicly stating her side of their affair and thus silencing the hypocritical pamphleteers who kept harping on her immorality. The attempt would prove vain. Pamphleteers like Breuillard would go on calling her a debauchee, while Proudhon was to adopt a tone of extreme virulence when speaking of her "obscene thoughts" and "unbridled shamelessness," or when attacking her autobiography: ". . . how did it not occur to her that in lifting her skirts in this manner before the public, she permitted the first comer to give her a good whipping, without her having any right to complain?" Such imagery evokes the vulgar character of the age.

The novel that signally failed in its intention was *Elle et Lui*, written in less than a month in May 1858, at Gargilesse, an enchanting village half hidden in the wooded hills above the river Creuse. Alexandre Manceau had purchased a small cottage there, with a handkerchief garden—an idyllic retreat. George loved to go walking in all seasons, looking down from the romanesque church upon the meandering river below or listening to the sounds—a word, the crack of a whip—carried a long distance in the clear air. The calm of this beauty spot could not have been further from the jealous passions of Venice in 1834.

Of *Elle et Lui*, set in the eighteen thirties—where she portrayed herself as the independent but supremely maternal woman painter Thérèse Jacques, Musset as the debauched and jealous artist Laurent de Fauvel, with Pagello as the improbable American, Richard Palmer—Henry James would say that it was less a work of rancor than of egotism.

The novel aroused a storm of discussion in the salons, so much so that one young woman admirer of George's, Juliette Lamber, declared that she could have recited the book by heart. Sainte-Beuve condemned "these excessively intimate revelations." Buloz, to whose *Revue des deux mondes* George had returned, would have liked Thérèse to be a little less sublime. Before publication, Buloz complained about the passage dealing with the way Musset-Laurent had wasted her hard-earned money—a passage George cut from the final manuscript. She was inclined to discover failings about money matters in her lovers when their time was up—Victor Borie had been criticized for irresponsibility in this regard.

No sooner was *Elle et Lui* concluded in the *Revue des deux mondes*, in March 1859, than it was followed in April by the periodical publication of Paul de Musset's attack, *Lui et Elle*. Afterward came Louise Colet's equally unfavorable *Lui*, though her novel served to demolish Léonce (or Flaubert, who had finally broken with the poetess four years before) even more thoroughly than Antonia (or George Sand). Mme Colet's relations with George, begun in the eighteen forties, had never really prospered. Self-regarding and running George a close second in the number of her eminent literary lovers, the impetuous Louise Colet, who once stabbed an abusive critic with a kitchen knife, had never been able to satisfy the suspicious author of *Jacques* as to her "character."

The storm over George's pallid novel stimulated the very scandal-mongering she had hoped to kill with it. In the preface to her *Jean de La Roche*, George defended her right to use her own experience in literature, though it was less her right than her method that seemed at fault. It occurred to her, though, that the best way to silence her critics might be to publish the correspondence with Musset, selectively quoted in *Elle et Lui*. (She had already contemplated publishing the letters exchanged with Jules Sandeau, which—so it was rumored—she had obtained by forcing his desk when he was absent in Italy in 1833.) Now George turned for advice about the Musset correspondence to her one-time father confessor, Sainte-Beuve (who had been helping Solange with a projected biography of her great-great-grandfather, Maurice de Saxe). In his turn, the critic consulted his secretary who, on reading the letters, declared them to be declamatory and vacuous, like a volume of Rousseau's *La Nouvelle Héloïse*. Sainte-Beuve advised George against publication during her lifetime.

Meanwhile, however, George had taken certain precautions. A number of the letters she submitted to the critic had already been trimmed:

"In the part I have copied out myself, I have made the necessary deletions, and I have even cut out with my scissors everything that could be wounding or compromising for other parties. While wishing to preserve the letters, I did not wish them to do any harm." It is in a mutilated and sometimes even rewritten form that a number of her letters to Musset have survived. Presumably her scissors were employed to protect her own image as much as that of the illustrious departed.

The problem continued to worry her. It seemed to be the one thing that weighed on her conscience. She acquired a much-valued young woman friend in Juliette Lamber who, in her *Idées anti-Proudhoniennes*, had defended both the author of *Lélia* and Daniel Stern against Proudhon's attacks. George enjoyed the influence she had gained over the beautiful, unhappily married but conventional Juliette, whose womanizing husband, La Messine, insisted on having his name on the second edition of her book, as he was perfectly entitled to do by law. Juliette learned how George had tried to save Musset, the drunken debauchee, from himself; how all the novelist's motives had been perfectly generous. You will defend me after my death, she urged Juliette, you will say that

> George Sand . . . has never deceived anyone, has never had two affairs at the same time! Her only wrong, in a life where art held the chief place, was to have chosen the companionship of artists, and to have preferred the masculine to the feminine code of morals, and I hasten to admit to you, my dear Juliette, that for a woman to lose her femininity is to become inferior.

Then she added, "If I had to begin my life over again, I should remain chaste!" That was, indeed, the one role largely left untried.

George went in quest of an identity, rather as she used to run after a rare butterfly, with the aim of pinning it down. In creating her personality as a woman writer, she had covered her original being with so many layers that she could no longer find the core, if core there was. Her widely divergent origins, her unstable and eccentric upbringing, and the demands made by her age upon women (in requiring that they be either whores or *ex-officio* saintly mothers) may be held partly accountable for her own confusion. Besides being a writer, she was—as Pagello had once noted—an actress. Now, in her declining years, she was about to embark on possibly the best role of all.

The Mask of Serenity

He [Montaigne] thought that man bears within himself all his elements of wisdom and happiness. He was not mistaken; and, in speaking of himself, in self-observation, in self-portrayal, in revealing his
innermost secrets, he taught as useful a lesson as inspired philosophers
and impassioned moralists.

George Sand, letter to Guillaume Guizot, July 12, 1868

Can one know oneself? Is one ever really SOMEBODY? . . . It seems
to me that one changes from day to day, and that after several years,
one is a different being. . . . Without knowing quite how, I have acquired a good deal of wisdom. . . .

George Sand
Sketches and Hints

REAT problem, to attain wisdom. I have often tried within
myself to resolve it, in order
to portray it," George confessed to Eugène Fromentin,
painter of North African
scenes, art critic, and author.
She was discussing his subtle
psychological novel *Dominque*
(which he dedicated to her).
Almost thirty years before, she
had defined the character of Trenmor, the stoic of *Lélia*, as "this beautiful
dream of philosophical serenity, of impassive resignation, that I have
frequently cherished . . ." while wondering whether she herself could
ever be Trenmor. In her fiction, she had sometimes depicted women in
the resolute calm of advancing years. She herself could even adopt a

pose of indifference, admitting that, despite inward spleen, "a calm face and a foolish word save one's secret from being read."

The lifelong attempt to acquire serenity appeared to be crowned with success during the eighteen sixties. After a serious attack of typhus toward the end of October 1860, when the characters of the novel she was writing, *La Famille de Germandre*, took shape and filled her delirium, George spent several months of convalescence with Manceau and Maurice at Tamaris, near Toulon. This frightening brush with death hastened the apparent acquisition of philosophical tranquility. At fifty-seven she could write to her "adopted" son, Dumas *fils*, about her earlier torments: "Weary of examining others and myself, one fine morning I said: I don't care about all that. The world is great and beautiful. Everything we believe to be important is fleeting and not worth thinking about." Having foolishly overlooked or despised the few serious things in life, she had been punished: ". . . I have suffered as much as anyone can suffer, I should be forgiven." Indeed, George was to adore her old age, which, she would suggest, performed the miracle of conferring long-desired tranquility of mind.

Probably the years with her devoted companion, Alexandre Manceau, had reconciled her to human nature, she told Dumas *fils*. So, too, had her son, whom she once called "the most perfect of my works" and a source of unalloyed happiness. From Tamaris, Maurice had crossed to Algiers, and from there to the strife-torn United States aboard Plon-Plon's yacht. A travel book was the result. Maurice undertook various occupations without acquiring mastery of any. He had succeeded Tony Johannot as his mother's illustrator (after George had bludgeoned Hetzel into accepting him). His professional name, indeed the appellation he commonly used, was Maurice Sand. He had created a pantomime; he wrote books on the theater, on the legends of Berry, or novels—which his mother reviewed favorably. When nearly thirty-nine, much to her pleasure, he announced his intention to marry young Lina Calamatta, daughter of George's old friend and portraitist. Lina proved to be thoroughly good-natured, an excellent housewife, intelligent, and musical.

Life at Nohant seemed pleasant enough, but it was far from wildly exciting, if Théophile Gautier is to be believed. He stayed there in the autumn of 1863, not long after the birth of Lina's first child, Marc-Antoine. The poet found among the house guests Dumas *fils*, together with the playwright's close friend and coeval, the bohemian painter Charles Marchal. This thirteen-stone Don Juan had been introduced to

George by Dumas *fils* two years earlier and had made a great impression upon her, spending several months at Nohant, ostensibly to paint her portrait. She soon busied herself obtaining imperial commissions for him.

According to Théophile Gautier, breakfast took place at ten o'clock. George descended, looking like a sleepwalker. A game of bowls in the garden seemed to revive her. Afterward, there was talk about pronunciation and jokes about bodily functions, but no mention of sexual matters. From three o'clock to six in the evening, George withdrew to write. (At this period, she used to produce three or four works a year, often traveling about the country to find new settings.) After dinner, she played patience. Then mineralogy and Jean-Jacques Rousseau were the subjects of conversation until one in the morning, whereupon George retired to continue writing into the small hours. What particularly amused Gautier was the way in which Manceau, ever the attentive spouse, placed pens, ink, lined writing paper, Turkish tobacco and cigarette paper within George's reach wherever she sat. Manceau had a deep respect for Madame (as he always called her) and her facility, which he once characterized as a "tap" to be turned on or off without bother.

Shortly after the death of Delacroix in 1863, her mask of serenity slipped a little. Hearing that the master's paintings were fetching high prices and that people were even snatching up his laundry bills, George thought it would be a good time to sell. To her new protégé, the artist Charles Marchal, she entrusted the delicate task of making it clear to all that it was not herself but Maurice who wished to dispose of the canvases. As it happened, the sale did not bring as much as anticipated, and three pictures were withdrawn.

Afterward, she sold "The Education of the Virgin," which Delacroix had painted at Nohant, to Edouard Rodrigues (known to her through Dumas *fils*). A Jewish stockbroker, Edouard Rodrigues assisted various charitable projects of hers. He liked to say that "Madame Sand has made me a better man." George kept the "Walpurgis Night" that Delacroix had bequeathed to her, but otherwise betrayed somewhat indecent haste for one who professed to worship the great artist.

The fact was that once again she urgently needed money, this time in order to move away from Nohant, where personal problems had arisen. Manceau was in the grip of that common scourge, consumption, and increasingly touchy. Besides, for a long while Maurice had found the engraver's authority and influence with his mother ever more objectionable. After a jealous quarrel concerning the Nohant theater, Maurice threatened to leave if Manceau did not. George hesitated, wounding Manceau by offering him his "freedom." Then she made the painful decision to depart with her sick companion.

A solid house was purchased, with Edouard Rodrigues's help, in the name of Manceau (who promised to leave the property to Maurice), in the village of Palaiseau, to the south of Paris. She let it be known to those who suspected the truth that the move was made so that she might be near the Parisian theaters without residing in town. Her new home was suitably quiet, situated among orchards and meadows. "I couldn't like it more in this little spot," she assured Edouard Rodrigues, to whom she gave lessons in disinterestedness where money matters were concerned. (An echo of their discussions may be heard in her novel *Monsieur Sylvestre*, in the views of the wealthy Jew, Gédéon Nuñez, and in young Pierre Sorède's variable attitude to him, his ideas and his entourage).

Then misfortune again struck the family. While Maurice and Lina were visiting Casimir at Guillery, their infant son fell seriously ill. George hurried south, accompanied by Manceau and a doctor. She arrived too late—the baby was dead. Casimir "was as moved as he can be and treated me in a very friendly manner," wrote George, who appeared to bear the loss with relative equanimity. She had not had time to become deeply attached to the infant.

It was her last meeting with her husband. Three years later, fearing lest Casimir might leave his estate to Rose, his illegitimate daughter by Jeanny Dalias, his mistress-housekeeper, George was to encourage Maurice and Solange to take Casimir to law. They won their case. Casimir in his old age had to sell Guillery in order to share the proceeds with Maurice and Solange. He would end a broken man, senile enough to solicit the Legion of Honor for "domestic misfortunes that belong to history." Jeanny Dalias and her daughter were an unmarried mother and illegitimate child who would not enjoy George's charity and protection.

Meanwhile, her true spouse was declining rapidly. As always, though, the approach of death made her clutch at life. She went off for a week at Gargilesse with Charles Marchal. Perhaps she was hoping to bind the painter to her as Manceau's prospective successor.

On her return to Palaiseau, however, George nursed Manceau devotedly throughout the long weeks of his painful last illness, when he lay desperately fighting for breath. She called in a specialist from

Montpellier, while making every effort to keep from the sick man the gravity of his condition. When Manceau died at Palaiseau on August 21, 1865, it was she who laid him out, placing flowers on the corpse and watching over it. George felt the full force of the solitude she dreaded so much: ". . . and tomorrow night . . . more lonely than ever! Now and always."

Soon, though, she started worrying about Manceau's will and the promised bequest of the house at Palaiseau to Maurice, commenting upon her late companion's lack of foresight and consideration. Her fears were laid to rest when Manceau's family resolved to make no claim upon the engraver's estate. Dumas *fils* was astonished by her resilience. Despite her absent expression and, as some thought, mummified appearance, she still possessed enormous vitality and a powerful will. In the playwright's view, few men would have been able to start a new life, after so many knocks.

Her recovery was doubtless greatly assisted by the birth of her granddaughter, Aurore, nearly five months after Manceau's demise. It was little Aurore who took possession of George, rather than Gabrielle (born two years later, of whom rather less is heard). Aurore, by virtue of her name, represented another self. Later, George would say that Aurore was "her passion," her "whole life."

Circumstances gave George the opportunity to shape her life as if it were one of her own novels. Instead of the brief, ideal relationship of her childhood shared by her grandmother, Marie-Aurore de Saxe, her father, Maurice Dupin, and herself, Aurore Dupin, she could enjoy the ideal family bond between herself in the role of grandmother, a second Maurice in the role of son, and another Aurore as grandchild. It was a perfect reprise of the basic trio.

Many writers who pass their half century, even though famous, often lose their following. Not so George, who kept her name before the public with her sometimes controversial novels, plays, and essays. By the eighteen sixties, George appeared as an established but large-minded literary figure, her mature works being read or seen by an entirely new generation. When Sainte-Beuve, believing her to be in financial difficulties, had put her name forward for the biennial prize of the Académie Française, George had guessed that she would not be successful, presumably because of her earlier views on matrimony and property and her anti-clerical reputation. Plon-Plon and his sister, Princess Mathilde, wanted her to accept a sum from the emperor equal to that of the prize should she be unsuccessful, but George declined gracefully. She was ready nonetheless to accept the Académie's prize, as "an external consecration of the morality of my supposedly immoral works." Jules Sandeau (an Immortal since 1859) remarked that if the Académie were dealing with a man of equal stature to George's, it would have been considering, not a biennial prize, but full membership. Despite the advocacy of Sainte-Beuve, Mérimée, and Vigny, the prize went elsewhere.

Two years afterward, a pamphlet signed S and entitled "Women for the Académie" recounted the imaginary reception of a certain Mme X— presumably George herself. The anonymous author suggested that the august institution had done wrong in failing to elect Mme de Staël or Delphine de Girardin, and that women would have provided a counterbalance to masculine materialism. George, suspecting the author to be Sandeau, replied with a witty pamphlet, "Why should Women enter the Académie?" The Académie Française could not be reproved for leaving outside "people who do not wish to enter" a purely literary establishment engaged in "not composing a dictionary." Women did not belong in this closed, conservative body, any more than in the Senate or the Army. Besides, it was too late. The Académie Française had lost its opportunity when it passed over Mme de Staël and Delphine de Girardin. Now women had nothing whatever to gain from this outmoded survival of literary feudalism. To avoid the accusation of sour grapes, George concluded that "those grapes are over-ripe." (More than a hundred years later, the body founded by Cardinal Richelieu to keep control over writers has not yet changed its statutes to admit a woman to its ranks.)

George's anti-clericalism had made her newly popular with the young. They admired her novel *Mademoiselle La Quintinie*, about a married woman under the baleful influence of her confessor, a counterblast to Octave Feuillet's dimly religiose *Sibylle*. Students and workers turned out in force outside the Odéon for the brilliant first night of *Le Marquis de Villemer*, attended by the emperor and empress, Plon-Plon and Princess Mathilde. "I came home escorted by students to shouts of 'Long live George Sand! Long live *Mademoiselle La Quintinie*! Down with the clericals!'" George told Maurice. The Latin Quarter was in an uproar. The police even broke up a student demonstration in the square in front of the Odéon. Young people tried to untie the horses of her hackney cab, so that they could lead her home in triumph.

Perhaps the most solid consecration that George received as a woman writer was an invitation to the select literary dining club founded by Sainte-Beuve for the elegant illustrator Gavarni and attended by writers and scholars like Gustave Flaubert, Ernest Renan, Hippolyte Taine, Dumas *fils*, the Goncourt brothers, Théophile Gautier, at Magny's restaurant. She had often climbed the cobbled street to this establishment, which stood next to the old coaching stop for Berry. This time, however, she was accepting an accolade. For when Princess Mathilde had asked Sainte-Beuve for an invitation, he told her Imperial Highness diplomatically that he would bring the guests to her salon. George made her first timid appearance at one of the regular Magny dinners to a warm welcome on February 12, 1866. She sat quietly, more swarthy-looking than ever with age, her tiny delicate hands half concealed by lace cuffs. Since at first she contributed little to the scintillating and sceptical conversation, which frequently turned on matters of literature and sex, one of the Goncourt brothers ventured privately to qualify her as "a nonentity of genius." When more at ease, George was to introduce another woman writer to the literary gatherings at Magny's, her young friend Juliette Lamber.

Of all the habitués at the Magny dinners, the one closest to George was a middle-aged bachelor, only slightly older than Maurice, with blotchy skin, drooping moustaches, and so tall that he touched the chandelier. To see this Norman giant, Gustave Flaubert, attentively bending over the stout but diminutive George must have been bizarre. "Only with you do I feel at ease," she whispered to him at her first entry. It was maliciously suggested that, on another occasion, she donned a peach-blossom gown with the secret aim of adding him to her list. Their superficially improbable friendship, one of the most touching and exemplary in literary annals, had taken root in 1863 with her favorable review of his bloodthirsty Carthaginian novel, *Salammbô*. Their association blossomed after the death of Manceau, when Flaubert was kind enough to call to cheer her at Palaiseau. In the main, though, it was conducted from a distance, by correspondence, for they met comparatively rarely.

One such meeting occurred in August 1866 when George visited Normandy. After staying with Dumas *fils* at Puys, a fishing village near Dieppe, where she commented unfavorably on the shoddy household management of his Russian wife—impossible servants, general grubbiness, no personal comfort, too much eating and formal dressing-up—George went on to spend a few days at Croisset, Flaubert's home near Rouen. Flaubert met her at the station with a carriage and drove her to see the great cathedral and the sights of the quaint medieval city. At

Croisset, she found the orderliness, cleanliness, and forethought so lacking in the Dumas establishment. George played cards with Flaubert's mother, "a charming old lady." Then she talked with the novelist in his book-lined study, whose windows overlooked the Seine, until two in the morning.

In November, she again traveled to Croisset, from Paris this time, accompanied by Flaubert himself. They liked to read to each other from work in progress, smoked, and chatted into the small hours—and, feeling hungry, went down to the kitchen for some cold chicken. The way in which the author of *Madame Bovary* introduced George to the privacy of his home, to his mother and his favorite niece, was fairly unusual for him. When his mistress, Louise Colet, had tried to see his mother, she had received her dismissal. Still, while George commented on the almost paternal warmth of his reception, he wrote to a married confidante, Mme Roger des Genettes, that the author of *Jacques* revealed much common sense except whenever she rode her socialist hobbyhorse.

Their relationship was a meeting of opposites. Like other men of homosexual tendencies, Flaubert moved between an ideal, impossible love (for Mme Elisa Schlésinger) and much-flaunted practical satisfaction with prostitutes. After the publication of *Madame Bovary*, he conducted a literary correspondence with two provincial spinsters, both known to George for many years as her disciples: the novelist Marie-Sophie Leroyer de Chantepie, who suffered from religious scruples, and the militant feminist and novelist, Amélie Bosquet. With George as a second mother, however, Flaubert moved onto a more exalted plane. Each enjoyed the opportunity of examining and defining a personal position for the other.

To Flaubert, who once thought he would like to be a woman and who told George that he partook of both sexes, she maintained, well in advance of her day: ". . . *there is only one sex*. A man and a woman are so much the same thing that the masses of distinctions and subtle arguments, on which societies subsist where that theme is concerned, are barely comprehensible." Maurice, she said, was another self, and therefore more of a woman than Solange ("a man who didn't come off"). Indeed, Maurice's wife Lina was her true daughter, not "the other."

As for the aging Sainte-Beuve, whose impotence Flaubert pitied so much, George felt little sympathy for him. "There he is, crying over what—as he understood it—is least to be regretted and least serious in life!" Sainte-Beuve might be clever, but cleverness does not teach one how to live or die. Flaubert objected to her severity toward the unprepossessing critic. Forgetting his cynical depreciation of women in other contexts, he tried to convince George that, for men, women represent the ribbed vault of the infinite. Nonsense, cried George. Sainte-Beuve was paying girls who were under age to revive his wilting appetites. There was no question of any "ribbed vault, infinite, male or female" but vice and filthy lucre. What really counted in life was affection untouched by sexuality, such as she had known with her true friend, her double, Rollinat, whose death in 1867 she continued to mourn.

On literary matters, as on sex, they could not but differ. Flaubert mostly lived like a recluse, agonizing over relative pronouns, spending hours over the choice of a word, stressing—though not without a touch of his customary exaggeration—his sufferings from the labor pangs of style. In contrast, George was one of the most facile writers who ever lived—"this excessively fecund writer," she had called herself when writing to Edouard Rodrigues. In her later years, she might bother more about punctuation and proofreading in general, but her style always flowed, as if indeed from a "tap." Her total of over a hundred volumes (excluding letters) occupies a far greater space on the shelves than Flaubert's small output, but in a sphere where quantity is not the prime consideration. He defined for her his concept of impersonality in literature, which she naturally could not accept, since it was the reverse of her own. Here, she was not entirely in the wrong, for she had perceived that the artist's vision could not be excluded, even when taking a daguerrotype. It was, doubtless, a question of degree and ability.

About her own writings she remained pleasantly—perhaps self-consciously—modest: "*Consuelo, La Comtesse de Rudolstadt*, what's that? Did I write it? I don't recall a blessed word of it." (She would tell Dumas *fils* that she found *Lélia* unreadable.) She was to say to Flaubert:

> I have not risen as high as you in my ambition. You wish to write for posterity. As for me, I believe that in fifty years time, I shall be thoroughly forgotten and perhaps severely misunderstood! That is the rule for things not of the first rank, and I have never imagined myself to be in the first rank. My idea has been rather to act upon my contemporaries, if only a few, and to make them share my ideal of gentleness and poetry. I have attained that end up to a point. . . .

Flaubert does not appear to have contradicted her, although he occasionally pleased her by expressing appreciation of aspects of her late works.

On politics and in their general view of the world, they could not see eye to eye. He enlisted her help for his researches into the Revolution of 1848 for his masterpiece, *L'Education sentimentale*, and she put him in touch with Armand Barbès. But Flaubert had been determined when quite young to avoid being a dupe—indeed, he had expressed a low opinion of humanity in his early youth—whereas she was the great dreamer about how humanity could and should be. His pessimism, his contempt for human stupidity and baseness, his elitism, for a long while stimulated her willed professions of faith. She would scold him for not counting his blessings (as well as for not taking enough exercise). Discreetly, she would try to help him when he was in financial difficulties. Always she would sustain and encourage him, even urging him to marry, for "To be alone is hateful, fatal. . . ." Their voices blend and divide like two immortal instruments in a great sonata, he admitting that he had been afraid of life, she the embodiment of the love of life and of the life force itself.

In the late eighteen sixties, George sensed that the Second Empire was approaching its end. "What spark will light the fire?" she asked. The façade had begun to show serious cracks. With some degree of liberalization, opposition grew vocal. Military adventures had too often ended in failure. Poverty and discontent were rife.

Hitherto, the regime had been largely successful, though, in attaching to itself such leading literary figures as Mérimée, Flaubert, Sainte-Beuve, through the award of decorations and sinecures, through invitations to Court, or through the outwardly more independent circles of Princess Mathilde and her brother Plon-Plon. Certainly, George herself had not been entirely immune to imperial blandishments of this sort. But as soon as Sainte-Beuve moved to *Le Temps*, an opposition paper, the "independent" Princess Mathilde lost her temper, called him a vassal of the empire, and banished him from her entourage. Only when he lay dying were they reconciled by letter. George attended the critic's nonreligious funeral and was surprised to find herself the unique object of a respectful demonstration. The crowd divided to let her pass, the men doffing their hats in silence.

The spark George had anticipated was the offer of the Spanish throne to a Hohenzollern prince. Provoked into declaring war on Prussia, the emperor engaged his country when it was totally unprepared. While students joyfully shouted "To Berlin!" on the Paris boulevards, the inhabitants of the provinces were appalled. George, writing to Flaubert,

railed against "this infamous war." To her sententious American ad-
mirer·Henry Harrisse, a lawyer and historian, she proclaimed her hatred
of the regime, her conviction that the Empire was finished. At Nohant—
whither she had returned three years previously, keeping only a Parisian
pied-à-terre at 5 rue Gay-Lussac—she watched and agonized over the
fate of her country. Her spontaneous responses were entered into her
diary, later published in somewhat milder form. On September 1, 1870,
after a series of crushing defeats, the emperor surrendered with over
eighty-six thousand men at Sedan. A Government of National Defense
was formed to pursue the war. George rejoiced—prematurely—at the
bloodless return of the Republic.

For months, Paris remained under siege, cut off from the rest of
the country, suffering dreadful privations. Charles Marchal kept for
George a sample of the unsavory bread the besieged Parisians had to
eat, though they were soon reduced to more ghastly fare. When peace
was ratified on March 1, 1871, the Prussians entered the capital and,
satisfied with inflicting this bitter humiliation, withdrew to the outskirts.
A week later, George learned of Casimir's death. Her comment was not
particularly generous: "The family loss . . . was, morally speaking, long
since accomplished. There was left in him neither intelligence nor sense
of life." Far more important to George was the state of the country
and the event that would reduce her to a quivering fury: the foundation
of the revolutionary Commune. For her, the Commune meant the
Saturnalia of the plebs after that of the Empire.

The Paris Commune was committed to prosecuting the war against
Prussia when all George wanted now was an end to bloodshed. Although
she could still consider herself a socialist of the deepest dye, in fact
she had grown completely out of touch with the progress of the Left
(and its ideological divisions among the followers of Marx, Bakunin,
Proudhon, Blanqui) since her avowed withdrawal from politics. She had
not associated with Dumas *fils* or Flaubert without being affected to
some degree by their pessimism or their contempt for the mob. Moreover, she was entirely dependent for information and opinion upon the
newspapers she received at Nohant and letters from friends mostly
themselves opposed to the Commune.

One of the most striking aspects of the short-lived but still controversial Paris Commune was the role played by women, whether
seamstresses, schoolteachers, writers—a role George appears to have
overlooked or misunderstood. Throughout the previous decade, the concept of the emancipated woman had been gaining ground, with writers

like Adèle Esquiros or Jenny d'Héricourt who did battle with Michelet or Proudhon. Renée Mauperin, "the modern young girl" who rejected numerous suitors in the novel by the Goncourt brothers, was contemporaneous with Trollope's Alice Vavasor in *Can You Forgive Her?*, so dissatisfied with the limited possibilities presented by marriage to a dull dog. From 1865 onward, a young woman as well-bred as Maria Deraismes could speak in public on female emancipation. Then Léon Richer initiated feminism as an organized movement, with its own newspaper, *Le Droit des Femmes*. By 1869, the "New Woman" had arrived.

In the same year, in England, John Stuart Mill published his epoch-making essay, *The Subjection of Women* (written in 1861), lauding therein the prose of George Sand, "whose style acts upon the nervous system like a symphony of Haydn or Mozart." Above all, in Russia, George Sand's example had produced a powerful effect upon women and, while turning the heads of some to disastrous effect, also encouraged others to study and to participate ever more actively in the movement for change. However, when questioned about free love by a young Russian lady, a relative by marriage of the novelist Ivan Turgenev, George denied responsibility and confessed that she was now worried about "the consequences of our conceptions of 'justice and liberty.'" George owned to a socialist friend, Edouard de Pompéry, author of *La Femme dans l'humanité*, that she had been criticized for being "behind the times" where feminist advances were concerned.

During the Paris Commune, women served as nurses and rifle-carriers, sometimes even fighting on the barricades. They also talked in clubs and discussed reforms. They wanted equality before the law, equal pay, family allowances, day nurseries, secular education, divorce. Their demand for the recognition of free unions (common among the working class) and of illegitimate children may well have owed something to George's writings. Among the leading figures was Elizabeth Dmitrieva, an elegant, studious young Russian member of the International and friend of Karl Marx. She was joined by Anna Krukovskaya, a well-born writer once courted by Dostoevsky and now married to a French doctor and Blanquist, Victor Jaclard. Other leading lights were the militant feminist, Maria Deraismes; the fiery schoolteacher and poetess Louise Michel, a follower of Bakunin, defiant orator, nurse, and fighter; the novelist Léonide Béra, who wrote under the pen-name André Léo and whose work George herself had recommended, but whom she later qualified as a virago. These were the women who, together with their less-celebrated sisters, the housewives and shoe-stitchers, entered history either as grandiose revolutionary heroines or as obscene, crazed harpies, depending on the political point of view.

Much of the hostility directed against these women, however, was antifeminist rather than political in character. One of the most vicious pamphleteers of the day was George's friend Dumas *fils*, who reduced the objects of his loathing to the position of animals: "We shall say nothing of their females, out of respect for the women they resemble—when they are dead." Some writers spoke of the women of the Commune as if they were members of a subject people, an inferior race, or congenitally insane. In an uncharacteristic moment, George even agreed with the remarks of Dumas *fils* concerning "the *non-right* of human *non-values* to influence society. . . . Now that everything of intellectual and moral value has left that den of madness [Paris], I confess that I am pretty hardened against the fate of those who remain behind," she added.

At Nohant, George shuddered to hear of the burning of the Hôtel de Ville and the Tuileries, the destruction of irreplaceable volumes in the national library. The perpetrators of such deeds were nothing but "hideous bandits." She was horrified to learn from the papers that the women of the Commune poisoned soldiers and set fire to the capital with the help of their children. Clearly, she believed all that she read about the *pétroleuses*. After government troops entered the city, any working woman caught in the streets carrying a basket would be summarily executed. Altogether, some thirty thousand men, women, and children were butchered on the Paris streets in one week of May 1871—more than perished during the entire revolutionary Terror from May 1793 to July 1794. "But executions, arrests, acts of repression continue. It is justice and necessity. But what becomes of civilization?" George wrote in her diary at Nohant.

Flaubert had noted George's increasingly bitter tone. He had already remarked to Princess Mathilde that his friend could now perceive the hollowness of her utopian ideals and that her republicanism seemed to be extinguished. When George wrote to Flaubert about awakening from a dream "to find a generation divided between cretinism and *delirium tremens*," in terms not so different from his own, Flaubert urged her to speak out against universal suffrage and compulsory free education. Much pained, she hotly refused to deny her republican faith and to hate with the venom he thought essential. In two open letters, she protested against such an interpretation of her current views. On no account would she be numbered among those who despised humanity or the people and who wanted government by mandarins. These open letters of hers preserved in public an image of George Sand that was often contradicted in her private correspondence and her diary during the Terrible Year. Afterward, she would return to her generous stance, protesting against terrorism; urging that mankind should not wallow in bestiality, even though descended from the apes; and insisting (with Zola in mind) that the depiction of the truth did not require writers to harp upon baseness and evil to the exclusion of all else.

Yet it was not George but Victor Hugo who, having learned from an eyewitness, Marie Mercier (soon his mistress), details of the atrocities committed by the victors, intervened on behalf of condemned men and women. George did not raise her voice for those who were sentenced to death, often on little evidence, or who, like Louise Michel, were transported to the penal colony of New Caledonia, locked in iron cages like animals. Some twenty years had passed since she had pleaded with Louis-Napoleon for the victims of repression.

During the early years of the Third Republic, George continued to write stories for children and novels and to contribute articles to the press. She participated in the weird pseudoscientific controversy that raged during 1872 over whether women form a separate and inferior species, to be ruled by men—a controversy in which several friends of hers, including Dumas *fils*, Emile de Girardin, and Henri Favre, were involved. Drawing upon her knowledge of natural history in an essay entitled "Man and Woman," she countered this thesis, declaring it to be a purely conventional fabrication, constructed out of nothing. To her mind, "the two sexes make manifest only the interlocking of organs necessary for fecund union. . . . There is thus only one type in each species, one being in two people, whose union is essential to reproduce life. . . ." All men and all women are needed to work together for the civilizing process. For a start, she would reject any view that tended to encourage hatred—fatal to the human race—rather than reconciliation. This, together with her second essay on Hortense Allart as free woman, may be taken as her supreme utterance on a theme that had occupied much of her working life.

At Nohant, she liked to gather around her a little court consisting of friends from the old days like Victor Borie and Eugène Lambert with their wives; later disciples like Edmond Plauchut and Henri Amic; the numerous offspring of close associates and relatives; and loyal sister souls like Pauline Viardot (with her husband, children, and entourage) or Juliette Lamber (now married to the republican politician, Edmond Adam).. George needed company, gaiety, and even flattery. As ever, absurdly childish pranks were practiced on the more owlish guests. Marionnette plays delighted the visitors. Discussions took place around the oval table in the late eighteenth-century drawing room, with its clutter of family portraits. Her charming accounts of these talks helped to shape the legend of Nohant in the imagination of her readers.

In the spring of 1873, both Flaubert and his friend, the novelist Ivan Turgenev, stayed at Nohant. (It was Turgenev's first visit, but Flaubert's second, the author of *Madame Bovary* having spent Christmas there in 1869.) Although the gentle Russian, with his white hair tumbling over his eyes and his high-pitched voice, had been deeply attached to Pauline Viardot for nearly thirty years, George had met him only briefly before. Now his hostess was thoroughly charmed by Turgenev's unfailing gaiety and childlike simplicity. His admiration for the author of *Indiana* dated from his youth, when she had dominated an entire generation of Russian writers. He had outgrown her influence, but he always acknowledged her as a writer who had dug the foundations of the modern edifice. For him, she was a "seer." He had once told Pauline Viardot that George possessed the gift to convey the most subtle and fleeting impressions, to "sketch" as it were the very perfumes or the slightest sounds—a gift he himself emulated.

On deepening personal acquaintance, his esteem for her grew. He would wax enthusiastic about her generosity and benevolence, calling her "one of our saints." Flaubert and Turgenev visited Nohant again in the autumn of the same year. The friendship between the three writers continued until George's death, though Flaubert knew moments of exasperation: "Mme Sand . . . is an excellent woman, but too angelic, too full of the milk of human kindness," he confided to Mme Roger des Genettes.

As George entered her seventieth year, she remarked to Flaubert that she was beginning to feel old. Sometimes her right arm was too stiff and painful for her to hold a pen. All the same, each summer, she went down to the river to bathe, as had long been her custom. She could still climb the curving stone staircase at Nohant as nimbly as her dog. Work continued and, for recreation, she painted watercolors as in her younger days. Flaubert admired her serenity. She assured him that it was not natural to her, but the result of a sense of duty and an effect of will.

Throughout the summer of 1875, George felt ill, but she was determined to work harder so as not to think about it. At times, it was difficult for her to walk without extreme pain in her stomach. Off and on she had been complaining of stomach cramps at least since 1851, and with renewed intensity after her illness in 1860. She had particular faith in her friend Dr. Henri Favre, whom some appear to have regarded as distinctly odd. "But, one part of my vital functions having almost entirely ceased," she wrote to Dr. Favre on May 23, 1876. "I wonder where I am going and whether I should not expect a sudden departure, one fine morning." By the time her old friend Dr. Gustave Papet was called in with other local doctors, George's condition had seriously declined.

From that day, May 23, she could not evacuate. Her abdomen swelled: "Just look at this belly, doctor," she said. George was in agony, with vomiting and nausea. Her screams could be heard at the bottom of the garden. Maurica, Lina, and two maids watched by her bedside. George did not want anyone else to come near her, because of the unpleasant nature of her illness. Papet and his colleagues suggested that a specialist should be called from Paris. A Parisian surgeon arrived at last and carried out a probe during which George suffered much pain, followed by momentary relief. Solange, notified by telegram, took command of her shattered brother and set about accomplishing the final betrayal of her mother's views by arranging for a Catholic funeral. George asked to see her granddaughters, Aurore and Gabrielle, and her dog. Then the pains returned.

"My God, death, death!" she cried during the night. George retained consciousness of the humiliating character of her illness until four hours before the end. She died on the morning of June 8, 1876. Some of her doctors suspected that she had been suffering from a latent cancer for many years. Her face was serene.

Epilogue

UCH a rage to live allied to a rage to write remain astonishing. The second seems to have been at least as powerful a force as the first. Who nowadays could toss off as fine a novella as *La Mare au diable* in as little as four days, or maintain so regular a literary outflow for more than forty years, regardless of private and public disasters?

Yet few things can damage a writer's reputation so badly as having written too much, and with a self-avowed desire for money. (Anthony Trollope, now restored to favor, long suffered in this way.) Never to lapse into lethargy like her grandmother: That was the aim she kept steadily in view. George Sand wrote out of a powerful inner compulsion to prove herself and justify her existence as a woman, a compulsion that she tended to express as financial need. Let the scoffers see that she could earn her living, provide for her family and others, negotiate her contracts! Once she was established, her numerous charitable activities served to maintain the constant demands on her purse and hence the constant urge to work to fulfill them. The end product, as she always ruefully admitted, never seemed quite to match the vision she beheld in her imagination.

If she had written less, and with greater care, perhaps she might have attained a more consistently high level. But then she would probably have lost her spontaneous musicality or her flashes of illuminating insight. She offered vast and varying largesse, in the manner of Victor Hugo—like her, an egoist on the grand scale. The range of her writings —short stories and novels of different types; autobiographical works; plays (many of which held the stage of her day); essays on books, art, music, drama, actors, acting, politics, society and religion; to say nothing of her voluminous letters—bears witness to her insatiable intellectual curiosity and her desire to explain and renew herself.

It has been said that she was no feminist. This is to take too simple and narrow a view of feminism. At different stages of her life, she urged different things. At first, half consciously, she laid claim to sexual equality, today still far from universally acknowledged. She broke the feminine stereotype, tried all the roles, expanded feminine possibilities. She opened windows and let fresh air into the stuffy drawing rooms and studies. Her words affected the outlook and the personal conduct of many thinking men and women, including some of the best spirits of the time, who never forgot their debt of gratitude to her.

Certainly, she desired more openings for women in general and better conditions for working women in particular. The question of woman's emancipation and future role was one that she struggled with throughout her life, though more attentively at certain key moments. In her person, by her example, and through her writings, she represented woman's aspirations for greater freedom and intellectual scope together with woman's fears about the limitations imposed upon her, if not by society, then by her own self-knowledge. She remembered her own weakness as well as her strength.

With considerable foresight, George Sand perceived that the vote, or a seat in parliament for the exceptional woman, would not count for much unless there were a profound change in social attitudes. Few in the nineteenth century worked harder to bring about that change in consciousness, or made a greater contribution to it. Henry James, who, as a novelist, owed her a good deal, could dryly but aptly observe that "Madame Sand's abiding value will probably be in her having given her sex, for its new evolution and transformation, the real standard and measure of change. . . . women are turned more and more to looking at life as men look at it and to getting from it what men get." That was no small aim, and it cannot be said, even now, to have become commonplace.

Meanwhile, however, the growing woman's movement at the turn of the century, and after, necessarily concentrated upon practical ends, for the most part unjustly neglecting her. It seemed for a while that she had been left behind. Now that a number of the more obvious reforms have been achieved, in France and elsewhere, the difficulties inherent in the human condition, as she foresaw, persist. The problem was not, after all, one that would be settled easily. In later life, she had made it plain that she did not want open or ill-disguised hostility between the sexes, but the acknowledgment of joint responsibility as equal human beings who share a common task—a possibility that seemed remote in the social conditions of her own day, and still to be fulfilled in ours.

When she died, Flaubert tried to console her son Maurice with the thought that there was no need to pity her, since she had lacked nothing. Still, she never found an equal partner in life (as distinct from a friend) to accept her on equal terms. She thirsted to have at all costs the esteem that, as a child, she had seen denied to her mother. With so many rich gifts and high attainments, she ultimately remains, through some deep inner flaw, a tragic figure. At the same time, George Sand the woman and writer stands, and surely will stand ever more firmly, as an enlightening and incomparable phenomenon in feminine, human, and literary annals.

Bibliography

I gratefully acknowledge here my particular debt to the scholarship of Georges Lubin, editor of George Sand's letters and autobiographical works, who has done so much to remove the varnish from her portrait and to restore her to her rightful place. Monsieur Lubin has very kindly granted me permission to quote from his editions of George Sand's correspondence and writings.

All translations from the French are my own. Unless otherwise stated, the place of publication is Paris.

Selected Works of George Sand

The year of the first publication of each novel, short story, or essay in nineteenth-century periodicals is given where it is relevant. If a modern edition of a work is available, for instance in the Classiques Garnier, this is named. Otherwise, her works may be found, all too often crumbling to pieces in libraries, usually in the nineteenth-century editions of the house of Lévy or in pirated Belgian editions.

The publication of George Sand's works in her lifetime and immediately after it appears as a tangle. Stories and essays were printed at the end of novels, and on more than one occasion, in order to pad the volume to commercial size. Articles on literature were published in collections on politics and vice versa. Most of these articles appeared in collections either during her life or posthumously. This muddle accounts for apparent oddities in the following list, presented here largely in order to give an idea of the variety as well as the quantity of her output.

1827   Mont-Dore Journal, afterward, *Voyage en Auvergne* (*Œuvres autobiographiques*, ed. Georges Lubin, vol. 2)
1829   *Voyage en Espagne, Nuit d'hiver, Le Voyage chez Monsieur Blaise* (ibid.)
        La Marraine (novel, unpublished)
1830   *L'Histoire du rêveur* (short story, ed. Aurore Sand. Montaigne, 1931)
        Les couperies (*Œuvres autobiographiques*, ed. Georges Lubin, vol. 2)
        Aimée (novel, destroyed)
1831   "La Molinara" (riddle in *Le Figaro*, March 3)
        Jehan Cauvin (published with *L'Histoire du rêveur*. Montaigne, 1931)
        Une Conspiration en 1537 (published in Paul Dimoff, *La Genèse de Lorenzaccio*. Droz, 1936)
        La Fille d'Albano (short story in collaboration with Jules Sandeau, published with *Les Sept Cordes de la lyre* in 1869)
        La Prima Donna (short story in collaboration with Jules Sandeau)
        Rose et Blanche (novel in collaboration with Jules Sandeau)

1832   *Indiana* (novel, ed. Pierre Salomon. Garnier, 1962)
     Valentine (novel)
     Melchior, La Marquise (short tales both in *Nouvelles*), *Le Toast* (short story, published with *La Coupe*)
     Sketches and Hints (*Œuvres autobiographiques*, ed. Georges Lubin, vol. 2)

1833   *Lélia* (novel, ed. Pierre Reboul. Garnier, 1960)
     Lavinia (short tale in *Nouvelles*), *Cora* (short story published with *Teverino*, 1846), *Aldo le Rimeur* (short tale published with *Isidora*, 1880), *Métella* (short story in *Nouvelles*)
     articles: on Senancour's *Obermann*; "Mlle Mars et Mme Dorval" (both in *Questions d'art et de littérature*)

1834   *Leone Leoni* (novel)
     Jacques (novel)
     Le Secrétaire intime (novel)
     Garnier (short story published with *La Coupe*)
     Journal intime (*Œuvres autobiographiques*, ed. Georges Lubin, vol. 2)

1834–36 *Lettres d'un voyageur* (ibid.)

1835   *André* (novel)
     Le Poème de Myrza (prose poem published with *La Dernière Aldini*, 1882); *Mattéa* (short story in *Nouvelles*)

1836   *Simon* (novel)
     Engelwald (novel, destroyed)
     Le Dieu inconnu (short story published with *Les Sept Cordes de la lyre*, 1869)
     "Souvenirs de Mme Merlin" (in *Questions d'art et de littérature*)

1837   *Mauprat* (novel, preface Claude Sicard. Garnier-Flammarion, 1969)
     Les Maîtres mosaïstes (novel)
     Le Contrebandier (short work published with *La Coupe*)
     Lettres à Marcie (didactic work)
     "M. Ingres et M. Calamatta"; "Marie Dorval" (both in *Questions d'art et de littérature*)

1837–38 *La Dernière Aldini* (novel)

1837–41 *Entretiens journaliers* (*Œuvres autobiographiques*, ed. Georges Lubin, vol. 2)

1838   *L'Uscoque* (novel)
     L'Orco (novella)

1838–39 *Spiridion* (novel)

1839   *Les Sept Cordes de la lyre* (Faustian drama, ed. René Bourgeois. Flammarion, 1973)
     Lélia (2d version, ed. Pierre Reboul. Garnier, 1960)
     Gabriel (novel in dialogue form)
     Pauline (short tale begun 1832, in *Nouvelles*)
     "Essai sur le drame fantastique: Goethe, Byron, Mickiewicz" (in *Autour de la Table*)

1840   *Cosima* (play)
     Les Mississipiens (play)
     Le Compagnon du Tour de France (novel)
     "Le Théâtre Italien de Paris et Mlle Pauline García" (in *Autour de la Table*)

1841   *Un Hiver au midi de l'Europe* (afterward *Un Hiver à Majorque*, in *Œuvres autobiographiques*, ed. Georges Lubin, vol. 2)
     "Quelques Réflexions sur Jean-Jacques Rousseau" (published with *Le Piccinino* in 1855); "M. de Lamartine, utopiste," "Les Poètes populaires" (both in *Questions d'art et de littérature*)

1841–42 *Horace* (novel)

1842   "Dialogues familiers sur la poésie des prolétaires" (in *Questions d'art et de littérature*)

Bibliography

1842–43   *Consuelo* (novel, ed. Léon Cellier & Léon Guichard, Garnier, 2 vols., 1959)

1843   *Carl* (short story published with *Les Sept Cordes de la lyre* in 1869), *Jean Ziska* (historical work published with *Consuelo* in 1856), *Fanchette* (social polemic published with *Isidora* in 1846 and with *Légendes rustiques* in 1877)

1834–44   *La Comtesse de Rudolstadt* (novel, ed. Léon Cellier & Léon Guichard, Garnier, 1959)

1844   *Jeanne* (novel)
Procope le Grand (historical work, published with *Le Compagnon du Tour de France* in 1885)
"Les Ouvriers boulangers de Paris"; "Lettre d'un paysan de la Vallée Noire"; "Pétition pour l'organisation du travail"; "La Politique et le Socialisme"; "Réponse à diverses objections" (all in *Questions politiques et sociales*); "La Fauvette du docteur" (in *Romans champêtres* 1860)

1845   *Le Meunier d'Angibault* (novel)
Le Péché de Monsieur Antoine (novel)
Isidora (novel)
Teverino (novel)
Preface to Leroux's supposed translation of *Werther*; preface to Magu's *Poésies* (in *Questions d'art et de littérature*); review of Louis Blanc's *Histoire de Dix Ans* (in *Questions politiques et sociales*); preface to *La Mare au diable*

1846   *La Mare au diable* (novella, ed. Pierre Salomon and Jean Mallion. Garnier, 1962)
Lucrezia Floriani (novel)
"Le Cercle hippique de Mézières-en-Brenne" (published with *Isidora* in 1880); "La Vallée Noire" (published with *Le Secretaire intime* in 1902); article on Deburau (in *Questions d'art et de littérature*)

1847   *Le Piccinino* (novel)
review of Louis Blanc's *Histoire de la Révolution Française* (in *Questions politiques et sociales*)

1847–48   *François le Champi* (novella, ed. Pierre Salomon and Jean Mallion. Garnier, 1962)

1848   *Le Roi attend* (play)
"Un mot à la classe moyenne"; Aux riches"; "Histoire de la France écrite sous la dictée de Blaise Bonnin" (all in *Questions politiques et sociales*); "Souvenirs de mars–avril 1848" (in *Œuvres autobiographiques*, ed. Georges Lubin, vol. 2); "Lettres au peuple," "Socialisme" (in *Questions politiques et sociales*); contributions to *Bulletin de la République*, *La Cause du peuple*, *La Vraie République* (in *Souvenirs de 1848* and *Questions d'art et de littérature*); preface to Victor Borie's *Travailleurs et propriétaires* (in *Souvenirs de 1848*); "A propos de l'élection de Louis Bonaparte" (in *Questions politiques et sociales*)

1848–49   *La Petite Fadette* (novel, ed. Pierre Salomon and Jean Mallion. Garnier, 1958)

1849   *François le Champi* (play)
"Aux Modérés" (in *Questions politiques et sociales*); preface to Gilland's *Conteurs ouvriers* (in *Questions d'art et de littérature*)

1850   *Histoire du véritable Gribouille* (popular tale)

1851   *Le Château des désertes* (novel, originally *Célio Floriani*, written 1847)
Claudie (play)
Molière (play)
Le Mariage de Victorine (play)
article on H. de Latouche (in *Autour de la Table*)
"Journal de novembre–decembre 1851" (in *Œuvres autobiographiques*, ed. Georges Lubin, vol. 2)

1851–56   *Œuvres illustrées. Préfaces et notices nouvelles*

1852   *Mont-Revêche* (novel)
        Les Vacances de Pandolphe (play)
        Le Démon du foyer (play)
        "Harriet Beecher Stowe : *La Case de l'Oncle Tom*" (in *Autour de la Table*)
1853   *La Filleule* (novel)
        Les Maîtres sonneurs (novel, ed. Pierre Salomon and Jean Mallion. Garnier, 1968)
        Mauprat (play)
        Le Pressoir (play)
        "Honoré de Balzac" (in *Autour de la Table*)
1854   *Adriani* (novel)
        Flaminio (play)
1854–55 *Histoire de ma vie* (begun in 1847; *Œuvres Autobiographiques*, ed. Georges Lubin, vols. 1 & 2)
1855   *Maître Favilla* (play, originally *Nello*)
        "Après la mort de Jeanne Clésinger" (in *Œuvres autobiographiques*, ed. Georges Lubin, vol. 2)
1856   *Lucie* (play)
        Françoise (play)
        Comme il vous plaira (play, adaptation of *As You Like It*)
        "Fenimore Cooper" (in *Autour de la Table*)
1857   *La Daniella* (novel)
        Promenades autour d'un village
        Le Diable aux champs (novel in dialogue form, written 1851)
        "Mme Hortense Allart" (in *Mélanges*); "Le Réalisme" in *Questions d'art de littérature*)
1857–58 *Les Beaux Messieurs de Bois-Doré* (historical novel, 2 vols. Taillandier, 1976)
1858   *L'Homme de neige* (novel)
        Légendes rustiques
        "Le Théâtre et l'acteur" (in *Œuvres autobiographiques*, ed. Georges Lubin, vol. 2)
1858–59 *Narcisse* (novel)
1859   *Elle et Lui* (novel)
        Jean de La Roche (novel)
        Flavie (novel)
        Marguerite de Sainte-Gemme (play)
        "La Guerre"; "Garibaldi" (pamphlets, both in *Questions politiques et sociales*)
1859–60 *Constance Verrier* (novel)
1860   *La Marquis de Villemer* (novel)
        La Ville Noire (novel)
1861   *La Famille de Germandre* (novel)
        Valvèdre (novel)
        Nouvelles (with preface of 1861)
1862   *Tamaris* (novel)
        Antonia (novel)
        Autour de la Table
        Souvenirs et impressions littéraires
        Le Pavé (play)
        Les Beaux Messieurs de Bois-Doré (play in collaboration with Paul Meurice)
1863   *Mademoiselle La Quintinie* (novel)
        "Pourquoi les Femmes à l'Académie?" (pamphlet); "Lettre sur *Salammbô*" (both in *Questions d'art et de littérature*)
1864   *La Confession d'une jeune fille* (novel)
        Laura (novel)

Le Marquis de Villemer (play in collaboration with Alexandre Dumas *fils*)
Le Drac (play)
1865   Monsieur Sylvestre (novel)
Le Don Juan de village (play in collaboration with Maurice Sand)
Le Lis de Japon (play)
1866   Le Dernier Amour (novel)
1867   Mademoiselle Merquem (novel)
1868   Cadio (novel)
Cadio (play in collaboration with Paul Meurice)
1869   Pierre qui roule (novel)
Le Beau Laurence (novel)
Lupo Liverani (play) (published with *La Coupe*)
review of Flaubert's *L'Education sentimentale* (in *Questions d'art et de littérature*)
1870   Malgrétout (novel)
L'Autre (play)
"Reprise de *Lucrèce Borgia*" (in *Questions d'art et de littérature*)
1871   Césarine Dietrich (novel)
Francia (novel)
Journal d'un voyageur pendant la guerre
"Réponse à un ami," "Réponse à une amie" (both in *Impressions et Souvenirs*); "Victor Hugo et *L'Année Terrible*" (in *Souvenirs et Idées*)
1871–76 Contributions to *Le Temps*
1872   Nanon (novel)
"L'Homme et la Femme" and "Un Livre curieux" (essay on Hortense Allart's *Les Enchantements de Prudence* published under the pseudonym Mme de Saman both in *Impressions et Souvenirs*)
1873   Impressions et Souvenirs
Contes d'une grand-mère (first series)
1874   Ma Sœur jeanne (novel)
1875   Flamarande (novel)
Les Deux Frères (novel, sequel to *Flamarande*)
La Tour de Percemont (novel)
Marianne (novel)
"Michel Lévy" (in *Dernières Pages*)
1876   La Coupe
Albine (novel, unfinished)
"Le Théâtre des marionnettes de Nohant" (in *Œuvres autobiographiques*, ed. Georges Lubin, vol. 2)

POSTHUMOUS PUBLICATIONS

1876   Contes d'une grand-mère (second series)
1877   Dernières Pages
Nouvelles Lettres d'un voyageur
1878   Questions d'art et de littérature
1879   Questions politiques et sociales
1880   Souvenirs de 1848
Mélanges
1882–84 Correspondance 1812–76, 6 vols.
1904   Souvenirs et Idées
Correspondance entre George Sand et Gustave Flaubert (collected by Lina Sand, preface by Henri Amic)
1926   Journal intime, ed. Aurore Sand
1928   Le Roman d'Aurore Dudevant et d'Aurélien de Sèze, ed. Aurore Sand
1964–   Correspondance, ed. Georges Lubin, vols. I–XII. Garnier (in progress)
1970–71 Œuvres autobiographiques, ed. Georges Lubin, 2 vols. Bibliothèque de la Pléiade, Gallimard.

Bibliography

PRINCIPAL WORKS CONSULTED

Adam, Mme Juliette. *Mes Premières Armes littéraires et politiques.* Lemerre, 1904.
———. *Mes Sentiments et nos idées avant 1870.* Lemerre, 1905.
———. *Mes Angoisses et nos luttes.* Lemerre, 1907.
Agoult (Marie de Flavigny, Comtesse d' [Daniel Stern]). *Mes Souvenirs 1806–33.* Calmann Lévy, 1877.
———. *Mémoires 1833–54.* Calmann Lévy, 1927.
———. *Correspondance de Liszt et de la Comtesse d'Agoult,* ed. Daniel Ollivier, 2 vols. Grasset, 1933–34.
———. *Histoire de la Révolution de 1848,* 2 vols. Charpentier, 1862.
Alain [pseudonym of Emile Chartier]. *Propos de Littérature.* Geneva: Gonthier, 1969.
Allart, Hortense. *Lettres inédites à Sainte-Beuve,* ed. Léon Séché. Mercure de France, 1908.
Alquier, Aline. *George Sand.* Pierre Charron, 1974.
Amic, Henri. *George Sand. Mes Souvenirs.* Calmann Lévy, 1893.
Arnold, Matthew. *Mixed Essays.* London: Smith, Elder, 1879.
Bachelard, Gaston. *La Psychanalyse du feu.* Collection Idées, Gallimard, 1949.
Bailbé, Joseph-Marc. *Jules Janin.* Minard, 1974.
Baldick, Robert. *Dinner at Magny's.* London: Gollancz, 1971.
Balzac, Honoré de. *Physiologie du mariage.* Garnier-Flammarion, 1968.
———. *La Peau de chagrin* (text of 1831, preface by Pierre Barbéris). Livre de Poche, Gallimard, 1972.
———. *La Fille aux yeux d'or* (preface by Pierre Barbéris). Livre de Poche, Gallimard, 1972.
———. *Béatrix,* ed. Maurice Regard. Garnier, 1962.
———. *Mémoires de deux jeunes mariées,* ed. S. de Sacy. Livre de Poche, Gallimard, 1969.
———. *Correspondance,* ed. Roger Pierrot, 5 vols. Garnier, 1960–69.
———. *Lettres à Madame Hanska,* ed. Roger Pierrot, 4 vols. Editions du Delta, 1967–71.
Barbey d'Aurevilly, Jules. *Les Œuvres et les hommes au XIX⁰ siècle: V. Les Bas-Bleus.* Palmé, 1878.
Barry, Joseph. *Infamous Woman. The Life of George Sand.* New York: Doubleday, 1977.
Barthes, Roland. *Michelet.* Seuil, 1975.
Baudelaire, Charles. *Curiosités esthétiques; L'Art romantique,* ed. Henri Lemaître. Garnier, 1962.
———. *Œuvres complètes.* ed. Y. G. Le Dantec and Claude Pichois, Bibliothèque de la Pléiade, Gallimard, 1968.
Bénichou, Paul. *Le Sacre de l'écrivain.* José Corti, 1973.
Berlioz, Hector. *Mémoires,* 2 vols. Garnier-Flammarion, 1969.
Bertaut, Jules. *Une Amitié romantique: George Sand–François Rollinat.* Renaissance du Livre, 1921.
Blanc, Louis. *Histoire de Dix Ans,* 5 vols. Pagnerre, 1842–44.
Bourniquel, Camille. *Chopin.* Seuil, 1973.
Bourniquel, Camille, et al. *Chopin.* Hachette, 1965.
Brandes, George. *Main Currents in Nineteenth-Century Literature:* Vol. V. *The Romantic School in France,* London: Heinemann, 1904.
Briquet, Jean, ed. *Agricol Perdiguier: Correspondance inédite avec George Sand et ses amis.* Klincksieck, 1966.
Browning, Elizabeth Barrett. *Poetical Works.* London: Smith, Elder, 1897.
———. *Letters,* ed. Frederic G. Kenyon, 2 vols. London: Macmillan, 1897.
———. *The Letters of Robert Browning and Elizabeth Barrett Barrett 1845–46.* London: Smith, Elder, 1899.
———. *The Unpublished Letters of Elizabeth Barrett Barrett and Mary Russell Mitford,* ed. Betty Miller. London: Murray, 1954.

————. *Letters of the Brownings to George Barrett*, ed. Paul Landis and Ronald E. Freeman. Urbana, University of Illinois Press, 1958.

————. *Letters to Mrs. David Ogilvy*, ed. Peter N. Heydon and Philip Kelley. London: Murray, 1974.

Browning, Robert. *See* Elizabeth Barrett Browning.

Buis, Lucien. *Les Théories sociales de George Sand*. A. Pedone, 1910.

Campos, Christophe. "Social Romanticism" in *French Literature and its Background: 4. The Early Nineteenth Century*, ed. J. Cruickshank. London: Oxford University Press, 1969.

Caro, E. *George Sand*. Hachette, 1887.

Carr, E. H. *The Romantic Exiles*. London: Peregrine, 1968.

Carrère, Casimir. *George Sand amoureuse*. La Palatine, 1967.

Catalogues. George Sand Exhibition, Bibliothèque Nationale, 1954.

George Sand: Visages du romantisme. Exhibition, Bibliothèque Nationale, 1977.

Cate, Curtis. *George Sand*. London: Hamish Hamilton, 1975.

Cellier, Léon, ed. *Hommage à George Sand*. Presses Universitaires de France, 1969.

————. *La Porporina*. Entretiens sur *Consuelo*. Grenoble: Presses Universitaires de Grenoble, 1976.

Charléty, Sébastien. *Histoire du Saint-Simonisme*. Paul Hartmann, 1931.

Chevigny, Bell Gale. *The Woman and the Myth: Margaret Fuller's Life and Writings*. New York: Feminist Press, 1976.

Chonez, Claudine. *George Sand*. Seghers, 1973.

Chopin, Frédéric. *Correspondance*, ed. B. E. Sydow, S. and D. Chainaye, 3 vols. Richard Masse, 1953–60.

————. *Lettres de Chopin et de George Sand 1836–39*, ed. B. E. Sydow, S. and D. Chainaye, Palma de Mallorca: La Cartuja, 1974.

Clark, T. J. *The Absolute Bourgeois: Artists and Politics in France. 1848–51*. London: Thames and Hudson, 1973.

Clough, Arthur Hugh. *Correspondence*, ed. Frederick L. Mulhauser, 2 vols. London: Oxford University Press, 1957.

Cobban, Alfred. *A History of Modern France*, vol. 2. 1799–1871. London: Pelican, 1961.

Colet, Louise. *Lui*. Librairie Nouvelle, 1860.

Delacroix, Eugène. *Journal*, ed. André Joubin, 3 vols. Plon, 1932.

————. *Correspondance générale*, ed. André Joubin, 5 vols. Plon, 1935–38.

Demar, Claire. *L'Affranchissement des femmes (1833)*, ed. Valentin Pelosse. Payot, 1976.

Deutsch, Helene. *The Psychology of Women*, 2 vols. New York: Bantam, 1973.

Didier, Béatrice. "Ophélie dans les chaînes: étude de quelques thèmes d'*Indiana*" in *Hommage à George Sand*, ed. L. Cellier. Presses Universitaires de France, 1969.

————. "*Consuelo* et la création féminine" in *La Quinzaine*, September 11–30, 1976.

Dimoff, Paul. *La Genèse de Lorenzaccio*. Droz, 1936.

Dolléans, Edouard. *Féminisme et mouvement ouvrier: George Sand*. Les Editions Ouvrières, 1951.

Dostoevsky, Fyodor. *The Diary of a Writer*, trans. Boris Brasol, 2 vols. London: Cassell, 1949.

Doumic, René. *George Sand: Dix Conférences sur sa vie et son œuvre*. Perrin, 1909.

Droz, Jacques. *Europe between Revolutions 1815–1848*. London: Fontana, Collins, 1967.

Du Camp, Maxime. *Souvenirs de l'année 1848*. Hachette, 1876.

————. *Souvenirs littéraires*, 2 vols. Hachette, 1882–83.

Dumas *fils*, Alexandre. *Théâtre complet*, 7 vols. Calmann Lévy, 1882–93.

Edwards, Stewart. *The Paris Commune 1871*. London: Eyre and Spottiswoode, 1971.

Eliot, George [Mary Anne Evans]. *Letters*, ed. Gordon S. Haight, 7 vols. London: Oxford University Press, 1954–56.

Evans, David Owen. *Le Roman social sous la monarchie de juillet*. Presses Universitaires de France, 1930.

Bibliography

──────. *Le Socialisme romantique: Pierre Leroux et ses contemporains*. Marcel Rivière, 1948.

──────. *Social Romanticism in France*. Oxford: Clarendon Press, 1951.

Evrard, Louis, ed. *Correspondance entre George Sand et Alfred de Musset*. Monte Carlo: Editions du Rocher, 1956.

Fahmy, Dorrhya. *George Sand, auteur dramatique*. Droz, 1934.

Ferra, Bartomeu. *Chopin y George Sand en Mallorca*. Palma de Mallorca: La Cartuja, 1974.

Fitzlyon, April. *The Price of Genius. A Life of Pauline Viardot*. London: John Calder, 1964.

Flaubert, Gustave. *Correspondance*, 13 vols. Conard, 1926–54.

──────. *Correspondance*, ed. Jean Bruneau, vol. 1. Bibliothèque de la Pléiade, Gallimard, 1973.

Forster, John. *The Life of Charles Dickens*, 2 vols. London: Everyman, Dent, 1969.

Fourier, Charles. *Vers la liberté en amour*, ed. Daniel Guérin. Collection Idées, Gallimard, 1975.

Fuller, Margaret. *Memoirs*, 3 vols. London: Richard Bentley, 1852.

──────. *Woman in the Nineteenth Century*. New York: Norton, 1971.

Gaskell, Elizabeth. *The Life of Charlotte Brontë*. London: Everyman, Dent, 1908.

Gattey, Charles Neilson. *Gauguin's Astonishing Grandmother. A Biography of Flora Tristan*. London: Femina, 1970.

──────. *A Bird of Curious Plumage. Princess Cristina di Belgiojoso*. London: Constable, 1971.

Gautier, Théophile. *Histoire du romantisme*. Charpentier, 1874.

Gavoty, Bernard. *Chopin*. Grasset, 1974.

Gerson, Noel B. *George Sand*. London: Robert Hale, 1973.

Girardin, Delphine de. *Le Vicomte de Launay: Lettres parisiennes*, 3 vols. Calmann Lévy, 1878.

──────. *Le Vicomte de Launay: Correspondance parisienne*. Michel Lévy, 1853.

Godeau, Marcel. *Le Voyage à Majorque de George Sand et Frédéric Chopin*. Debresse, 1959.

Goncourt, Edmond and Jules de. *Journal*, ed. Robert Ricatte, 3 vols. Fasquelle & Flammarion, 1956–59.

Green, Frederick C. *French Novelists from the Revolution to Proust*. London: Dent, 1931.

Grossman, Leonid. *Dostoevsky*, trans. Mary Mackler. London: Allen Lane, 1974.

Guillemin, Henri. *A Vrai Dire*. Gallimard, 1956.

──────. *Préface, Elle et Lui*. Neuchâtel: Ides et Calendes, 1963.

──────. *Pas à Pas*. Gallimard, 1969.

──────. *La Liaison Musset–Sand*. Gallimard, 1972.

Haight, Gordon S. *George Eliot*. Oxford: Clarendon Press, 1968.

Harrisse, Henry. *Derniers moments et obsèques de George Sand*, 1904.

Hayter, Alethea. *Mrs. Browning*. London: Faber, 1962.

Hedley, Arthur. *Chopin*. rev. ed. London: Dent, 1974.

Heine, Heinrich. *De la France*. Calmann Lévy, 1884.

──────. *Lutèce*. Calmann Lévy, 1892.

Herold, J. Christopher. *Mistress to an Age: The Life of Mme de Staël*. London: Hamish Hamilton, 1959.

Herzen, Alexander. *My Past and Thoughts*, trans. Constance Garnett, rev. H. Higgens, 4 vols. London: Chatto & Windus, 1968.

Holt, Edgar. *Plon-Plon: The Life of Prince Napoleon*. London: Michael Joseph, 1973.

Horne, Alistair. *The Fall of Paris. The Siege and the Commune*. London: Macmillan, 1965.

Houssaye, Arsène. *Les Confessions*, 6 vols. Dentu, 1885–91.

Howe, Julia Ward. *Margaret Fuller*. London: W. H. Allen, 1883.

Howe, Susan. *Geraldine Jewsbury*. London: Allen & Unwin, 1935.

Hugo, Victor. "Obsèques de George Sand" in *Depuis l'Exil (Actes et Paroles*, vol. 3), Hetzel & Quantin, 1884.

————. *Choses vues 1830–1885*, ed. Hubert Juin, 4 vols. Folio, Gallimard, 1972.
Hunt, H. J. *Honoré de Balzac*. London: Athlone Press, University of London, 1957.
————. *Balzac's Comédie Humaine*. London: Athlone Press, University of London, 1959.
Iwaszkiewicz, Jaroslaw. *Chopin*, trans. Georges Lisowski. Gallimard, 1966.
Jackson, Joseph F. *Louise Colet et ses amis littéraires*. New Haven, Conn.: Yale University Press, 1937.
Jambut, Monique ed. *George Sand: Femme de notre temps*. Châteauroux: Matarese, 1976.
James, Henry. *Notes on Novelists*. London: Dent, 1914.
————. *Literary Reviews and Essays*, ed. Albert Mordell. New York: Grove Press, 1957.
————. *Selected Literary Criticism*. London: Peregrine, 1968.
Jordan, Ruth. *George Sand*. London: Constable, 1976.
Karénine, Wladimir [pseudonym of Varvara Komarova]. *George Sand: sa vie et ses œuvres*, 4 vols. Paul Ollendorf & Plon-Nourrit, 1899–1926.
Kelly, Linda. *The Young Romantics*. New York: Random House, 1976.
Lacassagne, Jean-Pierre. *Pierre Leroux et George Sand: Histoire d'une amitié*. Klincksieck, 1973.
Lamber, Juliette. *See* Mme Juliette Adam.
La Messine, Juliette. *See* Mme Juliette Adam.
Launay, Vicomte de. *See* Delphine de Girardin.
Laver, James. *Dandies*. London: Weidenfeld and Nicolson, 1968.
Lidsky, Paul. *Les Ecrivains contre la Commune*. Maspéro, 1970.
Liszt, Franz. *See* Comtesse d'Agoult.
Lubin, Georges. *George Sand en Berry*. Hachette, 1967.
————. *Album: George Sand*. Bibliothèque de la Pléiade, Gallimard, 1973.
————. *Nohant*. Caisse des Monuments Historiques, 1976.
Mallet, Francine. *George Sand*. Grasset, 1976.
Marix-Spire, Thérèse. *Les Romantiques et la musique: le cas George Sand*. Nouvelles Editions Latines, 1954.
————, ed. *Lettres inédites de George Sand et de Pauline Viardot 1839–49*. Nouvelles Editions Latines, 1959.
Maurois, André. *Lédia ou la vie de George Sand*. Hachette, 1952.
————. *Olympio ou la vie de Victor Hugo*. Hachette, 1954.
————. *Les Trois Dumas*. Hachette, 1957.
————. *Prométhée ou la vie de Balzac*. Hachette, 1965.
Maurois, Simone-André, ed. *Correspondance inédite: George Sand–Marie Dorval*. Gallimard, 1953.
Maurras, Charles. *Les Amants de Venise*. Boccard, rev. ed., n.d.
Mazzini, Giuseppe. *Life and Writings*, 6 vols. London: Smith, Elder, 1864–70.
Mérimée, Prosper. *La Double Méprise* (1833) in *Romans et Nouvelles*, vol. 1, ed. Maurice Parturier. Garnier, 1967.
————. *Correspondance générale*, ed. Maurice Parturier, 17 vols. Privat, Toulouse, & Le Divan, 1941–64.
Michelet, Jules. *Journal*, ed. Paul Viallaneix, 3 vols. Gallimard, 1959–76.
Moers, Ellen. *Literary Women*. New York: Doubleday, 1976.
Musset, Alfred de. *Correspondance*, ed. Léon Séché. Mercure de France, 1907.
————. *Œuvres completes*, ed. Maurice Allem, 3 vols. Bibliothèque de la Pléiade, Gallimard, 1947–57.
————. *La Confesson d'un enfant du siècle*, ed. Claude Duchet and Maurice Allem. Garnier, 1968.
Musset, Paul de. *Lui et Elle*. Charpentier, 1868.
Pailleron, Marie-Louise. *Francois Buloz et ses amis*, 2 vols. Calmann Lévy & Perrin, 1919–24.
————. *George Sand*, 3 vols. Grasset, 1938–53.
Parménie, A. and Bonnier de la Chapelle, C. *Histoire d'un éditeur et de ses auteurs, P.-J. Hetzel*. Albin Michel, 1953.

Poli, Annarosa. *L'Italie dans la vie et dans l'œuvre de George Sand*. A Colin, 1960.

——. *George Sand et les années terribles*. Pàtron, Bologna, & Nizet, 1975.

Pommier, Jean. *Autour du drame de Venise*. Nizet, 1958.

——. *George Sand et le rêve monastique: Spiridion*. Nizet, 1966.

Pope-Hennessy, James. *Monckton Milnes*, 2 vols. London: Constable, 1951.

Pourtalès, Guy de. *La Vie de Franz Liszt*. Gallimard, 1926.

Proudhon, Pierre-Joseph. *De la Justice dans la Révolution et dans l'Eglise*, 4 vols. Marpon & Flammarion, 1870.

Raitt, A. W. *Prosper Mérimée*. London: Eyre and Spottiswoode, 1970.

Regard, Maurice. *L'Adversaire des romantiques: Gustave Planche*, 2 vols. Nouvelles Editions Latines, 1956.

——. "Charles Didier et George Sand," in *Revue des Sciences Humaines*. October–December, 1959.

Renan, Ernest. *Feuilles détachées*. Calmann Lévy, 1892.

Reybaud, Louis. *Jérôme Paturot*, 4 vols. Brussels: Méline, Cans, 1849.

Richardson, Joanna. *The Courtesans: The Demi-Monde in Nineteenth-Century France*. London: Weidenfeld & Nicolson, 1967.

——. *Princess Mathilde*. London: Weidenfeld & Nicolson, 1969.

Rocheblave, Samuel. *George Sand et sa fille d'après leur correspondance inédite*. Calmann Lévy, 1905.

Rouget, Marie-Thérèse. *Essai sur l'évolution psychologique et littéraire de George Sand*. Jean Renard, 1939.

Sainte-Beuve, Charles-Augustin. *Volupté*, 2 vols. Gallimard, 1933.

——. *Correspondance générale*, ed. Jean Bonnerot, 16 vols. Stock, 1935–70.

——. *Œuvres*, ed. Maxime Leroy, 2 vols. Bibliothèque de la Pléiade, Gallimard, 1956, 1960.

——. *La Cahier ver 1834–1847* ed. Raphaël Molho. Gallimard, 1973.

Salomon, Pierre. *George Sand*. Hatier, 1953.

Sandeau, Jules. *Marianna*. Charpentier, 1886.

Séché, Léon. *Hortense Allart de Méritens*. Mercure de France, 1908.

Seillière, Ernest. *George Sand, mystique de la passion, de la politique, et de l'art*. Félix Alcan, 1920.

Sellards, John. *Dans le sillage du romantisme: Charles Didier*. Champion, 1933.

Shephard, Esther. *Walt Whitman's Prose*. New York: Harcourt, Brace, 1938.

Shorter, Edward. *The Making of the Modern Family*. New York: Basic Books, 1975.

Silver, Mabel. *Jules Sandeau: l'homme et la vie*. Boivin, 1937.

Sitwell, Sacheverell. *Liszt*. New York: Dover, 1967.

Södergård, Östen. *Essais sur la création littéraire de George Sand d'après un roman remanié: Lélia*. Uppsala: Historia litterarum, no. 1, 1962.

——, ed. *Les Lettres de George Sand à Sainte-Beuve*. Geneva: Droz, & Paris: Minard, 1964.

Spoelberch de Lovenjoul, Charles de. *La Véritable Histoire de "Elle et Lui"*. Calmann Lévy, 1897.

Starkie, Enid. *Petrus Borel the Lycanthrope*. London: Faber, 1954.

——. *Baudelaire*. London: Faber, 1957.

——. *Flaubert: The Making of the Master*. London: Weidenfeld & Nicolson, 1967.

——. *Flaubert: The Master*. Weidenfeld & Nicolson, 1971.

Stendhal [pseudonym of Henri Beyle]. *Correspondance*, ed. Henri Martineau and V. Del Litto, 3 vols. Bibliothèque de la Pléiade, Gallimard, 1967–68.

——. *De l'Amour*, ed. V. Del Litto. Livre de Poche, Gallimard, 1969.

Stern, Daniel. *See* Comtesse d'Agoult.

Taine, Hippolyte. *Derniers Essais de critique et d'histoire*. Hachette, 1894.

Talmon, J. L. *Political Messianism: The Romantic Phase*. London: Secker & Warburg, 1960.

Thackeray, William Makepeace. *Paris Sketch Book*. London: Smith, Elder, 1866.

Thomas, Edith. *Pauline Roland. Socialisme et féminisme au XIX⁵ siecle*. Marcel Rivière, 1956.

Bibliography

————. *George Sand*. Editions Universitaires, 1959.

————. *Les Pétroleuses*. Gallimard, 1963.

Thomson, Patricia. *George Sand and the Victorians*. London: Macmillan, 1977.

Tocqueville, Alexis de. *Souvenirs*. Calmann Lévy, 1893.

Toesca, Maurice. *Le Plus Grand Amour de George Sand*. Albin Michel, 1965.

————. *Vie d'Alfred de Musset ou l'amour de la mort*. Hachette, 1970.

Tomalin, Claire. *The Life and Death of Mary Wollstonecraft*. London: Weidenfeld & Nicolson, 1974.

Tourneur, Michelle. *George Sand et Delacroix*. Lille: Université de Lille, 1972.

Trollope, Frances. *Paris and the Parisians in 1835*, 2 vols. London: Richard Bentley, 1836.

Troyat, Henri. *Tolstoy*, trans. Nancy Amphoux. New York: Doubleday, 1967.

Turgenev, Ivan S. *Ivan Tourguéneff d'après sa correspondance avec ses amis français*, ed. E. Halpérine-Kaminsky. Charpentier, 1901.

————. *Lettres à Madame Viardot*, ed. E. Halpérine-Kaminsky. Charpentier, 1907.

————. *Nouvelle Correspondance inédite*, ed. Alexandre Zviguilsky, 2 vols. Librairie des Cinq Continents, 1971–72.

————. *Lettres inédites à Pauline Viardot et à sa famille*, ed. Henri Granjard and Alexandre Zviguilsky. Lausanne: L'Age d'Homme, 1972.

Viallaneix, Paul. *Vigny par lui-même*. Seuil, 1966.

Vier, Jacques. *La Comtesse d'Agoult et son temps*, 5 vols. A. Colin, 1955–62.

Vigny, Alfred de. *Œuvres complètes*, ed. F. Baldensperger, 2 vols. Bibliothèque de la Pléiade, Gallimard, 1948, 1964.

Vincent, Louise. *George Sand et le Berry*, 2 vols. Champion, 1919.

Ward, Maisie. *Robert Browning and his World. The Private Face*. London: Cassell, 1967.

West, Anthony. *Mortal Wounds* (Mme de Staël, Mme de Charrière, George Sand). London: Robson, 1975.

Winegarten, Renee. *Writers and Revolution*. New York: Franklin Watts, 1974.

————. "The Reputation of George Sand" in *Encounter*, London: January 1977.

Zeldin, Theodore. *France 1848–1945: Vol. 1. Ambition, Love and Politics*. Oxford: Clarendon Press, 1973.

Zola, Emile. *Documents littéraires, Etudes et Portraits*. Charpentier, 1881.

Index

Index

Index

Maurice Dupin, 5–10, 12; as plebeian connection, 222–23; returns to Nohant (1822), 44–45; in Sand memoirs, 296; suffering under, 44–47

Dupin de Francueil, Marie-Aurore (grandmother of Aurore), 5, 7, 145; Aurore and, 8, 10–13, 15–27, 29–37, 39, 40, 42, 43; death of, 44; Sophie and, 12–13

Dupré, Jules, 248

Duras, Duchesse de, 98, 122

Duris-Dufresne, François, 95

Duteil, Alexis, 145, 175, 260

Duvernet, Charles, 43, 87, 95, 125, 145, 238, 258–60, 276

Duvaucel, Sophie, 148

Eckstein, Baron d', 168

Eichtal, Gustave d', 218

Eliot, George (Mary Ann Evans), 55, 109, 141, 148, 182, 227

Elle et Lui (Sand), 299–300

Enfantin, Prosper, 99–100, 124, 149, 164, 213, 218

Engelwald (Sand), 177

Esquiros, Adèle, 312–13

Essai sur le drame fantastique (Sand), 219–220

Eugénie (Empress of the French), 294, 307

Falcon, Cornèlie, 168

Famille de Germandre, La (Sand), 303

Fanchette affair, 238

Faulkner, William, 112

Favre, Henri, 315, 317

Feminism (feminist movement, women question), 124, 155–56, 162–68, 172; and concept of "human being," 270–71; divorce and, 176–77, 194, 262; freedom of childbirth, 187; French Revolution and, 98–101; and *Lettres à Marcie*, 193–95; in Paris Commune of 1871, 312–15; and questions of education and treatment of women authors, 181; reaction against women, 288–91, 297–99; in Revolution of 1848, 262–65; Sand as feminist, 319–20; working class and, 226–32

Feuillet, Octave, 307

Fieschi, Giuseppe (terrorist), 172

Fille d'Albano, La (Sand and Sandeau), 101

Filleule, La (Sand), 288

Flaubert, Gustave, 18, 202, 232, 263, 288–91, 300, 307–16, 320

Flavigny, Vicomte de, 189

Fleury, Alphonse, 43, 87, 93, 145, 155, 166, 238, 260, 281

Fleury, Laure 145, 155

Fourier, Charles, 98–100, 125, 182, 263

François le Champi (Sand): novel, 239, 252; play, 273

Franklin, Benjamin, 156

Freud, Sigmund, 117

Fromentin, Eugène, 302

Fuller, Margaret, 241

Fusinato, Antonietta, 138, 139

Gabriel (Sand), 220

Gabussi, Vincenzo, 152

Ganneau ("Mapah"), 100

García, Pauline (later P. Viardot), 223–25

Gautier, Théophile, 88, 94, 114, 223, 275, 291, 303, 304, 307–8

Gavarni (Sulpice-Guillaume Chevalier), 307–8

Gay, Delphine (later Mme Girardin), 98

Gay, Sophie, 215

Genettes, Mme Roger des, 316

Genlis, Mme de, 13, 34, 38, 41

George, Mlle, 108

Gérard, Baron François, 94

Gévaudan, Gustave de, 188, 190

Gide, André, 112

Girardin, Delphine de, 107, 307

Girardin, Emile de, 98, 275, 277, 288, 315

Gladkowska, Constantia, 210

Goethe, Johann Wolfgang von, 59, 86, 119, 219, 238

Goncourt, Edmond de, 209, 291, 295, 307–8, 313

Goncourt, Jules de, 290, 291, 295, 307–8, 313

Gouges, Olympe de, 99

Goya, Francisco de, 9

Grandsagne, Jules Ajasson de, 82

Grandsagne, Stéphane Ajasson de (Stény), 24, 84, 87, 89, 122, 123, 216; Aurore and, 38, 39, 41, 43, 44, 47; and birth of Solange, 82; love for, 80–81, 131; as Paris guide, 86; Sand on, 178; in Sand memoirs, 294

Greppo, Jean-Louis, 279

Gros, Baron Antoine, 94

Grzymala, Albert, 208, 211–12, 219–21, 249, 275

Guéroult, Adolphe, 161

Guizot, François, 96, 181

Guizot, Mme, 98

Gutzkow, Karl, 230

Handel, George Frederick, 234

Hanska, Eve, 201, 202

Hardy, Thomas, 112

Harrisse, Henry, 312

Haussmann, Baron, 200, 287

Haydn, Franz Josef, 234

Hegel, G. W. F., 189

Heine, Heinrich, 59, 100, 151–53, 155, 168, 199, 207, 212, 225, 226, 233

Helen, Sister, 34

Hérau, Mme, 224

Hérau, M., 224

Héricourt, Jenny d', 312–13

Herzen, Alexander, 232, 289–90

Herwegh, Georg, 232

Hetzel, Pierre-Jules, 249, 257, 274–76, 278, 282, 299, 303

Index

Index

Index

[339]